This Beautiful Britain

Golden Hands Books

Marshall Cavendish
London and New York

Acknowledgement
We are indebted to the Royal Automobile Club of Great Britain for their
invaluable advice and help in planning the routes described in This
Beautiful Britain.

Edited by Windsor Chorlton

Published by Marshall Cavendish Publications Limited,
58 Old Compton Street, London W1 V 5PA

Some of this material has previously appeared in the publication Route.

First printing 1974
Second printing 1975

ISBN 0 85685 064 0

Printed in Belgium by Henri Proost

About this book. . .

Britain, set like a jewel in the sea, presents a hundred dazzling faces to the discerning traveller. It is a land of contrast and, for those with eyes to see, each region has its own special flavour – a unique blend of people and places linked by the timeless thread of history.

This book helps you capture the rich diversity of Britain. Guided by a distinguished team of travel writers, you are taken right to the heart of each region, along a route specially chosen for its scenic grandeur and historical connections. Over 600 full-colour photographs illustrate the scenic and architectural treasures you will meet on the way. And for the seeker into the past, there are pages devoted to Britain's history – the men, myths and events which have shaped this island.

This Beautiful Britain is different. It is not for the traveller in a hurry. It is for the Wayfarer; the person who wishes to discover the real Britain – the one the other guides haven't discovered yet.

How to use this book. . .

Each chapter is devoted to a separate region. To set the scene, there's a lively introduction packed with information about the area, plus a pictorial map which presents an intriguing 'bird's eye' look at the pleasures to come. This is followed by a detailed, stage-by-stage account of the treasures that await you – the scenery, architecture, ancient monuments and battlefields . . . and much, much more.

When your wayfaring is over, you can relax by the fire and relive your holiday – capturing again, through the lavish illustrations, the 'feel' of each place visited. And, as you turn the pages, entranced by views of faraway places, the chances are you will begin planning fresh and exciting expeditions. . .

Contents

Devon and Cornwall –
the enchanted West Country

BRIAN WIDLAKE

The West Country, that thick peninsula of Britain bounded to the north by the Bristol Channel, to the west by the Atlantic and the warm caress of the Gulf Stream, and to the south by the swelling artery of the Channel as it flows into the ocean past the Lizard and Land's End: a region with the sea in its blood, a region of storms and gales where the ocean bursts on the rocks and chokes the coves of breath as the Atlantic breaks into cold hostility. But a region, too, that in summer sublimates the violent moods of the winter months so that the bare fingers of the coast are gloved with green and seagulls laze on the warm air and trippers take themselves off to the brash pleasures of Sidmouth and Torquay or the quieter Victorian charms of Minehead.

It's then that palm trees catch the surprised eye and prove that this part of England is warmer than any other: it's then that the great moors of the West — Exmoor, Bodmin and Dartmoor ("the last great wilderness of the south") — turn to rich browns and dark greens and the buzzard floats upward, quartering the moor for prey: it's then that the Devon Closewool and Scottish Blackface cut a neat figure after their spring shearing: and it's then that Devon lanes grow thick with fat hedgerows and there's cream for sale at every farm gate.

These are all contrary and opposite images, but that is what the West Country is at opposed ends of the seasons — the lushness of summer and the starkness of winter. There is always a hint of menace in the Scottish Highlands at any season. North Wales has an invariable quality of ruggedness, summer or winter. But the quality of the West Country is infinitely changeable, even when the climate is most hostile. On a winter's day, run up from Princetown on Dartmoor, one of the most desolate places in Britain, and look across to Sheepstor and then down and away through Sampford Spinney and the contrast is one of barren, primeval starkness — with dark, haunting tors — and the kind of green, fertile luxuriance which even this country can grow in its winter valleys.

Every county in Britain, of course, bears its own "motto", often precariously truthful. Kent, for example, is "the garden of England", Sussex is "by the sea", and "what Lancashire does today the world does tomorrow". They are not necessarily descriptive of the county, more often they're descriptive of psychological attitudes or pride or loyalty. But the West Country has been singularly badly served by descriptive epithets. Cornwall has been improbably called "the delectable duchy"; Devon has been taken in hand by the aggressively extrovert song and thumpingly dubbed "glorious"; while Somerset limps along with "smiling"

THE ROUGH AND THE SMOOTH

Any county "smiles" if you take the right bit — that bit, for example, from Minehead to Lynton along an exceptional coastline to the north, that saunters through Porlock Vale, that touches the beautiful village of Selworthy, and which nudges the northern flank of Exmoor. Oh yes, it smiles all right — in fact if you're looking for the typical West Country idyll it's all neatly packaged for you in these few miles: here there's sea and a soft coastline, there's the moor, there are old, nestling villages and winding, wooded lanes and tiny fishing ports. And if that's what you want, then linger over it because this route, all the way from Minehead to Falmouth, wasn't designed around "delectable", "smiling" or "glorious". It's rough and smooth, it's grand and barren, it's rugged and rambling, but it wasn't made for poetic charity and the tumbling

phrase. The native Cornish poet (and who could be more loyal?) had something, but only something, when he stigmatised his county in this rough verse:

> O Cornwall! Wretched spot of barren ground,
> Where hardly aught but rocks and furze is found,
> Thy produce scarce provides thy sons with bread,
> Nor finds them wood for coffins when they're dead.

There isn't much that's "delectable" about that, but the interests of truth aren't always well served by over-zealous versifiers. Don't be deceived by this poet, because he was probably drunk or hungry or both when he put pen to paper. Social conditions in Cornwall before the turn of this century would have wrung the withers of the most sublime optimist.

A CHERISHED LANDSCAPE

Yet he is symptomatic of the great change which has come over English attitudes towards their landscape and countryside. Even Daniel Defoe, who had no shortage of poetic imagination, called Exmoor "a filthy, barren ground" when he toured the West Country in the early 18th Century. Today, remarks like that would call down upon their author the vituperation of every rural and landscape preservation society from Land's End to John o'Groat's. There are two truths here. The first is that in Defoe's day the discomforts of travel were abominable. Roads were little more than gullies, worn by torrents in the rocks. William Marshall, one of the best-known writers on farming of that period, observed that "there was not, then, a wheel carriage in the district, nor, fortunately for the necks of travellers, any horses but those which were natives of the country".

Defoe would probably have travelled by coach on some of the better routes, but even then the time, the pace of long, horse-drawn journeys and the lack of frequent, comfortable inns would have jaded the most charitable traveller — especially in the rain and cold. The second truth is that the English have now learned to cherish in their landscape the dwindling remains which have not been encroached upon by industry, public construction and the demands of a rapidly expanding population. In this sense the West Country has been preserved from the worst depredations of the 20th Century. It is still comparatively difficult to get to, and industry prefers the convenience of the immediate south and south-east. Apart from china clay, there are few minerals left which are worth the bother of the extraction industries. But that is hardly a matter for complacency. If oil were discovered on the moors the battle for preservation would be a grim one, and Defoe, if called as an expert witness, would no doubt approve their spoliation.

Fortunately that hasn't yet happened and nobody now listens to Defoe. Most of this route takes you through the prime moorland of the south — moor formed by huge granite upheavals during our pre-history, which give the land its peculiar and distinctive character: the dark tors which crown the moorland hills (granite which poked itself through the subsoil and was then eroded by frost and weather); the miles of dry-stone walls and the grey granite cottages and farmhouses; hardy sheep and cattle and the tough, wild ponies of Exmoor and Dartmoor. There is harshness in this wilderness and the living doesn't come easy. It's taken centuries to learn the best methods of cultivation.

Exmoor — unlike its big brother to the south, Dartmoor — has the soft, rounded curves and mounds of a woman's belly; it is

Sunset over Henry VIII's castle at St. Mawes, near Falmouth

Malmsmead and Badgworthy Water in the Lorna Doone country

legends and old suspicions. You cannot lead what is often a solitary and lonely life as a hill farmer and not let the moor shape your pyschology and attitudes. It makes people sturdy and independent, and that is what the Devonians and Cornish are. They fought hard in the Prayer Book Rebellion and in the Civil War and they sent men like Drake to sea to become great captains.

> Drake he's in his hammock till the great Armadas come,
> (Capten, art tha sleepin' there below?)
> Slung atween the round shot, listenin' for the drum,
> An dreamin' arl the time o' Plymouth Hoe.

Not that the Cornish, apparently, didn't have their own brand of pride:

> And have they fixed the where and when?
> And shall Trelawny die?
> Here's twenty thousand Cornish men
> Will know the reason why!

Of course, the Cornish poet who said that his county could neither provide bread for the living nor coffins for the dying would, by today's standards, be accused of impoverishment of spirit and meanness of mind. All right, hurl what insults you like at the china clay industry whose excavations break out like grey boils along the Bodmin Moor skyline and foul the approaches to St. Austell. But this poet never looked across Carlyon Bay at St. Austell or dropped down to Truro or took the road from that cathedral city through serene and wooded pastureland to Probus and Falmouth where the Fal's fine estuary breaks so generously upon the Channel. Nor, by all accounts, did he ever go to Helford close by — that tranquil, wooded river — and guzzle oysters from its beds or fish for the incoming bass. No, he must have stumbled along the uncompromising shoreline in winter, searching for driftwood in the breaking sea or perhaps for kegs of brandy and bales of cloth from a hapless wreck. For the Cornish have never been rich — the duchy's mines have fallen into disuse and, anyway, were always a precarious form of living; and smuggling, even at its peak in the 18th Century, was not a form of illegal enrichment but an activity vital to the existence of the people. The Cornish have always had to wrest their living from the land and the sea, a perpetual struggle to keep body and soul together.

But what a business smuggling was! Stand on any Cornish headland and imagine that armed vessels of up to 300 tons used to put out from these shores to bring back spirits, lace and tea from France. In those days smugglers stopped at nothing — murder, theft and bribery were common tools of the trade. Even the advent of Methodism — spread by John Wesley stumping through Cornwall — could not dissuade the Cornish from their predilections for smuggling and drinking. And what drinkers they were!

The story goes that a Cornishman, after a drinking bout with friends, was pressed to have one more pint for the road. "No," he replied, "I can't get down a drop more, but I tell 'ee what you can do. Throw a pint ovver me if you mind to, so I shall be able to have the smill of un when I do wake up in the morning."

It takes a good man to put down a Celt. But the traveller is not engaged in such acts of aggressive indulgence. Let him taste the cider and the cream and the pasties, but let him remember, too, that here in the West Country — even among the three counties — you have a people as different from each other as they are from the Scots, the Welsh or the Irish.

lumbering and sensual, although that's not to say that when winter takes it in its grip it doesn't come alive in cold anger. This is the "Doone country". Look at it through the eyes of R. D. Blackmore who wrote the great romantic classic of moorland love, tragedy and murder, *Lorna Doone*. Stand in the Doone Valley — you can't miss it because they're more than conscious of tradition in these parts — and recall the words that Blackmore used of the Doones' robber stronghold: "She stood at the head of a deep green valley, carved from out the mountains in a perfect oval, with a fence of sheer rock standing round it, eighty feet or a hundred high; from whose brink black wooded hills swept up to the skyline. By her side a little river glided out from underground with a soft dark babble, unawares of daylight; then growing brighter, lapsed away, and fell into the valley".

The valley now doesn't bear much resemblance to Blackmore's description of it. There is no trace of the fearsome "water-slide" in the easy-flowing River Oare, but the great black wood that blocks off the western end of the valley like a sentinel and the fine east of the church and stone cottages still leave room for the workings of romantic fancy. The same is true at Lynton, at the Devil's Cheesering, those strangely formed sandstone rocks in which Blackmore set Mother Meldrum's cave and the dark drama of suspicion and witchcraft. The moorfolk, of course, are deeply conscious of

7

HARTLAND POIN

WAYFARER'S GUIDE 1

BODMIN MOOR

24 LAUNCESTON

25 ALTARNUN

26 BOLVENTOR

27 BODMIN

28 LANIVET

RIVER FOWEY

29 ST. AUSTELL

ST. IVES BAY

31 TRURO

30 PROBUS

32 FALMOUTH

LIZARD POINT

Photos: Peter Baker/B.T.A./Julia Brooks/Clifford R. Clemens/Colour Lib. Int./James Davis/Noel Habgood/Mansell Collection/Nat. Monuments Record/Picturepoint/Pix Photos/Bruce Scott/
Kenneth Scowan/Peyto Slatter/Spectrum/

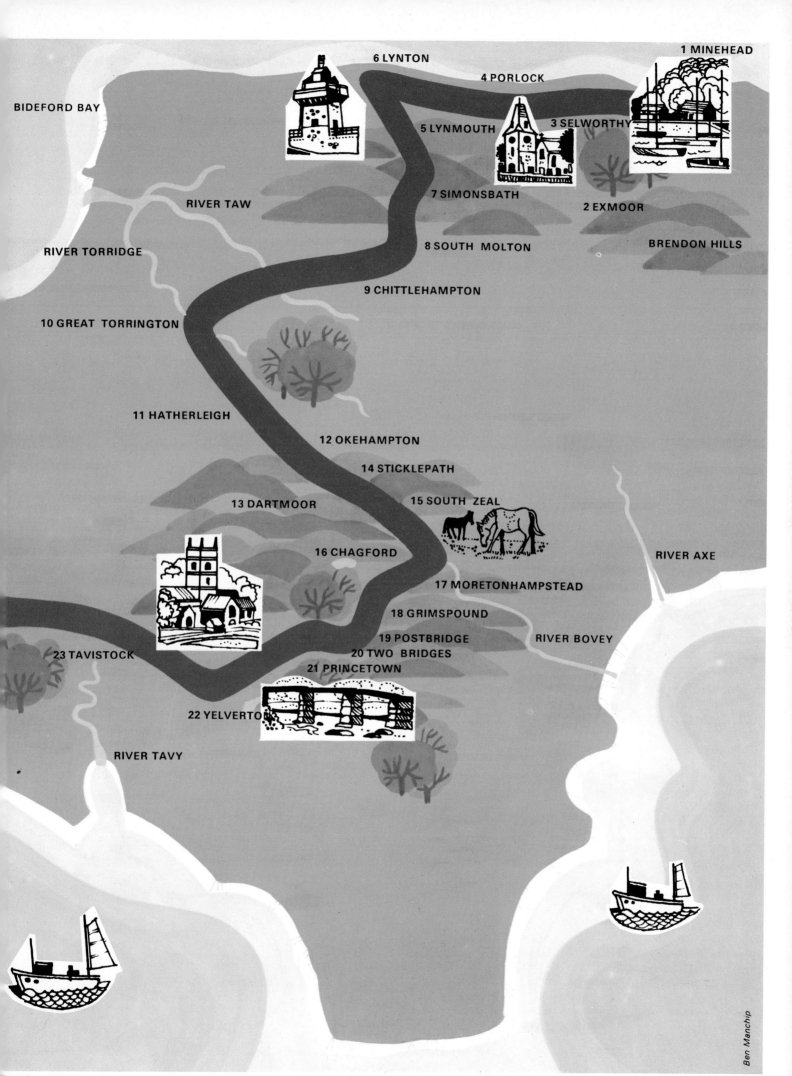

BIDEFORD BAY

6 LYNTON

4 PORLOCK

1 MINEHEAD

5 LYNMOUTH

3 SELWORTHY

RIVER TAW

7 SIMONSBATH

2 EXMOOR

RIVER TORRIDGE

8 SOUTH MOLTON

BRENDON HILLS

9 CHITTLEHAMPTON

10 GREAT TORRINGTON

11 HATHERLEIGH

12 OKEHAMPTON

14 STICKLEPATH

13 DARTMOOR

15 SOUTH ZEAL

RIVER AXE

16 CHAGFORD

17 MORETONHAMPSTEAD

18 GRIMSPOUND

19 POSTBRIDGE

RIVER BOVEY

23 TAVISTOCK

20 TWO BRIDGES

21 PRINCETOWN

22 YELVERTON

RIVER TAVY

Ben Manchip

Illustrations: Elsie Wrigley/Richard Hook   Plant Notes: Geoffrey Gilbert   Animals and Birds: Jeremy Johns

1 **MINEHEAD:** The old name comes from Mynheafdon, which means the hill above two rivers — the East and West Myne. The present town is of Anglo-Saxon origin on the site of an earlier Neolithic settlement. Its prosperity has always been closely linked with the sea, at first through fishing and trading, more recently as a holiday resort. In the 15th Century the town became a busy little port trading in fish and woollen goods. Despite plagues and raids by Welsh privateers, trade increased until, by the 17th Century, Minehead was second in size to Bristol among Bristol Channel ports, and ships from the town plied to the West Indies, Virginia and the Mediterranean.

By 1716, Minehead was importing coal from South Wales, cattle, wool and hides from Ireland, and exporting fish, grain and broadcloths produced by local cottage industries. But the 19th Century brought a slump in trade and the summer resort flourished. Minehead owes much of its development to the Luttrell family of Dunster Castle. The original quay was built by Sir Hugh Luttrell in 1488 and wa[s] enlarged to its present size nearly 20[0] years later by another Luttrell.

St. Michael's, the parish church on th[e] cliffs, has been a landmark for sailors fo[r] 500 years. A light in its window acted as [a] lighthouse. One of the treasures of th[e] church is a chest bearing the arms [of] Robert Fitzjames, a Tudor vicar, wh[o] became a bishop and built Fulham Palac[e]. There is a sculpture on the east wa[ll] showing St Michael weighing a soul, wit[h] the Devil clinging like an ape to th[e]

The old church steps, Minehead

Minehead harbour flourished until trade slumped last century

---

2 **EXMOOR:** One of the smaller National Parks, with an area of 265 square miles, Exmoor is bounded on the north by 29 miles of exceptionally beautiful coast. The moor's highest point is the 1,700 ft. Dunkery Beacon from which the tors of Dartmoor can be seen. To the east there is a beautiful view along Minehead Bay to the Quantocks. Northwards across the Bristol Channel are the mountains of Glamorgan and further still the Brecon Beacon and the cone of the Sugar Loaf above Abergavenny. To the south and east the National Park takes in the wooded valleys of the Exe, Barle and Haddeo. Exmoor is a plateau — a mixture of heather, bracken and grass moorland. Many of its combes are well wooded with scrub oak, birch, mountain ash and alder; others shelter big timber trees — oak, ash, walnut and various conifers.

The farming pattern of present-day Exmoor is based almost entirely on the pioneer efforts of John Knight and his son Frederic. Knight, an ironmaster from the Midlands, bought 15,000 acres — or, roughly, three-quarters of the Royal Forest — from the Crown in 1820 and centred himself at Simonsbath. An immensely able man, he was a keen agriculturalist but made the mistake of trying to introduce northern farming methods to the harsh and intractable moor. Among his mistakes were the construction of Pinkworthy Pond, the practical purpose of which has not yet been discovered; the cutting of miles of open drains on the moorland, which merely proved dangerous to horsemen; the failure to grow shorter belts; and the lack of any real attempt to colonise the estate. On the credit side, however, were the metalling of 20 miles of tracks across the moor, radiating from Simonsbath, and the breaking of some 2,500 acres of moorland, which produced ground for cultivation.

Much of the moor belongs to a handful of great landowners. Their tenants and the owner occupiers, farming between 50 and 300 acres each, account for the majority of holdings in the National Park.

On these farms they keep Exmoor Hor[n] or Devon Closewool, traditionally famou[s] for fine fleece and sweet mutton; o[r] perhaps Scottish Blackface, the hardies[t] of the hill breeds; or Cheviots.

Exmoor's wild life includes the ponie[s] and, of course, the red deer, the larges[t] remaining wild animals in Britain. The[re] are three packs of staghounds which hun[t] the deer in the National Park: the bigges[t] and most important is the Devon an[d] Somerset Staghounds, with their hom[e] at Exford; the Quantock Staghound[s] which hunt the Quantocks; and th[e] Tiverton Staghounds which search out th[e]

A quiet and lovely spot near Exford

weights and the Madonna trying to restore the balance by prayer.

The alabaster statue of Queen Anne carved by Francis Bird, a protégé of Grinling Gibbons, is a reminder that alabaster was once mined in Somerset. Originally, Queen Anne's statue stood in the church; now it is in Wellington Square.

Minehead's Hobby Horse, which dances through the town on May Day, introduces the Hobby Horse Fair. It is hard to say how old this custom really is. It has been suggested that it dates from 1722 when a cow was washed up on the beach on May Day Eve. It is far more likely to have its origin in the ancient fertility rites when a ship on wheels was trundled over the fields by the peasants. Between Minehead and Watchet, in the Flowery Vale, are the ruins of Cleeve Abbey. This was once a Cistercian monastery, and one of the noblest ancient monuments on the moor, despite the fact that for decades the cells of the monks were used as stables, and the refectory as a granary. At the time of the Dissolution of the Monasteries in 1537, Cleeve Abbey was granted to Robert, Earl of Sussex, and the "seventeen priests of honest life who kept hospitality there" were driven away.

The finest view of Minehead is from the top of North Hill, with a gentle climb to Selworthy Beacon (1,013 ft).

foothills to the south and west. There is a close season from springtime to the early part of August. The stag is hunted until late autumn and this is followed by a spell of hind hunting. Spring stag hunting finishes the season. The moor abounds with birdlife. Herons and carrion crows are common. The blackcock, although becoming scarce, can be seen; also red grouse. There are curlews and ring ouzels, and the two birds which nest by moorland streams, the dipper and grey wagtail. On the higher ground are the whinchat, stonechat, snipe, occasional golden plover, and a rarity like the snow bunting. On Exmoor, too, birds of prey can be seen high on the wing: buzzards, kestrels, sometimes the peregrine falcon.

It is likely that all the round barrows or burial mounds on Exmoor belong to the Bronze Age: they number between 300 and 350. Some fine examples occur within the boundaries of the National Park. Chapman Barrows, between Parracombe and Challacombe, comprises 11 large bowl-shaped examples; and just to the east are Longstone Barrow, and Wood Barrow. There are stone circles at Almsworthy Common, Porlock Common and Withypool Hill; hut circles (not known whether they are Bronze or Iron Age) at the Valley of the Rocks, Lynton; and numerous hill forts, perhaps the finest of which is Shoulsbarrow Castle, south-east of Challacombe.

UNDERWATER FISHERMAN

One of the most familiar sea-birds is the cormorant. This bird depends entirely upon fish for its diet and the craggy sea-cliffs provide both a safe and a convenient nesting site. Cormorants are easily recognised either in flight or perched by their distinctive shape, and their white face markings and larger size distinguish them from the similar shag. It is sad to note that the pollution of the sea has severely hit these birds, who depend so completely upon its threatened bounty. Unlike most sea-birds, cormorants do not produce waterproof oils and have to dry themselves out. They dive underwater, fill their crops with fish, then perch on posts or on buoys with widespread wings.

One of the loveliest villages in Somerset

3 SELWORTHY: Thatched cottages, dormer windows, trim hedges and gardens, with a "green" and a walnut tree as the centrepiece, make this one of the loveliest villages in Somerset. The road winds up past a 14th Century tithe barn to the Perpendicular church above — the Church of All Saints. There was once a 12th Century church on this site — a font of that period exists in All Saints. The present west tower is late 14th Century, but the rest of the building belongs to the early 16th. While the church is a remarkable building, its south side is distinguished by its grace, line and beauty which harmonise the church in all its parts — tower, porch and nave. The waggon roof of 1538 in the south aisle is one of the best in England. Each boss has four little sprays in the angle of the ribs and each rib is enriched with foliage. All Saints looks out across the lovely Vale of Porlock.

4 **PORLOCK** is famous for its person, and its hill . . . The person is unknown and unforgettable, because of what might have been. It was "a person from Porlock" who interrupted Coleridge and prevented the completion of *Kubla Khan,* one of the most famous fragments in the English language. Robert Southey, who stayed at the Ship Inn, said that Porlock was known as the end of the world, which it must have seemed like in the days when the only way of ascending the steep hill on the road to Lynmouth was by a "trackamuck" — a kind of sledge on two poles.

The first ascent of Porlock Hill by motor car was in 1901 — for a bet. An epic journey down it was made in 1899 when the Lynmouth lifeboat received a call to a ship in distress but could not launch the lifeboat in the gale. The crew decided to drag the boat across the moor, slide her down Porlock Hill and launch her in the quieter waters of Porlock. The boat was lashed to a cart and then began a night-mare journey which involved a team of 2 horses, aided by every available ma woman, and child to hang on the rope and act as a brake on the hill. En route, the had to widen the road in places, demolis a wall, and chop down a tree, but 10 hou later the lifeboat was launched fro Porlock. The ship, the *Forest Hall* (1,90 tons) on tow from Bristol to Liverpoo was found, and the crew of 15 saved.

Up to the early 1920s and the arrival the motor coaches, the coaches wer drawn by four-horse teams, with an extr pair, ridden postillion, being hitched on f the climb up Porlock Hill. With the help all the passengers and six horses the made it, which is more than can be sa for many of the early motor coaches. Th horse-drawn coaches, it is recorded, d the journey in three hours, and only onc failed to get through.

The 13th Century church is dedicate to St. Dubricius, (who is said to hav crowned King Arthur). The church has a unusual spire, covered with woode shingles, and the story goes that th original spire lost its top in a great ga around 1700, but this is only one several versions. Another explanation f the truncated spire was that workmen we repairing the tower when the hounds we

Beached at Porlock Weir: here no sand but pebble banks

5 **LYNMOUTH** was once a pictu esque little fishing village, at th mouth of the River Lyn, backed by towerin wooded cliffs. Thatch and roses, woo smoke and visiting poets. Much of tha has changed. The town has been largel rebuilt since the disastrous floods August 1952, when three thousand tw hundred million gallons of water fell o the Chains in about five hours in one of th

Rhenish tower and Mars Hill at Lynmouth

Watersmeet, near Lynmouth

huddle of masts in the picturesque harbour

through in full cry and, being good men of Somerset and great huntsmen, they downed tools and followed them, never returning to finish the job. Yet another story says that the bit which blew off the top of St. Dubricius' spire flew away and settled on Culbone Church like a pointed cap.

Like many other churches in the region it owes its origin to missionary Welshmen who are said to have crossed the Bristol Channel on improvised rafts. Culbone Church, which can seat no more than 24 people, is claimed to be the smallest parish church in England. It is 35ft. long, with a nave 21ft. 5 in. long and 12ft. 8in. wide. There was once an extensive charcoal burning industry in Culbone woods, not far from Porlock Weir. It is said that the original burners were members of a leper colony, who were not allowed across Culbone Water to Porlock.

Apart from a person from Porlock there is also a donkey which achieved a certain fame. There is a plaque in a church at Stoke Pero, 1,013ft. above sea level, which reads: "Be Thou praised, my Lord, with all Thy creatures. In the year 1897, when this church was restored, Zulu, a donkey, walked twice a day from Parson Street, Porlock, bearing all the oak used in the roof".

ost violent rainstorms ever recorded in e British Isles.

There are enough Shelley's Cottages in ynmouth to establish the fact that the oet stayed here, though the actual cottage here he lived with his first wife was estroyed by fire in 1907. The locals were ot always as fond of him as they are now, nd they told the Home Secretary of his volutionary activities, which mainly consted of writing pamphlets and floating em out to sea in bottles. Shelley left fore he became a problem.

Lynmouth was once a great herring shing port but by 1750 the industry had eclined and the curing houses were rned into cottages. A thousand feet oove Lynmouth, at the top of a one-in-ur hill, is Countisbury, which was once e site of an Iron Age camp. It is believed at during the reign of King Alfred, 1,000 ears ago, the Danes attacked a place lled Arx Cynuit on the Exmoor coast, at were beaten off by the defenders who shed down Countisbury hill, killed the ader of the Danes and 800 of his men, d captured their Raven banner. There as a church at Countisbury long before e Normans came, but the present church tes from the beginning of the 19th ntury, and is largely a do-it-yourself job the parishioners, who pulled down the d nave and rebuilt it, and then turned eir attention to the tower.

The Blue Ball Inn in Countisbury is here the coach slipped its extra pair of rses after the journey from Lynmouth.

6 LYNTON: A hamlet before Queen Victoria, now with Lynmouth, a main holiday resort. Set in the hollow of the hills above the sea, it is saved from exposure to the sea winds by the screen of trees on Summerhouse Hill and protected from the wet moors by a ring of hills. The hotels, boarding houses, shops and houses are Victorian. The first hotel was opened in Lynton in 1807, and three years later a visitor built himself a private house which is now the Royal Castle Hotel. Lee Abbey, which never was an abbey, was built in 1850. This was originally a private house and is now a retreat.

Railway enthusiasts will lament the lost railway from Lynton to Barnstaple, opened on May 11, 1898 and closed on September 29, 1935. It followed a beautiful route, past Chapman Barrows, the Chains, St. Petroc's Church and some of the most magnificent Exmoor scenery. On its last journey, along 19 miles of narrow gauge line, the little train carried 300 "mourners". There were four engines, *Lyn, Taw, Exe* and *Yeo,* and *Lyn* was nicknamed "Yankee" because it was built in America during a strike, and never really settled down, though it was loved for its eccentricities.

Sir George Newnes, the publisher, was chairman of the local company which built the railway. He also built the cliff railway between Lynton and Lynmouth. The cable railway was the invention of a local engineer, Bob Jones, who patented his invention in 1870. It was not until 1887 that blasting began and the cable railway

was officially opened on Easter Monday, 1890. The total cost was £8,000.

There is a prehistoric site at Castle Rock, including a pound some 40ft. in diameter, and in the Valley of the Rocks a collection of stones, probably the remains of hut-circles. The Devil's Cheesering, or Mother Meldrum's Cave, is to be found here. "Cheesering" seems to be an earlier form (used by Blackmore) of Cheesewring — a type of rock formation.

Countisbury Hill from Lynton

THE CUT-THROAT DOONES

R. D. Blackmore, who was educated at Blundell's School, Tiverton, wrote his famous romance in 1869 but set the book in the 17th Century. Blackmore did not invent the Doone legends, but he used the material as he thought fit — cutting, altering and embroidering to suit the needs of his story. *Legends of the West Country*, published in 1854, says this about the Doones: "The Doones of Badgworthy were a gang of bloodthirsty robbers who haunted. . . Exmoor about the reign of Charles I, and ravaged the whole country around. Many tales are still extant of their daring and ferocity."

The bare bones of the legends are these. Around 1620 a band of desperate men settled on Exmoor, taking possession of the old Badgworthy cottages. From here they established a reign of terror over the moor, robbing, pillaging and raiding the farms on the forest fringes. They abducted women from the villages and were responsible for many murders. Eventually, after a particularly vile outrage, the moorfolk could stand it no longer and rose against them. They expelled the cut-throats from their stronghold in 1690 and the few survivors fled.

Blackmore was amused at the belief, which some held, that he had invented the legends. When, in 1894, a correspondent sent him some Doone material, Blackmore replied: "I am pleased with your little fact, and should like to send it on to the man who lately proved — to his own good pleasure — that there never were any Doones, except in my imagination."

The novel shows a close acquaintance with the moor and has superb descriptive passages which evoke the topography and feeling of this wild place. It ought to be a traveller's companion for anyone touring the area.

7 **SIMONSBATH** is one of the highest points on Exmoor (1,599 ft.) The name has two possible sources. Richard Jefferies, the 19th Century author of *Bevis* and *Wild Life in a Southern County*, said the village was named after a man who tried to swim in a whirlpool but was sucked under and drowned. Which is not everyone's idea of a "bath". *Murray's Guide* of 1859 has a more probable, although remote, explanation — that it was named after an outlaw who enjoyed bathing in a crystal pool on the Barle just by the village.

Simonsbath Lodge, the first and only house in the Forest of Exmoor until the 19th Century, was completed in 1654 (date carved in a beam in the kitchen) by James Boevey, who bought the freehold of the Forest of Exmoor from the Crown in 1651. Boevey was a remarkable little man (less than 5 ft. tall) who was endlessly involved in lawsuits but found time to write many curious books — *The Art of Gaining Wealth, The Government of Amor Conjugalis* and two volumes on *Of Amor Concupisciente*. He also restored a famous Forest boundary by planting an oak tree to replace the original Hoar Oak Tree which died of old age in 1652. His oak, which survived until the 20th Century, was also a crafty compliment to King Charles II,

whose fondness for oaks was well know ever since he hid in one after the Battle Worcester in 1651.

The present Hoar Oak is one of thre saplings planted soon after the death Boevey's oak in 1916 and, though Exmo is notoriously unkind to the tree, it painfully holding its own.

Simonsbath church, dedicated to S Luke, was built by Sir Frederic Knight 1856. Sir Frederic and his wife and on son are all buried there. John Wesle preached at Simonsbath, and Charles als visited the town to try to help the miner whose expectation of life, according to survey of 1837, was 31 years.

Opposite the Exmoor Forest Hotel is path leading to a cairn, 1,500ft. up, bearin the inscription: "John William Fortescu Historian of the British Army". Th Fortescues (Strong Shields) earned the name at the Battle of Hastings when the fought for William the Conqueror. Th memorial is to Sir John Fortescue (185 1933), historian and librarian at Winds Castle.

Chapman Barrows, where the men the Bronze Age buried their dead, superbly situated, with spectacular view across the rolling moor as far as th Bristol Channel.

Simonsbath Lodge, completion date carved in kitchen beam

A GIANT AMONG FERNS

Devon and Cornwall rivalled the Lake District as hunting grounds during the Victorian craze for collecting ferns. There are about 50 British species varying from the minute filmy ferns to the royal fern, pictured here, standing 6ft. high. The sport of fern-hunting, so popular during the last half of the 19th Century, was encouraged by the intriguing mutations that crop up from time to time, which may look quite unlike the original plant. Interest in ferns is reviving, and the British Pteridological Society, still with its Victorian name, may once more be seen prowling through Devon lanes. The choicest ferns are likely to be found in damp, shady gorges. The South-West is notable for the shield ferns. The curious filmy ferns, with fronds only one cell thick, are found on rocks by waterfalls.

Detail from the George Hotel

SOUTH MOLTON has been a
market town for 1,000 years and
received its Royal Charter during the reign
of the first Elizabeth in 1590. It stands on
the River Mole. In 1655 Charles II, then in
exile, was first proclaimed King of England
in the High Street here. The loyal Royalists,
under Colonel John Penruddock, Lord of
the Manor of Compton Chamberlayne,
were attacked and outnumbered by the
Cromwellian cavalry, and the abortive
uprising was put down with great brutality.
Colonel Penruddock and all his officers
were executed. Other ranks were either
hanged, drawn and quartered or shipped
to Barbados as slaves.

Farmer Mole, whose disappearance in
the desolate heights above South Molton
gave rise to the legend of Mole's Chamber,
was riding home from market, so they say,
when he and his horse stumbled into a
bog. But ghost or no ghost, Mole's
Chamber is a place to avoid after dark
because it was once part of the mining
area — silver, lead and copper.

The famous hunting parson, Jack Russell,
who was born in 1795, was curate at
South Molton. Stories about him are
legion: he was accused of refusing to
conduct a burial service because it clashed
with a hunt; he fell from his horse when he
was 84, remounted after half-an-hour's
rest and rode the six miles home; he was a
friend of the Prince of Wales, and shared
his coach on the way to the hunt at
Minster Castle when 9,000 spectators
watched a meet of 2,000 riders at Hawk-
combe Head. The Prince of Wales sent a
wreath of wild flowers to Russell's funeral.
But, above all, Jack Russell is remembered
as a founder member of the Kennel Club,
and breeder of the fierce, tough little
terriers which bear his name.

The George Hotel claims to be 800 or
900 years old. It is thought that one of the
first clubs in England, the Hunt Club, used
to meet here. In the 18th Century the
George was known as the Posting Tavern,
a name derived from the fact that it lay on
the Barnstaple to London coaching route.
At one time the dining room was used as a
theatre, called the New Theatre, and on
the staircase there is a framed programme

for *Macbeth,* dated Friday evening,
January 17, 1834.

The Church of St. Mary Magdalene is
reached from the market place through
gilded wrought iron gates. It is 15th
Century and designed in the form of a
Latin cross. The aisles on each side of the
nave are separated by arcades, each of
five pillars, supporting Gothic arches of
Beer stone. Some of the pillar capitals are
grotesque, representing curious ceremonies
being performed by human figures. The
most conspicuous figure is that on the
north side of the chancel looking down the
church. Local historians assume this to
be the master mason looking down over
the church he had built.

The borough museum is in Market
Street, no more than an alleyway off the
market place. The building dates from 1620
and the collection includes MSS. and
documents relating to local history. There
is also pewter — some of which, from
Hanover, is dated 1585, and some marked
Sandringham; weights and measures from
the reign of William IV; a 1721 fire engine;
a 1750 cider press; 18th Century wigmak-
ing tools and other items of agricultural or
historical interest, including stocks and
man-traps.

The Guildhall is 1743, a stone-fronted
building of three bays crowned by a
cupola. Next to the Guildhall there is the
Panier Market, an under-cover market.

Bailiff's uniform, 1860

Front of South Molton Guildhall showing town crest

At the site of St. Teara's well

9 **CHITTLEHAMPTON** was originally a Saxon settlement on the site of the present village square. The church of St. Hieritha is dedicated to the saintly maiden whose piety so irritated her wicked, heathen stepmother that she provoked the village haymakers to murder the girl with their scythes. Chittlehampton is alleged to be the site of her martyrdom, with St. Teara's well at the eastern end of the village marking the actual spot.

There is a *Hymn of St Urith* (her proper name), a verse of which verifies the story:

For men's threats no fear she knew,
By her death the foe o'erthrew,
Foe o'er whom she triumphed;
Where the holy maiden fell
Water gush'd forth from a well,
And the dry earth blossomed.

The church has a 114ft. spire, with around 90 pinnacles. It has good brasses to the Cobley family and a mosaic reredos.

10 **GREAT TORRINGTON:** T town's original name was Chep ing Toriton, which comes from the wo "chepe", meaning market, and "tor (rough or violent) derived from the Riv Torridge on which the town stands. O of the most important market towns north Devon in the 14th Century, it wa by the 16th, second only to Exeter, with very important cattle market..

To the right of the main entrance to t parish church of St. Michael there is a sto commemorating the bleak fact that: "Th Church was blowen up with powc Febr.ye 16th anno 1645 and rebuilt 1651". In fact the date of the explosic by our modern calendar, was February 1 1646. The "blowing up" occurred durin the Battle of Torrington. It was in th battle that Fairfax and the Roundhea defeated Hopton and the Royalists a thereby ultimately gained command of t

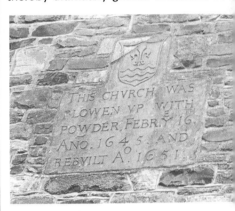
Commemoration stone

11 **HATHERLEIGH** is a cob-wal market town with a Perpendicu church possessing a fine carved roof. C is basically mud, mixed with chopp straw, chalk, gravel, pebbles, broken sla and anything else available, with li added to make it set. The cob was th laid in layers, about 4ft. wide and a f thick, and trodden down while still s It was left for a week to dry out before next layer went on, which meant tha could take a couple of years to buil two-storey house. But it was built to l "All cob wants is a good hat (overhang roof) and a good pair of shoes" (stone pebble foundation). Many cob walls d from the 16th and 17th Centuries.

The history of the parish church g back over 1,000 years. In the Domes Book of 1086 Hatherleigh is referred under the possessions of Tavistock Abb The church is mentioned in a Bull of P Celestine III, dated May 29th, 1193, as "Church of St. John the Baptist".

The tower contains a fine peal of ei bells, which were recast and rehung 1929. Nothing now remains of church chapel which existed in Saxon days. font is Norman and the greater part of present building dates from the 14th a 15th Centuries.

Cobley family brasses in Chittlehampton church

outh-west. The Royalists used the church an arsenal and had stored 80 barrels of npowder inside. As the Roundheads ained more ground, and more prisoners, ey decided to use the church as an ternment camp. Originally it was a 14th entury building but was itself on the site f an older one. The vestry (approx. 1485) rvived entirely, but the waggon roof — hich is a fine example of the type — elongs to a later period.

There was once a Norman castle here, parently founded by Richard de Merton the reign of Edward III. All that can be en now is the enclosure of a bowling reen and an 18th Century gazebo. From e castle there is a dramatic, almost sheer op of several hundred feet to the River orridge below, and a fine view across to e other side of the valley.

The town has some pleasant and tractive houses. In Fore Street, the White lobe Hotel, 1830. In South Street, No 28, two-storeyed, red brick house with five ays and a hooded porch, inside which ere are carved trophies. Date 1701. In ew Street there is another red brick use, Palmer House, built in 1752 for Sir shua Reynolds's brother-in-law; both eynolds and Dr. Johnson stayed there. ere is an interesting four-armed cross the junction of South Street and Mill reet — at Windy Corner.

Hembury Castle, five miles west of the wn, is the site of a prehistoric encamp- ent and was occupied by the Royalists ring the Civil War.

The hooded porch in South Street, Great Torrington

ocks now used as a bench outside 1,000-year-old church at Hatherleigh

Detail from church window

The Norman font, still in use

Picturesque Okehampton Castle

12 **OKEHAMPTON** was founded by Baldwin de Brionne, the Norman Sheriff of Devon, just before 1086. It is often called the capital of the north moor. From Roman times onwards it had been recognised only as a staging point for those crossing central Devon to and from Exeter.

Okehampton is the birthplace of James Meadows Rendel, who gave London one of its most famous views: he designed the little suspension bridge over the lake in St. James's Park. Rendel was a farmer's son who learnt surveying under Telford in London. He designed Brixham harbour and the breakwater at Torquay.

The highest points in Devon — High Willhays and Yes Tor (both above 2,000ft) are to the south of Okehampton. The castle, one of the largest in Devon, is situated in a remarkably picturesque situation on a knoll east of the River Okement and protected by a valley on the west. It was built by Baldwin de Brionne and mentioned in Domesday but there are no remains earlier than 1300.

At the northern end of the town there is Oaklands, a Grecian mansion of 1830 with an Ionic four-column portico on one side and two-column loggia on the other, all of pink sandstone and perfectly flat-roofed. The town suffered badly in the plague of 1625.

Sampford Courtenay, the village where the Prayer Book Rebellion started, is just north-east of Okehampton. The rebels refused to change from the Latin Prayer Book to the new English version, and despite the attempts of the local magistrate William Hellyone to dissuade them, they marched on Exeter and besieged the city. They were driven back to Sampford Courtenay and massacred in the streets.

William Pitt, Earl of Chatham, was MP for Okehampton.

13 **DARTMOOR** is based on a granite plateau formed by a series of volcanic upheavals in the remote past. In the course of this land change the granite was seamed with minerals — among them tin (which led to the formation of the tin mining industry, now dead); arsenic, copper, iron, wolfram, quartz and fluor. The origin of the tors — those castle-like formations of rock which can be seen all over the high uplands of the moor — is open to geological argument. But it seems most likely that these prominent, over-lying rocks were split and formed by frosts into blocks which are not unlike the towers we know better in architecture. The name "tor" is another version of tower.

Running downhill from these tors there are cascades or avalanches of smaller rocks, known as "clatters" or "clitters", which were almost certainly eroded by the weather from the main granite outcrop.

Farming is Dartmoor's main industry, as it has been for centuries. But the altitude of the moor, the frequent rain and mist, and the rugged, stony and acid nature of the soil, have all imposed their conditions on the nature of farming in the area. Few cereals are grown, except in some favoured and sheltered valleys.

The core of the Dartmoor hill farm is livestock — cattle, sheep and ponies. A fairly typical "mix" on a traditional Dartmoor farm would include a herd of South Devon cattle, Whitefaced Dartmoor sheep, some Dartmoor mares, pigs and poultry. Other farms, on the edge of the moor, might have a dairy herd of Friesians, while on the high ground above 1,000ft. farmers tend to be restricted to the hill breeds of sheep and cattle.

While there is no record of settled habitation on the moor between 400 B.C. and A.D. 700, Dartmoor has one of the richest concentrations of prehistoric remains and monuments in Britain. There is evidence of human life on Dartmoor during the Mesolithic period (15,000 to 3,500 B.C.). Numerous artefacts of the period have been found among the 30,000 flints turned up during ploughing at such places as Postbridge, Gidleigh Common and East Week. These suggest that these were temporary camping sites based on a subsistence of hunting, fishing and the gathering of edible fruits and roots. The "homes" were bound to be extremely rudimentary and probably consisted of scoops in the ground which were covered over with branches and turves.

It also seems probable that these early hunters began the long process which helped to create the physical appearance of today's moorland. Recent research indicates that they lit fires in the forest

Widecombe-in-the-Moor, high up on Dartmoor and scene of the song about Uncle Tom Cobleigh

ake clearings for camps and to drive
nimals out of the woodland into open
round where they would be easier to kill.
he conifer plantations are new and have
ostly been planted by the Forestry
ommission.

The monumental record of Dartmoor
egins with the Bronze Age (2,000 to 500
.C.) when primitive man acquired the
nack of making implements and weapons
om bronze (copper alloyed with tin). This
ill was introduced by the Beaker Folk,
ho were itinerant craftsmen and pros-
ectors from the Continent. The name
beaker" is associated with a particular
pe of pottery vessel which was frequently
terred in their graves. Beaker burials have
en found in *kistvaens* (rude sarcophagi
chests formed of stone) in barrows at
atern Down, at Fernworthy, and on
akehead Hill. They have yielded up
eakers, stone wrist guards, and flint and
opper knives.

Most of the stone rows and circles on
e moor are probably early Bronze Age
nd are largely ascribed to the Beaker
olk. The large stone circles were possibly
mples to the gods, and the stone rows
ocessional ways which led up to
arrows. The finest Bronze Age settlement
the moor can be seen at Grimspound.
There are now virtually no deer left on
e moor. In the late 18th Century,

following numerous complaints from
farmers, the Duke of Bedford sent his
staghounds down from Woburn and
exterminated all the stock. Tavistock was
so glutted with venison that only the
haunches were kept, the hounds getting
the rest.

Apart from deer, Dartmoor is fairly rich
in wildlife. Foxes are common on the moor
(there are about three or four to the
square mile). Otters can be seen in
Dartmoor streams. Badgers often frequent
the open moor — some even dig their setts
up by the tors. Stoats and weasels can be
found among the clitter of the tors, and
even some long-tailed field mice. In the
woodlands there are mice, voles, hedge-
hogs, rats and squirrels.

Bird life in the area is also vigorous,
although a good deal of it is in coniferous
plantations which provide habitats for the
merlin, chiffchaff, siskin and redpoll. In
summer the moor abounds with skylarks
and meadow pipits. A survey (1968) of 15
square miles of the moor recorded 75
breeding species and 41 non-breeding.

The largest landowner on the moor is the
Duchy of Cornwall, which holds Dartmoor
Forest. The word "forest" is not used
literally: it means a place where the king
used to ride. Since 1336, when Edward III
created his son Edward, Prince of Wales,
Duke of Cornwall, any subsequent Prince
of Wales has also been Duke of Cornwall
and Lord of Dartmoor.

The moor was designated a National
Park in 1951 to preserve the environment
and prevent any development which could
detract from the park's natural beauty.
Conservationists do not believe that the
ideal has worked very well in practice.
They cite the extensive china clay workings
in southern Dartmoor, whose waste tips
rear up far over the skyline and can be seen
for miles into the moor. Overhead power-
lines have been erected in beautiful places,
when they could have been put underground. A pumping station has been built
on Taw Marsh. Extensive areas of open
moor have been ploughed up, and heli-
copters often use the moor for exercises.

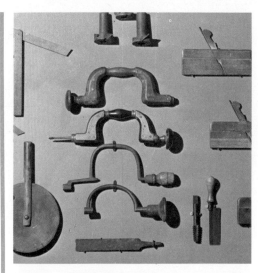

Handmade tools at Sticklepath

Finch Foundry's old trip-hammer system

14 **STICKLEPATH:** The name means
steep road, from the Saxon word
sticele. "Stickle" is the West Country word
for a *rapid.* Stickles and ranges are the
rough shallows and smooth reaches of a
stream.

The Finch Foundry Trust and Sticklepath
Museum of Rural Industry (on the main
road) is on the original site where the
Finch family worked their foundry from
1814-1960. Their hand-made agricultural
tools — such as scythes, billhooks and
shovels — were of a very high quality and
famous throughout the south-west of
England. The business stopped in 1960,
partly through competition from mass-
produced tools and partly because demand
for hand tools on the farm has become
less and less.

The machinery, most of which is still in
place, was powered by water from the
River Taw and consisted of three water
wheels — one to operate the trip hammers,
a second to power a fan which provided
air for the forges, and a third to drive the
grinding mill.

The foundry is considered to be extremely important in industrial archaeology, and
a charitable trust has been set up to
restore the machinery and building.

The granite rock of Hay Tor on Dartmoor

Drake's Golden Hind: Tired of waiting for Drake, Oxenham sailed in his own ship — to his death

The ancient stone at the Oxenham Arms

15 **SOUTH ZEAL** is the site of a former copper mine. The Chapel of St. Mary has a stately cross, about 18ft. high, considered to be one of the finest in Devon. Probably 14th Century, it was repaired in 1838 by John Stanbury, a native of South Zeal, who was home on a visit from America where he worked as a carpenter. He cut his initials and the date of the repair in the base, an action which infuriated the villagers who destroyed the inscription and thereby made a panel which can still be seen on the north side.

The Oxenham Arms, virtually next door to the chapel, was built by lay monks in the 12th Century around a great granite menhir (long stone), thought to be about 5,000 years old. It can be seen in a room at the back of the bar. At one time the inn was the manor house of the Burgoyne family and later the Oxenhams, who created the legend of the white bird.

Charles Kingsley relates how a former John Oxenham, "a brave lad of Devon", saw the white bird and what happened to him afterwards. He was with Francis Drake at Nombre de Dios in 1572, when they climbed a tree to look at the Pacific Ocean. Drake then and there made a vow to Oxenham that he would "sail that water, if I live and God give me Grace", to which Oxenham replied that he was with him "to live or die".

But the promised voyage showed no sign of coming off and Oxenham decide[d] four years later to go without Drake. H[e] reached Panama and, after capturing tw[o] barques laden with gold and silver, h[e] and his crew were incautious enough [to] pluck some hens whose feathers fell in[to] the water and thus enabled the Spaniar[ds] to track them down. Oxenham had [to] abandon his booty.

The crew made their way back [to] Nombre de Dios, where they were ca[p]tured and put to death. Oxenham wa[s] taken to Lima and hanged as a pirate. S[o] ended the life of the first Englishman [to] sail the Pacific and who, despite "h[is] two great sins of wrath and avarice", wa[s] yet "a noble and gallant gentleman".

16 **CHAGFORD** was formerly a stannary, or tin town. During the Civil War, so the story goes, the Royalists made an attack on the town and during the course of the fighting lost one Sidney Godolphin, " a young gentleman of incomparable parts. He received a mortal shot by a musket, a little above the knee, of which he died on the instant, leaving the misfortune of his death upon a place could never otherwise have had a mention in the world".

This slighting reference by the writer to Chagford's obscurity takes no account of the Church of St Michael, at least 700 years old, which has the Tinners' sign (three rabbits) in the centre boss of the chancel roof — the church is being restored under the direction of Mr. Dykes Bower, a leading church architect; or of the Three Crowns, close by; or of Chagford House, late Georgian, behind the church; or of Whiddon House (two miles to the north-east), a picturesque granite building of late 16th or early 17th Century.

Inside St. Michael's Church, Chagford

17 **MORETONHAMPSTEAD**: Chi[ef] feature is the Church of S[t] Andrew set on its own at the higher en[d] of the village. It has Perpendicular window[s] and the west tower is of four stages [—] granite-ashlar built, diagonal buttresse[s] polygonal stair-turret and short obeli[sk] pinnacles. There is a two-storeyed battl[e]mented porch.

The almshouses are thatched and bu[ilt] of granite over an open colonnade facin[g] the street. Although built in 1657, t[he] crude columns make the building lo[ok] much older.

George Barker Bidder, "the calculati[ng] phenomenon", lived here as a boy, a[nd] grew up to baffle the Institute of Ci[vil] Engineers when he read a paper to [its] members on his methods of ment[al] arithmetic in 1822. Bidder built railwa[ys] and constructed London's Victoria Doc[ks] and was a great friend and disciple [of] George Stephenson. He had a brain li[ke] a computer and could carry up to [?] numbers in his head.

18 GRIMSPOUND is the site of a remarkable Bronze Age village. In his book, *The Hound of the Baskervilles*, Sir Arthur Conan Doyle gave Sherlock Holmes the remnants of a prehistoric hut, set in the wilds of Dartmoor, in which to bivouac for the night. Grimspound was the model for this eerie experience. A stone wall, some 9ft. thick, surrounds a rough circular area of about four acres, in which there are the remains of 24 circular huts each measuring about 15ft. in diameter.

Bronze Age village at Grimspound

This clapper bridge at Postbridge has slabs thought to be of Celtic origin

19 POSTBRIDGE has a clapper bridge to the left of the road, crossing the East Dart. "Clapper" literally means "heap of stones". There are two central piers overlaid with stone slabs, each 15ft. long and roughly 6ft. wide. The central part has two of these slabs, laid side by side. probably Celtic in origin, although some sceptical authorities think they might be of much later date.

George Bidder, "calculating phenomenon"

20 TWO BRIDGES: Another clapper bridge, this time over the West Dart. The Two Bridges Hotel was once the Saracen's Head, built by Sir Francis Buller in the 18th Century. His estate was centred on Prince Hall, which he rebuilt. Buller was a judge of the King's Bench and received his baronetcy in 1790.

Another clapper bridge — at Two Bridges

21 PRINCETOWN: The man who created Princetown, desolate and bleak at 1,400ft., was Thomas Tyrwhitt who became friendly with the Prince of Wales when he was up at Oxford (originally it was known as Prince's Town). He became the Prince's private secretary and then auditor to the Duchy of Cornwall. Well before he was knighted in 1812, and appointed Gentleman Usher of the Black Rod, Tyrwhitt started operations at a spot a little south of Two Bridges, which he called Tor Royal after his patron.

Not content with creating a large estate here, Tyrwhitt decided that he wanted to make a self-sufficient community and chose to make Princetown the nucleus. It was high, bleak and quite hostile to his dreams of acres of corn and flax, root crops and plantations. He needed something else to make his scheme work. It turned out to be the prison.

Alarmed at the numbers of prisoners from the Napoleonic wars who were confined in hulks at Plymouth, the authorities were looking around for alternative accommodation. Tyrwhitt was influential and persuasive and on March 20, 1806,

These prehistoric hut circles, just east of Merrivale Bridge, can be reached by turning off the route at Two Bridges and following the 384 towards Tavistock for 3½ miles.

he laid the foundation stone of Britain's most forbidding prison. By 1809 — at a cost of some £200,000 — 5,000 prisoners were accommodated at Princetown. Eventually the figure rose to 9,000 and the gross overcrowding became the cause of much Parliamentary criticism.

The prison, however, brought Princetown a short-lived prosperity. A thriving market was established; a corn-grinding mill was constructed; and a brewery went up behind the building now known as the Duchy Hotel, which had been built to house officers. But by 1816, when the last prisoners left, Princetown declined, and it was not until 1850 that it was decided to make it a permanent convict settlement.

The Church of St Michael was built in 1813 by prisoners of war, and the east window was given by American women in memory of their men who died in prison.

22 YELVERTON: Distinguished by the Church of St Paul built 1913-14. Devonian interior, with painted waggon roof. Early 20th Century at its best, but still adhering to tradition.

River scene near Yelverton

SNAKE? NO, A LIZARD

The mild climate of the South-West provides an excellent situation for one of England's most fascinating creatures, the slow-worm. At first sight this lizard appears to be a snake. It has no legs and moves in serpentine fashion. But beneath the slow-worm's skin are vestigial remains of a lizard's limbs, made redundant through evolution. Also the slow-worm has eyelids and a tongue that is notched rather than forked, features not shared by snakes. It does look remarkably like a serpent with thin tapering body, usually a foot long, yet the slow-worm, like the more orthodox lizards, sheds its tail with surprisingly little provocation. But the process of regeneration never seems successful, and most slow-worms have an untidy stub, an indignity no snake would endure.

23 TAVISTOCK is one of the oldest inhabited parts of Devon — prehistoric settlers were attracted by the tin found on the surface. The town grew rich in the wool trade and had sole rights to make a certain kind of cloth known as Tavistocks, or Tavistock kersies. Much of the town is associated with the Bedford family. Henry VIII gave Tavistock Abbey to John Russell, first Earl of Bedford: it is a Benedictine foundation and the ruins can be seen in the grounds of St Eustachius. Russell was a Dorset squire who rose high in Henry's favour — he was responsible for suppressing the Catholic Rebellion of 1549, sometimes known as the "Prayer Book Rebellion", with unusual ferocity and zeal.

Tavistock is an ancient stannary town — one of the few where mined metal could be weighed, stamped and assessed for duty. From the 12th Century large quantities of tin had been mined — the Devon Great Consols mines were once the richest source of copper in Europe.

The statue of Sir Francis Drake at the junction of the Plymouth and Tavistock road was designed by Joseph Boehm, erected in 1883 and paid for by Hastings, ninth Duke of Bedford. It has bronze panels on three sides: one depicting Drake being knighted by Queen Elizabeth I, another showing a burial at sea; and one, of course, of the famous bowling scene at Plymouth Hoe. Drake was born at Crowndale Farm on the outskirts of the town in 1542 and made his home at Buckland Abbey, only a few miles away. Opposite the Drake statue is Fitzford Gatehouse, originally the entrance to the mansion of the Fitz family. Built before 1568, it was restored in 1871.

The town's focal point is Bedford Square, flanked by the parish church of St Eustachius and the town hall. The square was built in 1860 as part of the redevelopment carried out by Francis, the seventh Duke of Bedford ("the beneficial dictator"). The town hall has a lovely vaulted, beamed ceiling and can seat up to 500 people. The Guildhall, rebuilt in 1848, has battlements and pinnacles which are matched in the town hall, and also has stone mullioned windows.

Chevalier's House is one of several in Devon with equestrian statues on the roof, said to indicate to Royalists that supplies could be had within.

Statue of Francis, Duke of Bedford

Tavistock's statue to Francis Drake. The panel (left) shows the bowling scene on Plymouth Hoe.

24 LAUNCESTON (pronounced "Lanson") is just inside the border, only a mile from Devon. It was the most important Cornish town in the Middle Ages, and the county town until 1835. At Launceston, on mayor-election day, it used to be the custom to elect a mock mayor as well, known as "Mayor of the Pig Market". Before his election the mayor was made drunk, his hat was removed and his head well powdered with flour. If he had really long hair a frying pan was attached to it and allowed to hang down his back. Then he was led away, pelted by the mob, to the New Inn, which bore the nickname of "Shindy Arms", and here the proceedings usually ended in general uproar.

St Mary Magdalene church is 16th Century, with granite exterior walls and elaborately carved buttresses. Of remarkable workmanship, the church was the gift of Sir Henry Trecarrel, who had hoped to build a house for his beloved wife and son. When they died, he had no heart to build the house and diverted the money and material to the church.

An Augustinian Priory was founded here in 1136 by a Bishop of Exeter. The church

Launceston Castle — in Domesday Book

of St. Thomas has the largest Norman font in Cornwall, with corner faces and rosettes in circles.

The castle was the chief fortress of Richard of Cornwall, Henry III's brother, and was mentioned in Domesday Book. Some of it may be 12th Century. White Hart Inn was once a great coaching inn which also housed a theatre.

26 BOLVENTOR is a former haunt of smugglers. Daphne du Maurier used its Jamaica Inn in her novel of that name. Dozmary Pool, on the fringe of a circle of Bronze Age remains, is about 1,000ft. above sea level, and more than a mile in circumference. It is supposed to be the lake where Sir Bedivere hurled the dying King Arthur's great sword Excalibur, and saw it caught by the arm "clad in white samite". It is alleged to be haunted by the giant Jan Tregeagle, wicked steward of Lord Robarts in the 17th Century, who sold his soul to the Devil. He is condemned to spin endless ropes of sand, and bail out Dozmary Pool with a leaking limpet shell.

Dozmary Pool at Bolventor

25 ALTARNUN: Birthplace of sculptor Nevill Northey Burnard (1818) son of a stonemason, whose sculptured profile portrait of John Wesley is above the door of the Methodist meeting house. Burnard was a protégé of Sir Charles Lemon, M.P. for Carthew, who took him to London, and set him up in a studio, where for a short time he became fashionable. He was ruined by drink and returned as a tramp to his birthplace in 1875, dying three years later in the workhouse at Redruth.

His statue of Richard Lander is in Lemon Street, Truro, where there is also a bust of Richard Trevithick in the County Museum and Art Gallery.

Burnard also had a gift for drawing with a sharpened nail on stone slabs and in the churchyard at Altarnun is a stone engraved with an eagle flying into the rays of the sun.

The church of St Nonna's west tower is 109ft., one of the highest in Cornwall. It has a large Norman font, decorated with bearded faces at the corners and large rosettes between. There is a Bronze Age stone circle two miles south-east.

27 BODMIN was once famous for its "riding", a festival which commemorated the return of the body of St. Petroc, patron saint of the parish, which had been stolen by a Breton priest and taken to the abbey of St Meen. The original festival lasted several days starting with a beer tasting. The festival died out at the end of the 19th Century after it had degenerated into a drunken shambles.

Part of the hangman's rope from Bodmin Gaol was believed to have miraculous properties, and it was believed that if a sufferer wore a little of the rope around his neck — in a bag! — and buried another small piece, as the rope rotted so would he be cured.

The Church of St. Petroc is a Perpendicular building, mostly rebuilt in 1469-91.

John Wesley's profile at Altarnun

Norman font at St. Nonna's Church

Bodmin Moor is an 800 ft. high plateau

28 LANIVET

28 LANIVET once noted for tin mines and quarries, now has a radio station. The Feast of Lanivet was famous, and attracted hordes of visitors from all over Bodmin, whose revelling was frequently rough. Their local game of hurling would pass for a war in less rugged towns, and at the beginning of the 19th Century one hurling (a kind of stepped-up Rugby) encounter turned into a two-hour running battle which left scores of wounded as the men from Bodmin were routed by the local opposition.

Church interior at Lanivet

29 ST. AUSTELL: Centre of the china clay industry which succeeded tin mining as the main occupation. White mountains of clay and quartz to the north of the town are local landmarks. Sir Josiah Wedgwood was one of the industrialists who developed the industry in the 19th Century, but it was a Quaker, William Cookworthy, who found the clay, which gave Cornwall a new industry.

Connoisseurs of holes in the road will be impressed by Carclaze quarry, first quarried for tin by the Phoenicians. In 1851 it was first worked for china clay. The quarry is a mile at least in circumference, and 150 ft deep.

The 15th Century church has a 90ft. tower, a massive Norman font, and a quaintly carved little reading desk showing a fox preaching with his pad on the pulpit and his eye on a lady nearby.

The town and market halls are in the Italian Renaissance style, and there is a Quaker meeting house of 1829.

A wishing well (Holy Well) will be found at Menacuddle on the Bodmin road.

Pentewan beach, near St. Austell, a typical Cornish seascape

30 PROBUS: The Church of St Probus and St. Grace (1523 was once attached to a Priory founded in the 10th Century and rebuilt by the Normans. It has the highest tower in Cornwall — at 125ft. it is said to be one o the eight finest in England. and closely resembles that of Magdalen College Oxford. The villagers helped to carry the granite from the moor. The church also ha the heaviest peal of bells in Cornwall — the tenor weighs over a ton. There are si: bells and 134 steps to the belfry.

Skulls found last century were said t be the remains of St. Probus and St. Grace believed to have been buried under th altar.

The church of St. Probus and St. Grace

31 TRURO: The cathedral foundations were laid in 1880, and the church was completed in 1910. The architect was J. L. Pearson. The south aisle of the original 16th Century church of St. Mary has been incorporated into the design. Mainly Cornish stone has been used — granite, Polyphant, china clay stone, serpentine — and the brilliant green roof of the clock tower is weathered Cornish copper. In the Jesus Chapel is a painting by Ann Walke showing Christ blessing the Cornish industries.

Wedgwood plaques of Shakespeare and Garrick are all that remain of the old Assembly Rooms — the freestone front at the west end of the cathedral, facing High Cross.

One notorious episode used to be remembered in Truro by burning effigies in the streets. These represented the Truro millers who profiteered during the Napoleonic wars by mixing china clay with the flour, and caused great illness at home and among the troops serving abroad.

The County Museum and Art Gallery has paintings by Rubens, Kneller, Lely, Hogarth, Gainsborough, Constable, Millais and John Opie, the son of a St Agnes mine-carpenter, who became Court portrait painter to George III. At the head of the stairs leading to the art gallery is a full-size portrait of Anthony Payne, the Cornish Giant. Payne stood 7ft. 4in. in his stockinged feet.

The museum has large collections depicting Cornish life from early times: Bronze Age jewellery and funeral urns, items connected with tin and copper mining, ship models, vehicles, agricultural implements, coins and tokens. There is also English pewter, pottery and porcelain, and a fine collection of Cornish minerals.

A quiet river scene at Truro

THE GENTLEMEN GO BY!

If you wake at midnight
  and hear a horse's feet,
Don't go drawing back the blind
  or looking in the street,
Them that asks no questions isn't
  told a lie.
Watch the wall, my darling,
  while the Gentlemen go by!
Five and twenty ponies
  trotting through the dark —
Brandy for the parson,
  'baccy for the clerk,
Laces for a lady, letters for a spy
And watch the wall, my darling,
  while the Gentlemen go by!

These lines from "A Smuggler's Song" from Puck of Pook's Hill *epitomise Cornwall in the 18th Century, when a large part of the county's wealth came from illegal tobacco, tea and liquor imports. The smugglers used to land their wares by night in hidden coves — such as the one described in* Frenchman's Creek, *the novel written by that famous daughter of Cornwall, Daphne du Maurier. There are many smuggler's tales, and sights to see. Such as the sign of the King of Prussia Inn, at Fowey. One side of this sign shows a former landlord and his brother in their Sunday best; the other in smugglers' gear.*

32 FALMOUTH

32 **FALMOUTH:** One of the largest towns in Cornwall, it has a harbour, a dockyard, and a seaside resort. Founded in Elizabethan times, it is protected by two castles, built by Henry VIII, at the mouth of Carrick Roads — Pendennis Castle and St Mawes. Much of its early development was in the hands of the Killigrew family — first, Sir John who developed it as a port; then Sir Peter who built the Church of King Charles the Martyr (1662-5) and the quay in 1670.

In 1661 Falmouth was given its charter and this took away a good deal of valuable trade from Penryn and Truro. From 1688 until 1852 it was the headquarters of the Royal Mail packets (even the captains of these packets engaged in extensive smuggling) but lost this important business to Southampton. Eleven years later (1863) the railway arrived and this began the development of Falmouth as a seaside resort.

The Church of King Charles the Martyr was entirely paid for by Sir Peter Killigrew. The building is a mixture of 17th and 18th Century additions, subtractions and alterations. Arwenack House, the Killigrew manor, is at the end of Grove Place, opposite a plain obelisk to Sir Peter erected in 1737.

Trelissick, a grand early 19th Century house in the Grecian style, with gardens of almost tropical splendour should be seen.

Bananas were growing out of doors in Falmouth before World War II and the average number of days with over nine hours sunshine is 64 in Falmouth; 44.4 at Kew. Above all, it is an even climate. At Penjerrick Gardens the boast is that everything possible that grows in England grows here. Famous for rhododendrons, azaleas and camellias. Fox Rosehill Gardens received an award for acclimatising over 200 species of foreign plants. Here are abutilons 20ft. high, tobacco plants 14ft., and daturas with a diameter of 15ft. Gyllyngdune Gardens are noted for magnificent ferns, including a fine example of the New England tree fern.

The *Cutty Sark*, the famous clipper, was bought back from the Portuguese by Captain Dowman, himself the former master of a sailing ship. He saw the *Cutty Sark* in Falmouth harbour, and decided there and then that he wanted her for a training ship. She stayed in Falmouth until just before World War II, when she was taken to Greenwich, but she might have been lost to Britain for ever if it had not been for the sharp eyes of an old sea captain in Falmouth harbour.

Haven for small craft

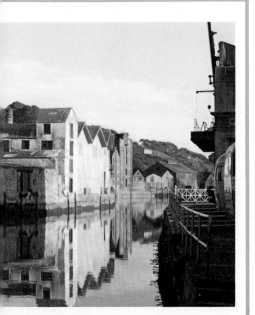

The beach at Falmouth from the cliffs

An Iron Age village

The idea that our prehistoric ancestors in Britain were a tribe of semi-naked apes, spending most of their time cowering in caves, rubbing bits of wood together and hacking one another to shreds with the jaw bones of mastodons, has taken a rude hammering in recent years. They may well have originated in this manner many thousands of years ago but all the evidence now goes to show that "civilisation" of a sort was fairly well established in these islands when Pericles was orating in Athens and the first stones of the Parthenon were being laid.

By the sophisticated standards of Periclean Greece, Iron Age Britons — around 500 B.C. — were a pretty primitive crowd. But, like their Bronze Age predecessors, they were capable of very creditable and, at times, beautiful craftsmanship.

Look at the objects on this page. The famous mirror discovered at Desborough in Northamptonshire is one of the very finest examples of Iron Age craftsmanship and design. The mind behind the hand that fashioned this exquisitely graceful exercise in the symmetry of curves was certainly not that of a naked savage.

The large shield with its red enamelled boss and the jet bead necklace date from the early Bronze Age (which in Britain began around 1900 B.C.). Many of their torques or clasps were, as our specimen shows, fashioned with a delicate intensity which is a hallmark of fine craftsmanship. The curious object which looks a bit like a Russian fur hat is in fact the two halves of an Iron Age hand mill used for grinding corn. The groove in the "lid" has a hole in the centre through which the corn was poured. A stick was put in the groove and this served as the handle to the grinder.

Chysauster, south-west of St. Ives in Cornwall, was an Iron Age village of some eight houses clustered beneath the fortress stronghold of Castle-an-Dinas. Village life in Chysauster began around the second century B.C. and continued well into the Roman occupation. Perhaps the villagers worked the tin mines in the area and traded with the La Tene people of Eastern France, who in turn traded with the Etruscans of Italy and the Greek colonists of Marseilles. The highly civilised Southerners sent their wine to the La Tene people, and in this way La Tene became familiar with the pottery and bronze vessels, often finely made, of this advanced culture.

The details of Iron Age clothing are

anybody's guess but there are indications that these early Britons might well have dressed as we show them. Razors of the period have been recovered so it is quite possible our hero shaved his chin. It is quite possible that an Iron Age man and his mate would not cause too much alarm if they appeared at a 20th Century "hippie" festival.

Their pottery was of a high standard with simple, geometric patterns worked into the glossy red surface. These bowls were often highly polished to imitate bronze.

Iron Age houses were built round a circular main room with smaller rooms branching off. The semi-circular courtyard was apparently used as a cattle pen.

There is no evidence that Chysauster came to a violent or sudden end. It seems that the population simply drifted away — possibly to move to other tin mine workings when the Romans were redeveloping Cornish tin mines around A.D. 300.

In the Chysauster period the axe and spear had reached a high point of development. Axe heads had a shaped socket with a ring for thonging the head to the shaft.

M. MacGuinnes

The Southern Counties – 4,000 years of history

JOHN TAYLOR

The best way to start this journey is to stay where you are, for at least a short tour of Winchester. There has been a town here since before the Romans – and though some 12ft. of earth has covered the ancient town during the centuries, much is still left above the surface to mark the pageant of history: The Roman layout of the streets – a rectangular grid with main roads running north to south and east to west, the ancient gates, the vast low-lying cathedral, the castle with its apocryphal Round Table of King Arthur, all now merged painlessly into a bustling middle-class market town with impingements of passing centuries.

The last of these you witness as you drive past the old West Gate at the top of High Street hill and branch left on to the A31 for Romsey. The country soon begins to undulate, with here and there, the post-card beauty of thatched, moss-covered cottages to set a scene of sentimentalised England. Romsey itself is an unassuming town but excused by its sturdy Norman Abbey, just off to the right of the route, and "King John's House" which possibly saw him once upon a time. Broadlands, on the south side of the town – once the home of Lord Palmerston – is now the property of Earl Mountbatten. The Queen and Prince Philip spent part of their honeymoon there. The main advantage to the route now is that it gets us quickly to Cadnam and the beginning of the Forest. A few miles through Cadnam and just north of the A31 at Canterton Glen, before you get to Stoney Cross, you can see the Rufus Stone which marks the spot where William II met his death by Tyrrell's arrow, but if you take the east-bound lane off the 31 to Minstead, you can see the curious little church there – and the grave of Sir Arthur Conan Doyle, creator of Sherlock Holmes.

Turn right when you come to the 337 and you will reach Lyndhurst. Now you're deep into the New Forest. Thick-coated ponies line the roads, quietly cropping the grass verges into green cushioned picnic places and straying casually out on to the tarmac. About two and a half thousand mares wander the Forest, with a limitation of stallions to around one hundred – a seeming encouragement to an equine permissive society. Their picturesque alternative is the deer, mainly fallow deer, which are less popular with the locals because of their more destructive habits. At Lyndhurst, turn for Beaulieu, and you're soon out into a part of the Forest which simulates moorland rather than woodland. Heather and gorse, brackish streams and standing ponds, the long views punctuated by the munching bulk of fat ponies, distant woods on the right emphasising the variety of New Forest vista. Approaching Beaulieu the road winds through gentle beauty, farms and Friesian cows, and the wooded estate – until you turn a bend in the road and the near distant huddle of Beaulieu itself lies across a reach of silent water.

HEARTS OF OAK

Later make for Buckler's Hard – along a narrow winding road, tree-lined, hedged and ditched – and leave the car to see the funny old single street, stepping down to the water's edge where once the ships of Nelson lay. Two ancient terraces line the road to the reach, one including the tiny Chapel of St. Mary – an unseparated cottage in the terrace which seems to offer accommodation in the floor above. The end of the terrace on this side features the Master Builder's House, home of the man who once designed the hearts of oak constructed of the wood so handily growing in the nearby forest. *Sic transit gloria* . . . Now it is a small and picturesque hotel.

Now back through Beaulieu, take the road for Brockenhurst, across the Forest again. After Brockenhurst you avoid the built up areas of Lymington by turning off before Sway on the lanes that go through Burley and Moortown towards Ringwood. Already you can notice the West Sussex look of Hampshire clearly changing to the more moorish aspect of Dorset and the Hardy country. As you branch left on the road from Ringwood, on to the 348 at Trickett's Cross, you cross the county border. Passing through Wareham you drive across Middlebere Heath to Corfe Castle.

HUDDLE OF SOFT, GREY STONE

Craggy Corfe Castle suddenly appears against the sky high on its mound, but just around the corner the real surprise is the village that nestles at its foot and shares the castle's name. A beautiful huddle of soft grey stone cottages and houses, it is entirely out of character with anything yet seen upon the route. From Corfe Castle turn left across country towards East Lulworth. Now you cross the Purbeck Hills – an outstandingly beautiful drive with a marvellous rolling drop of several hundred feet away on your right, hilly moorland all the way, and finally a glittering revelation of the sea down on your left through the lower upland. On unlucky days the road is closed because it includes a great area of Army firing ranges, and one must drive further north through Wareham. The cottages and houses here are built of stone from the local quarries of the Isle of Purbeck (it isn't, and never was, an island) and with plenty of thatch it could be a piece of the Cotswolds that lost its way home.

East Lulworth is dominated by the remains of a 16th Century castle. At West Lulworth, leave the car and walk down the narrow sloping lane to Lulworth Cove – where the surrounding cliffs enclose the cove in practically a fully symmetrical circle. The high chalk walls, the green grass atop them, and the blue sea, offer colouring to rival Mediterranean localities. Lulworth Cove is a delight to botanists, ramblers, geologists, bathers, fishermen and those who just like to sit and listen to the grass grow.

Our next target *en route* is inland to the county town of Dorchester; and by taking the road back through Wool, we can see the town that Hardy chose for Tess to spend her honeymoon – though he called it "Wellbridge". One of the oldest houses in Dorchester is Judge Jeffreys' lodgings in High West Street and another reminder of past oppression is the old County Hall which staged the trial of the Tolpuddle Martyrs. Outside Dorchester, on the road to Sherborne, the early countryside is scrubland, but fork right off the A37 back on to the 352 and you find a narrow winding road with high hedges and farmland all the way. Through places with lovely names like Cerne Abbas, with its pre-Roman turf giant cut out of the hill 200ft. high, his club alone measuring 30ft.

You drive over Blackmoor to Sherborne and reach Somerset near Sandford Orcas; and after Marston Magna (surely this area has the most charming names in England) you cross the main 303 on the other side of Queen Camel – leaving Cadbury Castle on your right and a few miles on your left the Fleet Air Arm Museum at the Royal Naval air station at Yeovilton.

Make for South Barrow and North Barrow now, along a twisting narrow lane delightful in its rural scenery. Through Lovington

nd Hornblotton Green, and villages where almost the only vidence of the internal combustion engine is your own, and over ne A37 in the direction of Parbrook, to join the 361 at West ennard for Glastonbury and its abbey. The A39 joins Glaston-ury to Wells, where the cathedral offers possibly the most omprehensive menu of beauty and historic interest available in est country ecclesiastical history.

Out of Wells, the signposts point an easy drive to Wookey, here the local church has a 13th Century font, seeming uriously young compared with the 10,000 centuries the under-round rivers needed to carve out the grottoes of Wookey Hole aves deep below the surface. Leaving Wookey, keep the Ebbor ocks directly on your right and follow the narrow road via riddy. Already you have a toehold on the Mendip foothills. After riddy the 3135 will take you down through the grand canyon into heddar. If you have never seen the Gorge before, you will find it ifficult to believe you are still in Britain. Thickly wooded all the ay, the winding descent is a mile long and would swallow St. aul's Cathedral with 100ft. to spare. And at the bottom lie the ntrances to the weird and spooky caves, and the more cheery ttle town of Cheddar – from whence comes one of the finest, and robably the most underrated, cheeses in the world. Climb back up rough the winding canyon on the 351 again and, after the sum-it, turn left on the 3371 towards the Bath road (368) which you in at West Harptree.

If there is no countryside in England like Cheddar Gorge, there no town quite like Bath. Its seemingly unending stone terraces ve a sense of continuity unmatched anywhere else in Britain – d its historical links with ancient Rome are immense. The oman Baths, the superb abbey, Pulteney Bridge across the Avon where you can sit in a cafe on the bridge itself and watch the urning water of the weir below – all these are simply a few items a long list of things which even separately could dub the city

unique. And from the top of Beckford Tower, at the summit of Landsdowne Hill and nearly 1,000ft. above the river, on a clear day you can see six counties and almost for ever.

THE GREAT WHITE HORSE

The route out of Bath takes the 363 fork to Bradford-on-Avon. The country runs through a hilly wooded area, the hedgerows thick with honeysuckle and the land falling steeply away to your right and sloping upwards on the left hand side. Over the Wiltshire border the countryside flattens out and begins to throw off the wilder western influences of Somerset. Bradford-on-Avon and Stonebridge at the bottom of the hill, are the last hints of the now distant Mendips, as you climb out on the 3053 to join the 350 at Melksham. We need to drive through Chippenham, however, and turn on to the pleasant A4 before we really begin to get the feel of Wiltshire proper. Now it is rolling agricultural country, great squared-up meadows and wooded copses like casual punctuation. Ahead and to the southeast lies the Vale of Pewsey, and Marl-borough Down begins on your left after you get to Beckhampton.

But first there is a great white horse cut in the hill on the right when you leave Cherhill; and beyond it Oldbury Castle. The curious great mound of Silbury Hill rears up beside the road as you approach West Kennett, and only Fyfield and Manton need be traversed before you see a second great white horse cut in the down to your right by the boys of Marlborough School. Sweep beneath the college archway which spans the road, and turn the corner into the magnificent High Street of Marlborough town. St. Peter's Church (where Thomas Wolsey was ordained) stands at one end of this great wide thoroughfare and St. Mary's at the other. Geographically placed to great advantage, the High Street does not, somehow, seem to make the most of itself. One expects, perhaps, a deeper medieval feeling to the place; but since the countryside around is a great natural museum of pre-history rather than the Dark Ages, we may be expecting too much. As you drive through and take the road (346) towards Burbage you skirt old Savernake Forest on your left with its reminiscent warnings of wandering deer, and a latticework of scenic roads.

By turning hard right at Burbage, you launch out on to the Vale of Pewsey itself – making for the town. Pewsey is a pretty, thatched and timbered place and sends you on your way through thatched Upavon, to villages where one sees the brick beginning to replace the stone of the farther west country. Then to Bulford, and a right turn on to the dual carriageway of the 303 until you reach the prehistoric star of Wiltshire – the great enigma of Stonehenge.

Here you may well feel slightly disappointed that the stones are not bigger (perhaps one's early consciousness of them as a child has left a larger impression than they make upon the eye in maturity). The unwittingly ribald notice which requests visitors "not to picnic on the monument" is so Frankie Howerdian in its connotations as to bring a touch of anti-climax to this, the climax of a journey which, in a little over a quarter of an hour, will end in the great cathedral city of Salisbury – almost 300 miles along the road since you let in the clutch at Winchester.

In those 300 miles you've seen four counties, a myriad of scenic splendour, wildlife and countryside in profusion, architectural achievement unmatched in all the world – and thousands of years of history.

van Green, typical thatched cottage scene in the New Forest

23 BATH ABBEY
24 COSTUME MUSEUM
25 ROMAN BATHS

MENDIP HILLS

26 PULTENEY
BRIDGE

21 CHEDDAR GORGE
22 CHEDDAR CAVES

20 WOOKEY HOLE

19 WELLS CATHEDRAL

GLASTONBURY
TOR

18 GEORGE AND PILGRIMS
(GLASTONBURY INN)

17 GLASTONBURY (ABBEY)

16 CERNE ABBAS

15 TOLPUDDLE

13 BOVINGTO
TANK MUSE

WAYFARER'S GUIDE
2

14 THE HARDY COUNTRY

12 LULWOR
COVE

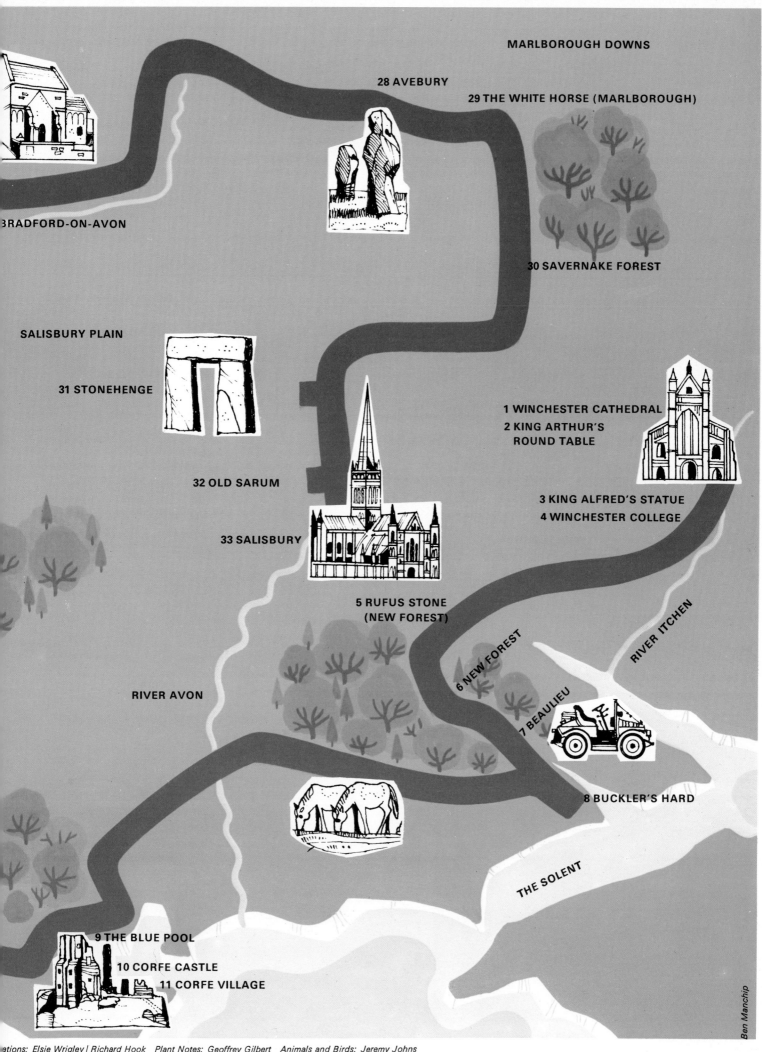

MARLBOROUGH DOWNS

28 AVEBURY

29 THE WHITE HORSE (MARLBOROUGH)

BRADFORD-ON-AVON

30 SAVERNAKE FOREST

SALISBURY PLAIN

31 STONEHENGE

1 WINCHESTER CATHEDRAL
2 KING ARTHUR'S
  ROUND TABLE

32 OLD SARUM

3 KING ALFRED'S STATUE
4 WINCHESTER COLLEGE

33 SALISBURY

5 RUFUS STONE
(NEW FOREST)

RIVER ITCHEN

6 NEW FOREST

RIVER AVON

7 BEAULIEU

8 BUCKLER'S HARD

THE SOLENT

9 THE BLUE POOL

10 CORFE CASTLE

11 CORFE VILLAGE

ations: Elsie Wrigley / Richard Hook   Plant Notes: Geoffrey Gilbert   Animals and Birds: Jeremy Johns

Ben Manchip

1 WINCHESTER CATHEDRAL: Its architectural grandeur is obvious, even to the most insensitive; but what are some of the curiosities of this standing monument to more than 1,000 years of Christianity? Least ecclesiastical, perhaps, is the plain marble slab which marks the burial place of Jane Austen. She was taken there after dying in a little stucco fronted house still standing in College Street, just outside the Cathedral Close.

The stone calls God's attention to the memory of "Jane Austen, youngest daughter of the late Reverend George Austen, Rector of Steventon . . . she departed this life in the 18th of July, 1817, aged 41, after a long illness suffered with the patience and hopes of a Christian. The benevolence of her heart, the sweetness of her temper, and the extraordinary endowment of her mind obtained the regard of all who knew her, and the warmest love of her intimate connections. . . . in their deep affliction they are consoled by a firm though humble hope that her charity, devotion, faith and purity, have rendered her soul acceptable in the sight of her Redeemer."

Nowhere is there any reference to her literary greatness, to the happiness, in- struction, entertainment and gentle pleasu[re] she afforded so many millions.

Two other resting places vie curious[ly] with her gentle soul. The much-abuse[d] William Rufus is buried here — not to[o] far from the Rufus Stone which marks th[e] scene of Walter Tyrrell's "accidenta[l]" arrow shot; and here, almost befor[e] memory, they buried St. Swithun in 86[2]. Legend has it that Swithun's humility wa[s] so great he insisted on being burie[d] outside the precincts of the house of God — and that when his grave was opened i[n] 971, to redress the self-imposed injustic[e] the Heavens wept copiously for 40 day[s]

At 556 ft external length, Winchester is the longest cathedral in Europe. Walkelin, the first Norman bishop, began the building in 1079

The nave, 78 ft high, was remodelled in the 14th Century

The famous black Tournai font

he City Mill, restored in 1744

ospital of St. Cross

he Isaac Walton memorial window

2 KING ARTHUR'S ROUND TABLE:

The Great Hall of Winchester Castle is almost all that remains of the castle since its demolition was ordered by the Parliamentary Army after it had been besieged and captured by Oliver Cromwell in 1645 during the Civil War.

The Hall was the scene of the trial and condemnation to death of Sir Walter Raleigh, and also of some of the vicious sentences of the infamous Judge Jeffreys.

All that time, the great Round Table of King Arthur hung on the wall — as it does today — staring down on passing history. Is it *really* King Arthur's Round Table? Who knows? There are a hundred places and associations with Arthur on our route, but few so genuinely antique.

It is known with certainty that this great piece of solid oak has hung upon that wall for at least 600 years. John Hardynge wrote (*circa* 1400) that "The rounde table of Wynchester beganne, and there ended, and there it hangeth yet . . ." so the Table was regarded as ancient history even in those days; and Caxton in his preface to the *Morte D'Arthur* refers to this table as a surviving proof of Arthur's existence.

Ornamented like an enormous regal dart-board, it sports the Tudor Rose in the centre (a result of being repainted in the reign of Henry VIII) and bears place names for 24 of Arthur's knights, each named. They are Sir Galahad, Sir Lancelot, Sir Gawain, Sir Percival, Sir Lionel, Sir Tristram, Sir Gareth, Sir Bedevere, Sir Blubrys, Sir Lacote, Sir Lucane, Sir Plomyd, Sir Lamorak, Sir Bors, Sir Saser, Sir Pellens, Sir Kay, Sir Ector, Sir Dagonet, Sir Degore, Sir Brumeur, Sir Lybyus, Sir Alinore, and Sir Mordred.

Solid oak, 600 years on the wall

A symbol of regal power

3 KING ALFRED'S STATUE:

It is ironic that the most generally popular fact remembered about Alfred the Great is that he wasn't much of a cook — but the great statue in Winchester High Street is a symbol of more power and intelligence than is contained in a legend about burning cakes.

Alfred was the first great regal administrator this country had ever known, and the fine bronze statue of a genius who held his court in this city and was finally buried here (the site is unknown), seems the least that posterity can do for him. By Hamo Thorneycroft, it is relatively new — being erected in 1901 as a national monument to mark the millenary of the great Saxon king.

Backed by St Giles Hill, with a public park on its summit, the environs have historic interest, too. For on St Giles Hill is the site of a famous medieval annual fair which originated in a grant made by William the Conqueror to the Bishop of Winchester. The line of the High Street today, from Broadway up to the old Westgate, still follows the route of the main street laid down by the Romans — almost 1,000 years before Alfred himself strode the land.

Alfred succeeded to the crown of Wessex in 871 — and to a kingdom largely under the domination of the Danes. He drove them northwards and across to the other side of the Thames and was thenceforward able to develop the kingdom in peace. The first mention of Winchester, indeed comes as "Vintancaester" in the Venerable Bede's *History of England* — the five volumes of which were translated in English from the Latin by Alfred's order.

The quadrangle of the college founded in 1382

4 WINCHESTER COLLEGE: More than any other English school, this has a reputation for the British stoic preparation for the rough knocks of life to follow. The college was founded by Bishop William of Wykeham in 1382. It was envisaged as an academy which would ensure a regular supply of 70 young scholars for the Church and its original personnel consisted of "70 poor scholars, 16 choristers, a Warden and Headmaster, 10 Fellows, 3 Chaplains, 3 Clerks, an Usher, and 10 Commoners".

There are still 70 "scholars" at Winchester, though in 1885 the scholarships were thrown open to "intellectual competition", but the number of fee paying "commoners" has been considerably in-creased from the original ten.

Bishop William hoped that his 70 original scholars would continue their education eventually at New College, Oxford (which he had founded some few years earlier) and there is still a tenuous traditional connection between the two. Much of the College Chapel was rebuilt in the 19th Century, but some original glass exists at the south-west end, some Flemish tapestry of around the late 15th Century, and some 14th Century stall ends.

The wall of the adjoining hall — where the boys ate from wooden platters — has some 16th Century panelling. The atmosphere reflects the grandeur which makes this college — with Eton and Harrow — one of the three most historic in England.

*THE WINTER CHORUS
OF LINNETS*

The linnet, favourite cage-bird of the Victorians, now seems a forgotten pet. The bird is little over five inches tall and prefers the open heath or moor of Hampshire or Dorset, to the confines of a garden. The hen is a dull striated brown colour but the male has vivid crimson patches on his forehead and breast and a rich chestnut back. The crimson patches play a part in mating — they fade and disappear during the Autumn. The song of the linnet is usually compared to a canary's but it is deeper, more sonorous and considerably more varied. "Choral singing" has been noted during the winter when the birds come together to forage in flocks for food.

5 RUFUS STONE: If you drive ou of Cadnam and along the A31 th Rufus Stone is just north of the road before you come to Stoney Cross. The ston stands in a little woodland area known a Canterton Glen. Here, it is claimed, th arrow of Walter Tyrrell killed William (The Rufus); and how much th "accident" was preconceived history ha never been able to decide.

There was a rough justice about Wil liam's death, however, as the New Fore had been the scene of considerabl oppression of the inhabitants by Williar Rufus on behalf of the Forest Law William's father — The Conqueror — ha been blamed for laying waste great area of the countryside to create happy nev hunting grounds—but, in fact, the area ha been hunted by Saxon kings for centurie before he arrived in England. William th Conqueror more or less formed the Nev Forest in terms of drawing up the area as royal playground in 1079, and introduce legislation prohibiting hunting there to an without the royal consent. But it is doubtfu if much of the area had been farme beforehand, because of the poor natur of the soil.

The Rufus, on the other hand, was a oppressor of the first class — and h continually enforced savage penalties fc any killing of deer without royal per

6 NEW FOREST PONIES: The fir thing to know about the New Fore ponies is that you may be in trouble if yo feed them. Notices everywhere warn yo that indulging their equine appetite renders you open to a fine of £20. It is n official spoilsport attitude which prompt the legislation. Over recent years th number of accidents to cars and ponie through the animals being attracted to th road side areas in the expectation c goodies, has mounted alarmingly. The poc soil of the Forest area offers no easy an luxurious living to these animals, who winter have to forage continuously, an the chance of an easy meal prompts ther to locate a picnic with uncanny instinct.

Most of them look fat enough thoug to be sure; like an errant collection of thos frolicsome quadrupeds cartooned by The well. And the male should look happy least: stallions are limited to 100 — to kee the breeding figures under control — o of a pony population of some 2,500.

The ponies do not stray far away fro their chosen locality, and stick loose together in herds. Mostly they keep to th wooded areas where the soil, and there fore the grazing, is kinder. They a generally thought to be the descendan of small wild horses here before the doma of the Forest was officially drawn up. The can be spiteful, which is another reasc for discouraging them from coming tc close.

ission. These regulations were the fore-
nners of those which promised death
d perpetuated outlawry for Robin Hood
r killing game in Sherwood Forest in the
ign of King John.

The spot where William Rufus died

Russet tints highlighted by autumn sunshine in the New Forest

Wild ponies at Rhinefield, near Brockenhurst

7 BEAULIEU: The Montagu Arms Hotel is not an old building compared with the Palace House and the Abbey nearby, but it can claim a successful merging of the tastes and decor of passing centuries. Interestingly enough, the area is one of the oldest wine growing centres in England, and still produces a rosé which cannot be *dismissed* as "modest" because no rosé wine is ever anything more.

Fittingly, the bar counter is fashioned from an ancient wine press.

In the vicinity the restless traveller can amuse himself with sailing on the Solent and Beaulieu River, hunting and beagling over the New Forest area, pony trekking and hacking, fishing in the Avon and the Test for trout and salmon, and walking with pure delight through the animal and bird sanctuaries of the Forest.

Just down the road, is the best-known vintage car museum in the world. Founded in 1952 in memory of John, Second Baron Montagu of Beaulieu, by the present Lord Montagu, it commemorates one of the pioneers of British motoring and possibly the first parliamentary champion of the motorist's cause. Its mechanical charm is enhanced by the pastoral and architectural delights which everywhere surround it.

An Alldays and Onions veteran

Lord Montagu at the wheel of a vintage Daimler at Beaulieu

A 1911 Renault

8 BUCKLER'S HARD: A fascinating little hamlet which 200 years ago was a thriving boat-building centre. The river bed of the Beaulieu River is private property — owned today by Lord Montagu of Beaulieu whose family inherited it via the first Earl of Southampton. The Earl acquired it after the dissolution of the monasteries had wrenched it from the Cistercian monks.

Now devoted to sailing, the area has a considerable naval history, marked by a Maritime Museum opened by Earl Mountbatten in 1963. H.M.S. *Agamemnon* was built and launched there in 1781 and was later commanded by Horatio Nelson, who described her as his favourite ship. Later she took part on the Battles of Copenhagen and Trafalgar.

A scale model of the Hard, with the great wooden ships H.M.S. *Euryalus* and H.M.S. *Swiftsure* waiting on the stocks for launching, sets the scene of Buckler's Hard in the year 1803 (two years before Trafalgar), and the whimsical addition of a case containing the baby clothes worn by Nelson as a child is a sentimental touch. But even without these historic references, a visit to Buckler's Hard is well worth the journey for the picturesque sweep of the water and the fascinating old buildings.

Overlooking Beaulieu River near Buckler's Hard

lue Pool, near Stoborough Green

he quay at Wareham

9 THE BLUE POOL: About a couple of miles out of Wareham on the road o Corfe Castle (the 351) take a right fork own a minor road to The Blue Pool. It lies nidway between Stoborough Green — vhere you took the fork — and East reech. The Blue Pool is a flooded clay pit vhich really is a very pretty blue, and urrounded by several acres of hills overed in pine trees. Open as an especially leasant pleasure garden, it is there to be njoyed all the year round except for a rest eriod during the months from January to aster.

The Blue Pool is some 38 ft at its eepest and about three acres in area. It is a erfect place for picnics, and unfortunately widely patronised therefore. But there is a rge car park and you can find pleasant hough seclusion if you will take the ouble to strike out and explore the ections furthest from the inevitable re-eshments shop. The colour of the water is credibly brilliant.

Creech Grange is nearby too; an nposing Tudor house with fine furniture nd paintings and a garden full of peacocks.

10 CORFE CASTLE: The village and the castle itself are of the local quarry stone — and the very name is supposed to come from the Anglo-Saxon word *ceorfan,* meaning "to cut". The original date of building is lost in history — but, certainly, a stone fortress was standing here in the reign of William the First, and some kind of settlement must have existed that was important enough for the visit of a king. A sign in the village square attests to the murder of King Edward the Martyr.

Violence was never far away. In the 12th Century, King Stephen besieged it against Queen Matilda and almost a century later King John imprisoned 22 of the noblest knights of France, who had supported the succession of Prince Arthur — and starved them to death. Edward the Second was imprisoned here, too, before he was removed to the larger and more important castle of Berkeley for his murder.

In 1644 Corfe Castle was the only stronghold between Exeter and London still standing out for King Charles, but it fell in 1646 and was demolished by the Parliamentarians. It remains today much as the spoilers left it.

A novel touch is the scale reconstruction of castle, village and church, as they stood in the 17th century prior to the siege.

11 CORFE VILLAGE: Possibly the tiniest museum encountered on the route, the Corfe Castle Village Museum is on the left of the main street after you pass through the square leaving the castle behind you. It is a collection of improbable exhibits. There is for example a box of Victorian slate pencils alongside a 1923 battery wireless set. There are things which, if you are over 40, hit the bell of distant memory — curious relics which one may have seen at grandmother's house when one was a small child.

Here is an example of the earliest cigarette machine — with slots for six-penny pieces for the luxurious brands, and for two single penny pieces for cheaper brands. Facing it is a genuine motorised scooter (one suspects a steam motivation) of 1919, and a pair of hand stocks from far more distant times.

Exhibited as a kind of afterthought is the Corfe Castle School Bell — with an addendum on its label stating that it was "Last used as an Air Raid Warning by Mr. Sid Paine". Most whimsical of the exhibits, possibly, are a brace of mechanisms claiming to be "mole traps", delightfully described in Winnie the Pooh terms by the qualification beneath their notice explain-Ing they are "For Trapping Moles".

Corfe Castle — the museum is on the right going uphill

Like a lake, Lulworth Cove nestles between two great arms of stone

12 **LULWORTH COVE:** Stop here for tea and you could ask for "Dorset Nobs" with it. These are so called after the buttons they resemble — the making of which was one of the main cottage industries in Dorset in the 1800s. But think of more than your stomach. The place is beautiful if sometimes spoiled by an influx of trippers who come there incessantly but somehow never seem to pay its beauty the respect it deserves.

The cove is almost circular and seems to be entirely enclosed until you focus closely on the Pillars of Hercules, the two monuments of Purbeck and Portland stone which stand guard at the doorway to the cove.

Durdle Door is there too — a great rock arch, shaped by the waves of for ever, through which a small boat may make its drifting way. There are lovely walks along the cliff tops on either side and views to take away your breath. And for the man who really takes his pleasures prehistorically, the cove can boast a Fossil Forest which becomes visible at low tide.

13 **BOVINGTON:** Later in the route we can drift off a few miles to the west to see the Fleet Air Arm Museum at Yeovilton in Somerset. But Army loyalties can be served now at Bovington Camp, a couple of miles north of Wool. It is not far from Lawrence of Arabia's cottage at Clouds Hill. So Army and Air Force are well represented in terms of Lawrence's service life.

Armoured vehicles of all kinds from 1900 onwards — both British and foreign — are interestingly well presented and comfortably unbelligerent.

At Moreton, two or three miles to the right off the 352 between Wool and Dorchester, is the grave of Lawrence of Arabia. He was killed on his motor cycle on the heath road near Bovington, and buried in the small cemetery beneath the simple inscription "To T.E.L. — who should sleep among kings".

German Panther and Tiger II in the tank museum

14 **THE HARDY COUNTRY:** Dorset is the Hardy Country, of course. Since the end of its confused partisanship in the Civil Wars of the 17th Century, there has been little to remark Dorset as a political area, and much of the county's pride rests in the memory of its most famous literary figure. The Dorchester Museum, next to the church, at the end of the narrow main street has a reconstruction of Hardy's study at the Max Gate, which is just on the edge of the town. The detail has been watched carefully — down to small points such as keeping the calendar standing at the day of his death in 1928. At Higher Bockhampton, not far away, the site of his birthplace 88 years earlier is tended by the National Trust.

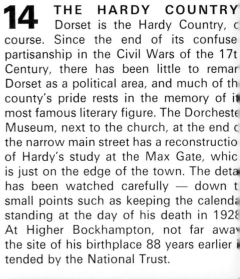

Maggie Richardson's bust of Thomas Hardy

Hardy's walking-stick

Hardy's birthplace, the cottage at Higher Bockhampton, tended by the National Trust

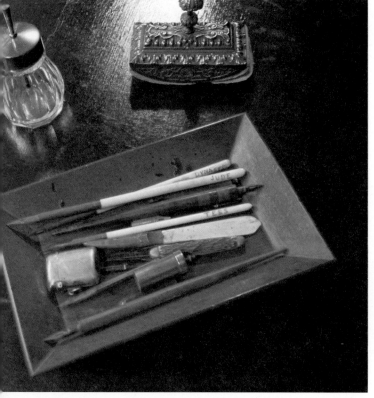

Pens, ink pot and blotter used by Thomas Hardy

Reconstruction of Hardy's study

Tolpuddle village — home of the six trade union martyrs

Abbey gatehouse at Cerne Abbas

The turf giant with a 90 ft club

15 **TOLPUDDLE:** Before we proceed from Dorchester up the 352 towards Sherborne, we could pay our respects to the Trade Union Martyrs of Tolpuddle. Tolpuddle lies astride the Poole road (A35) out of Dorchester, and still boasts the famous sycamore tree (now the property of the National Trust) where the Six Men of Dorset met stubbornly to form a trade union aimed at improving the lot of farm labourers.

They were adjudged guilty of conspiracy — the first of the trade union "martyrs" — and transported in chains to Australia. Exactly a century later — in 1934 — the trade union movement recognised their bold and sacrificial initiative by erecting six cottages and other memorials in the village to their memory.

There is, apart from the cottages, a roadside shelter made out of the timbers of H.M.S. *Hercules.* There is, too, a memorial gateway to the martyrs in the foreground of the Wesleyan Chapel.

Gravestone of martyr James Hammett

16 **CERNE ABBAS:** Along the 35 about a third of the way betwee Dorchester and Sherborne, you encount the village of Cerne Abbas — which offe more than the picturesque simplicities the average village. It is beautifully site and is where much of the film *Tom Jone* was photographed. Remember the huntin scene? That was on the downs abov Cerne Abbas, and near the ruins of the o abbey stands a farm also featured in th film.

The area has practically everything f tourists: There's a jolly little stream, and 15th Century church with a Norma chancel. The village has houses wit strains of Tudor, Regency and Georgia influences, and an abbey gatehouse wit mullioned windows to mark an ecclesia tical palace where Margaret of Anjou said to have slept the night.

And there is the Cerne Abbas Turf Gia cut out of the hill above the village nearly 200 ft high in itself and wielding club 90 ft in length. He is believed to I Roman and the fact that his clubless han carries a lion's skin has identified him as facsimile of Hercules. But all the ancie earthworks and burial mounds in whic the area is rich seem to take the figure bac close to pre-history. Cerne Abbas is a bus afternoon in itself.

THE WEASEL'S DANCE OF DEATH
In Hampshire the weasel is given the local name of "Carne", a familiarity that has been used to argue a high population of weasels in the county.

This small predator seldom measures more than nine inches from tip to tail and is renowned for its ferocity and reckless courage in tackling animals far bigger than itself and for its skill and subtlety in luring its prey with a strange dance reminiscent of the mongoose.

Fortunately the weasel's true value to the farmer is at last being recognised and the animal enjoys a much safer existence than it once did.

7 GLASTONBURY ABBEY:

Among beautifully kept lawns and trees, these lovingly tended ruins are all that remains of what was one of medieval England's finest ecclesiastical buildings. Pillaged after the dissolution, the stones themselves were finally dragged away for use in the building of much of the town that now surrounds the ruins.

But there is still much to amuse and fascinate. The two huge whales' jawbones, which constitute the arch to the original entrance; one of several graves specified as the tomb of King Arthur; and of course the Holy Thorn Tree which is claimed to be a cutting of that planted by St. Joseph of Arimathea when he came to England to preach the Gospel in A.D. 60. Traditionally, he is supposed to have stuck his staff in the ground on nearby Weary-All Hill and it forthwith sprouted and flowered. The Thorn blossoms twice a year — in the Spring and at Christmas time.

Pilgrims came from all over England in ancient times attracted by an impressive collection of holy relics and by the belief that Joseph of Arimathea buried the chalice used at the Last Supper under a spring on Glastonbury Tor. Certainly the history reaches back to the foundation of a church on this spot by the Saxon King Ine, around the year A.D. 700. The Great Church itself was not built until very much later, towards the end of the 12th Century.

Abbey gate at ancient Glastonbury

Majestic ruins at Glastonbury, hinting at the glory of what was formerly one of England's finest abbeys

Historic George and Pilgrims Inn

18 GEORGE AND PILGRIMS:

This historic old inn has been standing for five centuries. It was built originally by the Benedictine Abbot Selwood of Glastonbury Abbey in 1475 — as its contemporary equivalent of a luxury motel offering more comfortable accommodation for pilgrims than given to the free board and lodgings meted out at the Abbey itself. The architecture is uncompromisingly ecclesiastical still. But the beautiful mullioned windows and the four-poster bedrooms upstairs bring a beautifully welcoming touch to the glory of the magnificent superstructure.

Inside, a long hallway is floored with the original stone flags, inclining gently with the lie of the land and worn by the tread of ages, and the whole place successfully captures that happy blend of history and comfort without confusing the eye and the mind with the hang-overs of succeeding centuries. Warrants to the building's great age are the three shields placed above the main entrance in Glastonbury High Street. They bear the arms of St. George of England, King Edward IV — and a blank face still waiting to receive the arms of the patron builder, who somehow never quite got around to adding them.

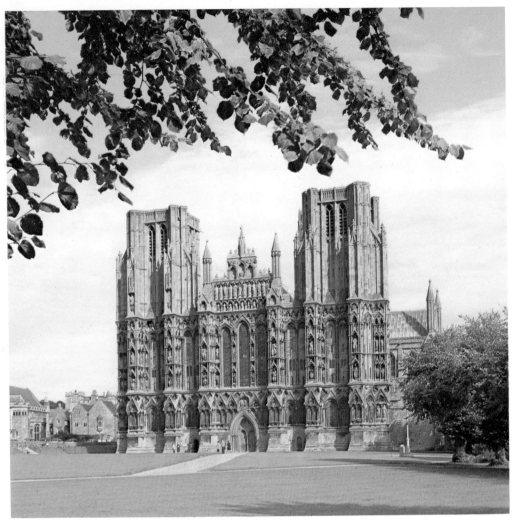

Wells Cathedral — "the finest assembly of medieval sculpture in Britain"

Cheddar Gorge — a fabulous sight

10,000 centuries under the earth

19 **WELLS CATHEDRAL** has what may be the finest assembly of medieval sculpture in Britain. Arthur Mee thought so. He described the cathedral and its surroundings as "the most complete example we have today of what an ecclesiastical city was like in days when the Church ruled the world". The chain bridge, the moat, the great clock, the introspective boundaries turned towards the palace, all these suggest the isolated splendour of churchmen in days when none dared flaunt them. And the prelates who ruled this great place have left a line of individualities to mark their personal phases of power.

Bishop Ralph's chapel still contains its original 14th Century altar stone. In two chapels of the north transept a pompous lump of 18th Century sculpture recalls Bishop Kidder; and this is paralleled by the figure of Bishop Still (17th Century) to whom has been attributed that undying fragment of children's satirical verse *Little Jack Horner*. Bishop Marcia, of the 14th Century, lies beneath a canopy of three bays in the south transept, and a stone lying above the grave of Bishop Bytton is one of the first engraved figures ever made in Britain. A visit to his tomb was long regarded as a certain cure for toothache. Bytton's coffin has been opened recently and his own teeth were noted to be in almost perfect condition after a rest of more than 600 years.

In the aisles lie the remains of nearly all the long line of faithful Bishops of Wells — to point up again how much our English churches seem to give their floors to the memory of the ancient and medieval times, their walls to monuments of the 17th Century and later. When all at last is decorated, perhaps the 20th Century will have access at last to the roofs decorated mainly nowadays by figures of angels.

The cathedral itself is a wonder — but its clock is a delight of whimsicality which evades classification in aesthetic references. The legendary Jack Blandifer sits way above the cathedral's north transept, kicks his heels each passing quarter of an hour and sets in motion the cheerful prancing panorama of mounted knights galloping around the transept below him. And as they go, they set in motion the two great knights without the walls who strike the hours with their huge battleaxes. It is a magnificent piece of medieval mechanism — stretching in its idea way back to the late 14th Century — and though many of the working parts have been replaced, the old works are still actually ticking away in a London museum. The great clock registers the hour, the minute, the day of the month, and the current phase of the moon. The face is supported by angels controlling the four winds and measures more than six feet across. Well worth a visit.

20 **WOOKEY HOLE:** As you lea Wells on the way to the w caverns of the Cheddar Gorge, a stop Wookey Hole will get you in the mood cave dwelling — or at least test yo reaction to the claustrophobic. Not impressive as Cheddar, Wookey has t advantage of not being quite so popu and not so tripperish. Like the Chedd Caves, which are but a few miles away, t whole natural underground temple h been slowly nagged into its weird evo tions by four distinct slow-moving wa courses, and their tiny water dropl shaping the stone over a period of 10,0 centuries or more.

Prehistoric finds have been made h wholesale; for its size, its historical cont may be considered more impressive ev than Cheddar. It seems like referring yesterday to point out that Wook Church has a 13th Century font.

21 CHEDDAR GORGE: While sensibilities may be assailed by the grotesque formations of the caverns themselves, the fabulous sight of the Cheddar Gorge itself can delight everyone. If possible, it should be visited out of season, when its 400 ft. high cliffs, sliced apart like two great layers of a stone cake, stand lonely monuments to Ice Age erosion.

There are nearly two miles of road from the bottom to the flat country of the Mendip Top, and the steepness happily forces any car into a crawl which allows a fuller appreciation of the breathless beauty you are passing. Inside those cliffs on each side, a billion streams of trickling water continue to shape the fantastic geological excrescences that decorate the caves.

Cheddar itself is worth a visit for its 15th century market cross, and for its magnificent 15th Century church — a gentle human homage to the vasty grandeur of the caves.

22 CHEDDAR CAVES: Whether you regard their weird, twisted convolutions as marvellously beautiful or hideously obscene, there is no denying their curious grandeur. A host of small caves had been known to local residents for centuries, but only in the middle years of the 19th Century did Richard Cox Gough begin to excavate through the smaller, basic, and relatively normal rock holes into the fantastic natural architecture deeper inside the hills. The wild stalagmites and stalactites are now there for all visitors to see (shun them if you are claustrophobic), but rock falls in the mists of time may have sealed off from the outside world a formation of natural palaces inhabited by primitive man for aeons.

Flint implements found in Soldier's Hole are identified as belonging to the Early Upper Palaeolithic Age (roughly between 0 and 30 thousand years ago) and contemporary with the times of woolly mammoths and woolly rhinoceri. The Late Palaeolithic Age is even more fully represented — by many thousands of simple flint and bone instruments, and by the complete skeleton of a man of the period whose bones have been established as being more than 10,000 years old.

x's Cave in Cheddar Caverns

23 BATH ABBEY: An extraordinary town like Bath demands an extraordinary edifice like Bath Abbey. Building was started in 1499 and the Gothic love of grotesque or seeming primitive statuary is much in evidence. See the fabulous carved oak west door presented to the Abbey by Lord Chief Justice Sir Henry Montague in 1617. See the curious decoration, and the wealth of it, on the faces of the turrets on the west front, with the angels climbing into and descending from Heaven; and note the elaborate and intricate carving of the stone rebus of Bishop Oliver King.

Be enthralled by the fantastic wrought iron screen in the north transept, and the brilliant colourings of the heraldic glass window (17th Century) in the north aisle. Do not miss seeing the superb fan vaulting in the Chapman Aisle. It is not short of exquisite; and pay homage to the "King" of Bath at the plain tablet to Richard "Beau" Nash, Master of Ceremonies at Bath during the first half of the 18th Century. He made Bath the centre of Fashion in its day, unwittingly laying a nicely historic trailer for the present-day Museum of Fashion.

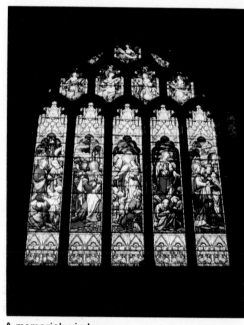
A memorial window

Bath Abbey with its magnificent carved oak door

24 COSTUME MUSEUM: The immense boom in fashion interest since the end of the Second World War, makes this collection a "must" to any traveller who likes his history spiced with a dash of the sociological. It is possibly the largest collection of fashion and costume in the world — based on the original collection assembled by Doris Langley Moore at Eridge Castle near Tunbridge Wells, Kent, under the patronage of the Marquess of Abergavenny, and now in the Bath Assembly Rooms.

It was Doris Langley Moore who first exploded the myth of those tiny 16, 17 and 18-inch Victorian ladies' waistlines. She measured more than 1,000 women's costumes from the period and did not discover one with a smaller waist than $20\frac{1}{2}$ inches. The Manchester Gallery of Costume bears out her findings — having no dress on show of less than 21 inches, despite the rigour of Victorian lacing.

But to make up for this disillusionment, there are caps and doublets embroidered when William Shakespeare was still in breeches, brocades and damasks from the Beau Nash period, and charming muslin dresses which would have graced the polite social set of Jane Austen's heroines. For the more esoteric, one room concentrates entirely on underwear — and in the Modern Room an annual adjustment brings the collection up to date with a representative ensemble of the current season.

19th Century carriage dresses

Minerva head: a national treasure

25 ROMAN BATHS: Rediscovered, accidentally by builders in 1775, these Roman Baths were encapsulated for centuries by the rubble of succeeding generations — each layer piled atop the other until a workman's pick brought the ancient hot springs gushing to the surface. Excavation found the baths almost as they were more than 1,500 years ago. Here is the finest collection of authentic Roman remains that this country can boast.

It is centred on a magnificent suite of baths developed between A.D.80 and A.D.400 around hot water springs which have been on the boil for time uncounted. The baths are surrounded by magnificent archaeological finds which this tomb of treasure surrendered up with its steamy rediscovery. All the unused water still makes it way to warm the River Avon down the stone duct the Romans placed there for the purpose — and the floors are still covered with the lead the Romans mined in the Mendip Hills.

There is a gilded bronze head of Minerva which may be numbered among our greatest national treasures, and a weirdly menacing head of the Medusa, writhing in snakes but carved in still and solid stone — as if the fearsome thing had suddenly seen its own hideous head mirrored in the waters, and suffered the petrified fate of all its victims.

26 PULTENEY BRIDGE was bu[ilt] by Robert Adam. Like an en[g]raving of old London Bridge, it stand[s] with its shops and buildings lining th[e] narrow way across and reminds us of [a] time when bridge space was never waste[d] as it seems to be today.

You can sit in a neat little café restaura[nt] here, by the open window, and watch th[e] Avon river rushing over the weir belo[w] you, its trapped froth "creaming an[d] mantling like a standing pond" to remin[d] us of the growing modern hazard [of] detergent pollution. But the blemish is a[s] yet a minor one, and the view across th[e] water, to the unbroken continuity of Bath['s] never ending terraces, is unequalled fo[r] novelty anywhere.

Half a mile away, climbing up toward[s] the London Road, is another delightf[ul] bridge — the bridge of Cleveland, also hig[h] across the Avon. With a span of about 1[00] ft. it was rebuilt in 1927 but retains th[e]

The King's bath in the baths — the finest collection of Roman remains in Britain

arm of much greater antiquity. The two
tle Greek temples at each end (formerly
ll gates) are largely responsible, and the
k with history is made clear by the 20
ins of the Roman Emperor Constantine
hich were unearthed in the original
undations.

st like **Old London Bridge**

e bridge at **Bradford**

27 **BRADFORD-ON-AVON:** Like
many of Britain's historic trea-
res, the Saxon church here was dis-
vered by accident. From the top of the
l above the little town, the Vicar of
adford-on-Avon in 1858 noticed the
ape of a cross among the roofs of
ildings huddled together below him.
search revealed that in the chronicles of
lliam of Malmesbury, a Saxon church
dicated to St. Laurence is mentioned,
d the Vicar took a closer look.
n effect the church had disappeared —
t structurally it remained virtually un-
uched. Within the original shell stood a
o-storey cottage, a school, and a small
use where the schoolmaster lived. Before
e incumbents could be moved, twelve
ars were to pass — but finally, from the
red remains, emerged the almost un-
oiled example of a Saxon church. And,
link with our route, it is believed that
ne stones found in the nave are
gments of a shrine in which were buried
bones of King Edward the Martyr who
s murdered by his mother at the village
Corfe Castle.

SEAT FOR THE GNOMES

*The pretty fly agaric is familiar to everyone,
for this is the pink toadstool with white
spots well-known as the seat of gnomes in
children's story books. Look out for it under
birch trees, for trees have their favourite
partners and these two go together.*

*Toadstools, so abundant in woodlands,
have always mystified people, for they appear to spring from nowhere and to have no
roots. In fact, top soil everywhere is threaded
through and through with fungal mycelium,
which is the name of the underground part
of the plant. It is virtually invisible because
it is so thin, perhaps half the thickness of a
cobweb and only noticeable as a white
silky mass when unusually fertile soil
produces a dense cluster of threads. It has
been estimated that a cubic inch of good
top soil contains over 100 miles of mycelium,
a figure that baffles imagination.*

*Of the vast family of fungi, most are
benign, but there are exceptions such as
the dry rot fungus or the honey fungus.
Many are edible and good but it should be
remembered that identification from books
can be treacherous.*

29 **THE WHITE HORSE:** You see
it up on your right, on the hill
just before you come into Marlborough
beneath the gantry arch at the western
end of the High Street. About the time of
Waterloo it was cut into the hillside by a
band of schoolboys under the direction of
Headmaster Greazeley. From your car on
the road it seems to be a bright beast,
prancing briskly with its tail up, but you
miss a true appreciation of its size. It is
62 ft. long and 47 ft. high.
The boys came from Marlborough
College, which was built on the site of an
old castle. One of the houses here entertained Charles II and Samuel Pepys. It later
became the Castle Inn — a popular stage
between London and the West Country —
and in 1843, the nucleus for the new
college at Marlborough.

28 **AVEBURY:** Most of the village
of Avebury lies inside its famous
stone circle and earthworks. These form
the largest prehistoric monument of the
kind in the country and were probably
built about 1800 B.C. The stones, which
are sarsen (local sandstone), seem to have
been chosen specially for their shape. Some
are tall with vertical sides. Others are
diamond-like, resting on one corner.
Several weigh over 40 tons, the biggest
four being at the entrances.
Several theories have been put forward
to explain the stones. They may have been
religious meeting places, or they may have
had some astronomical significance. With
the primitive tools available, the construction would probably have taken 200
men about nine years.
The stones were brought from the
Marlborough Downs, probably mounted
on large rough sledges and run on tree
trunk rollers. Well over 100 men may have
been needed to move each stone, using
ropes of cow hair or leather. It is believed
that to erect the stones a pit would be dug
with one side vertical and protected by
wooden stakes. The bottom would be flat
and the opposite side would form a sloping
ramp. The stone, base first, would be
rolled to the sloping edge of the pit and
wedged up until it was almost vertical.
Ropes would be used to pull it into the
final position. The sloping side of the pit
would then be filled with hard clay.

The stone circle at Avebury

East front of the College

30 SAVERNAKE FOREST: We pass down the right hand side of Savernake as we leave Marlborough and drive the first easy miles on the way along the 346 before we branch off across the Vale of Pewsey towards Stonehenge. A foray into its cool, dim, trees is worth any extra hour or two on the route. The forest covers more than 4,000 acres.

A stone obelisk in the grounds of the house of the Marquess of Ailesbury was optimistically erected as a monument to King George III's recovery from insanity; though, clearly, it was not destroyed with his relapse.

Solitude will be no problem here, though there is a beautiful Grand Avenue four miles long with eight other roads feeding it, and a feast of elms and beeches is everywhere you care to look.

Savernake Forest covers more than 4,000 acres

32 OLD SARUM: Out of c Sarum comes Salisbury, ar Old Sarum comes out of a hill fort of t early Iron Age. A great castle mound w built in the centre by the Normans. Befo them, for hundreds of years, the pla changed hands between Britons, Roma and Saxons. The luckless Ethelred t Unready used the place as a mint — ar doubtless struck coins for the infamo Danegeld which did him such little go in the long run. But 500 years before h time, according to the *Anglo Sax Chronicle*, in A.D.552, ''Cynric the Sax fought against the Britons at the pla called Searoburh and put the Britons flight . . .''

Searoburh may not sound much li Salisbury — but trace it through: Duri the Saxon period, the name lost its 'o' giving Searburh; and after the Norma the change developed into Seresberi. A

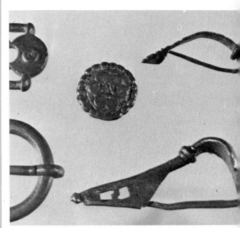

Brooches found at Old Sarum

31 STONEHENGE: One thing is certain about Stonehenge — it was not built by the Druids (a general misconception). Druids were priests in France and Britain during the last couple of centuries before Christ — but by that time Stonehenge had been standing already for more than 1,000 years.

There are three Stonehenges, built in the same place but successively over the centuries. The rudimentary circle, possibly with wood and some stone appendages, was created in the Neolithic or New Stone Age period, about 2,000 B.C. The second wave came four or five hundred years later, when the first circle of stones was erected. Bluestones were fetched all the way from Pembrokeshire in South Wales and sarsen stones from a radius of some thirty miles, possibly by raft along the Bristol Channel and up the River Avon, and dragged by sledge across the land. They were set up in two semi-circles about six feet apart and the middle of the opening faced towards the point of sunrise on the longest day of the year.

Excavations show that the arrangement was never completed — the builders changing their minds and neglecting to

Stonehenge — mysterious monument to the ingenuity of primitive man

fficial or civic name was invented to give
ne place prestige and for some reason —
ue possible to the basic similarity — the
tinised form of Salzburg was borrowed.
he latinised form was Salisburia. Over
ne centuries the "l" and the "r" seem to
ave been switched according to the mood
f the writer. Sarum comes from a devel-
oment in the Middle Ages when clerks
obreviated the name so.

In more modern times, the area was a
vourite of Constable who painted many
ictures in the area. One picture, exhibited
the Academy in 1834 dramatises the
reat mound with a forbidding Constable
y as background. St Osmund lived there,
o. He died in 1099 but 51 of the books he
ollected for his famous library still lie in
e cathedral.

In 1734 William Pitt the Elder first sat as
ne of Old Sarum's two Members of
arliament, elected by 10 voters.

d Sarum jugs in Salisbury Museum

ect about half the stones for which they
ad prepared the ground. Something
milar seems to have happened during the
ird phase, about a century later. Holes
ere prepared to form a certain circular
attern of stones, but the design was
arranged at some point during construc-
on. As Stonehenge was apparently some
nd of ritual calendar, as well as some
rm of temple, it is possible that the long
eriod connected with the building of the
ird phase (between two and three
undred years) cast some doubt on the
athematical calculations or heavenly
oservations necessary.

Whatever it stood for then, Stonehenge
ill stands as a monument to the infinite
genuity and patience of relatively primi-
ve man. If you need some pointer to their
atience as you regard these huge slabs,
alise that they were not shaped with
odern tools — but simply by pounding
e surfaces to dust with another round
one — until the shape was achieved.

Known as *trilithons* (from the Greek for
hree stones") their top sections —
rming a lintel — are all fixed by tenons
the top of the standing stones. The
nons protrude as much as nine inches.

Works of the oldest clock in England

Alabaster monument of Sir John Cheyney

33 SALISBURY CATHEDRAL:

The original cathedral was a
Norman one, built at Old Sarum — some
mile and a half from the centre of the city.
The present cathedral was started in 1220
— a remarkable monument to the then
new Gothic style architecture.

In the very capstone of the spire a lead
casket was placed with a holy relic, said
to be a fragment of the Virgin's robe, inside
it — to shield the spire from peril. In 1559,
however, the spire was struck by lightning.
It is reported that the relic was found still
in its box in the capstone, was replaced —
and discovered again in 1762 when
workers were adding a weathervane. In
the 19th Century, it was apparently
replaced by a more substantial container —
for during repairs in 1950, a copper box
with a lead lining was found. Due to the
weather, the contents were unrecognisable.

The cathedral contains the works of the
oldest clock in England. Made in 1386, it
was originally housed in the detached bell
tower which was done away with in the
year 1790. Until 1884 it stood in the
cathedral's central tower. Older still, within
the cathedral lies one of the only four
known copies of Magna Carta — a neatly
written sheet of some 1,000 words.

Salisbury Cathedral — its 404 ft spire is the tallest in England

The birth of England

The famous Alfred Jewel, fashioned from gold and showing the enamelled figure of a man holding two sceptres.

The Peace of Wedmore between King Alfred and the Danes was one of the most memorable in English history since "in saving Wessex it saved England". The Danes had conquered Northumbria, Mercia and East Anglia and had pushed up the Thames to Reading. Advance units of the Danish horde had advanced into the heart of Wessex — to the heights overlooking the Vale of the White Horse. Finally, Guthrum the Dane sailed for the south and from there raided Exeter. Alfred negotiated a temporary peace but a fresh "horde eager for plunder" swooped on Chippenham. Alfred withdrew to the Isle of Athelney among the marshes. From there he called the Saxon thanes of Somerset to his standard and marched through Wiltshire to meet Guthrum and the Danish horde. He defeated Guthrum in a great battle at Edington. Guthrum was baptised a Christian and was bound by a solemn peace pledge taken at Wedmore — and apart from a few brief skirmishes Guthrum kept his word.

Although all Northumbria, all East Anglia and half of central England was given over to the Danes (or became Dane-law), Saxon Wessex was preserved. In addition, Alfred retained his grip on the upper part of the Thames Valley, the whole of the Severn Valley and the rich plains of the Mersey and the Dee. In one sense Alfred can be described as the father of English literature. He was a considerable translator and gave a West Saxon form to Bede's famous Anglo-Saxon Chronicle. With Alfred England's consciousness as a nation may be said to begin.

The late 7th Century Saxon church at Bradford-on-Avon. The church was restored in the 19th Century. Its carved stone angel is one of the finest pieces of Anglo-Saxon sculpture.

The pommels of Anglo-Saxon swords were often of gold and were finely wrought. Only the richer warriors would have shields with iron boss. Mostly they were made from wood and leather.

After the Peace of Wedmore, King Guthrum of the Danes visited Alfred at the village of Aller and was there baptised. Guthrum is seen in his white robe — worn for eight days after the ceremony. Alfred holds the white band, sprinkled with holy oil, which he is about to bind round the pagan warrior's head. The font in the church at Aller may have been the one used for Guthrum's christening.

It was Alfred who consolidated the rule of the royal house of Wessex as the controllers of the Anglo-Saxon kingdom.

The map on the right shows the principal divisions of England at that time. In the late 6th and 7th Centuries there were many little kingdoms in the country. At one time or another Northumbria (divided into Bernicia between the Tees and the Forth, and Deira between the Humber and the Tees), Mercia (roughly the present Midlands), Essex, Middlesex, Kent, Wessex and Sussex all had kings who traced their ancestry from the old Germanic gods!

Anglo-Saxon houses were simple affairs. In early settlements the walls were often made from wattle, supported by a timber framework. These were the forerunners of the later Saxon style which developed the great beamed halls. Thatch was used for roofing but wooden tiles were also developed.

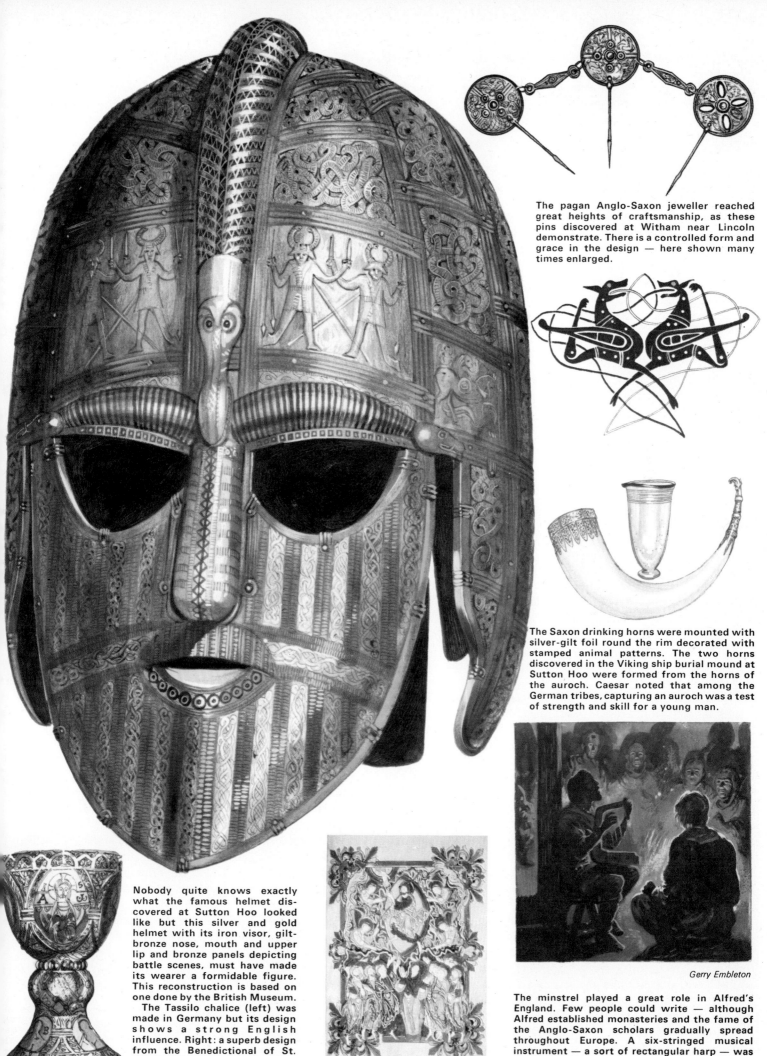

The pagan Anglo-Saxon jeweller reached great heights of craftsmanship, as these pins discovered at Witham near Lincoln demonstrate. There is a controlled form and grace in the design — here shown many times enlarged.

The Saxon drinking horns were mounted with silver-gilt foil round the rim decorated with stamped animal patterns. The two horns discovered in the Viking ship burial mound at Sutton Hoo were formed from the horns of the auroch. Caesar noted that among the German tribes, capturing an auroch was a test of strength and skill for a young man.

Gerry Embleton

Nobody quite knows exactly what the famous helmet discovered at Sutton Hoo looked like but this silver and gold helmet with its iron visor, gilt-bronze nose, mouth and upper lip and bronze panels depicting battle scenes, must have made its wearer a formidable figure. This reconstruction is based on one done by the British Museum.

The Tassilo chalice (left) was made in Germany but its design shows a strong English influence. Right: a superb design from the Benedictional of St. Ethelwold done at Winchester.

The minstrel played a great role in Alfred's England. Few people could write — although Alfred established monasteries and the fame of the Anglo-Saxon scholars gradually spread throughout Europe. A six-stringed musical instrument — a sort of rectangular harp — was among the treasures found at Sutton Hoo.

Sussex and Kent – the garden of England

TONY ASPLER

Between Midhurst in West Sussex and Canterbury, the jewel of Kent, lies some of the most tranquil and lush scenery in Britain. The fertile clay valleys of the Sussex and Kentish Weald separate the tough grasslands of the North Downs from the softly rolling green velvet of the South Downs, stippled with flowering gorse and laced with chalk trails that shepherds followed 5,000 years ago. The famous breed of Southdown sheep has all but disappeared from the Downs now, abandoning the steep pastures to herds of dairy cattle or the plough.

The irregular plain of the Weald, the wonderfully rich soil of the Hastings Bed which is aptly called "The Garden of England", was once thickly wooded. It was described in the Kentish section of the Domesday Book as inaccessible and so it remained well into Elizabethan times. When the Roman engineers cut Stane Street across the Downs from London to Chichester, the road plunged like a switchback down into thick Wealden forests of oak and beech: oak in the clay of the valleys and beech out of the lighter chalk soil of the hills. The voracious demands of the ironfounder's furnace over the centuries and the shipbuilders of the Tudor and Georgian navies decimated the forests and denuded the lower slopes of the Downs leaving them bare-shouldered. Industrial England violated the Downs further by mining their chalk and leaving behind great white wounds. The process had already been started on a smaller scale by medieval builders who quarried the chalk for their churches, as at Aldingbourne.

THE CONQUEROR'S LEGACY

The story of the two counties stretches back into pre-history when Stone Age man fortified his settlements with long barrows, like the mound at Chilham; and his Iron Age ancestors left their mark at such high points as the Trundle, overlooking Goodwood, Mount Caburn near Glyndebourne, the spectacular oval defensive earthworks at Chanctonbury, and Cissbury Ring, the site of an early flint mine.

The Roman colonisers left their monuments in stone and mosaic in addition to their network of roads in the south of England. After St. Augustine brought Christianity to Britain by converting Ethelbert, King of Kent, at Canterbury in 597 the stones from Roman walls were consecrated and used to build Saxon churches and monasteries. The legacy of great castles in Sussex we owe to William the Conqueror, the last successful invader, who divided the county into five "rapes"—parallel blocks of territory running to the sea, each with a port, a river and a forest. Trusted Norman lords built their castles at Hastings, Pevensey, Lewes, Bramber and Arundel to consolidate their power. The building boom which followed the Conquest, inspired by Norman craftsmen, left behind it scores of churches, particularly in West Sussex.

In fact the whole route is rich in ecclesiastical architecture from Saxon to Perpendicular, including some of the finest early wall paintings in Britain, at Hardham and Clayton. From the sturdy simplicity of the church at Singleton, with its weathered mossy tombstones, to the majestic lacy spires of Canterbury Cathedral almost every parish offers the visitor a unique and unexpected artefact—a lead font perhaps, a well-preserved brass or painted monument, a fine stained glass window or an eccentric doorway.

The early prosperity of the South-East owed much to Edward III who encouraged the Flemish weavers to settle in England and to practice their traditional skills. The cloth halls of several

Down by the river at Bury, Sussex

An oast house at Smarden, Kent

Wealden villages and the looms in the attractive Weavers' House in Canterbury are evidence of this bygone craft. The "hurst" villages of the Kentish Weald were already thriving iron centres but only the hammer ponds, which drove the mills, and the decorative wrought iron to be found on church doors hint this vanished industry.

Sheep that graze in winter under apple and cherry trees inland were reared on the Romney marshes in summer, a hardy breed that punctuates a flat, isolated landscape broken only by the clumps of elm, alder and willow that cluster around lonely church steeples. The Romans began draining the windswept marshes which are now some of the richest pastures in England, abundant with rye grass and white clover. It was the Romney Marsh sheep and the Southdown whose wool enriched the merchants of such villages as Cranbrook, Tenterden and Biddenden until the 18th Century and they displayed their wealth in the fine houses they built, vying with the iron barons in the magnificence of their homes and furnishings. If beautifully preserved cottages like the Old Shop at Bignor are anything to judge by, the medieval yeoman lived high on the hog as well. The business acumen of those industrious farmers is summed up in the old rhyme:

A squire of Wales, a Knight of Cales,
And a laird of the North Countrie,
A Yeoman of Kent, with half a year's rent,
Will buy them out all three.

The affluence of ancient ports like Bramber and Steyning, Rye d Smallhythe diminished in the 17th Century when the Rivers other and Adur (both excellent fishing grounds now) silted up. As e legitimate sea trade foundered, the smuggling fraternity took er and, for the next 150 years, the lonely Kentish coast became e illicit beachhead for French brandy and silk, Dutch tobacco and emish lace. In those dangerous days the forests of the Weald were ve with the sound of packhorses carrying contraband luxuries hide-outs like Owl House at Lamberhurst. (The men who in- lged in this lucrative trade were known as "owlers" because of e hours they kept.)

The great houses of Goodwood, Parham and Firle bear witness an earlier age of gracious living when titled families hunted rough their woods and fields untroubled by roads or railways. me private estates like Cowdray Castle and Scotney Castle are egant ruins today but they still evoke a romantic sense of their n time and they prove that medieval builders needed no lessons om contemporary architects on where to site their buildings.

Impressive as these noble houses are, it is the domestic archi- cture of the region that comes as a revelation. The enduring flint rmhouses of West Sussex, thatched, tiled or slated, set in rolling stureland, give way to the brick and weatherboarding of East ssex and the characteristic local ragstone of Kent, a sandy yellow at time and the elements have weathered to honey. Fat brick oast uses, square or round, suddenly appear in East Sussex but they long to Kent, a ubiquitous and handsome feature of the county's yline and a symbol of its leonine share of Britain's annual p harvest. Whatever the season the landscape is dramatic here: xuriant blossom of pink and white in spring, boughs heavy with uit in summer, and in winter vistas of symmetrical rows of trees d hop poles marching over gently undulating fields.

The coastal plain around Aldingbourne and the flat marshlands rth of Rye are separated by the great belt of the South Downs at command a breathtaking view inland — a patchwork of lage, field and forest. Embraced by the Downs where the River use cuts through stands the capital of Sussex — Lewes, which ows its red-brick face before it presents the stone, timber and hitewashed plaster of its ancient heart. Lewes is an object lesson r planners on how to preserve the medieval fabric and character of town while allowing its citizens to pursue the economic necess- es of the 20th Century. The view from the castle keep over the wn to the amphitheatre of the Downs that encompasses it proves at modern industry need not desecrate a natural beauty spot. he same holds true for Rye, the most elegant medieval town in the uth. The ancient core of the town supports shopkeepers and sinessmen in buildings of rare beauty and antiquity.

The Vales of Sussex and Kent have few centres of dense popula- n — these stretch in a glum, thick ribbon along the coast — so lage life continues to flourish behind the South Downs and over e greensand hills of the Weald. The villages appear very much lf-contained, inward-looking along their rich streets of Tudor d Georgian shops, inns and dwellings. In spite of the proximity fast modern highways, especially at Charing and Chilham, they ll remain happily sequestered.

Driving through Sussex and Kent one is continually reminded at the history of the two counties is virtually the history of Eng- d. What happened here shaped our heritage and our modern institutions. Sussex was the scene of two of the most momentous struggles of our past: the battle for Senlac Hill in 1066, which laid the foundation of Norman supremacy in Saxon England, and the Battle of Lewes in 1264, where the democratic ideology of Simon de Montfort triumphed over Henry III's despotism to pave the way for our parliamentary system of today. And in the skies over Sussex and Kent another battle was fought to drive off a new in- vader. Canterbury suffered badly from German bombs but mirac- ulously the cathedral sustained no broken windows. Like St. Paul's, the Bell Harry tower (once known as "Angel Steeple" when it was surmounted by a great gilt angel) was a symbol of resistance against tyranny during the last war. There is a timeless quality about the cathedral and its precincts, removed from the hurly- burly of the London Road (the Roman Watling Street).

JOURNEY'S END

Approaching through the narrow Mercery Lane you can only stand in awe before the towering mass of the cathedral, which gives the impression of immense strength in its lines and yet a delicate lightness in its tracery and pinnacles, and you begin to feel like a latter-day pilgrim come to worship at the shrine of Thomas à Becket. As the Mother Church Canterbury attracted pilgrims long before Becket's martyrdom in 1170 but his shrine became a potent attraction for the faithful all over Europe, including the first French king to set foot on English soil, Louis VII, who in 1179 offered jewels at Becket's tomb as a result of his son's recuperation. And to Canterbury came Richard the Lion Heart, on foot from Sandwich, to offer his thanks "to God and St. Thomas" for his safe return from the Siege of Acre. Becket's fame reached its height in the 15th Century but in the reign of Henry VIII, that most pragmatic of monarchs, his shrine was desecrated by royal command. Tried posthumously for treason and found guilty, Becket's bones were disinterred and burned, which summarily put an end to the pil- grimage business as described so graphically in Chaucer's Canter- bury Tales. Yet the physical facts of the pilgrimages can still be seen in the many old hospices around the city.

If Henry VIII stopped a ready source of income for Canterbury by closing Becket's shrine, his daughter Elizabeth cannily allowed the French and Walloon weavers, religious exiles, to settle in the city (on the tacit understanding that they would pursue their calling in English interests) and let them worship in the Norman crypt of the cathedral.

It is perhaps fitting that any journey through Sussex and Kent should end at Canterbury, where the visitor experiences the un- deniable feeling of having reached his destination. If the eye could look back across the two counties and take in the varying features of hill and plain, cottage and castle, the mind could comprehend the magnetism of the region and how it inspired those most English of writers, Kipling, Chesterton and Belloc, to rhapsodise in verse about the scenery and sunsets.

This area of England has been the longest civilised; it is Saxon England and the Saxon heritage lives on protected by the Downs, as durable as the flint of its buildings and as unmistakable as the solid oaks and towering beeches that remain of its forests. The Romans, Danes, Jutes, Franks and Normans all shaped the terrain, but the spirit of the land is Saxon for all that and Sussex and Kent stand proudly at the gateway to England, a direct link back to the days of King Harold.

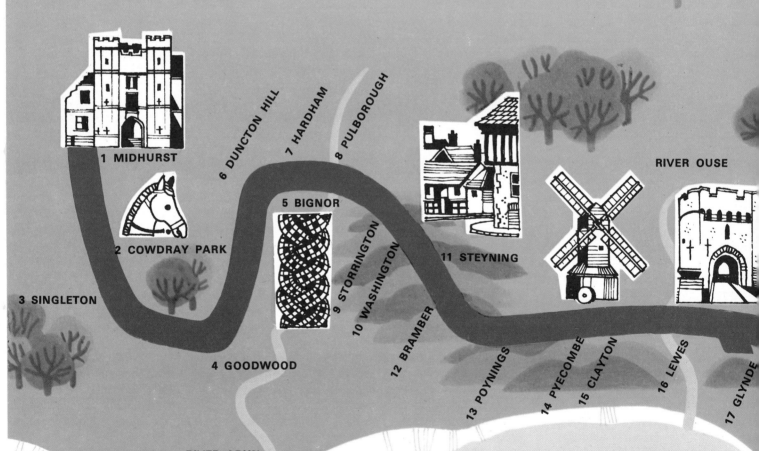

WAYFARER'S GUIDE 3

27 CRANBR[OOK]

24 LAMBERHURST

26 BAYHAM ABBEY

1 MIDHURST

6 DUNCTON HILL

7 HARDHAM

8 PULBOROUGH

RIVER OUSE

2 COWDRAY PARK

5 BIGNOR

11 STEYNING

3 SINGLETON

9 STORRINGTON

10 WASHINGTON

12 BRAMBER

13 POYNINGS

14 PYECOMBE

15 CLAYTON

16 LEWES

17 GLYNDE

4 GOODWOOD

RIVER ARUN

SELSEY BILL

Photos: Peter Baker / B.T.A. / Colorific / J. A. Dixon / Noel Habgood / Geoffrey Harper / Michael Holford / Picturepoint / Kenneth Scowan / Bruce Scott / Spectrum / Sussex Life / Tourist Photo / Transworld Features

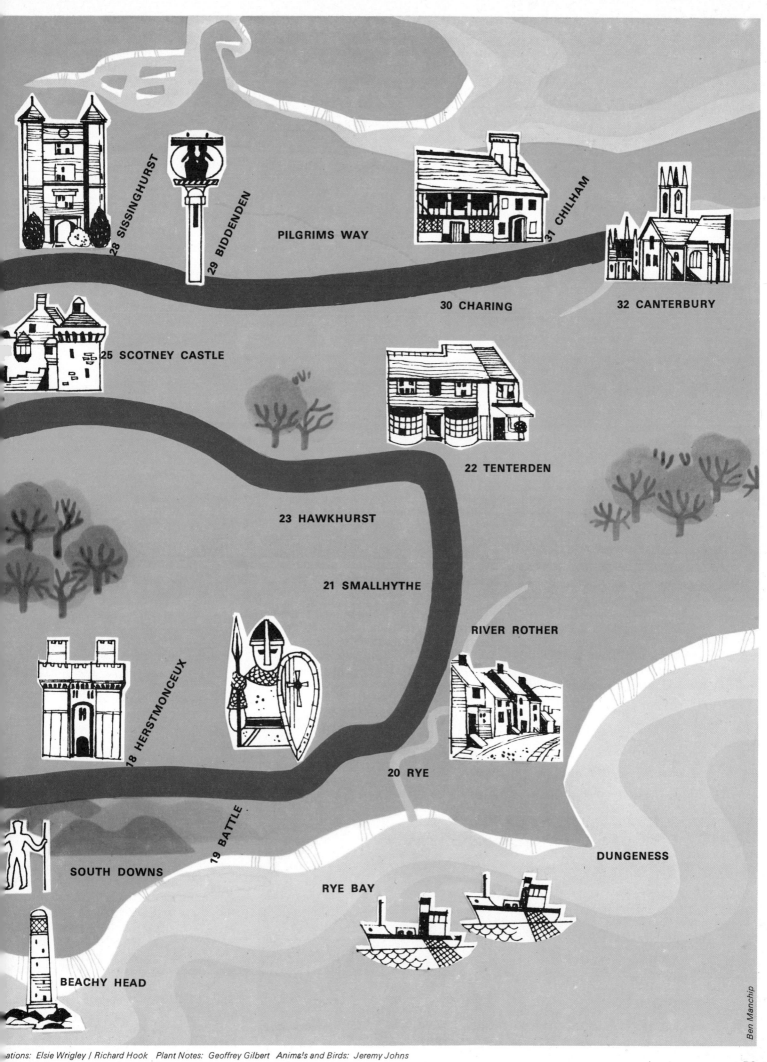

28 SISSINGHURST

29 BIDDENDEN

PILGRIMS WAY

31 CHILHAM

30 CHARING

32 CANTERBURY

25 SCOTNEY CASTLE

22 TENTERDEN

23 HAWKHURST

21 SMALLHYTHE

RIVER ROTHER

18 HERSTMONCEUX

20 RYE

19 BATTLE

SOUTH DOWNS

DUNGENESS

RYE BAY

BEACHY HEAD

ations: Elsie Wrigley / Richard Hook   Plant Notes: Geoffrey Gilbert   Animals and Birds: Jeremy Johns

Ben Manchip

1 MIDHURST: This old market town on the River Rother with its narrow right-angled streets is best discovered on foot. The busy High Street with its 16th and 17th Century buildings culminates at the southern end with the dramatic juxtaposition of the Spread Eagle Hotel, with its black and white half-timbered façade and over-hanging upper storey, and the ancient decorative brickwork and timbers of the Old Market House. Near the Church with its partly Norman tower is an old pillory which could accommodate three miscreants. Along West Street stands a beautifully preserved black and white timber frame cottage dated 1660, now a butcher's shop. There are many delightful picnic spots in the area.

Midhurst on the River Rother is best discovered on foot

2 COWDRAY PARK: In 1793 a family curse was fulfilled when Cowdray Castle was consumed by fire. The view from the 18th fairway of Cowdray Park golf course, especially evocative in the morning sun, presents a majestic 16th Century fortified mansion, surrounded by farm cottages. Approaching from Midhurst the spell is broken since Cowdray Castle is a shell of the building once owned by Sir Anthony Browne, a favourite of Henry VIII and the Chief Standard Bearer of England. Sir Anthony was a considerable property tycoon in his day who owned six estates, including the Bayham and Battle Abbey.

On the courtyard lawn, surrounded by neat cottages, is a timber and brick granary elevated on staddlestones. Under the shadow of the castle ruins are the polo grounds where Prince Philip used to play. At nearby Benbow Pond picnickers can share their sandwiches with wild duck.

Cowdray Castle, destroyed by fire in 1793, to fulfil a family curse

3 SINGLETON: The miniature green with its pond and weeping willow set the mood for this tranquil sprawling village of thatched flint cottages tucked away in the Lavant Valley. The Saxon tower of St. John Evangelist was built nearly 1,000 years ago. The nave and its window date to the 11th Century.

The village pond at Singleton

18th Century granary

Charcoal burner's kiln

The Weald and Downland Open Air Museum stands in 35 acres of meadow and woodland south of Singleton, near Chichester. The museum has re-erected ancient buildings of the Weald and Downlands of Sussex, Surrey and Kent whose removal from their original position was considered unavoidable. The emphasis is on small, timber-frame domestic buildings and craft shops. The Bayleaf Farmhouse in the centre of the museum stood at Edenbridge for 500 years before being moved here. Some of the buildings illustrate wood crafts based on the use of oak from the Weald. They include: A blacksmith's shop and forge; reconstructions of a sawyer's pit and of a Saxon weaver's hut; and a charcoal burner's hut and kiln, built by members of a family who were charcoal burners from the Conquest until the Second World War.

Sèvres china (left) on display in Goodwood House, family home of the Dukes of Richmond and Gordon viewed (right) from across the park

4 GOODWOOD: A winding road leads up 600 feet to one of the most beautifully set racecourses in the country – Glorious Goodwood, its horse-shoe shape overlooked by the earthworks of a Stone Age camp on top of the Trundle ("the hoop").

Archaeologists have uncovered pottery dating back 4,000 years here. Lines of Tote windows now scar the lower slopes of the hill, but on the crest the ramparts of a later fort (*circa* 250 B.C.) can still be seen. The Trundle offers one of the most panoramic views of Sussex, as millions of racegoers will testify.

Goodwood House, family home of flint and stone, belonging to the Dukes of Richmond and Gordon, is surrounded by extensive forests. It was built originally in 1720 as a hunting seat close to the first regular fox hunt in Britain, the Charlton Hunt. An air of 18th Century elegance is preserved inside the house with an internationally famous collection of paintings, Louis XV furniture, Gobelin tapestry, as well as other curiosities including a shirt which belonged to Charles I. In the Yellow Drawing Room graced by Rubens' portrait of his wife, is the silver plate from which Napoleon breakfasted on the morning of Waterloo. For sporting enthusiasts the long hall is hung with sporting paintings, and the dining room contains canvasses by Reynolds and other prominent English painters. The nobly proportioned stable block adjoins the house and 40 varieties of oak as well as some ancient Cedars of Lebanon grow in the surrounding parkland. Set on a hillside is a Shell House, a small pavilion made completely from intricately patterned coloured shells by the Second Duchess in the 1740s.

5 BIGNOR: Some of the best Roman mosaics in Britain are to be seen in the remains of a villa lying west of Bignor, dating back to the 2nd Century, which spread over 4½ acres in a complex of 70 buildings. Five thatched farm buildings now protect the mosaic pavements remarkable for the tiny dimensions of the stones which give an artistic quality to the designs – especially the head of Venus with a frieze of Cupids dressed as Gladiators dancing below her. Remarkable too is an example of Roman op art in the geometric pavement where cubes appear to leap out of the floor in three dimensions.

In the hamlet of Bignor stands the Old Shop (now a private house), a 15th Century yeoman's cottage with a variety of decorative brick in-filling, flint, stone and plaster. A precipitous drive up to Bignor Hill affords an ideal picnic spot and time to trace the route of Stane Street, the Roman road constructed in A.D. 70 to link the port of Chichester with London.

A scale model of the village as it was in its heyday can be seen in the museum.

Mosaics to be seen at Bignor: Medusa (top left), Winter (bottom left) and Venus (right)

6 **DUNCTON HILL:** A parking area half-way down the hill on the road to Petworth affords a magnificent look-out point over the Vale of Sussex from the South Downs, 398 ft. above sea level. It commands a view as far north as Bexley Hill and Telegraph Hill.

View over the Weald from Duncton Hill

8 **PULBOROUGH:** The walled gardens and deer park of Parham House seem to have protected this Elizabethan manor from the march of progress outside. The vistas from the high mullioned windows of the great hall and the bay windows along the Long Gallery (158ft) across lake, forest and down have not changed since Tudor times. The house contains some magnificent period carpets, tapestries and needlepoint, as well as 300 paintings.

Pulborough is a deservedly popular fishing centre. The bailiff who issues fishing permits proudly claims that you can catch "every coarse fish here except for barbel". The bridge across the Arun is one of the oldest in Sussex. There are some interesting 15th Century frame cottages in the town: when the road was cut in the 18th Century one attractive half-timbered cottage was left high and dry like a fortress commanding the approach.

The bridge over the River Arun

7 **HARDHAM:** The whitewashed St. Botolph's Church, just south of Pulborough, is typical of West Sussex ecclesiastical architecture but to by-pass it would be to miss the most complete series of early wall paintings in the country. Dating from shortly after the year 1100 the paintings depict scenes of the Nativity and 'The Torments of Hell'. On the south side of the chancel is a "squint" — peep-hole into what used to be an anchorite's cell; the last known occupant was Prior Richard who ended his days in hermit-like solitude there in 1285.

The whitewashed church at Hardham with (inset) one of the 12th Century wall paintings

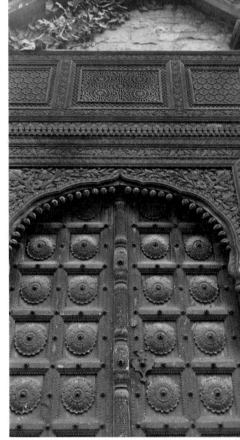

Famed mahogany door at Storrington

9 **STORRINGTON:** The Victorians seems could build Tudor-style convincingly as the Elizabethans: at lea that is what the St. Joseph's Convent Church Lane would suggest. Certain worth stopping for is an outlandish wood door set into the garden wall surroundir the modern Abbey House at the corner Church Lane and Brown's Lane. The do (and its twin inside the wall) are copies the famous doors at Lahore. The toug Indian mahogany which gives the illusi of steel has happily defied the *graff* artists over the years.

arham House, near Pulborough, preserves its Tudor atmosphere

Early in this century London Zoo had too many North American squirrels and set a number of them free in Regent's Park. These grey squirrels, rapidly spread to other London parks and gradually colonised the South-East. Now they can be found in most parts of the country and the grey squirrel, with his larger size, hardiness, and rapid reproductive rate, has almost ousted his British cousin, the tiny red squirrel.

WASHINGTON: The Downs meet the Weald at Washington here the sons of Wassa established a ttlement in Saxon times. Overlooking the llage and commanding a spectacular ew of four counties stands Chanctonbury ng, an Iron Age hill fort delineated by a g of beech trees planted in 1760 by harles Goring who lived at nearby Wiston ouse. There are still traces of the oval efensive mound on which the Romans ilt two structures, one a temple, towards e end of the 3rd Century.

A 1½ mile footpath provides a healthy mb to the encampment from Washington urch past Chancton Farm where in 1866 crock of Saxon coins was unearthed, now the British Museum. The southern proach towards Steyning is less energetic d those who venture to the top to picnic ll be rewarded by the view. From the top other local Iron Age fort, Cissbury Ring, n be seen to the south and for the mbler a five mile cross-country footpath ks the two ancient sites. For those who efer to admire Chanctonbury Ring from e road, one of the best vantage points is Wiston Pond from where the Dutch-bled façade of Wiston House stands ectly below the Ring. Wiston House is t open to the public.

ston House

Chanctonbury Ring, Iron Age hill fort — the trees were planted in 1760

11 STEYNING: Church Street is the pride of West Sussex. Some of the best examples of houses from the 15th to the 18th Century vie for the visitor's attention. To drive past them is to miss some of the most attractive architecture in the county packed into one street. It is perhaps invidious to single out specific houses from the picturesque series of gables, overhanging storeys, leaded windows and bulging whitewashed cottages, but for those who cannot linger here the 15th Century Brotherhood Hall, Holland Cottage and Saxon Cottage will give an immediate impression of the village. Legend has it that St. Cuthman the Shepherd founded Steyning in the 8th Century at the place where the wheelbarrow in which he was pushing his invalid mother from Devon broke down. He built a church on the site where now stands the 12th Century St. Andrew's with its mighty Norman arch and late Norman nave. Not far away King Alfred's father, Ethelwulf, lived and was buried in the church until his remains were re-interred in Winchester. The old headstone in the porch might have been over either his grave, or St. Cuthman's.

The South Downs from Poynings

13 POYNINGS: A stone Norman church was mentioned in the Domesday Book where now stands the squared flint fabric of Holy Trinity. Michael de Poynings, Guardian of the Sussex Coast, willed the church to the parish after his safe return from the Battle of Creçy. He died in 1369. The Perpendicular church has relics of the Norman structure in beautiful glazed tiles on the altar. A fragment of stained glass dating back to 1421 can be seen in the east window of the north transept, depicting the Annunciation. The south window of the south transept, mid-17th Century, is an importation from Chichester Cathedral.

From the village a 2½-mile climb leads to Devil's Dyke with a fine view across West Sussex and the Weald. According to local legend the Devil, incensed by the rapid spread of Christianity, tried to bring it to an abrupt halt by flooding the Weald. He began to dig a dyke from the Channel, but a woman caught him and exorcised him by holding out a lighted candle. The Devil, taking this for the rising sun, fled leaving his dyke unfinished.

Church Street, Steyning, a treasury of 15th to 18th Century architecture

12 BRAMBER: Like Steyning this attractive village was a prosperous port when the Adur was tidal enough to carry ships up river. A provincial capital of William the Conqueror, the port was protected by Bramber Castle. Built by William de Braose 20 years after the Conquest, the castle stands on a natural mound. James Temple, the regicide, successfully defended it against the Royalists in the Civil War, but soon after it was dismantled and only a slab of the tower-keep, standing 76 feet, remains of this once impressive fortress. The view from the mound across the Weald gives an idea of its commanding position, and a scale model of the castle can be found in the forecourt of Potter's Museum and Exhibition of Humorous Taxidermy. This curiosity created by Walter Potter over 70 years until his death in 1918 was inspired by his memory of his nursery book. "The Death of Cock Robin" is just one of the tableaux he brought to 'life' with stuffed creatures.

At the end of the village is St. Mary's, a 15th Century timbered home for the Wardens of the Bridge — monks from Sele Priory at nearby Beeding. Well restored in the 19th Century, the house is a splendid example of Elizabethan close timbering. The panelling in one of the upstairs rooms is painted and the fine collection of furniture, tapestries, lace and fabrics is on view to the public.

All that remains of Bramber Castle

Painted leatherwork on view at Bramber

14 **PYECOMBE:** An odd gate that swivels on a central pivot opens on to the churchyard; the gate handle is in the shape of an iron crook, evidence of the small forge directly opposite. The Downland village of Pyecombe used to be an iron-founding centre and the traditional home of crook-making. It is said that no sheep caught with a Pyecombe crook could hope to escape. Though the sheep are disappearing from the Downs and nowadays there is little call for shepherds' crooks, there is still thriving production of crooks for bishops. Whether the same legend holds true for spiritual flocks is a matter of speculation.

Pyecombe Church itself, built in the 13th Century, contains one of three remaining lead fonts in Sussex (the other two are at Parham and Edburton); 6 ft around and 5 in deep, this fine example of Norman lead-work was probably made in 1170.

Pyecombe Church, built in the 13th Century, contains a Norman lead font

The 'Jill' mill at Clayton, built in wood, dates from 1821

15 **CLAYTON:** This hamlet offers more surprises than its size might suggest. Looking down on what used to be a centre of population in ancient times are the twin windmills, Jack and Jill — he in brick and dating from 1876, she in wood of 1821. Parallel below the road runs the London to Brighton railway and the entrance to the tunnel is dignified by a magnificent mock-Tudor castle gate in yellow brick built with flamboyant extravagance in Victorian times. Between the turrets is a railwayman's cottage. But the glory of Clayton is its church. Contained within the 2½ ft thick walls of flint and lime building are some of the oldest and best preserved wall paintings in England, thought to be the work of Cluniac monks around 1150. The elongated figures depicting Christ and the Apostles around the nave are in proportion with the tall walls, that belie their height from the outside. There is an interesting small brass of Richard Idon (1523), a parson, set in the south wall, and outside in the churchyard west of the porch is a large round stone thought to be the base of an early font.

A tortuous climb leads to Ditchling Beacon which commands a wonderful Downland view, including Wolstonbury Hill, the site of an old Saxon camp, 670 ft above sea level.

THE BEE ORCHID

In their characteristic style, waxy, opulent looking, orchids are handsome plants. In addition to being beautiful flowers, however, they have some strange habits. They impersonate insect odours to attract pollination, giving rise to such names as Fly Orchid and Bee Orchid. Another peculiar habit is that of spending long periods underground, sometimes all their lives. Orchids are much sought after and many species have almost disappeared. However, the charming Bee Orchid, illustrated here, can still be found on chalk Downs.

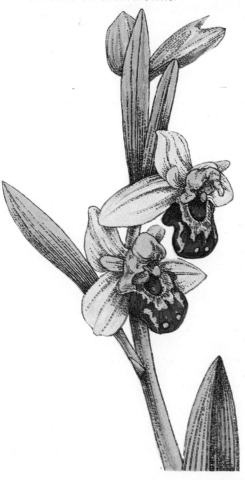

The massive 14th Century Barbican still stands guard at Lewes

16 LEWES:

16 **LEWES:** The view from the battlements of the castle shows just how this fascinating East Sussex county town developed. The flint faced castle is the focus and from it run the streets and alleys of Tudor and Georgian buildings down to the River Ouse. The castle was built around 1100 to consolidate the Norman Conquest. The walls at their base are 30 ft thick, narrowing to 4 ft at the top from where you can see Mount Harry to the north-west, the site of the Battle of Lewes (1264). The defeat of Henry III there by Simon de Montfort and his barons paved the way for parliamentary democracy.

In the gardens of the castle stands an original panel of the iron railings from St. Paul's Cathedral which were cast at Lamberhurst. Adjacent to the castle gatehouse is the Barbican Museum which houses prehistoric remains as well as objects of local interest, particularly some superb Sussex Wealden encaustic pottery.

The High Street, a hill to the river, presents a mixture of Georgian facades of grey and red brick chequer, as well as weatherboarding and timber frame houses with overhanging upper storeys. More intimate are the steeply raked cobbled and bricked pedestrian ways of Keere Street and St. Martin's Lane with their picturesque cottages of flint, brick and timber. The same variety of styles is echoed in the walling alongside with its continually changing patterns.

In Southover Street stands one of the finest Tudor buildings in England, the Anne of Cleves' House, now the Sussex Folk Museum. Its fine timbers stand over 14th Century cellars and in one corner of the splendidly equipped kitchen is the Sussex marble table on which the knights who slew Becket in 1170 are reputed to have put their arms and trappings. (The table refused to support such blasphemous paraphernalia and threw everything to the floor, twice!) The house was built in the early 16th Century as part of the Priory of Lewes. After the Dissolution Henry VIII gave it to Anne when he divorced her. Ten of the rooms are devoted to the social history of Sussex, including an incongruous Victoriana room complete with furnishings and wax figures.

Not far away is 16th Century Southover Grange where the diarist John Evelyn lived as a boy. The timber fireplace is especially fine. Other buildings of note are St. Michael's Church in the High Street with its 13th Century round tower and beautiful stained glass windows, St. Anne's with its low doorway and drum-shaped font, and the 15th Century Old Bull where Thomas Paine, author of *The Rights of Man* lived between 1768 and 1774.

Lewes celebrates November 5th with spectacular torchlight processions in period costume and huge bonfires.

MEDIEVAL BRICKS

In the 15th Century many castles wer built of brick. Herstmonceux (about 146C is one of the finest examples of mediev brickwork. Medieval bricks were burr with wood fuel in a kiln or a clamp. The cost about 4s. 6d. a thousand.

Most of the bricks used in England in th early Middle Ages were apparently im ported from the Low Countries. Howeve bricks were made in England from 143 onwards. The masons who laid the brick were called 'breakemasons'.

A medieval brick would measure rough $10\frac{1}{2}$in. x $5\frac{1}{4}$in. x 2in. A deficiency in th colour of the brick was made up by paintir them over with red ochre. Usually brick were employed only where there was shortage of local building stone. Their us was restricted to larger houses and it wa not until the end of the 17th Century th they became a common material in th houses of ordinary people.

Early English masonry was often bour together with a cement "composed wax and pitch or resin, applied in moulten condition". There is a startlir reference in some records of 1279 to " lbs. of wax, 4 stone of pitch, sulphur to th value of $1\frac{1}{2}$d. and 1d. worth of eggs" all said to be "for cement". Sulphur, wa and resin were also used in 1324 f cement in St. Stephen's Chapel in Wes minster. This type of cement was wide used throughout a period of three centurie

Traditional types of brickwork

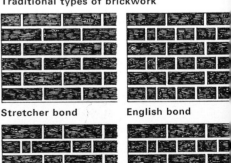

Stretcher bond   English bond

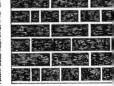

Flemish bond   Gardenwall bond

7 GLYNDE: Looking down from the Iron Age fort on Mount [C]aburn, Glynde Place in its 160 acres [st]ands as a monument to the gracious life [of] 16th and 17th Century England. This [fe]eling is reinforced inside the house with [a] fine collection of paintings, bronzes and [ne]edlepoint. In the churchyard adjoining [th]e estate lies the agriculturalist John [E]lman who bred what is now the famous [bl]ack-faced Southdown sheep.

Glyndebourne, where opera lovers have [be]en picnicking in dinner jackets by its [la]kes since 1934, is 1½ miles north. The [or]iginal Tudor house was small, but [en]largements in Victorian times and in this [ce]ntury by the late John Christie who [cr]eated the Glyndebourne Opera Festival [ha]ve given the house a grandeur in keeping [w]ith its latter-day international reputation [fo]r opera. The modern opera house blends [w]ith the ancient Tudor manor in spite of [th]e 400 year span between them. A [re]staurant has been built around two oak [tr]ees which sprout through the roof.

To the south below Glynde is Firle Place. [O]riginally built by the Gage family about [14]87 the house has been owned by the [fa]mily ever since. A Thomas Gage became [C]-in-C British Forces during the American [W]ar of Independence and after Bunker Hill [he] retired to England with some of his war mementoes which are on show in the house along with an outstanding collection of paintings, furniture and porcelain. Another Thomas Gage is reputed to have grown the first greengage in England in the handsome grounds of Firle Place where today pheasants stalk about and sit imperiously on the balustrades around the house. In the 13th Century Firle Church, where members of the Gage family are buried, are some of the finest brasses in Sussex. A path leads from the village of West Firle up to the Firle Beacon, 713 feet above sea level.

Glyndebourne (left), home of the famous opera festival. Right: the forge at Glynde

18 HERSTMONCEUX: The castle was built by the Fiennes family in the 15th Century as a lavishly fortified mansion, with moat and castellation. Dismantled in 1777, it was restored between the World Wars. In 1948 the Royal Greenwich Observatory took it over and in 1967 built the Isaac Newton telescope, one of the most powerful in the world, which stands in its aluminium-domed silo. The telescope and the magnificent grounds are open to the public, but not the castle. The warm terracotta coloured brickwork of the castle gives it a romantic air which is more appealing than the grim stone of Bodiam Castle which it resembles. In All Saints Church there is a superb brass of Sir William Fiennes (1402) and the spectacular Dacre memorial tomb. In the town the ancient craft of trug-making (baskets with sweet chestnut frames and curved willow boards) is still carried out by hand.

[He]rstmonceux Castle, a fortified mansion built in the 15th Century

All Saints' Church dates from 1180

19 BATTLE:

Saxon England died with Harold at Battle on October 14, 1066 and where he fell the conquering William dedicated a church to God in thanks for his victory. Recent excavations have unearthed the foundations of this church and on the site of the high altar — the spot where Harold died — is a stone erected by the Souvenir Normande in 1903. Benedictine monks built an abbey close by but when Henry VIII dissolved the monasteries he gave the property to his favourite, Sir Anthony Browne. The building was subsequently destroyed by fire in this century but was restored and is now a girls' school. Visitors can still wander round the shell of the abbey dormitory and the monumental gatehouse (1338) which is one of the finest in the country.

Sheep now graze on the battlefield which can best be seen from the abbey terrace where the English troops were drawn up in a long battle line against the advancing Normans. Had Harold's men stayed on Senlac Hill (the abbey terrace) instead of rushing down on the retreating Normans, Saxon England might have lived on. Outside the magnificent gatehouse cars are now parked on what used to be an 18th Century bull-baiting pit on the village green. Adjacent is the 15th Century Pilgrim's Rest, once an almshouse and now a popular restaurant. Other noteworthy buildings: Battle Lodge, Battle Hospital (formerly the workhouse) and the buildings along Mount Street where a pleasant hour can be spent browsing in the antique shops.

20 RYE:

In the Middle Ages whe the sea came up to the walls this magnificent hill town, Rye enjoyed th prosperity of a thriving fishing industry but the sea washed away its eastern sid silted up its harbour in the late 16th Ce tury and then receded leaving the tow two miles inland at the mouth of the Riv Rother. Ravaged by marauding Frenc buccaneers in the 14th and 15th Centurie the town became a refuge for Hugueno who brought with them their tradition weaving skills. But by the 18th Century, port inoperative, Rye's economy reste precariously on the proceeds of wool ar spirits smuggling. The turbulent history the town has left its mark on its building The Ypres Tower, built as a fort in 125 was burnt by the French in 1377 and w sold as useless less than 100 years later John de Ypres who gave it its name. T corporation bought the Tower back in 15 and used it for three centuries as a cou house and jail. Today it is a museum of t Cinque Ports. The cobbles of Merma Street once rang with sound of horse hooves and the muffled cries of despera

The magnificent gatehouse leading to the ruins of Battle Abbey

The Ypres Tower, Rye, built in 1250

men secreting contraband in the vaults the 15th Century Mermaid Inn. In the tov hall can be seen a fine pillory (a favourite photographers whose subjects have ke the ancient wood shiny with use) and t skull of a butcher, set in an iron cage who tried to murder the mayor of R in 1732.

The 12th Century St. Mary Church is impressive mixture of styles spanning t Norman and Perpendicular periods. No able are the stained glass windows and t carved mahogany altar. Its pride is a tur clock still functioning on the original wor made in Winchelsea in 1560. An 18 pendulum has been mesmerising inatte tive congregants for 400 years while t twin Quarter Boys outside have be

Interior view of the abbey ruins

The shell of the abbey dormitory

ermaid Street once echoed the cries of smugglers hauling contraband to the cellars of the 15th Century inn on the right

dling the quarter hours.

To enjoy the ancient fabric of the town e visitor should walk from the 14th Century Land Gate, which secured the northern pproach, up the High Street and around e kidney-shaped cobbled lanes of Meraid Street, Church Square (where the dest building in Rye, the Friars of the ck, is to be seen) and Watchbell Street, on Street where the playwright Fletcher ed in a 15th Century house, and West reet where the novelist Henry James ayed at the 18th Century Lamb House.

South of the town are the ruins of mber Castle, built by Henry VIII against e French; it was torn down in 1643 when e River Rother altered course and is now ccupied by a variety of seabirds.

Fishing boats still sail from Rye

The Land Gate, 14th Century lookout

21 **SMALLHYTHE:** In medieval days when the River Rother was tidal this tiny hamlet was a bustling port where Henry VIII commissioned one of his warships to be built. Only a drainage ditch now remains of a once proud river. Smallhythe Place (built around 1480) with its attractive red tiled roof was the Port Master's House. For 30 years this magnificent timbered yeoman's cottage was the home of Ellen Terry, the world-famous actress, who lived here until her death in 1928. The house was presented to the National Trust by her daughter as a theatrical museum. The house contains the personal and theatrical possessions of Ellen Terry as well as other legendary actors like Sir Henry Irving, Mrs. Siddons, and David Garrick. The barn at the back has been turned into a private theatre club by Ellen Terry's daughter. The neighbouring cottage, known as Priest's House, belongs to the estate which Miss Terry bought in 1899. In the church next door the 15th Century font stands over an old millstone presented by her.

23 **HAWKHURST:** A monke puzzle tree greets the visitor o entering this small town from the east. I medieval times Hawkhurst followed Cran brook into the clothmaking industry an was a large ironfounding centre in th 17th Century when William Penn, th founder of Pennsylvania, owned the smel ing furnaces. West of the valley that divide the town is Hawkhurst Moor, a large gree The Marlborough House School is a worth while stopping point. In the High Street is a attractive weather-board shopping arcad The church of local sandstone was des troyed during the war but has now bee restored and is especially noteworthy for th decorative tiles around the altar, th wrought-iron work on the door and th small thatched well in the churchyard. S John Herschel, who came from a family famous astronomers, had his observato south of the church and received th accolade of burial in Westminster Abbe near Isaac Newton in 1871. The churc wardens accounts for the parish of Hawl hurst dating back to the 16th Centu contain some curious expenditures — f instance twopence paid "to blast f kepying the doggs out of the churche".

Ellen Terry lived here for 30 years

Friendship beads presented to Ellen Terry

The High Street at Tenterden, an attractive shopping street where Tudor, Georgian and modern buildings mingle

tar tiles in Hawkhurst church

24 LAMBERHURST: Names like Furnace Wood, Furnace Field and Furnace Farm are the only reminders of the iron industry that flourished in this wooded village. The railings that once surrounded St. Pauls were cast here, lyrically described by one travel writer of yore as "the most magnificent balustrade perhaps in the universe.' The railings now surround a cemetery in Toronto after being salvaged from a ship that sank in 1870, presumably under their weight — over 200 tons. A panel of the railings can be seen in the castle keep garden in Lewes.

The 14th Century church contains a fine painted Royal coat of arms of Queen Anne. The Owl House, a 16th Century tile-hung timber building was a smugglers' retreat in the 18th Century and they must have enjoyed the beautiful grounds if they were as luxuriant in shrubs and flowers as they are today.

Typical Kentish farm near Lamberhurst with oast houses in the background

22 TENTERDEN: The prosperous air of this Wealden town owes much to the wool trade that flourished from the time of Edward III.

A market town which enjoyed port privileges as a member of the Ancient Town of Rye, Tenterden boomed in the 18th century as can be seen by the number of fine houses built by wealthy wool merchants. The High Street is one of the most attractive shopping streets in Kent. Tile-hung Tudor cottages and Georgian brick lodge against modern supermarkets. The old inns like the 15th Century Woolpack and the William Caxton are a delight — the latter named for the father of English printing reputedly born here. As was the daughter of Nelson and Lady Hamilton, a certain Horatia Ward who subsequently became a vicar's wife. St. Mildred's Church tower, built in the late 14th Century and standing 100 ft high, commands a fine view of the Weald and on a clear day the French coast. An old legend suggests that "Tenterden steeple is the cause of the break Goodwin Sands" because the stones earmarked to be used for the repair of the sea wall east of Deal were diverted on the instructions of the Abbot of St. Augustine's at Canterbury to make the church tower.

As a result the Earl of Sandwich's estate, according to the legend, is now submerged. The bells of St. Mildred's are said to be the best parish peal in the South-East.

Tenterden is one of the many villages and towns in a radius of a few miles which ends in the suffix "den". This means "a wooded valley affording pasturage".

The haunted moat at Scotney Castle

25 SCOTNEY CASTLE: The ghost of an 18th Century revenue man drowned in the moat is said to come knocking at the castle ruins — a vine-clad Plantagenet and Elizabethan house with later additions. Most spectacular is the round tower (1387) which rises out of the lake of lilies, the boundary between Sussex and Kent. Modern Scotney Castle is a Gothic Revival house of 1837 commanding a view of the wooded valley and the gardens. An iguanodon, whose skeleton was found at Wittersham, seems to have left his mark some ten million years ago in the quarry.

The ruins of Bayham Abbey

26 BAYHAM ABBEY: Across the Sussex border, two miles west of Lamberhurst, along twisting country lanes is Bayham Abbey, one of the most splendid 13th Century ruins in England, with creeper-covered piers and arches rising romantically from a carpet of grass. The Abbey, founded before 1200 by White monks, passed to Cardinal Wolsey at the Dissolution, but the Crown reclaimed the property on his fall. The 15th Century dower house was the original home of the Pratt family before they built the neo-Elizabethan manor on the hill.

Picturesque Cranbrook with its 72 ft mill, the second highest in England

27 CRANBROOK: Flemish weave invited over by Edward III creat a flourishing cloth industry at Cranbro and when Queen Elizabeth I came to I the foundation stone for Cranbrook Scho in 1574 (now the headmaster's house) it said she walked for a mile to the neighbou ing parish of Coursehorn on a path broadcloth made by Cranbrook weavers.

Cranbrook's parish church is known "The Cathedral of the Weald", an impre sive Perpendicular structure in local san stone. Old Father Time gazes down fro the church clock (an older version stan inside) and above the porch is a roc called "Baker's Jail" — a prison f Protestant martyrs convicted by Sir Jo Baker, whose over-zealous persecuti earned him the name of "Bloody Bake Once the market town of the Wea Cranbrook has many fine 18th Centu buildings and above the town stands t 72 ft wooden Union Mill, the seco highest windmill in England, which is ke in full working order.

28 SISSINGHURST: Two miles west of this former weaving village with its weatherboard houses stands Sissinghurst Castle, built in 1550 by Sir John Baker on the site of a fortified manor house. When Horace Walpole visited it in 1752 he wrote, "There is a park in ruins and a house in ten times greater ruins . . ." and this was before the castle became a jail for 3,000 French prisoners during the Napol- eonic Wars ! Rescued in 1930 by Sir Harc Nicolson and his wife the author Virgir Sackville-West, Sissinghurst Castle no stands a proud Tudor house in some of t most beautiful Elizabethan-style gardens the country. The soft red brick of the buil ings is continued in the magnificent oa houses of the farm attached. The garde are open to the public, as is the room which Miss Sackville-West wrote her book

Statues in Sissinghurst's gardens

Sissinghurst Castle, once the home of writer Virginia Sackville-West

ddenden village and church

he sign of the Siamese twins

29 **BIDDENDEN:** A signpost on the triangular green perpetuates e legend of the Biddenden Maids: Marie nd Eliza Chulkhurst, the Siamese twins ined at the hip and shoulder who, so the ory goes, were born about 1100 and urvived 34 years in the parish. Under their ill they left a plot of land whose rent was to rovide cheese and bread for each of the arish poor on Easter Day. The continuing rgesse of the Maids is distributed from a indow in the White House (formerly the ld Workhouse) near the church. Biscuits earing the image of the Biddenden Maids re still handed out on Easter Monday "to l who apply, Strangers and Parishioners."

Driving from the west, past modern ousing, a bend in the High Street reveals e sudden surprise of a curving sweep of 5th Century cottages and shops. A delight, o, are the ancient pavements set with uge smooth stones of marble from ethersden quarries four miles away, also sed in Canterbury Cathedral.

30 **CHARING** High Street is a peaceful hill up to the Downs with some marvellous timbered houses (particularly Pierce House) that stand as silent witnesses to the pilgrims who would have rested here on their journey to Canterbury from Winchester. From the 8th Century to the Dissolution the Archbishop's Palace belonged to Canterbury. Cranmer was its last episcopal tenant before he discreetly handed it over to Henry VIII. The King probably mentioned that he'd taken a liking to it when he stopped there on his way to the "Field of the Cloth of Gold" meeting with Francis I in Artois. Now the 14th Century great hall is a barn. In the ruins — now called Palace Farm — can still be seen traces of herringbone masonry, tiles and carvings. The church beside it was gutted by fire in 1590 as a result of "a gun discharged at a pigeon then on the roof" and only the tower and walls survived. So fierce was the blaze that the steeple bells melted. Over the entrance to the church is a sundial and the roof has splendid painted beams. One oddment is the Vamping Horn in the vestry, an instrument like an old gramophone horn, one of eight extant in England and used for amplifying the choir leader's voice.

The road snakes up to Charing Hill over which runs Pilgrims' Way and it offers a wonderful view of the Upper Stour Valley and the Weald.

Charing Church, scene of a disastrous fire

This Vamping Horn was used by the choir

Old school table found in Chilham Church

31 **CHILHAM:** The compact village square allows the visitor to take in at a glance the timber and brick houses with their projecting gables and dormer windows and the impressive gates of Chilham Castle. Set back in gardens laid out by "Capability" Brown the octagonal keep of this Norman castle stands on Roman remains next to a fine red brick Jacobean manor built in 1616.

Chilham was a battle site of the Romans

Chilham Castle's Jacobean mansion

and Britons and many Roman relics have been unearthed here. A 1½-mile walk down the High Street, past the Woolpack Inn, across the railway tracks, past an old mill and over two bridges leads to Julieberry's Grave, originally a Stone Age long barrow.

The Perpendicular Church of St. Mary, with its flint and stone chequer, is surrounded by lime trees and the holes in the oak door are said to have been made by Cromwell's muskets.

32 **CANTERBURY:** As the cradle of English history and religion, Canterbury is arguably the most important city in the country. Dominated by the soaring Bell Harry tower of its magnificent cathedral, the city has survived Danish raiders, Henry VIII's demolition men, Cromwell's musketry and Hitler's bombs over a 2,200-year period of changing fortunes. Julius Caesar captured the area in 54 B.C. from Belgic tribes and the second Roman invaders established their walled city of Duroverum here in A.D. 43. The Saxons welcomed St. Augustine in 597, and on the conversion of King Ethelbert England became a Christian country with St. Augustine being made the first Archbishop of Canterbury.

The square half-mile of the medieval city, its walls built on Roman stonework, contains some of the finest examples of ecclesiastical and domestic buildings in Britain. Half of the ancient walls can be seen but only the 14th Century West Gate remains of the original seven entrances to the city. Once a jail and now a museum with a splendid view from its battlements, the Gate sits uncompromisingly over the busy A2, which bisects the city. Canterbury is best discovered on foot because of its narrow byways and unexpected lanes off the main street.

From East Bridge the old Weavers' House seems to rise out of the River Stour. In its upstairs rooms, over what is now a tea shop, are the looms the Huguenots used. In the garden at the back a ducking stool is poised over the muddy river. Opposite is

The ancient walls from Westgate gardens

Lofty pillars, graceful arches and mellow stone make Canterbury Cathedral a fitting cradle of English history and religion

Pilgrims' Hospice with its marvellous Norman undercroft, one of Canterbury's almshouses. Up Stour Street is the 14th century Poor Priests' Hospital adjoining the Buffs Regimental Museum. The Saxon and Norman ruins of St. Augustine's Abbey surround the site of the original wooden church built by Augustine — and his first tomb. East of the city, past the County Jail and House of Correction, is St. Martin's church with its Saxon font where for nearly 1,400 years there has been continuous worship. King Ethelbert is reputed to have been baptised here.

The best view of the cathedral is from the modern campus of Kent University on Tyler's Hill. Nothing remains of St. Augustine's cathedral or the later Saxon one, but Norman architecture is preserved in the vast crypt, the largest in Britain. Most memorable features are the exquisite medieval and modern stained glass, the tombs of Henry VI and Edward the Black Prince, the 12th Century choir, and, of course, the Trinity Chapel — the shrine of Thomas à Becket.

The Marlowe Theatre perpetuates the name of a native son, the Elizabethan playwright. Not far away are the Dane John Gardens with a prehistoric mound and the world's first passenger train engine, the *Invicta,* which used to run between Canterbury and Whitstable, at a loss. Other buildings worth noting are the ruins of Greyfriars, the first Franciscan house in England, on the banks of the Stour, and the Roman house in Longmarket with its mosaic pavement which was unearthed by a German bomb.

The high altar from the choir

The cathedral dominates the square half-mile of the medieval city

The stained glass in Canterbury is among the finest to be seen in Britain. Much of it is devoted to St. Thomas à Becket such as this scene depicting his martyrdom in the Cathedral

...ah, in 13th Century stained glass

The old Weavers' House seems to rise from the waters of the River Stour

London –
by the royal Thames

BENNY GREEN

In nominating London as the most amazing, most enriching, most diversified, most personalised city in the world, I am perhaps antagonising the good citizens of Paris, Rome, Vienna, Brasilia, Caracas and Tokyo among others, but, being a Londoner, I do not really care. Perhaps London remains the one city on the planet which, unassisted, can provide a man with a comprehensive liberal education, the one urban conglomerate which may fairly be defined as a three-dimensional history book, the only metropolitan point on the map which can claim at the same time vast antiquity and a life unbreached by either of those twin destroyers of tradition, the heel of the conqueror and those terrible deeds of impersonal wrath defined in insurance policies as Acts of God.

London has suffered no obliterating earthquakes, no enveloping seas of molten lava. It has trembled neither at adjustments in the earth's crust nor at the caprice of a victorious enemy. Not since William of Normandy had himself crowned at Westminster has London been obliged to pay obeisance to an interloper.

It became a commonplace a long time ago to describe London as a cluster of self-determining villages, and like most cliches, it is quite true. But London is more than that. It is a cluster of interdependent cities, a series of inter-locking worlds. Fleet Street is a city on its own, the City of Terrible Moonshine perhaps, as independent of and as separate from the shipping empires of Leadenhall Street as the theatrical entrepreneurs of Shaftesbury Avenue are unconcerned with the juridical serenity of the Inns of Court; as the unbreached walls of bureaucratic Whitehall are impervious to the intellectual casuistry of Bloomsbury; as the riparian dreamers at Chelsea and Kew, committed to the contradiction of boats that cannot sail anywhere, live in blissful ignorance of the amazing world just down the river in Dockland.

THE FOCUS OF HOPE

In this fantastical place a man can live and work all his life and never know what is going on three streets away, so that in a sense there are as many Londons as there are Londoners, to say nothing of the provincials and colonials and foreigners who have flocked to it for at least the last 200 years as to the focus of hope. London has always opened its arms. Karl Marx wrote his irascible masterpiece in a house in Dean Street, Soho, on whose site there now stands, ironically, an establishment devoted to the gastronomic gratification of the *bon viveur*. Bolivar, en route to the liberation of the state soon to be named after him, rested awhile near Baker Street; and not far from Euston Station there stands the house where Mazzini conceived the baroque idea of a united Italy. The London that Marx and Bolivar and Mazzini knew was more highly coloured than ours, more ramshackle, more personal, less daunting in physical scale for the specimens of *homo sapiens* who walked its streets. The last of the fleets of multi-coloured omnibuses disappeared in the 1930's (although not for another generation did the chromatic gradations of the bus tickets fade to all-embracing white). The skyline today is punctured by specimens of the new shoebox school of architecture, and by the idiot finger of the Post Office Tower. The quantity of public lighting consumed by the capital becomes vaster with each year, so that in the 1970's the dumb scream of neon casts a tubercular flush over the night sky as seen from the vantage points of Hampstead Heath or Primrose Hill.

London is all things to all men. For the student of political science it has always been a city of crowned heads, ever since the

days when strategy was a mere matter of commanding a fe approaches to the river and a few roads to the north and west. early as the 9th century, Alfred, wary as he was of the fier independence of the town, knew that London must be secured ever the Danes were to be thrown back into the sea. To the histori it is a gated city whose old strongpoints have enjoyed wide differing fates; some to survive as names on an undergrou railway map, Aldersgate, Aldgate, Moorgate; others to retain least the cachet of modern usage, Billingsgate, Bishopsga Ludgate; still others, like Cripplegate, to decline; or even, li Dowgate, to disappear altogether from the tongue of the London

Topographically London is a place of palaces and of parks, "t lungs of London", as the Earl of Chatham once described the two of the most vital being royal "legacies" — Hyde Park, open to the public by Charles I, and Regent's Park, designed by Na for the Prince Regent, later George IV. And for tourists it is t place of panoply and pageantry whose links with the monarc who rule it, either in fact or in name, are reflected in the nome clature of its myriad streets. Most people know that Regent Str is so called because the Prince Regent decided to have a road ru ning from Carlton House to Marylebone Fields. It is less w known that George II thought of Rotten Row in 1737, or th Henry VIII created the dockyards at Woolwich and Deptford. B perhaps the oddest fact in the list is that to this day there rema only one freehold property on the south side of Pall Mall, N Gwyn's old house, and that the king made it freehold because "N had always conveyed free under the Crown and always would"

This intimate link between London and its rulers accounts the richness of anecdotage about public ceremonies which, in t modern age, reached their zenith of patriotic fervour in the sligh hysterical reaction to Queen Victoria's diamond jubilee processi in 1897, and perhaps slumped to an equally spectacular nadir le than a generation later when, for the coronation procession George V, Londoners stayed away in their tens of thousands, mu to the astonishment of Lord Kitchener who, fearful of the met politan temper, had thoughtfully installed a couple of field guns Pall Mall. Monarchs have usually displayed a great affection London life, or at least a keen regard for its good opinion. George liked the town, even though one day a highwayman held him up Kensington, depriving the king of "his purse, his watch and buckles". It was in Kensington Palace that the same king die thus following the examples of Mary II, William III and Que Anne. Victoria was made of sterner stuff, enjoyed a happy chil hood at the Palace, and left her dolls behind as evidence that s had once been amused. The dolls are on view to the public.

VANISHING LANDMARKS

Today the traveller through London, whether he moves on fo or on wheels, is travelling through a town which is beginning last to lose the outlines for which it has been famous for at least t centuries. Many of the old landmarks will disappear during t 1970's. Many already have. Some changes have not been the better; others, oddly enough, have hardly been changes at a so much as name-juggling, label-switching, performed for t convenience of the bureaucratic mind, which has obliterated so boroughs, forced the shotgun wedding of others, and inform Middlesex that it no longer exists. It is an incredible thing, but r until 1888, when the population of the town had climbed to fi

WAYFARER'S GUIDE 4

illion, did the London County Council come into being. Seventy ven years later the L.C.C. gave way to the Greater London ouncil, and the boundary adjustments to the boroughs began, though it has to be said that the man today who attends the Cup nal still considers he has travelled to Wembley rather than to rent, and that the schoolboy sitting in the Mound Stand at Lord's nows he is on the property of the Marylebone Cricket Club, no atter what the Westminster street signs outside may suggest.

Today London is a city in transition, a city struggling to keep ce with its own development, a city fearful of the possibility that may outgrow its own strength, in the way that an 8 ft man is ddenly perceived to be not a giant but a tragic weakling. There e twice as many residents of London today as there were in *the hole of England* when Samuel Pepys began his diary. In 1563 ere were 90,000 Londoners, in 1600 more than 200,000, by 1700 o-thirds of a million, by 1830 one and a half million. From time time there have been disasters, like the Plague, the Fire, the itz, which seemed to offer an opportunity to the planning mind regulate London's growth, but always the human tide swept rward, ignoring the blueprints and creating a distinctive aura of ganised architectural chaos which has made London the delight d despair of humanity.

REATION OF WRITERS

Today there are two significant sounds floating on the metro- litan air, the rustle of official forms condoning the destruction of me ancient monument, and the splutter of petitions protesting ainst the self-mutilation. The student of London affairs soon tices that these disputes are hardly ever rational; and he also tices something else, the most fantastic truth of all about this ntastic city, and it is this: that a great deal of its dazzling beauty, hypnotic power, its priceless heritage, its immortal soul, has ver really existed at all. To a great extent London has been the eation of those writers, very often provincials, who came to love it, en who created a different London from the one we tramp and ive through, coeval with it but living a quite independent life. d it is this spectral city, dying slowly of dry rot and the 20th ntury, which is at the heart of so many anguished cries against e pick and the bulldozer.

In fact, that sound of crashing masonry you can hear is London ying goodbye to its own fictitious Victorian image, Lon- n looking back for the last time to that wistful imperial f that never was; saying goodbye to the wharves of . W. Jacobs' bargees; goodbye to that back street taurant where the Three Men in a Boat celebrated eir escape from the river and the Beaune was od at 3s. 6d. a bottle; goodbye to the shipping parishes H. M. Tomlinson, where in lost Edwardian pubs the p-faced masters of tramp steamers downed their ale, der framed photographs of forgotten tea-clippers slowly fading o sepia oblivion. Goodbye most of all to that magic den, snug yond the point of claustrophobia, where the muted clop of the proaching hansom seemed to set the tempo for Sherlock lmes' Stradivarius.

Perhaps it is impossible to park a vehicle outside 221B Baker reet, but that does not disqualify the building, or others like it, m bulking disproportionately large on that relief map of London which every resident and every visitor will do well to refer.

Edward VI
1547-1553

Mary I
1553-1558

James I
1603-1625

George II
1727-1760

14 KEW GARDENS
KEW BRIDGE

Oliver Cromwell
The Commonwealth

Charles I
1625-1649

George V
1910-1936

Anne
1702-1714

OLD DEER PARK

RICHMOND BRIDGE

EEL PIE ISLAND

15 RICHMOND
RICHMOND PARK

Charles II
1660-1685

Mary II
1689-1694

William III
1689-1702

James II
1685-1688

George III
1760-1820

17 HAMPTON COURT

16 KINGSTON
KINGSTON BRIDGE

Edward VII
1901-1910

George VI
1936-1952

George IV
1820-1830

Elizabeth II
1952-

Edward VIII
January-December
1936

William IV
1830-1837

Victoria
1837-1901

Georg
1714-

REGENTS PARK
THE ZOO

KENSINGTON GARDENS
HYDE PARK

12 WORLD'S END
11 THE KING'S ROAD

9 ST. JAMES'S PARK

BUCKINGHAM
PALACE 10

PALL MALL

8 WHITEHALL
7 PARLIAMENT
HOUSES OF PARLIAMENT

6 WESTMINSTER
ABBEY

RIVER THAMES

5 CLEOPATRA'S
NEEDLE
4 EMBANKMENT

2 THE TOWER
TOWER BRIDGE

3 LONDON BRIDGE

13 PUTNEY
BRIDGE

LIMEHOUSE REACH

1 GREENWICH
ROYAL NAVAL COLLEGE
NATIONAL MARITIME
MUSEUM

Ben Manchip

WAYFARER'S GUIDE
4

Illustrations: Elsie Wrigley / Richard Hook   Plant Notes: Geoffrey Gilbert   Animals & Birds: Jeremy Johns

1 GREENWICH: Once, on a trip of exploration at the Isle of Dogs on an afternoon grey under a fine rain, I stumbled on to a scrap of forgotten foreshore strewn with the detritus of a great estuary, rubber boots, anchor chain, a capstan bearded with rust. And there, on the far shore, mocking all this rubbish, lay the vista of London past, the fine lace filigree of the *Cutty Sark's* rigging, tricked by the perspective into sitting in the Arcadian lap of the Greenwich Maritime Museum. London today is a jostled, congested city, but to start a passage through it at Greenwich is to catch a glimpse of a more spacious age, and to get a dim conception of what a planned, ordered city might be like.

It is the architecture that does it. The hand of genius has touched so many of Greenwich's set architectural pieces that the whole area has been affected, touched

Golden Cherubs figurehead in the Cutty Sark

with grace. The Maritime Museum, for instance. It was James I who asked Inigo Jones to supplement the old Tudor Palace with a new building, which Jones called "a curious device", and which we call the Maritime Museum. Today the spirits of dead sea-dogs are preserved here, in the models of old ships, the navigational instruments, the maps and the manuscripts, Nelson's Trafalgar uniform, and the essence of words like "binnacle" and "spinnaker".

It was at Greenwich that Charles II installed John Flamsteed as Astronomer Royal at an annual salary of £100 and solved the pressing problem of longitude once and for all. Since 1958 the work of the Royal Observatory has been carried on at Herstmonceux Castle in Sussex, away from the smoke and neon of London. But the visitor to Greenwich can still enjoy the feeling of being at the literal centre of the world's affairs by going to the Octagon Room of Flamsteed's house, and standing astride a brass strip on the path outside. That strip marks the zero meridian of longitude, so that one has a foot in each hemisphere.

And it was here at Greenwich that Christopher Wren and John Evelyn jointly laid the foundation stone of the new palace which the 20th Century Londoner knows to be the Royal Naval College, although Wren was only one of seven architects required to complete the plan. The royal naval section of this grandiloquent complex was the idea of Queen Mary II, who, in 1692 while her husband William was away at the Dutch Wars, was saddened by the thought of the "large numbers of maimed and wounded soldiers arriving at our naval ports" after the triumphant victory over the French fleet at La Hogue. Two years later, after William had finally agreed to the idea

Flamsteed House in Greenwich Park

of a hospital, the joint monarchs issued patent for "the encouragement of seamen giving "a parcell of ground . . . eight acre two roods and 32 square perches . . . fo the reliefe and support of seamen servir on board the shipps or vessells belongir to the Navy Royall of us, our heires, successors".

It was from Greenwich that Gener Wolfe sailed to death and glory on the Heights at Quebec, and here too that *Gip Moth IV* lies at rest after its lone journe round the world in 1966-67 with S Francis Chichester at the helm. In fact the entire borough is redolent of England's pa maritime greatness, unlike the rest of the old dockyard sites which, being still com mercially viable, have lost their aura pastness. Indeed, to move in from Gree wich to Deptford is to be flung abrupt into the century of the Common Peop Once the site of the great naval dockyar founded by the Tudor kings and closed 1869 with the passing of the wooden ship Deptford today is a thronging workin class borough; and a road pointing central London indicates one of the mo famous of all London thoroughfares, t Old Kent Road, where redevelopment a new housing schemes have reduced t old music hall connotations to a faint ect

The celebrated tea clipper Cutty Sark in dry dock at Greenwich

The Tower of London and Tower Bridge, although so often linked in one picture, are eight centuries apart

THE TOWER: Of all the architectural symbols of London visible to the naked eye of the traveller, there are two which are known and accepted all over the world as representations of the city, structures whose disappearance would instantly render London incomplete, and perhaps incomprehensible. One is that Westminster complex which the eye has learned to take in at a single stroke, the cluster of neo-Gothic rhetorical gestures comprising Big Ben, the Clock Tower and the Houses of Parliament. The other symbol is Tower Bridge, a claim which would have baffled so recent a professional Londoner as Charles Dickens. For the first of the million misapprehensions that some Londoners have about their city is that Tower Bridge is anything like as venerable as the grim fortress on its northern extremity from which it takes its name. Tower Bridge, bursting with historical symbolism as it appears to be, is a mere whippersnapper of

a building, an afterthought added as late as 1894.

The Tower is another business, being so old and so encrusted with the barnacles of myth and history that it is impossible to know where one starts and the other ends. We know that in 1067 William the Conqueror, extremely respectful of the Londoners he had suddenly acquired, retired after his coronation "while certain strongholds were made in the town against the fickleness of the vast and fierce populace". We know also that one of these strongholds was the White Tower, that it became in part a royal palace, that young Richard II was blockaded here in the Peasants' Revolt of 1381, that Cromwell

A Yeoman Warder at the Tower

pulled down the royal quarters, that Charles II perversely revived the custom of a new monarch spending the night before his coronation within its walls, that it was the last residence of Anne Boleyn and Lady Jane Grey, and that when the royal zoo was removed to Regent's Park in 1834 the ravens were left behind.

Tower Bridge can offer nothing so ancient. On the other hand, it is one of the most extraordinary buildings in the world, a road that can be made to split in two and point to heaven, a bridge which can be adjusted to suit the demands of ships of different sizes, a ridiculous, eccentric gesture that has proved to be as sternly practicable as the most fanatical utilitarian could demand. Its twin, 1,000-ton bascules open as smoothly as some beautifully conceived toy, allowing ships to pass upstream between the Tower and that delightfully named landmark of the Thames, Pickle Herring Stairs.

Edward's Crown in the Crown Jewels

Queen's House — now the Governor's residence

3 LONDON BRIDGE:

The motorist who sets out to travel westward from Tower Bridge through the vast, belittling, metropolitan maze is beginning at the very heart of the London mystique. For a while his progress is linked to the river, the main artery which has dictated for 2,000 years the shape and extent of the city's growth.

There has been a London Bridge for more than 1,000 years, and the first one may have dated back to the Roman occupation. We know that Ethelred the Unready was ready enough to levy a toll on ships using the bridge, and that later he joined forces with a King Olaf of Norway to destroy the bridge. Later attempts to rebuild the bridge were shortlived, their wooden structures being blown away or burnt down. It was not till 1176 that the first stone London Bridge was erected, 910 ft. long and 20 ft. wide with 19 arches. Houses built on it reduced the practicable width to 12 ft. Henry II, King John and Henry III all operated different schemes for raising revenue out of the bridge, and in 1281 Edward I decided to charge a farthing per crossing to create a maintenance fund. This was the bridge across which Henry V paraded on his return from the field of Agincourt. We are inclined to forget today that until 1750 this was London's only bridge, by which time both the bridge itself and the houses built upon it were in a sorry state. The houses were eventually demolished, the last disappearing about 1760,

but it was not for another 70 years that the Rennies, father and son, designed and built the new bridge.

The Rennie bridge lasted till 1967, when it was decided that both pedestrian and motor traffic had grown to a point where renovations to the old structure would no longer solve any problems. During the morning and evening rush hours 20,000 pedestrians and 3,000 vehicles an hour were crossing the bridge, and on November 6, 1967 work was begun on a new structure to cost £4½ million, and have dual three-lane carriageways and 41 feet of pedestrian footways. Londoners can still admire the Rennie bridge, but only if they go to Lake Havasu City in Arizona where the original stones have been reassembled, after being bought by an American oil corporation.

Still, the Londoner can console himself with the thought that there are many other bridges spanning the Thames whose age does not compromise their usefulness, and as the motorist follows the line of the Thames, he will pass several of them. At Blackfriars, where the road swings away from the modern bastions of *The Times* and *The Observer*, circumvents the Mermaid Theatre and runs alongside the water, the traveller will be reminded that London is, after all, a maritime city. He may think of the great mercantile complexes behind him at Millwall, Deptford, Rotherhithe, and of that 18th Century influx at Greenwich.

THE CITY WITHIN A CITY

At the heart of London's 620 squa[re] miles is a city within a city, the home of t[he] most sophisticated financial machine t[he] world has ever seen. This is the true Londo[n] founded by the Romans and once enc[om]passed by protective walls. It is kno[wn] simply as "the City". Only about 5,000 [of] London's 8,000,000 citizens live in t[he] Square Mile. But 400,000 commuters [go] there after breakfast and earn on an avera[ge] workday about £2,000,000 for Britai[n's] balance of payments.

More than 1,000 years of independen[ce] have produced a special blend of ente[r]prise, self-assurance and expertise to he[lp] give the City its dominant role in wor[ld] commerce. It was this independent sp[irit] which extorted a charter of rights fr[om] William the Conqueror and forced Ki[ng] John to concede more liberties in Mag[na] Carta. Today the City is still largely se[lf]governing through the Lord Mayor, t[he] Court of Common Council, alderm[en] sheriffs and craft guilds, all observi[ng] medieval rituals which give historic sa[nc]tion to modern duties.

This sense of continuity is daily evide[nt] even in the greatest institutions. The Ba[nk] of England's messengers still wear t[he] first Governor's pink and scarlet livery a[s a] reminder of its foundation by royal char[ter] in 1694. The Old Lady of Threadnee[dle] Street used to be guarded at night by [a] piquet from the Brigade of Guards beca[use] in 1780 her reputation was threatened [by] rioters. The Stock Exchange transacts de[als] worth about £150,000,000 on a normal d[ay] and has a telephone system big enough [for] a town of 40,000; but it still has attenda[nts] in blue and red uniforms who are cal[led] "waiters", because early stockbrokers [did] their business in coffee houses. At Lloy[d's] underwriters who cover almost any ty[pe] of insurance risk anywhere in the world [sit] at pew-like desks, present-day equivale[nt] of the high-backed benches used by th[eir] predecessors, in Edward Lloyd's Tham[es]side coffee house. Important announ[ce]ments are heralded by the ringing of [the] bell of H.M.S. Lutine which sank in 17[99] with a £1,000,000 cargo insured at Lloy[d's.] One stroke for bad news, two for good.

Artist's impression of new London Bridge

Down comes Rennie's bridge

Engraving of Old London Bridge which spanned the Thames for more than six centuries

ne of the dragons on the City boundary

4 EMBANKMENT: As he drives along the Victoria Embankment, the traveller will find what is before him too fascinating to bother too much about what is behind. From Blackfriars Bridge on, the texture of London becomes progressively richer, like some great orchestra building to a climax. On the left are those training ships of the Royal Naval Reserve, *President* and *Chrysanthemum,* on the right the City of London School. Then, overlooking the water, the Submarine Memorial. Twin winged dragons mark the limits of the City of London. From now on the policemen will have blue sleeve-cuffs instead of red, there will be no bump of knowledge incorporated into the design of their helmets, and they will be called the Metropolitan Police.

The cool lawns of the Middle Temple on the City side of the dragons help to preserve the illusion that London remains a spacious, elegant place, an effect soon dissipated by the blackened facade of King's College. But it is on the left that most

of the action is taking place. The sheer variety of the statuary and the memorial plinths on the Embankment is surprising even to the most experienced Londoner. There is the arch marking King's Reach, and commemorating the 25th anniversary of George V's reign in May, 1935. There is the memorial to that intrepid journalistic crusader of the 1890s, W. T. Stead, another to Walter Besant, founder of the Society of Authors, and, best of all, the memorial to that most gifted and remarkable of Victorians, William Schwenk Gilbert. There is a dual reason for the location of Gilbert's robust features here. The site of the Savoy Theatre, which he helped to create with the incandescence of his lyrical wit, is a few yards to the north, and it was along this Embankment, gas-lit in those days, that he paced on the first nights of his operas. While Sullivan stood in front of the orchestra milking the audience for applause, his irascible partner walked through the night, turning up from the river into the theatre when the performance was over.

e Polar ship Discovery moored alongside the Embankment with St. Paul's in the background

Watergate marking the old river bank

Thames-side gardens at Charing Cross

A beloved piece of statuary and a masterpiece of irrelevance

5 **CLEOPATRA'S NEEDLE** on the Embankment is perhaps the strangest sight the motorist through London will ever see. This is a masterpiece of imperial irrelevance, its name false, its connotations with royalty spurious, its utility nil and its aesthetic appeal minimal. In some odd way this unimposing piece of statuary is deeply beloved by most Londoners. In fact, it is much older than Cleopatra, having been hacked into shape at least 1,000 years before she ever made eyes at any of the Caesars. How the British acquired it is not clear, except that in the 19th Century the British generally managed to acquire anything they took a fancy to. It was shipped to England, abandoned during a storm in the Bay of Biscay, retrieved and set up in its present position — and chipped by the first German bombs ever to fall on London, on September 4, 1917.

But the oddest thing of all about Cleopatra's Needle is not the Needle itself but what lies underneath, and it is this aspect of the question which perhaps underlines the superb aplomb of the British when Victoria presided over them. In 1878 somebody decided that posterity, certain to find London fascinating, should be given a few hints. Sealed jars were therefore placed under the obelisk once described by a famous London traveller as "that sad stone", the said jars containing symbolic artefacts of the British way of life. These items included a man's lounge suit, the complete dress and toilet perquisites of a lady of fashion, some illustrated papers, Bibles in several languages, some children's toys, a razor, some cigars, photographs of the most beautiful women in England, and a complete set of coinage from a farthing to a five pound note. Who decided on the most beautiful women? Did they include a pictorial representation of the Queen? One question which can be answered with certainty is, who was responsible for sticking the Needle up in the first place. In 1878, on the first night after the deed was done, an unknown hand inscribed on the stone the words:

This monument as some supposes .
Was looked on in old days by Moses,
It passed in time to Greeks and Turks
And stuck up here by the Board
of Works.

Soon the nature of the terrain will abruptly change as the route swings north towards the liveliest, most vulgar, most robust and raucous part of London, its West End. But first there is the serenity of the Gothic towers of Westminster, the last hint of such a quality for some miles to come.

6 **WESTMINSTER ABBEY:** In 106 Edward the Confessor consecrate his new Abbey at Westminster. A few day later he died, and after a brief interval th Conqueror thoughtfully staged his ow coronation there. Henry III rebuilt th Abbey in the 13th Century, the chantry Henry V was added in 1441, Henry VI chapel was completed in 1519, and Wre added the west towers. St. Margare Church, next to the Abbey, is a mere 70 years old, rebuilt around 1500, refaced Portland stone in 1735 and restored in 187

Every sovereign has been crowned in th Abbey since William the Conqueror, exce Edward V and Edward VIII: many are buri there. Monarchs of a different kind in Poets' Corner, including Tennyso Chaucer, Kipling, Spenser, Hardy an Browning, the actors Garrick and Irvin and, nearby, Handel and Dickens. In Hen VII's chapel lie Henry VII and his quee Edward VI, Mary Queen of Scots, Edward and his brother (the Princes in the Towe Queen Mary Tudor, Elizabeth I, James Charles II, William and Mary, Queen Ann and George II. The Chapel is memorab for two other reasons: its eastern en dedicated to the pilots and crews who die in the Battle of Britain, with its memori window, roll of honour and national flag and its status as the chapel of the Order the Bath, with the swords, banners an helmets of the knights hanging above.

The Houses of Parliament

Big Ben: the nation's timepiece

Henry VII's Chapel in Westminster Abbey is said to be the finest example of Perpendicular Gothic

The Houses of Parliament cover eight acres, the biggest buildings of their kind

7 PARLIAMENT: The Houses of Parliament, perhaps the most renowned puncturer of London's skyline, was built after the old palace had been destroyed by fire in 1834. Its Gothic-Romantic style was the work of Sir Charles Barry, who had the pleasure thereby of constructing the biggest building of its kind in the world, covering nearly eight acres. Sadly, Barry used Yorkshire limestone to build his masterpiece, and as Yorkshire limestone is notoriously fragile, all eight acres need to be under constant surveillance and repair. In 1941 the old House of Commons was destroyed by fire, and the new chamber, a replica of the old, was opened by George VI in 1950. The Churchill Arch at its entrance is constructed of stone from the original chamber.

The Clock Tower housing Big Ben continues to reassure Londoners, and indeed everyone else, that things are much as they always were. In a riot of statistical curiosity, I discovered that there are 374 steps up to the top of the tower, but no lift, that the minute hand is 14 feet long, that each Roman numeral is two feet high and that the space between each minute marker is one foot. The pendulum is 13 feet long and the bob at the end of it weighs four hundredweight. To which your average Londoner, either glancing up casually at one of Big Ben's four identical faces, or setting his watch right by the chimes on radio or TV, says "So what?"

8 WHITEHALL: Today the symbol of the State, synonym for red tape, bastion of the Rule of Law, Whitehall did not take on its present shape for some centuries after its emergence. It began as a mansion called York Place, owned by Walter de Grey, Archbishop of York in King John's reign. This property later became the possession of Cardinal Wolsey, and then of Henry VIII, who renamed it Whitehall. It was Henry who also acquired much of the surrounding land, including Green Park and St. James's Park, and who did much building for sporting purposes, including a tennis court, bowling greens, a cockpit and a tilt-yard. Henry married Anne Boleyn in Whitehall Palace, and died there 14 years later.

It was with the building of the Banqueting Hall by Inigo Jones around 1620 that Whitehall as we tend to think of it began to form. With the exception of Wolsey's wine cellar, now buried under office buildings, Jones's Banqueting Hall is the only structure of the period which still stands. Charles I was executed outside the Hall in 1649, Cromwell died in the Palace in 1658, and so did Charles II, in 1685. In 1698 the Palace was destroyed by a fire started by a laundress's carelessness but, due to the efforts of William III in raising a special fire-fighting force to deal with the blaze, the

Banqueting Hall was saved. Modern Whitehall really began to rise in 1829 when the Metropolitan Police set up headquarters at Scotland Yard, named after the Scottish Embassy which was once situated there. The Treasury Offices were built in 1846, the Home Office in 1868 and the War Office in 1899. Between 1895 and 1963 the Banqueting Hall housed the Royal United Services Museum.

Perhaps the most world-famous of all the Whitehall ceremonials is the Changing of the Guard, a daily performance dating back to the days of Charles II. Henry VIII's old tiltyard can be found by walking through the arch on to Horse Guards Parade. There, among various items of statuary, stand the two effigies in black stone of Lords Roberts and Wolseley, those two Victorian generals whose distaste for Indian mutineers, Egyptian rebels, Afghanistan marauders and Zulu warriors was nothing compared to their distaste for each other.

Out in Whitehall proper stands Sir Edward Lutyens' memorial to the dead of the world wars, the Cenotaph. Unveiled by George V on Armistice Day, 1920, a new inscription was later added and unveiled by his son George VI on Remembrance Day, 1946. Nearby is one of the most famous streets in British history, Downing Street,

built by Sir George Downing in the lat 17th Century. Downing must have bee one of the most brilliant diplomats of a time, for after trying to persuade Cromwe to become King Oliver I, he succeeded i getting into the good books of Charles I No. 10 Downing Street has been th official residence in London of the Prim Minister since 1731, and after more tha two centuries' accumulation of dry rot i the building, was remodelled in the 196C without altering Downing's original facade

No. 10, home of Prime Ministers

Whitehall, viewed across the flower beds of St. James's Park

The Cenotaph — memorial to the dead of two world wars

he aviary at the London Zoo

THE PRINCE REGENT'S PARK

Regent's Park, perhaps the most subtle
nd endearing of all the royal parks of
ondon, had its beginnings in one of the
rince Regent's schemes. The Prince
egent's original intention was the wrong
ne, as usual. His plans would have broken
o the fields of Marylebone and spoilt their
pen character by dotting them with villas
ncluding a house for himself). But John
ash dissuaded him by insisting that you
n have elegant crescents and lodges and
ill retain the open country. Nash had his
ay and created a London masterpiece,
hich the Prince very much enjoyed taking
e credit for, announcing when the park
as opened: "I would wish this park to be
quented by only the very best people, a
rk where one could see breeding in every
ace". Apart from the fact that his last four
ords were most unfortunately chosen,
s wishes were sadly thwarted. Regent's
rk has since become world famous for
e Royal Zoological Gardens, opened in
28, and beloved for its gracious
oportions and its amenities.
But the visitor will be surprised by the in-
cacy of the regulations of the royal parks.
o stage coaches may be driven inside their
its, and while cycling is permitted on peri-
ter roads, it is allowed only on condition
t the rider is not "cycling furiously".
rse-riding is permitted on specified paths,
t no mules, asses or donkeys. Dogs, yes, but
t if they are mangy. Sale of soft drinks, yes;
oholic beverages, definitely no. Organ-
d prize fights and wrestling matches, no.
litary evolutions, no. A man must not
mble in the royal parks, or ride in a stage
ach, and, by a recent amendment to the
de, he is banned from playing transistor
dios. The visitor cannot help noticing that
many of these regulations are ambiguous,
hen does an itchy dog become mangy?
hen does a cyclist become furious?
When George II opened Kensington Gar-
ns to the public, he did so only on
ndition that visitors wore "formal dress",
d when William IV further opened up the
ritory, he only made matters more con-
sing by insisting on "respectable dress".

St. James's Park, where Charles II and Samuel Pepys used to walk

9 **ST. JAMES'S PARK:** Up to
Trafalgar Square, where Landseer's
lions, their tails tweaked many times now
by the winds of change, look more than
ever like visitants from Wonderland or the
Looking Glass land; then west towards St.
James's Park and Buckingham Palace, at
which point royal history becomes so thick
on the ground that it becomes impossible
not to tread all over it. The first news which
history recalls of the park is a remark by
Samuel Pepys, who in 1666 confided to
his diary: "Walked in St. James Park, where
three hundred of the London unemployed
were digging a large hole". The hole turned
out to be Charles II's desire for a private
swimming pool. Charles was never actually
seen using the pool although he used to
walk his spaniels in the vicinity. He was
one of the great walkers of English royal
history, a robust strider-out whose courtiers
could hardly keep up with him and who
once remarked in the park to the visiting
Prince of Denmark, a corpulent young man:
"Walk with me, hunt with my brother and
do justice to my niece, and you will never
be fat". The Prince's reply has not been

recorded. Another of Charles's bright ideas
— one which the authors of *1066 and All
That* forgot to define as "a Good Thing" —
was his creation of a private bowling alley.
This favourite game of his was really a kind
of croquet played on a hard court, and was
known as . . . Pall Mall.

Springtime in the park

The symbol of the monarchy, but Buckingham House became a palace by accident

10 **BUCKINGHAM PALACE,** which symbolises the monarchy more than any other building in Britain, is, like so many other artefacts of our history, not at all what it appears to be. One might be forgiven for assuming that the world's most famous royal residence had been intended as such, that it had been planned and erected by a dutiful Parliament, that it had been conceived in a democratic state as a necessary appendage to the pomp and circumstance of constitutional monarchy. In the event Buckingham Palace happened more or less by accident. The story begins, like so many outrageous ones, with George IV who one day decided that his home, Carlton House, was "antiquated, rundown and decrepit". His father, poor old George III, considered quite mad in his own day but since discovered to have been suffering from a disease called porphyria, had bought the site of Buckingham House for £28,000 and the Prince Regent now decided to build on the site of this property a lavish new home.

In fact the Hanovers generally were extremely troublesome over this business of palaces. George III could never stand St. James's Palace, which he considered too grandiose for the kind of quiet domestic peace he preferred, and so used to retreat to Buckingham House. Later he gave Buckingham House to Queen Charlotte for

use as a Dower House. And having now become the queen's property, it became known as the King's House. But the Prince Regent now decided that Buckingham House must come down, and summoned his friend John Nash to perform the feat. Nash, who had been busy improving St. James's Park by planting many trees and landscaping new walks, began to plan a new palace, at which point the House of Commons started to make ominous noises.

Parliament had granted the sum of £200,000 for the building, but by the time Nash, who was building new stables, pulling down wings and putting them up again, laying out gardens and erecting colonnades, had spent the whole allowance, there was still nothing remotely resembling a palace to show for it. Joseph Hume argued that "the Crown of England does not require such splendour. Foreign countries might indulge in frippery, but England ought to pride herself on her plainness and simplicity". There was a general feeling that as Englishmen were starving, this was the wrong time to spend all this money on yet another palace. Others criticised Nash's architecture, and it must have looked at times as though the palace would never be completed at all.

But George IV was nothing if not obstinate, and decided that he must celebrate his birthday there in 1830. To

Victoria memorial in the Mall

Decorative panels on the gold State coach

Changing the Guard

...commodate him, 1,000 workmen slaved ... hours a day, to prepare the palace in ...e for the celebrations. But George never ...ved in after all. He died and was suc-...eded by his tactless sailor-brother ...lliam IV. The work on the palace con-...ued. By now Nash, fed up with the whole ...siness, had become so depressed by the ...ht of two wings of the building that he ...led them down again. And so, when ...orge IV died, Nash was dismissed. Still ... work went on. William died and ...ctoria succeeded. Still the work went on. ...en Queen Victoria moved in, the palace ...s still not ready.

...he cost had now stopped rising at ...00,000, and Victoria was understand-...ly disenchanted with the place when she ...nd that few of the lavatories were ...ntilated, there were no sinks for the ...ambermaids on the bedroom floors, the ...ins were faulty, the bells would not ring, ...ne of the doors would not close, and ...ny of the 1,000 windows refused to ...en. The Queen never did get it all ...ightened out. As late as the 1880s it ...s discovered that the royal apartments ...re ventilated through the common ...ver. In view of all this, perhaps the least ...sterity could do for the Queen was to ...ow Sir Thomas Brock to take 2,300 tons ...white marble and create the Victoria ...morial in front of the palace courtyard.

11 THE KING'S ROAD: As the route west leaves Westminster behind and threads its way through Belgravia towards Bohemia, the traveller gets a sense of the sheer vastness of London. Not only does he have far to go yet, but he is only just about to enter on one of the most frenetically urban areas in the whole of Britain, a long, confused street known in five continents as a centre of — what?

The King's Road, which begins before Sloane Square but which is usually thought to start life at the Royal Court Theatre, is enjoying a notoriety which is of compara-tively recent vintage. Its present stylish reputation was really created in the 1960s when a Mr. Plunket Greene opened the first coffee bar in the thoroughfare, and later a dress shop in partnership with Mary Quant. Since then the King's Road has resembled nothing so much as a fancy dress ball. It sports beyond question the most bizarre sartorial fashions and, perhaps more to the point so far as the motorist is concerned, presents desperate problems of parking and movement.

Those who come to the Royal Court Theatre, or to Peter Jones' store across the road, those who flock to the bars and restaurants, those who come rummaging for Edwardian junk, all these seekers after chic, are resigned to the fact that a parking ticket is almost a daily incident of life. And once the broad expanse of Sloane Square funnels back into the continuation of the King's Road, the stream of movement is always likely to congeal into a mere ooze. As the years go by the shops in the road seem to be edging closer and closer to the kerbside, so that walkers and drivers alike suffer from the illusion of persistent con-striction of their freedom. Car radios become superfluous, owing to the fact that boutique owners provide their own music free, which bellows across the pavements for most of the day.

A reactionary cynic might say that this is what you get when you start having democracy, for there was a time when the King's Road was really a king's road. Charles II required a private route from his palace at Whitehall to his other palace at Hampton Court, and part of the route is the present-day King's Road. Not till 1830 did it become a public thoroughfare, although long before then the Londoner had learned to regard Chelsea and particularly the King's Road with that peculiar derisory affection which has obtained to this day. When, in 1711, Jonathan Swift wanted some fresh air, he went to lodge in Church Lane, and wrote to Stella: "I got here with my servant and my portmanteau for sixpence, and pay six shillings a week for one silly room, with confounded coarse sheets".

Oscar Wilde's children used to enjoy bus rides along the King's Road. The ageing Ellen Terry, half-blind, was once discovered marooned on a traffic-island here, smiling to herself at the thought that she had eluded her minders if only for a little while. And in June, 1936, Lady Sybil Colefax, the King's Road's indefatigable lion-huntress, gave the last of her famous parties. The guests that day included King Edward VIII and Mrs. Simpson, Winston Churchill and Noël Coward. As a recently published book on Chelsea remarked; "Higher than that you cannot go". Today the only celebrities to be found in the King's Road are not royal, merely popular. It is therefore an irony that the old Chelsea Palace, once the home of the music hall idols, has now vanished. On the northern side of the road, just past a huge cinema done in the tradi-tional Odeon-Moorish-Egyptian-Rococo style, the old Palace lingered on into the 1960s as a television studio, but even that did not last, and the whole corner site finally came down.

For hippies who regard the King's Road as the heart of the nation, the central point of psychedelic awareness, the old Palace site marks the end of the Great Happening. On the south side of the road is the Chelsea Town Hall and the Chenil Galleries, after which boutiques graduate into antique shops, fancy dress into mere flamboyance.

The flavour of the King's Road in its signs: Six bells (a pub, of course) and antiques

RUB OFF A LITTLE HISTORY

Brass rubbing is a simple way of collecting a personal record of the past. There are several thousand memorials to tradesmen and servants, knights and their ladies, merchants, monks and bishops, which give us a picture of fashions between the 13th and 17th Centuries.

Taking rubbings requires care and patience. It is courteous and advisable to ask permission of the vicar. The materials required are white lining paper; a block of heelball, from an art shop or cobbler; adhesive tape; a soft brush and a rag. Clean the brass with the brush and rag and fasten the white paper with tape. Rub evenly with the heelball, from the head.

12 **WORLD'S END:** Not for nothing is the great bend in the King's Road called World's End; and the end of the world was exactly what it must have seemed like to the rakes of the town in 1877 when Cremorne Gardens were closed. Cremorne Gardens once spread across the area which is today represented at one end by Lots Road and at the other by World's End. By day the Gardens were respectable enough, but after dusk their personality subtly changed, and among those who thought that this was wrong was the Prince Consort. In 1855 a spectacular attempt was made to raise the tone of the district by holding an enormous military fete, including "A Colossal Panorama of Sebastopol", which promised "The Storming of the Memelon Vert and the Rifle Pits, effectively pourtrayed by 500 soldiers and three battering trains". These dubious delights were presented under the "direct patronage of Her Majesty the Queen and His Royal Highness the Prince Consort".

Even so, Cremorne continued to sink in the eyes of the bourgeoisie, and George Augustus Sala, that tireless man-about-town reported that it was "not a place that ladies were in the habit of visiting, unless in disguise or on the sly". Another commentator, writing in 1870, said: "At sunset, calico and merry respectability tailed off eastward by penny steamers, and at the Grand Entrance in King's Road hansom cabs drew up, freighted with demure immorality in silk and fine linen". In 187[_] Monsieur de Groof, "The Flying Man[_]" attempting a balloon flight, sailed ov[_] King's Road and plummetted into Sydne[_] Street, never to fly again, or indeed do any[_]thing else. When in 1877 a licence wa[_] refused for the Gardens, there was a sale [_] relics, among which was "Lot 1084, [_] Large Balloon, The Cremorne, with ca[_] ropes, etc". And so to the World's End.

From now on the social tone of th[_] journey changes. From Belgravia [_] Bohemia to Social Realism, the bourgec[_] world of Fulham. A little to the north, in [_] cul-de-sac off the Brompton Road, [_] penniless Irishman came to live with h[_] mother in 1876. Half a lifetime later, th[_] man, whose name was George Berna[_] Shaw, recalled the district when he fi[_] arrived there:

"The land between West Brompton a[_] Fulham and Putney, now closely pack[_] with streets and suburban roads, had s[_] plenty of orchard and market garden to gi[_] it a countrified air and to make it possib[_] to live there, as I did for years, witho[_] feeling that one must flee to the country [_] wither in the smoke. All the parallel Grov[_] connected the Fulham Road with King[_] Road, Chelsea, where Cremorne Garder[_] an unlaid ghost from the eighteenth ce[_] tury, was desperately fighting off its fir[_] exorcism as a rendezvous of the half-wor[_] Hence these now blameless thoroughfar[_] were then reputed Bohemian."

The Boat Race, London's annual unofficial celebration, starts at Putney

13 **PUTNEY BRIDGE:** All this tir[_] the river has never been very [_] away, and now the route comes right [_] to its ragged fringe once again. As [_] travel south-west, the line of the Tham[_] takes a north-westerly bend, and our inte[_] section comes at Putney Bridge where [_] arrive at the focal point of one of the gre[_] institutions of English public life. The Bc[_] Race, which starts here, is one of tho[_] idiosyncratic events which long a[_] graduated from its original status, whi[_] was a sporting event in the Oxfor[_] Cambridge calendar, into a kind of u[_] official London celebration, involvi[_] hundreds of thousands of people who [_] university connections may best [_] described as extra-mural. For at least t[_] last 100 years Londoners have sported lig[_] or dark blue rosettes on Boat Race day.

In fact the first Boat Race was row[_] quite a distance away — at Henley in 18[_] It proved so riotous a success that nobo[_] bothered to arrange another one for sev[_] years. Since then the history of t[_] ceremony has been fraught with drama. [_] 1843 Oxford turned up with only sev[_] men and still managed to win. In 1858 t[_] Oxford stroke caught a crab, fell back a[_] knocked all the other oarsmen over, a[_] while this was going on the Cambrid[_] crew, so intrigued by the antics of th[_] rivals, failed to look where they had be[_] and crashed straight into a moored barg[_]

Street scene in Chelsea near the World's End

The sign at the World's End

n 1859 Cambridge sank. In 1868 one of he Oxford men, relaxing on the eve of the ace by cleaning his revolver, accidentally lew his brains out. The official result for 877 was "A dead-heat to Oxford by five engths". In 1903 the starting pistol ammed. In 1912 *both* boats sank. In 1951 he Oxford boat sank with its crew continuing to row to the end. Best of all was he race in 1880, when the crews entered he water at Putney in a snowstorm, so that when the starter dropped his handkerchief, nly the Oxford crew noticed. The race was little one-sided.

The beauty of all this is that even in nodern times there is nothing to stop the oat Race from being a wild extravaganza n which boats disappear and then reppear, in which men above the surface top rowing while other men below the urface keep on rowing. In these publicity-onscious times the whole ceremony is rranged with an eye for television chedules, but the Boat Race, which is run ver a course to Mortlake of rather more han four miles, remains the same as ever as. And as our own route, slicing across he long northern loop that the river takes o Mortlake, arrives therefore at Duke's Meadows much faster than any boat could ope to match, we are inclined to forget at we have performed the great symbolic ondon act. We have crossed for the first me to the south side of the river.

BLOOMING AGAIN
The primrose is coming back to London. This lovely woodland Spring flower last bloomed on Hampstead Heath about 1900. Nostalgic poems were written in memoriam but no effort was made to replace the loss. The primrose suffered chiefly from misguided "flower lovers" but probably would have died out from loss of its natural habitat: hedgerows and coppices. About 70 years later a positive approach was initiated by Geoffrey Gilbert with support from Prince Philip, Sir Julian Huxley and others. Now efforts are being made to re-establish primroses and other wild flowers, to watch them and repair damage without delay.

HOME OF THE SWANS
Royal London with its parks and palaces offers the best opportunities to see that royal bird, the mute swan. Despite its name this swan can produce a wide variety of hissing or whooping noises when alarmed. According to legend it was introduced into England by Richard the Lionheart in 1194. Today the mute swan has become a common wild-breeding bird. The custom of swan upping still exists on the Thames and two Norfolk rivers. Young cygnets are caught in July and August and their beaks notched for identification; the birds that escape this indignity are the Crown's by right.

The great curved-glass Palm House in Kew Gardens was completed in 1848. Here the temperature is kept at 80 degrees Fahrenheit

14 **KEW GARDENS:** In crossing Putney Bridge, Barnes Common and then turning north-west towards Kew, we have crossed the great divide, for there is a sense in which London is not one town but two, and a further sense in which the south side is the neglected one. Further east lie the great working-class hinterlands of Wandsworth, Southwark, Lambeth, Lewisham, but for the motorist cutting across Barnes Common, covering rather more than three and a half miles from Putney Bridge to Kew, this is a very different south side, an altogether more sylvan place.

By heading straight for Kew Bridge and then turning abruptly south, we may run alongside one of the most extraordinary monuments to English disinterested scientific curiosity still extant in the country, an institution which has perhaps given as much pleasure to as many people as any building, park, theatre, palace or al fresco location in the kingdom. The Royal Botanical Gardens at Kew begin their story in 1759 when Princess Augusta, mother of the prince who was to become George III only a year later, initiated a botanical garden of nine acres at her private estate, Kew House.

This entire enterprise was dominated by the Hanoverians, for over on the west side of the present Holly Walk was Richmond Lodge, where the future George III was then living. Sadly, both Kew House and Richmond Lodge have vanished, although a few of the original trees from their gardens do remain. Between 1759 and 1841, when the State finally took over,

there was a constant stream of one-way traffic from the royal family to the population, as more and more of Kew Gardens were handed over. Today the Gardens extend over an area of 300 acres, and the royal ramifications are so numerous and so interwoven that probably the best way to impart the information is to list them item by item.

The Pagoda, perhaps the most spectacular of all the Kew Gardens outbuildings, was designed in 1761 for Princess Augusta. In 1837 was erected King William's Temple, which once housed a number of royal busts, long since removed to Windsor Castle. Then there is the Reference Museum, once the gardeners' quarters and the vegetable and fruit storehouse for Augusta's kitchen garden. The Wood Museum is housed in the cottage that was once the home of the Duke of Cambridge, while in the south-western extremity of Kew Gardens is the most picturesque of all the royal items, Queen's Cottage. This building stands in a railed-off area constituting 37 acres of woodland, once the grounds of the cottage. In 1897 Queen Victoria, moved by the demonstrations of affection towards her at her Diamond Jubilee, bequeathed the cottage and grounds to the nation, expressing the wish, since respected, that they should remain in their semi-wild condition. Queen's Cottage itself, surely one of the most whimsical and sentimental structures of any kind to be seen in London, was built by George III in the year of his accession, 1760, and in Queen Victoria's time was used as a

Kew's Japanese Gateway

shooting-box and as a summerhouse fo picnics. The guidebook shatters a few illusions with the news that the cottage ha no water, light or sanitary fittings, and tha although there are four entrances to th building, it has only two rooms.

But apart from the heavy scent o historical connotation which saturates th atmosphere at Kew Gardens, there is als the geographical aspect to be considere for it is doubtful if any more all-embracin

The Chinese Pagoda is 165ft high

Bluebell time in the Gardens

collection of flora has ever been so gathered together. The traveller by-passing the borders of the 300 acres of the Gardens may care to ponder the fact that he is now alongside such items as a Javanese fern with 12 ft. fronds, a giant water lily, a tree as old as King Alfred, and a rhododendron whose sap can give you blisters. Most remarkable of all, the Royal Botanical Gardens are strictly speaking not dedicated to pleasure at all, but to the spirit of scientific inquiry. There is the Library for research workers, containing 55,000 volumes, the Economic Museum, again for specialist workers, the Jodrell Laboratory, devoted to research into the cytology, genetics and physiology of plants. And yet the general impression one gets strolling down the beautiful glades of Kew is that somebody once tried to build, plan or in some way to bring about a kind of Arcadia. Indeed it is almost with reluctance that one drives away from Kew Gardens. Like that other aura far back to the east at Greenwich, this air and these generous buildings induce in us a suspicion that we might somehow now have slipped through a chink in the space-time continuum and ended up in some forgotten corner of the 18th Century. Oddly, as one leaves Kew behind, the impression, so far from being destroyed, is soon to be confirmed.

15 RICHMOND:

We are approaching the unique area known as Richmond, a place which conforms, perhaps more than any other in the whole metropolis to the old definition that London is a series of villages. Blackheath, miles away over in the Kentish purlieus of London, is the only place comparable to those sections of Richmond which chance and the eternal vigilance of the local residents have saved, at least in part, from the relentless encroachment of the 20th Century.

At first the view contradicts this idea, for the central shopping area of the village turns out to be a permutation of stores in every other High Street. But there is also the village proper, and here at least one can be reminded of other times, other cultures, other sets of values.

There is Richmond Bridge, for instance, judged by many experts to be among the finest along the whole length of the river. It was opened in 1777 and widened in the 1920s, spanning a section of the Thames where fact and fiction start to mingle until one is indistinguishable from the other. Turner painted Richmond Bridge; and to nearby Twickenham came Pope, Gay, Reynolds, Johnson, Garrick. But of all the districts we have so far travelled through, Richmond is the one with the most royal connections. For hundreds of years the rulers of England, dynasty after dynasty, succumbed to the charm of the place, sometimes for reasons of state, often for pleasure. The village of Richmond seems rarely to have been altogether out of the social or political reckoning.

In the days when young Richard II brought his court here, the place was known as Shene, and it was not until the reign of Henry VII, who built Richmond Palace, that the place was given its present name, after the town in Yorkshire where the Tudors owned land. Henry VIII brought Richmond into the Great Game in a most unexpected way. Being a man who was often too preoccupied with his next wife to spend much time with his current one, he ordered Anne of Cleves to Richmond while

Deer in the Park where Charles I hunted

he enjoyed himself in London with Catherine Howard.

Charles I had different tastes, being more interested in hunting deer. In the teeth of local opposition, he started "acquiring" Richmond Park for this purpose. After his execution, Richmond Palace was knocked down to the highest bidder, but when Charles II came home to confirm the Stuart succession, the park also was restored to royal status. Charles II had great affection for the place, and William and Mary would have agreed with him, for they too loved to hunt there.

However, the moment the Hanovers arrived, there was trouble. They had a genius for internecine squabbling, and squabble they did when it came to Richmond. The future George II, who detested his father, took his wife Caroline off to live at Richmond Lodge, where the Old Deer Park now lies. It was a gay court they formed at Richmond, and to this day street names behind Richmond Green preserve the memory of the period. In the houses in Maid of Honor Row Caroline's

Thames scene at Richmond

ladies once resided. As for George III, he built an observatory in Richmond Gardens which can still be seen in the Old Deer Park. Unfortunately, he also decided to build there a crenellated palace, which he designed himself.

George III's design for this palace was, to put not too fine a point on it, eccentric, and it turned out in the end to be one of the architectural disasters of his reign. There were so many Gothic towers and turrets that the architect working under the king's supervision described the outcome as "an image of distempered unreason", a remark which could not have made him very popular with a monarch who was by this time already beginning to persist in the belief that he was a tree. Before the crenellated folly was ever completed it was pulled down, possibly in one of the king's more lucid moments. However, for all his bunglings and ramblings, George III has been somewhat restored to grace by modern researchers, who see him more as an unfortunate person whose old age was imbued with a pathetic Lear-like sadness.

Dinghies race on the Thames at Kingston

16 KINGSTON:

In a sense Kingston proper is an object-lesson in the steadily advancing anonymity of modern British town life. For the shops, their window-displays, their lights and their juxtaposition are all so uncannily evocative of what we saw only a few minutes ago in Richmond that on a winter evening one might be pardoned for mistaking one borough for the other. We pass Kingston Grammar School on our left, mentioned as long ago as 1264, rebuilt as recently as 1878, and then spot Kingston Bridge.

We know there was a Kingston Bridge as early as 1223, but the present stone structure was erected in 1828, and widened without being ruined, in 1914. Motor boats and launches, blue-and-white sails, trips on the water to Hampton Court, all this creates a general effect of an ease and expansiveness which vanished from English life in the year of the renovation of the bridge. Today the town may be seen at the moment of its dissolution. For Kingston seems about to drift to a uniformity which has already levelled so many other parts of the country. The medieval market square and its quaint statue of Queen Anne somehow miraculously survive, and the bones of the old town can still be discerned under the flesh of modernism. Outside the Guildhall is the Saxon Coronation Stone from which this 1,000-year-old borough takes its name. As we cross the bridge, we sense that the one factor which has slowed the pace of Kingston's desecration is the river. It is the Thames which persists in this attitude of unhurried delight, the Thames indeed which has been the hero of our entire

A mixture of ancient and modern

journey, the Thames which is now about to leave our route once again, before rejoining it for its finest hour.

Over Kingston Bridge and a left turn down a long vista which creates the startling illusion that there are almost no buildings before us. But as we proceed along a road flanked on either side by walls and what looks like open country beyond, we realise that it is no illusion. The dumb scream of Kingston town's neon, its congested shopping area and its crowds of people, these were in effect the last throw of the dice by London proper, the last urban gesture of a city whose heart lies eleven miles to the south-east at Charing Cross. For as we drive westward into Surrey, still a little confused by the uncanny duplication of appearances at Richmond and Kingston, we cruise along something very like a wide country road and proliferation begins to drop back behind us.

17 HAMPTON COURT:

The road out of Kingston is, in a sense, a road back to at least two earlier periods of English history than our own, one factual and therefore extremely hard to take literally, the other fictitious and therefore utterly plausible. It has to be remembered that not so very long ago, a trip this far out of the city constituted a run into the country. It is therefore hardly surprising that this road before us was the high road to high jinks for the late Victorians and Edwardians out on a day's spree; and, for the Tudors, those distant monarchs whose presence has made itself felt so persistently and so incongruously at various points on our route, they must have regarded this road as one of the squares of the giant chequerboard of power politics, the route to a square in a distant corner of the board, where nonetheless, a king might settle the fate of a few of the lesser pieces.

On our right we pass a small domestic cluster named Victoria Villas, and soon after, as the countrified style of the road imperceptibly changes, there is the Greyhound Hotel. We are now in Hampton Court, up to our necks in Tudor history – and as we shall see, Victorian slapstick. The road turns left and we suddenly realise that we are circumnavigating a building more superb than anything we have seen so far, more regal even than our mental image of Greenwich, or the Clock Tower of Big Ben. This building appears to have been conceived by somebody so profligate with time and space that an acre seems to have been flung down here, a lawn there, with absolutely no regard for the cost. This is Hampton Court Palace, built by Cardinal Wolsey in such a style that even his gift for casuistry must have been stretched to their limit to reconcile the architecture with the renunciation of worldly goods.

However, Wolsey did not retain Hampton Court Palace for quite as long as he might have desired. The official reference books tell us that Wolsey "presented the palace to Henry VIII in 1526", but it seems that Wolsey had little choice in the matter. Hampton Court immediately became Henry's favourite residence, and he started to enlarge it, adding wings on either side of the Great Gatehouse, behind which is the Base Court and Anne Boleyn's Gateway leading to the Clock Court. Over the gateway is the clock built for Henry in 1540, although the Great Hall named after the king was in fact built later by Sir Christopher Wren, who was responsible also for the king's staircase and colonnade. There is a George II gateway leading to Fountain Court, rebuilt by Wren for William III (George II was in fact the last reigning monarch to occupy the Palace). It was Queen Victoria who threw the State Rooms open to the public, and assigned nearly 1,000 rooms as "Grace and Favour" apartments for the widows or children of distinguished Crown servants. In the gardens laid out for William III in a style expressing

Formal gardens at Hampton Court Palace, the Banqueting House in the background

calculated to make him feel homesick for Holland, may be found a vine planted in 1768, two orangeries along the south side of the Palace, a wilderness and — a maze. At this point — at the mention of the Hampton Court Maze — the kings and queens fade away and are replaced by three young Victorian sightseers and a mongrel, the Three Men in a Boat — those three comic prototypes, Harris, George and Jerome K. Jerome's narrator, who set out with the dog Montmorency in 1889 to boat up the Thames and who met with misadventure at every turn of the river. Jerome had intended his book to be a primer of the

The Palace Gatehouse

river's history, but he wrote another book altogether — and made Hampton Court Maze familiar to millions who have never stepped within five miles of the river.

The story of Harris and the Hampton Court Maze is an object lesson in the art of comic writing. Harris, the bumptious, self-confident member of the party, studies the map of the maze, finding it so "simple that it was foolish". Taking a friend in, he says: "We'll just walk round for ten minutes, and then go and get some lunch". Once inside the maze, they meet several others who have been wandering round for hours and are hopelessly lost. Harris tells them to follow him, which they do. Some time later one of the party notices a penny bun on the ground which they have passed several times. Harris starts to lose his temper.

Till now the episode has developed along conventional, not to say predictable lines, but there now comes a touch of Jerome's personal style. Harris starts out from the centre of the maze, but some of his followers, so sceptical, don't bother to follow him, but stay where they are and wait for him to come back to the same spot, which he does. Even better is Jerome's next stroke, which seems about to end the episode, only to provide its best joke of all. Eventually Harris admits defeat and the lost party calls for the keeper to come and rescue it. The keeper does, but he is a young keeper and gets lost too.

Jerome finally ends his episode on a curiously homely note somehow redolent of the late Victorian period, with its apparently unlimited supplies of time and patience. "They had to wait until one of the old keepers came back from his dinner before they got out".

It would not be pushing the truth too far to suggest that so far as the 20th Century is concerned Hampton Court Palace is as much the province of the Three Men in a Boat as it is of Wolsey and Henry, or Charles II, who had the moat filled in, or the neo-Georgians, who had it uncovered again. Perhaps this is the most unexpected thing about our journey, that it should have arrived in the end at the very symbol of pomp and circumstance, not to the trumpet fanfares of history, but to the sound of belly-laughter wafting across the broad sweep of the Thames as it floats under Hampton Court Bridge.

Across the road from the bridge lies the Mitre Hotel, whose exterior strikes just the right balance between the efficient and the picturesque. The traveller can now take his choice. Due south lies Surrey, spread out, as some sentimental expatriate once said, like a well-tended golf course; to the west lies Staines and the very distant echo of the west country; to the east, Croydon and the promise of Brighton; or further east to the very limits, the Kentish marshes and the English Channel.

Windsor—England's Royal castle

Even as a skyline attraction, Windsor Castle is everyone's idea of what a castle ought to look like. The solid emphasis of the Round Tower and the massive ramparts of the walls seem the very embodiment of the 'fortress castle' and yet there is also a delicacy of tracery in many of the buildings — the magnificent St. George's chapel, for example — which gives a special grace to the whole. Windsor has an ancient history. There was a Saxon palace a couple of miles down the river which was taken over by William the Conqueror who moved the castle to the hill above the river because of its obvious strategic value. Nothing remains of William's work. Most of the early buildings were almost certainly constructed of timber. In these early days the castle was primarily a military establishment and it only became a royal residence in 1100 when Henry I moved there from Old Windsor. The earliest architectural features, among them the famous Keep, date from the reign of Henry II (1154-1189), and Henry III (1216-1272) strengthened the castle's defences and built the western wall.

Edward III — the next major royal builder at Windsor — was born in the castle on November 28, 1312. It was Edward who, probably in 1347, founded that most famous of all the orders of chivalry, the Order of the Garter, with Windsor as its headquarters. Actually, the order was at first only intended as a jousting competition but it was solemnly consecrated on August 6, 1348. When Geoffrey Chaucer, the poet, was clerk of works in 1390 he supervised the restoration of St. George's Chapel. The famous north terrace was built by Queen Elizabeth I. During the Civil War the castle was a Roundhead stronghold and Charles I was imprisoned there for a few days shortly before his execution. He is buried beneath the choir in St. George's, near the remains of Henry VIII and Jane Seymour.

The castle was popular with Charles II who made extensive alterations. Then followed a period of neglect. It was really in the reign of Queen Victoria that Windsor achieved its prime position as the home of the British reigning monarch. The Prince Consort loved it. He died there in 1861.

Windsor has been a focal point in many famous episodes. King John stayed at the castle during the week of June 15-23, 1215, when he was forced to sign Magna Carta (see picture above) at Runnymede, a couple of miles away.

Above: this drinking glass was used by Queen Elizabeth I and is now preserved at Windsor Castle.

Right: a suit of armour belonging to Henry VIII. This one was made in 1540 and shows the king's increasing girth! This armour can be seen at Windsor.

Below: a pair of bellows said to have belonged to Nell Gwyn and now preserved in the State Appartments.

Left: Edward III picking up the garter — incident that led the creation of the world's most famous order of chivalry.
Above: a model Knight of the Garter in full regalia.

Above: Henry VIII in a jousting tournament at Windsor.

A bird's eye view of Windsor showing 1. The Curfew Tower 2. The rooftops of the Horseshoe Cloisters 3. The Garter Tower 4. The Salisbury Tower 5. King Henry VIII's Gateway 6. The main door of St. George's Chapel 7. The Albert Memorial Chapel, below which lies the Royal Tomb House 8. Henry III's Tower 9. St. George's Gate, which leads into the Great Quadrangle.

10. Edward III's Tower 11. George IV's Gateway 12. The Visitors' Apartments 13. The Queen's Tower 14. Where the Principal Dining Room is situated. On the left are 15. The State Apartments. 16 The Round Tower 17. The Norman Gate 18. The Winchester Tower.

East Anglia – Fenland and Sky

TREVOR RAY

Flat, treeless, empty, this country. And dominating all, the sky. There is more sky here than anywhere else in Britain. It floods the black fen, illuminates the marsh and makes splendid the great canvases of the East Anglian painters. A country of sharp horizons and of close people. A country of splendid medieval building which has grown slowly and which escaped the grinding cultural mills of the 19th Century and the grey horrors of the Industrial Revolution. Can it survive the 20th Century? Its natural boundaries are losing their terrors: the fens are drained, major road schemes develop, overspill towns are nominated. London and the Midlands approach. The week-ender proliferates. But still the country is empty, waiting and, in an odd way, passively resisting the change of pace. Spend one day here for refreshment, a week for a complete change of character. Spend a year here and leaving will become impossible. It has something to do with the quality of the light, the constant ten-times-a-day change of scene as the weather moves the sky.

GUERRILLA ACTION

The fens were drained in part before the Romans cut their great Carr Dyke and Fosse Dyke but it was not until the 17th Century, when Charles I desperately needed cash, that the Crown backed the efforts of companies which realised that there were huge profits to be made in land reclamation. A Dutchman, Cornelius Vermuyden, succeeded in devising the great drainage schemes which form the basis on which modern authorities improve year by year. Not without opposition, though. The fenman, who had lived a damp and uncomfortable existence on the few "hards" that existed among the moving bogland, resented the acquisition of "his" land by the outsiders and fought a bitter guerrilla action which lasted for centuries, broaching dykes, sabotaging sluices and resisting improvements. The struggle of the small man here was one issue which fed the Civil War, during which time Dutch settlers had a bad time at the hands of the embittered fenmen. Vermuyden made little profit from this and other ventures, dying a poor man — but to him is owed a great deal of the agricultural wealth of England, for the fens are now the most fertile farmland in Britain.

Today money is poured into atomic energy research, space exploration and other great projects. In medieval times spare wealth was invested in soul-building, a sort of divine insurance, resulting in extraordinarily beautiful ecclesiastical architecture which still delights. Domestic architecture flourished later, when the merchants were able to contain much of the outward power of the church. This part of the world has an incredibly large number of truly impressive medieval buildings and the Marshland churches are by far the most remarkable of these. The large towns have their share of grandeur in their cathedrals and large houses but it is the villages of the Marshland which bear the finest testimony to the greatness of early English architectural form — and contain something else, too. Something indefinable. A quality. These are not *just* churches — they were built by masters who knew something and took pleasure in attempting to express it.

The great expanses of open fen and looming marsh no doubt gave our forefathers ample opportunity to indulge in the morbidity of introspection and its resulting passions are still to be felt today. Nonconformism flourished in this part of the world from the time of the Pilgrim Fathers on, and proselytizing men have been listened to and followed avidly. They gave an expression to the pent-up feelings of these lonely places, an outlet for those energies which cannot be sublimated in mere hard work. Puritanism, the Baptist movement, Congregationalists, all found their earliest and stoutest followers here, the Wesleys toured and had tremendous impact and these influences are still strong hereabouts.

The agriculture of the fenland is today chiefly given over to the production of grain and root crops, the development of flowers and bulbs — see the bulb fields in spring, when the black billiard table flatland is flooded again, this time with the richness of the coloured blooms. Market-garden crops flourish in the fen soil which is in many places being used up at an alarming rate as the peat decomposes. The land has long been *sinking* due to the contraction of the peat after drainage, the organic exhaustion due to intensive cropping and from erosion, which in dry times is considerable. But meanwhile soil technology improves and there need be little reason to fear the eventual exhaustion of this great land.

The marshes have long been dry land and have been farmed for centuries. The difference in the quality of the marsh villages compared to those of the fenland is very noticeable. They have existed so much longer — there is hardly a domestic building of great age in the fen. The fens were formed by the flooding of dry land, caused by the silting-up of rivers — the "fresh" marshland was laid down by the silting of the river deltas at the coastline and grew under tidal sea conditions. It is not peat but a rich loam which farms almost as well as the fenland.

The Marshes border the Wash — indeed the sea once covered much of the marshland and Roman seabanks are to be found in many places now miles inland. The Wash has long dominated the everyday life of this area, for it is from this unpredictable sea that the flood-danger has always come. In times of great rain and high spring tides water from the fens cannot escape fast enough and the build-up bursts banks and floods farmland. Many times in past centuries the sea itself has burst across sea defences and flooded great areas with disastrous effect on crops and animals. Calm and placid with the heat-haze shimmering inverted mirages of Boston Stump or Hunstanton, the Wash can change within hours to roaring white fury, threatening even the great defences of modern man. Once a fishing ground, the Wash has long been denuded of everything but small shellfish by the huge colonies of breeding seals which bask on the banks, miles offshore. Once heavily slaughtered for their skins, they lead a more protected life now but try talking to a Wash fisherman and learn what is thought locally about these sea-wolves. Very descriptive, some of these local terms! Large catches of shrimp and cockle continue to be made, although deep-sea fishing has dwindled and the Greenland and Iceland fishery boats which sailed out of Boston, Wells and Lynn have seen their greatest days. On a bright summer's day the offshore channels present a thrilling image as the coastal and cargo ships wait for a making tide to get into the Witham, Ouse or Nene. Gibraltar Point, on the northern corner, and Blakeney, on the east are two great protected wildlife areas which shelter many rare breeding species.

MIGRANT VISITORS

In winter the Wash is the haunt of Bewick's swan, widgeon, pintail, mergansers and both brent and pink-footed geese. Spring brings the waders, redshank, plover, knot and others. In summer the tern, oystercatcher and the occasional kittiwake. Many oc

onal visitors drift here and careful watching may be rewarded by
e sight of ortolan buntings or, very rarely, a black redstart or
d-backed shrike. Autumn sees huge wheeling clouds of thrush,
arling and lark; and study over the whole year provides a fascinat-
g canvas of British shorebirds. In the rivers flowing into the
ash pike, perch, and lesser fin are to be found, the delicious
cumber fish, smelt, is here seasonally and the eel is everywhere.
el with green sauce or smoked and served with horse-radish
eam is food both for gods and men. But it is the large herds of
mmon seals which are one of the great sights of the Wash sand-
nks. Grey seals breed here, too, when man allows.

There is a good deal of shooting to be had along our route,
me of the large estates having famous beats and a cold night
a freezing punt can easily be arranged for the masochist. It was
economic necessity for Wash fishermen to become wildfowlers
t so many winters ago. Skating was a great fen sport which bred
own famous men who competed against Dutch champions,
ne out of mind. The championships continue today and are
tirely concerned with sheer speed.

AITH AND COURAGE

Bordering fenland beyond the Isle of Ely lies the curious desert
Breckland, for centuries the most heavily populated part of
st Anglia. Early man found the light sandy soil easier to culti-
te than the fertile forest elsewhere but the Angles and Danes
andoned the area, having the skills to develop the richer lands.
he abandoned heaths quickly reverted to desolate wastes and
re only marginally productive. Neolithic man mined flint in the
eat workings at Grimes Graves, near Brandon, but otherwise
eckland was for centuries a sandy steppe and a fine breeding
ound for rabbit. Today, all is changed — myxomatosis and the
restry Commission have ravaged whatever the army has allowed
em. Rabbits gone, tank tracks now score the mereland and
etford Chase is covered with 50,000 acres of Corsican pine in
ried rank after boring rank. The deer and red squirrel survive
t many smaller mammals and very many birds have gone.

Nothing that the Victorians have added to the two great cathedrals on the route can spoil the delight of a visit to Ely or Norwich.
Superb examples of English ecclesiastical building set in precincts
of quiet charm. Ely towers above its island town — imagine the
flooded fens with only the causeway to Stuntney, where relatively
dry land began. Medieval man had both faith and courage to
begin building in such surroundings. The fen now spreads black
and fertile as far as the eye can see, thanks to poor Cornelius
Vermuyden. Norwich Cathedral is a brilliant example of Norman
and Perpendicular work, breathtaking in its initial impact and
rewarding to detailed study. These buildings were not so much
built as places of worship, more as acts of worship. We are
fortunate to inherit such statements. Our own statements are in
other fields, architecture no longer absorbs our passions, as
witness the modern building throughout the route, which is
practical, unadventurous and oddly *temporary*. Nowhere is there
the feeling that the cement and steel is here to stay — with the
exception, perhaps, of the truly monolithic Tail Sluices at Lynn.

Looking to the past in practical ways, the junk shops of Boston,
Lynn and Norwich are still worth picking over. The whole area
is in a changeover period, releasing a new flood of bygones onto
the market. Many villages, too, have shops in which a few moments'
search may unearth the very thing that's needed. Anyway, it is a
good way to get chatting — a story may be the greater bargain. . . .

Apart from the civil strife during fen drainage, the area has
been little troubled by war. Cromwell swept through, supported
by all save King's Lynn, which held out in opposition for months,
finally capitulating. The greatest rumble of discontent came
from the land enclosure riot led by William and Robert Kett who
took Norwich in 1549 and were put down by the Earl of Warwick
and 12,000 troops sent from London. Both brothers were hanged
alive in chains, one at Wymondham, the other at Norwich. Since
then all has been relatively peaceful.

Continue, if there is time, into Broadland, where a different
country again comes into view. Fine rivers, reeded broads, a
"prettier" feel to villages, friendly people and hospitable hotels.
And always, above all, the sky.

aven for yachtsmen at Blakeney Quay, Norfolk

1 TATTERSHALL

2 CONINGSBY

3 BOSTON

5 GOSBERTON

4 SUTTERTON

6 MORTON

8 BOURNE

11 HOLBEACH

9 SPALDING

7 GRIMSTHORPE

DEEPING FEN

10 CROWLAND

THE WASH

RIVER WELLAND

RIVER NENE

GREAT OUSE

14 GEDNEY DROVE END

15 LONG SUTTON

12 FLEET

13 GEDNEY

19 WEST WALTON

16 TYDD
ST. MARY

17 WISBECH

18 WALSOKEN

20 WALPOLE ST. PETER

21 WALPOLE
ST. ANDREW

27 STOW BARDOLPH

23 KING'S LYNN

22 TERRINGTON ST. CLEMENT

24 WIGGENHALL ST. GERM

25 WIGGENHALL
ST. MARY THE VIRGIN

26 WIGGENHALL
ST. MARY MAGDALEN

28 DOWNHAM MARKET

HUNDRED FOOT DRAIN

TWENTY FOOT RIVER

BEDFORD LEVEL

29 WELNEY

VERMUYDEN'S DRAIN

30 LITTLEPORT

OLD BEDFORD RIVER

31 ELY

33 ISLEHAM

32 SOHAM

Photos: Peter Baker / W. H. Brighouse / B.T.A. / Conway Pic Lib / Fox Photo's / Noel Habgood / Michael Holford / S. Jennett / A. F. Kersting / Mansell Collection / Joe Monk / C. V. Nic
Pictor / The Picture Lib / Picturepoint / R.S.P.B. / Bruce Scott / Kenneth Scowan / Spectrum

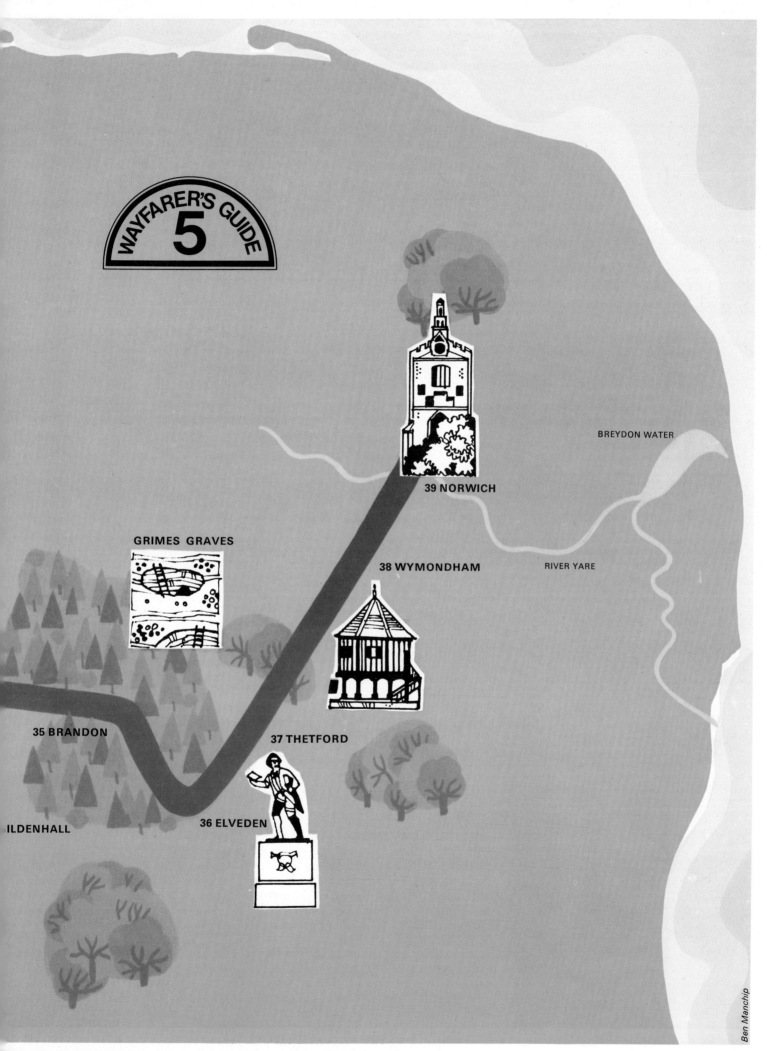

WAYFARER'S GUIDE 5

39 NORWICH

BREYDON WATER

GRIMES GRAVES

38 WYMONDHAM

RIVER YARE

35 BRANDON

37 THETFORD

ILDENHALL

36 ELVEDEN

ations: Elsie Wrigley / Richard Hook   Plant Notes: Geoffrey Gilbert   Animals and Birds: Jeremy Johns

Ben Manchip

1 **TATTERSHALL:** Dominated by its castle keep, the village huddles opposite Coningsby, on the once-navigable Bain. Originally the site of Robert de Tateshalle's moated stone castle, the present building has had a remarkable career, being saved from the depredations of Edwardian speculators by the generosity of Lord Curzon of Kedleston who restored the almost total ruin in 1912 and presented it to the National Trust. Ralph, Lord Cromwell, Lord High Treasurer of England in the reign of Henry VI, together with William Wayneflete, Bishop of Winchester and founder of Magdalen College, Oxford, planned the present group of buildings as the centre of a great castle/church college complex but there is some evidence that the plans were never fully realised. Once one of the finest medieval brick buildings in England, the restoration, though careful and inventive in its detail, still leaves the feeling that what we see is Edwardian "medievalism". But as a restoration it must be considered perfect.

The cruciform collegiate church of 1438-55 has also been much restored but one is more aware of patchwork here. The few fragments of original glass remaining are gathered in the kaleidoscopic east window — the rest was the subject of dispute in 1757 when it was given to Lord Exeter by the Fortescues, causing a certain amount of heartburn among local residents who threatened loudly enough but who never quite made the rescue journey to Stamford where the gift still glows in St. Martin's.

The remarkable one-handed clock

Tattershall Castle, restored by Lord Curzon in 1912

A detail from Sutterton church

2 **CONINGSBY:** The bridge over Bain gives a good view of Tatt shall's castle and church and of village church which contains a m remarkable clock in its 15th Cent tower. The face is huge and has only hour hand. The tower stands on curic tall stone arches, so that it is possible pass under the tower on three sides. clock mechanism is mainly oak, with i bits at salient points, and the clock weig are stones suspended on steel wire rop The pendulum, which swings only on every two seconds, is hung some dista away on the tower and is connected various rods to the clock. Half a m towards Tumby is the Lea Gate Inn wh Thomas à Becket is said to have ta refuge when Henry II was after his blo There are ruins in the grounds that m have been a hermitage and an old i beacon bracket to light night travellers the tollgate. On the way to Boston pass Brothertoft, once called Goose where in July a vast sheep fair was h each year. Thousands of geese w reared hereabouts and driven to ma even as far as London.

4 **SUTTERTON:** Once close to the sea, the village has been left by drainage miles inland, surrounded by fertile marsh. The fine cruciform Norman and Early English church had some restoration in the 18th and 19th Centuries. However it didn't suffer nearly as badly as the church of Kirton which was "restored" with gunpowder, everything but the nave being destroyed, by a barmy Gothick architect named Hayward. The treasure here must surely be the fine 18th Century ring of eight bells and the Sanctus bell inscribed to bellmaster Symon de Hazfelde, who cast it in the 13th Century.

AT HOME ON THE WATER

e Moorhen is very much at home in the ater-laced flat lands of this area. The bird easily recognised since of all our water-wl only the larger Coot is similar. It is edominantly black with white flashes on tail and wings and a scarlet bill and rehead. The Moorhen's flight is poor and short, stubby wings seem hardly ade-ate to lift it from the water.

oth sexes are alike in colouring and are of milar size at a little over a foot long.

e Moorhen makes its home by fresh ater, resting in densely covered areas side ponds, rivers or lakes. The bird's name is, in fact, a corruption of "mere". There is a brisk air of busyness about its staccato dashes across the water, which, with following chicks, may suggest a total devotion to domesticity. In fact, they are fierce defenders of their own territory and resolute fighters.

Nests are built on platforms of dried pond-side plant debris. The male has a special posture in courtship: it cranes its body up-wards, spreads its wings, fans its tail to show the white marking and points its head downwards. A pair may hatch out two or three broods between March and July, the chicks swimming within a few days.

BOSTON: From miles away the Stump towers above the Fen town, ce the second largest port in all England. landmark for centuries both for seamen d fen travellers, the great church tower the glory of the place which gave its me to the Massachusetts town when ritan ships sailed from here carrying rly settlers to the colony. Still a trading rt though dwindled in importance since e great Hanseatic League days, cargoes m Europe and Russia still line the busy narves. The River Witham has been epened and straightened in the last ntury and is the centre of the town's life d prosperity. Spain Court and the ectory of the Dominican Friary, the ildhall and the wharves all fascinate.

But the focal point is undoubtedly the splendid Stump church built, as were Lavenham and Long Melford, Clare and Cavendish, "on wool". From the top, 272 ft. up, a vast stretch of England can be seen, Hunstanton across the Wash to the east, Lincoln towers 30 miles north, Tattershall relatively close at hand. Mostly 14th Century, there are modern roofs and a quite beautiful medieval oak door in the south porch, above which is the church library. The interior is splendidly spacious and a mass of carvings both medieval and modern. The roof bosses spell out the town's history, the stall misericords are superb, modern glass records various moments of interest as well as being memorials to past dignitaries. Monuments are few but good and there are defaced brasses of ancient worthies.

On the left bank of the Witham lie the Market Place, the Bargates (Strait, Wide and End), the Central Park, Pescod House, and the grand Maud Foster windmill, in good order. Good lanes round the Close buildings lead to Church House, the County Hall and the Sessions House. Boston suffered much over the years from the floodwaters, even after Fen drainage was complete, and there are records of the high-water marks recorded on the base of the church tower. Many times in the past the Fen has become a great inland sea and the farms have suffered badly, crops and cattle being washed away.

A splendid mass of carvings

ton Stump, a landmark for centuries for travellers

The Maud Foster windmill

5 **GOSBERTON:** A very "alive" feeling here, maybe due to its crossroads position. It is still very much a village and seems to keep its proportion well. The church has a curious feature that it shares with Sutterton and other villages in this area — the paving has risen over the years and some of the pillars are buried in the floor by two ft. or more. Outside is an amusing elephant gargoyle, and inside the reredos is painted with copies of Old Masters by a woman who in recent years lived in Gosberton House, now a council school — a good 18th Century mansion in fine, mellowed red brick with a splendid white cupola.

Gargoyles outside church

An impressive Fenland church

6 **MORTON:** The journey here has been across land reclaimed from bog and fen in fits and starts since Roman days. The Carr Dyke and South Forty Foot Drain have long brought the land to use, every muddy cubic inch slopped out by hand — no machinery, just honest imported Dutch labour. This village stands right on the edge of Fenland and has a most impressive approach to the west front of the church along a main street lined with attractive small houses. The church interior is spacious and impressive and contains some good groups of carved medieval heads and a fine 15th Century font. Just as fine is the welcoming 18th Century look of the King's Head.

7 **GRIMSTHORPE:** Cross the valley of the Eden here. After the fat farming flatlands the gentle hills are almost a surprise. There are few great houses in Lincolnshire but Grimsthorpe Castle ranks among the greatest in England — standing on a rise within a huge park with "English" vistas in every direction. Avenues of chestnut and hornbeam, a splendid lake and herds of deer beneath age-old oaks. The early history of the house is lost but legend suggests it was built quickly to house Henry VIII on one of his tours. The castle was extended later and Sir John Vanbrugh added the grandly pompous north front in 1722. Stone for the building was quarried within the park and although Vanbrugh's plans for the house were never completed, the beautiful Hall with a double stair at each end within colonnades, decorated with family portraits and busts, is ample evidence of Sir John's magnificent thinking. Other great rooms in the castle

Wood carving head of Christ

Medieval pew end

contain treasures such as are rarely se[en] outside national museums. The Willough[by] de Eresby family have held the heredita[ry] title of Lord Great Chamberlain of Engla[nd] for more than 300 years and many of t[he] treasures are connected with royalty — coronation robes worn by monarchs fr[om] the first James on, chairs and canopi[es] used at coronations, gold plate and ma[ny] other splendid perquisites of the fam[ous] office. There are paintings by Van Dy[ck] Lawrence and Reynolds.

Edenham church has grown throug[h] the centuries along with the great folk [of] the castle and is filled with monuments [—] in some cases marbles which some peop[le] find so grotesquely tasteless as to [be] awe-inspiring and put to shame by t[he] figures of earlier times whose memori[als] rest beneath the tower. A 15th Cent[ury] brass, thought to be of Thomas à Beck[et,] was once fixed on the outside wall of t[he] tower but is now protected in the churc[h.]

12th Century font with unusual double lobed arches to the decorative columns

8 BOURNE: A splendid small market town with a fascinating history of resident heroes. Those days are long gone but the marks remain. The Roman Carr Dyke passes here, channelled 56 miles from Peterborough to Lincoln, at once a canal and a catchment dyke for the water coming down into the Fens from the toplands east of Grantham. It was an important Roman camp, the Saxons were here in force and the Normans built a moated castle and an abbey, the ruins of which are still the parish church, restored and developed during the 15th Century. Apart from the good 15th Century font the church interior is not well endowed. In the early 14th Century, Robert Manning or Robert de Brunne as he called himself, produced *Handlyng Synne,* a doggerel translation of a French poem, the first literary work composed in English as we know it, "in simple speech for love of simple men". It dealt with a wide variety of interests of the period while illustrating the results of sinful doings.

Apart from the ecclesiastical buildings and remains of the old Elizabethan grammar school in the churchyard, the Burghley Arms Hotel — the birthplace of William Cecil, Lord Burghley, Elizabeth's great statesman and founder of the Cecil family history — leaps to mind whenever passing through Bourne. The great hero of the town is Hereward the Wake, the early English guerrilla who fought the Normans through the Fens. Legend says that he was born and buried here, and Charles Kingsley compounds the tale in his romance. More recent fame was brought to the town by Raymond Mays, who developed the BRM Formula One cars in his workshops here. It is a small, friendly, town that has lost the bustle and clang and has settled into the solid routine of the rich surrounding farmland.

Abbey restored as parish church

h Century brass, thought to be St. Thomas à Becket

In the Springtime . . . acre upon acre of dazzling colour

9 SPALDING: The most important of the Fenland towns, famous as the centre of a rich agricultural area, with potatoes, sugar beet and bulbs as its main crops. Springtime is an extraordinary sight with acre after dead flat acre blinding the eye with colour — a landscape flooded with the brilliant blooms of tulip, daffodil, narcissus and hyacinth. A rich market-garden land which turns easily to the more plebian rootcrops when the seasons change. A visit to one of the large bulb producers is a must for the spring visitor. In recent times the local engineering industry has developed machinery that keeps pace with the economics of some of the most fertile farmland in the country. The Welland gives the town its centre and main artery, rather in the manner of Dutch towns. Good buildings line the banks and make a pleasant walk. Cross the High Bridge into the older part of the town, into Church Gate and Church Street and visit the slightly tarted-up White Horse Inn.

On the river bank by Church Gate is Ayscoughfee Hall, now a museum and once the home of the prolific Maurice Johnson, friend of Newton, Pope and Addison and a founder of both the Society of Antiquaries and the Gentlemen's Society of Spalding, which still exists, in Broad Street. The church of St. Mary and St. Nicholas is splendid and odd in that it is almost as broad as it is long, secondary aisles having been added to the original 13th Century cruciform plan, while the nave was lengthened and the superb north porch built. Sir Gilbert Scott was let loose here, expensively, but without causing too much obvious rapine which is more than can be said for his two other efforts in the town, St. Paul's and St. Peter's. In all, a handsome, prosperous town, pleasant to live in and good to visit.

10 CROWLAND: Close to the po where Lincolnshire joins Ca bridgeshire and Northamptonshire, t ancient market town has dwindled little more than a village when it mi well have become a city. The basis of early fortune and eventual decay was great Benedictine Abbey founded in 713 memory of St. Guthlac. Then a patch relatively high dry land in the seas of m which stretched many miles around, became a place of pilgrimage and grew importance. The Abbey was destroyed a rebuilt three times before Cromwell bo barded it in 1643, helping towards its fi ruinous collapse in the 18th Centu which left only the north aisle to serve the parish church among the splen decayed stones. Prior to the draining the Fens the parishioners suffered grea from "Fen ague", thought to be a type malaria among the quaking bogs. Fenm doctored themselves with laudanum a opium, probably on the basis that wh it might not cure them it was a better w to go. Even after the attacks faded aw we find a Mrs. Burroughs in 1850 decryi the fact that the habit of drugtaking had r stopped. The West front of the church superb as is much of the interior: the 15 Century oak chancel screen and the tw fine fonts have much good detail. oddity is a very small stone coffin actually the top of a heart burial cask

In the middle of the town is the Triangu Bridge which has three legs spanni streets which were navigable rivers wh the bridge was new in 1370. Unique u a few years ago, the same simple sche has solved a similar bridging problem Thetford where the new three-legg bridge over the Thet has won an importa design prize.

Detail of statue at Crowland church

THE PERFECT POACHER IS WELL EQUIPPED

The flat lands around the Wash are interlaced with rivers and streams which are sanctuary to the otter. Until recently the otter has been persecuted, for his crime comes so close to the hearts of many Englishmen He poaches fish. What is worse, he is perfectly equipped. His body is about four feet long and tapers to a broad tail reminiscent of a rudder. His paws are webbed and his legs powerful and efficient in and out of water. The otter's coat is a sort of animal double-glazing. Closest to the skin lie fine, closely packed, grey hairs; on top of these are longer, thicker dark brown hairs, coated with a hydrophobic secretion. The water cannot penetrate the grey layer and the otter inside remains warm and dry.

TRAVEL BY STEAM AROUND THESE FAMOUS GARDENS

he gardens and steam engine museum at ressingham Hall near Diss, Norfolk, are oth hobbies of Mr. Alan Bloom, who has geniously combined the two loves of his e — flowers and steam — by taking sitors round his gardens and nursery in eam engines.

Mr. Bloom's business is farming and orticulture: the hardy plant nursery on his 50-acre farm is one of the largest in urope. As a relaxation, he created a beauti- l five-acre garden on his farm, stocking with uncommon hardy plants from all over e world. Although not originally intended a showpiece, so many visitors came to e it and enquired where they could buy e more uncommon plants, that he now fers a limited number of these for sale.

When his garden was finished, he cided he needed another hobby and ught Bertha, a ten-ton traction engine. nding his visitors as enthusiastic about eing Bertha in steam as he was, he ught another eight engines and pains- kingly restored them to their former glory.

It was a short step to acquiring railway comotives and now there are narrow uge and standard gauge engines running sitors to all parts of the gardens and rsery. The mightiest of them all, the 143- n Britannia Class Pacific No. 70013 iver Cromwell, was the last steam loco- otive to haul a British Rail passenger in.

Now run as a non-profit-making trust, s unique collection gives visitors a ance to "see, hear and smell" steam gines in working condition.

11 **HOLBEACH** is reached across yet more reclaimed Fen, where once a main crop was woad (used for dyes) and now is beet and potatoes. Mustard fields are a great attraction when in full bloom, the colour seeming to affect even the quality of the light. Holbeach is really a marshland town and from here until King's Lynn is reached, the marshland journey must be given over to the great churches. Its own church has a soaring plain spire and a fine clerestory. Inside is the 15th Century tomb of Sir Humphrey Littlebury, the head of whose effigy rests on the life-sized head of a woman in a netted hood. Opposite the church is the Chequers Inn, the home of a quaint gambling legend "made into a rhyme by Mr. Rawnsley of Bourne about the year 1800" and quoted by elderly locals.

15th Century tomb at Holbeach

Detached tower and spire

12 **FLEET:** As the sea bank indicates, much of the marsh north of the village has been reclaimed and the sea, once close, is now eight miles away, no 'flete' or creek in sight. The church has a detached tower and spire with splendid gargoyles and flying buttresses springing from the tower pinnacles to the spire. There are also some 19th Century van- dalisms but the vast west window is good to see. On the north wall there is a carving of a Lincoln Imp. Not too far away stands Hovenden House, of the type called neo- Georgian, in this case George V. Now it is a Cheshire Home, run by the group who do so much for the seriously disabled. A visit will be welcomed.

A charming early brass

13 **GEDNEY:** It has been pointed out that the churches along this road are exactly three miles apart, though the significance is obscure. At this distance of course, the spires serve well as markers for marsh travellers, but the Holbeach-Lynn road is certainly older than any of the churches. Gedney church has a charming early brass of a lady and her lapdog. It is claimed that the registers go back to 1558, around about the time that Richard Hakluyt (author of *Principall Navigations, Voiages and Discovries of the English Nation*) was vicar here. The spirelet of the church is curiously stumpy and may indicate some truth in the belief that the tower and church were built without foundations, being floated in the peat bog on a raft of timbers.

14 **GEDNEY DROVE END:** There are places which are marinaded in a feeling of world's end — and this half-village certainly has the vintage flavour. Walk from here and you will eventually come in sight of the Wash and there is no more splendidly bleak and unwanted spot on earth. That legends abound in this part of England can be no surprise, the gloom of a January day here lurks on well into the summer. Marsh birds wheel slowly and the mud sucks and waits. Keep to the higher, harder ground and don't linger. In spring you may catch sight of seals far out on a bank. In winter, pneumonia is more likely to strike. But stunningly.

15 **LONG SUTTON:** A good 19th Century town with a bustling air on market day. A few good Georgian houses help the honest look of the place, but the treasure is the soaring 13th Century steeple claimed to be the greatest lead-covered spire extant. The tower is detached and originally stood on arches (now closed up) as at Coningsby. The interior is a well-restored patchwork of the centuries with a couple of curious, carved bosses; a pelican and a double man/woman face with two tongues that makes one wish the carver had scribed captions to his cartoons. The two-storey sacristy is curious as are the memorials to a sexton and to a Dr. Bailey who was the victim of a murderer. "Alas, poor Bailey", cries the stone. Not far away is a well-kept six-sailed tower mill, one of the few remaining. Once mills pumped water along the ditches, raised water from the fields into the rivers and milled grain and woad; but no longer. First steam and now electricity has swept away the turning sail.

A six-sailed windmill

Town sign at Tydd St. Mary

16 **TYDD ST. MARY:** Once boasted Nicolas Brakspere as rector. He later became the only English Pope. Imagine his translation from the modest beginnings of this typical Fen church to the grandeur with which he found himself invested! There is great charm in the Trafford family monuments within and in the usual pattern of development and restoration from the splendid Norman arcades onwards in time. Fen drainage is very much in evidence here with two major dykes emptying into the nearby Nene. Outside the village we leave Lincolnshire for Cambridgeshire.

In the great flat country of Norfolk windmills stand tall like the old sailing ships — and, like them, are today both beautiful and rare. More than any other part of Britain, East Anglia was the land of the windmills. Once they stood for the latest in mechanical ingenuity with their varied arrangements of gearings, bearings and cogs for harnessing the wind to the best advantage. A century and a half ago some 10,000 windmills dotted the countryside, pursuing their mundane tasks of draining fens and broadlands or grinding the local corn. Now few remain, decayed, pensioned off or switched to other occupations. Anxious to save survivors from extinction, Norfolk County Council decided in 1960 to sponsor a

1. Burnham Overy Mill.   **2.** Cley-next-the-Sea Mill, near Blakeney, now a private house.   **3.** Denver Mill nea

campaign for the restoration of 18 mills within the county boundaries. Four examples are pictured here. Three are tower mills which used to grind East Anglian corn. Tower mills became popular in the 18th Century. They have tops which rotate to catch the wind — in contrast to the older post-mills, the whole of which had to be revolved. Burnham Overy Mill which overlooks the A149 in the north of the county, was built in 1814, continued working until 1914, became a private house in 1926 and was presented to the National Trust in 1958. The odd mill out of the four is a restored drainage mill at the head of Thurne Staithe. It is a familiar landmark to people boating on the Norfolk Broads.

market. **4.** Drainage Mill at Thurne.

17 **WISBECH:** An excellent town, attractive in the Anglicised Dutch style that is so common in East Anglia. Long called the capital of the Fens, it was until a century ago an important port and flourishing market town despite the huge tidal rise and fall of the Nene which makes such difficulties for watermen. The quaysides and warehouses show the scope of the former trade, now much reduced. Will the recent move to a restoration of waterborne traffic bring back a share of prosperity to the town which, like Spalding, is now a centre for the surrounding

Georgian houses on the bank of the Nene

farmland? The sight of a busy small port so far inland is exciting to contemplate. The town contains some splendid 18th Century architecture, the result of merchants turning their new-found coin into comfort. Walk along the Nene on North or South Brink and you will find a superb Georgian street, very Dutch but very English too. The finest example of this nouveau-riche architecture is probably Peckover House, built in about 1727. Don't miss, either, the White Hart Hotel facade nor the Rose and Crown in Market Place on the corner of the High Street. The brewery on the North Brink has scented the air with something other than mud and oil for many years.

It is difficult to enthuse enough about Wisbech. It has the grand air in miniature and, if its planners get it safely through the next generation, it could well become a place of pilgrimage for all that has been good in England. Miss out the badly mutilated church unless the huge brass of Thomas de Braunstone (1401) attracts. There is also a memorial by Nollekens who must have made a fortune out of glorifying his clients.

This font is the showpiece at Walsoken's Norman church

18 **WALSOKEN:** Out in the suburbs of Wisbech, across the border into Norfolk, stands one of the glories of the journey. Nikolaus Pevsner, the architectural authority, speaks of All Saints Church as the grandest Norman parish church in the county. It is very late Norman, developing into Early English

easily with beautiful effect. The interior has some very delicate touches, slender piers, carved roof timbers, and good screen tracery. But the font is the show piece. In the north aisle a heart-burial is recorded and there are some grand tombstones in the yard outside. The immediate surroundings have little to make you linger.

Detached bell tower at West Walton

19 WEST WALTON: Within a few square miles it is possible to see superb examples of every period of English architecture and St. Mary's here is an exciting start to the sequence. If it is justly called "the finest 13th Century church in Norfolk" new and equally grand credits will have to be found for Walpole St. Peter and Terrington St. Clement. The beauty of the Early English concept and design comes to mind years after one's first sight of the building and puts into true perspective the copybook restorers of the 19th Century. Here there is the feeling of originality, the prayer expressed in stone. The wall paintings between the clerestory windows may date from about 1250, but everywhere there is good detail and again we see the tower on arches, detached by some 20 yards from the church.

One of the most beautiful parish churches

20 WALPOLE ST. PETER is often labelled Queen of the Marshes. One of the most beautiful parish churches in England, it is quite remarkable in its splendour. While at first sight Lavenham seems a paean of praise, the effect here is sharper, more of an offering of gratitude. The half-drained land, dominated by enormous skies, may have inspired the master-mason in his attempt to communicate his thanks. A grand Jacobean font cover and Tudor eagle lectern stand out from the splendid minor detail — look for the sedan chair type shelter (which was used by the vicar during rainy funerals).

21 WALPOLE ST. ANDREW: Otherwise intelligent people spend much time and money here in attempts to find King John's baggage train which was overtaken by the tide nearby, perhaps . . . Has anyone put forward the uncharitable suggestion that he sold all the good stuff in Lynn and set up the bagwash story as a cover? The deed was not beyond him.

King John loses his baggage

"Cathedral of the Marshes"

22 TERRINGTON ST. CLEMENT: The sort of village that a Suffolk man would label "a good place to come FROM". Perhaps no more boring visually than many nearby but a good deal more obvious. The main road does not help and apart from the delicious Lovell's Hall, look only to the church, yet again. For this, too, has a tag tied to its spire, this time "The Cathedral of the Marshes". It is a title impossible to quarrel with anywhere else in England, St. Clement's might well serve a city. The west front and window are superb and the fact that the sundial is kept in the splendid porch should not lead to uncharitable thoughts about the local weather. The interior surpasses, if that is possible, the two previous churches. Find a guide and spend time here, some of the minor moments will last a lifetime.

Away north, towards the Wash, lies Orange Row, a straggle of housing in which the Prince of Orange took refuge from the French. All around lie protective sea-walls with the great detached tower of St. Clement as the final safety from an encroaching flood.

23 KING'S LYNN: A deliciou town by any standard, perhap the most pleasant urban spot on th journey and a fine centre for exploration – ancient port and market on the right ban of the Great Ouse, full of fine houses an superb architectural monuments to it lively trading past. This was, above all, th home of merchants, a rival of Boston, it sister town across the Wash. Betwee them they supplied, through their grea inland river communications, towns an villages of nine or ten counties. The trad was mostly with the European countrie bordering the North Sea but even toda Baltic ships are to be seen waiting for th tide to bring them alongside the medieva warehouses in the heart of the town. Th streets are crowded with rich medieva merchants' houses. The Guildhall of S George, which has been used since th 15th Century for many purposes, is onc more equipped as a theatre and rightly sc for there is a very good chance that this i the only public building extant in whic Shakespeare himself played — certainl his company is recorded as having bee here. The town was once centred on th two markets, the Saturday Market and th Tuesday Market, and it is in the streets c these locales that the buildings of greate: interest lie.

The men of Lynn were great fisherme in the Greenland Fisheries but no fish com to the Wash now. Shellfish are sti harvested, however, and men spend hou out on the banks, miles from land, rakin them from the mud and sand. The market centre around the two main churches c

Pew ends at Wiggenhall St. Germans

24 WIGGENHALL (St. Ge mans): This small Marsh villag has the feel of having been "lived-in" f longer than the Fen villages and this ma well be so. Certainly the domestic buildinç in the Marshland have older traces tha most Fen villages. Once this was a stop ping-off place for lightermen, but no there is a great sense of quiet. The church medieval and contains excellent origin bench ends, with copies in the aisle.

Customs House, King's Lynn

Tower Gardens at King's Lynn with church in background

Lynn: St. Nicholas in the Tuesday area a Chapel of Ease to the parish church of St. Margaret, which is in the Saturday Market. Out on The Walk is the curious octagonal 15th Century Red Mount Chapel, built as a wayside chapel for Walsingham pilgrims. St. Margaret's contains a fine rococo 18th Century organ case, a splendid lectern and two of the biggest brasses in England — and perhaps the best known.

The beautiful Flemish work of these plates to Adam de Walsokne and Robert Braunche and their wives are not to be missed. Braunche's brass records the famous feast which he laid on for Edward III's visit to Lynn in 1349 when peacocks figured largely on the menu. The Town Hall is a great civic centre and has on display the Lynn Regalia, a sword given to the town by King John and a remarkably beautiful

gold and enamelled cup bearing his name, but dating from about 1340. Oliver Cromwell had Lynn under siege during the Parliament troubles and 80 or so people were killed during the bombardment. The odd thing is that such a merchant sort of town should side with the King, but it did, and was one of the few places in East Anglia to do so. Today their are some proper pubs and places to eat well.

Unique pelican font cover

25 WIGGENHALL (St. Mary The Virgin:) On the way from St. Germans stands a great pumping station which raises water from the Middle Level Main Drain to the level of the Great Ouse. The village clusters around the church which has echoes of St. Germans, a grand lectern of 1518 and a pretty Jacobean pelican font cover. The carved benches in these churches are considered the finest in the country. St. Mary's Hall is a 19th Century rebuilding of the original house.

15th Century stained glass window in North aisle

26 WIGGENHALL (St. Mary Magdalen): Yet another church of splendour in its proportions, although perhaps not so well endowed as its sisters.

The glass in the North aisle is 15th Century and there are some good Jacobean panels. Priory Cottages near the church are a pretty 17th Century group.

27 STOW BARDOLPH: The park looks splendid in autumn when the beeches provide welcome colour. The cottages are unremarkable, except in one case, but the Hall is mock Tudor on the site of the original house. The same architect restored the church in the mid-19th Century. The older North chapel contains the family monuments and here, in their modest setting, they again illustrate our ancestors' attitudes. Sir Thomas is frozen marble, bewigged and in Roman armour. Sarah Hare, who died in 1744, ordered that a waxwork figure of herself, dressed in her own clothes, should be exhibited in a large cupboard in the chapel.

Sir Thomas Hare in marble and daughter Sarah in wax

28 DOWNHAM MARKET: A charming small town on relatively high ground overlooking the Great Ouse, it once boasted a large river trade before the coming of the railway and the re-organisation of the drainage system via the new channel to Lynn. The use of Carr stone is mellowing and in certain lights blends with the freely used yellow and red brick to give an "old print" tone to the town. The Nonconformists built in strength here but apparently never with joy. The parish church stands high and fails to excite after the surfeit of the Marshes. Perhaps the Victorian hand lies a little too heavy here again.

15th Century oak chest in parish church

Unique 17th Century glass chandelier in Downham Market church

29 WELNEY: Until 50 years ag the fenland flooded even in goo winters and the famous skating fairs too place here, at Cowbit near Crowland an on Whittlesey Mere. Speed races we skated against Dutchmen, both here an in Holland, and great men were alive. Th Smarts, "Fish", and the legendary "Turkey "Gutta-Percha" See and others equal famous, were natives of Welney. The spo is more organised now and perhaps le popular. The great fen drainage system well shown here as we cross the O Bedford River, the River Delph and th New Bedford River within the space of few hundred yards. Think again of thos Dutch navvies and poor Cornelius Ve muyden, whose brainchild much of th system was. He died in debt after leadin his "Adventure" in the face of oppositio from the fenmen.

Farm cart typical of the area

Parish church of the "Martyrs"

30 LITTLEPORT: The Littlepc Martyrs are remembered loca in a story of one of the most futile gestur made by poor men and one of the mc savage replies any demonstration of bitte ness ever received. In 1816 land enclosu had brought hard times to the district a out-of-work labourers marched on E After a good deal of rampaging about t streets and minor damage to proper everyone went home. Some time la eighty men were arrested and tried by t Temporal court of the Bishopric of Ely. Fi were hanged, five transported and the re imprisoned. The surrounding fenland nc grows neat market-garden crops a flourishes mightily on farm subsidies.

31 ELY: A small town, a market and port of sorts. Splendid in its isolation and seen well from its approaches, it keeps the Georgian character of its domestic architecture well and glories in its cathedral. The river was for long its surest connection with the world and in some measure still performs that function. The road south-east to Soham was the first causeway built to the Island of Eels from outside Fenland and it is from this road that the most "fairytale" view of the great church is seen . . . Hereward the Wake took refuge here during his campaign against the current invader.

The earliest remains date from the end of the 11th Century, but the building is mainly a superb example of English architecture of the 14th Century. There is much beautiful exterior detail, including the great Octagon which is such a splendid feature of the cathedral. Sir Gilbert Scott is represented here by some very restrained and attractive work, including the timber lantern. The interior has had many hands developing and improving on the original Norman glory and some details are fascinating, much dating from the middle 19th Century but carefully done in most instances. The misericords demonstrate the difference in approach between the old masters and Scott and his contemporaries. Comper's chantry chapel reredos is nowhere near as good as the one he did for Wymondham.

Practically all the glass is Victorian and livid with doom. Monuments are many and good. Outside again the much-altered, much ruined buildings in the precincts are happily grouped and of interest. King's School and St. Michael's should be noted.

Cathedral, in which Hereward the Wake took refuge

Cathedral choir with 14th Century stalls (left) a gargoyle (centre) and a detail of the South transept stained glass window

32 **SOHAM:** The Danes destroyed the cathedral here in the 7th Century and today there is little of grandeur about this pleasant yellow-brick village. The church's only real contribution is in the view of the typical flushwork tower. The interior has a dead feel. The interior of The Fountain has a much livelier and more refreshing aspect. This was once a great area for mills and several remain in varying stages of disrepair. The marshland is fully reclaimed and prospers splendidly on rootcrops. There have also been discoveries of Anglo-Saxon burials on a nearby site. Not far away is Wicken Fen, a rare stretch of waste fenland that is preserved for its wild life values by the National Trust. This is how Fenland was before the drainage schemes succeeded.

The bittern is returning to the Fens

The church at Mildenhall

Two of the elegant brasses to the Peyton family at Isleham: Richard Peyton and his wife, 17th Century

33 **ISLEHAM:** St. Andrew's is a splendid 14th Century flint and rubble cruciform church with a boring later (much later) addition in the west tower, quite out of keeping with the riches within. The detail of this interior is superb in many points and the monuments and early memorial brasses, particularly of the Bernard and Peyton families, are elegant and touching. There was a Benedictine Priory here in the 11th Century and a perfect example of an early Norman chapel still survives.

Crest on the tomb of John Peyton

Brass of Thomas Peyton's first wife

34 MILDENHALL: Where the Fens meet Breckland, and once an important river port, now even more important in an unconsidered way, as a military airport dormitory, part of our defensive network. Does this sound unexciting? It should not, for the past is splendid and the present comfortable enough, thank you. The countryside that has known and absorbed the invasion of Dane, Saxon, Roman and Dutch settlers has coped without bloodshed with the Americans who fly from the nearby bases. Indeed, the social prosperity of the area has been much aided by the excellent community schemes run by the USAF in partnership with the Ministry of Defence and an opportunity to visit one of the bases during the frequent "open days" should not be missed.

From the approach roads the gigantic aircraft and hangars are a superb testament to engineering capabilities, the sight of such huge craft getting airborne instils the sort of thrill that Dounreay or Fylingdales (from a distance) engender and something of the first sight of Ely Cathedral.

The church has a glorious roof, as good as nearby Lakenheath, filled with beautifully carved angels, birds and beasts. The 16th Century Cross is the centre of a good area and The Bell welcomes as a free house should. The Mildenhall Treasure, ploughed up from the fen, is a collection of Roman silver, perfectly preserved, including the great dish showing Bacchus and Hercules, and now displayed at the British Museum.

35 BRANDON: Flint flushwork everywhere, which makes the flush of modern infill look like bad dentistry. Flint formed the basis of Brandon's former importance and the place still has oddly leisurely moments to it; a street lined with pollarded trees, a charming limewalk to the playing field — a good approach to the church, which although of no great interest, has a churchyard which at first sight seems to have been divided between the living and the dead — one half headstones, the other allotments! At Grimes Graves, a few miles away, there are the mines which supplied the flints we see in every building. Thirty-odd acres of clearings in the forest mark the spot where Stone Age men first started the mines. Other workings in the area have provided flints for the last century or so for local flintknappers who carried on their trade there until recently. The Department for the Environment now have the site of Grimes Graves in hand and it may be visited — and a very strange experience it is, too.

The mines at Grimes Graves

36 ELVEDEN: A long, undulating straight through Thetford Chase, the verges softened by deciduous planting, brings us to one of the great follies of East Anglia — but a folly which has been made to work. In the 1860's the Maharajah Duleep Singh, exiled from Lahore, built this huge Indian palace, with a copper dome, acres of carved Carrara marble, a beautiful park and later the first Lord Iveagh added the oddly Baroque front. And the church received his blessing, too. Caroe was employed to update what was basically Norman and 14th Century and what a riot of "Art-Nouveau Gothick" now is here. The detail is superb and it is impossible not to like the sheer confection of it. The estate is now one of the largest and most intensely farmed in the country and with the prior permission of the agent, may be visited though the interior of the house is not open to the public.

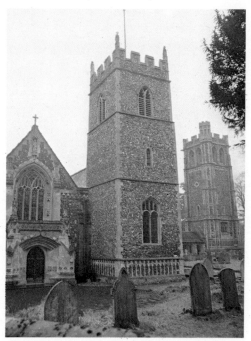
Mock Gothic tower of Elveden church

37 THETFORD: A rapidly expanding town with a varied past and a definite future. Having elected to absorb some of the excess population of London, the local authority (together with the Greater London Council) has started the development most promisingly.

Once an important ecclesiastical centre with many monastic remains, the town's social history has fluctuated, dying a savage death at the Dissolution, reviving slightly as a spa, later boosted when light engineering works provided economic impetus — but before World War II the town was stumbling along again. The present revival brings new and promising life to a most pleasant town, set in a curious part of the country. The Forestry Commission has had the grace and foresight to border its murky forests with ash and beech, birch and oak, inducing the return of some of the bird and animal life that had fled the early years of afforestation. The army, too, have lingered on in these parts and much of the mereland of the Breck is out of bounds to civilians during most of the year. Agriculture has spread as soil technology has improved and even previously barren ground is now bearing. A potentially productive town.

Statue of Tom Paine born at Thetford

The carved oak town sign

38 **WYMONDHAM:** Small, intimate and sedate, the town leans heavily on the past. The Abbey, long a bone of contention between the town and the clergy, is now the pride among a series of small town houses of unpretentious good quality. In the countryside nearby are a half-dozen large houses of some interest. The county library is housed in the former Chapel of St. Thomas a Becket near a grand half-timbered house, the Green Dragon Inn. The splendour of the Abbey will concern us most, Sir Ninian Comper's 20th Century mock-Gothic reredos matching anything done in England since 1550, the work of a grand artist. Packed with gorgeous detail, the roof, Norman arcades and 15th Century clerestory are delights. Perhaps the favourite is the beautiful work of the two towers, (the octagonal tower and the west tower) from one of which William Kett was hanged alive, in chains, after the failure of the great rebellion in 1549.

Abbey church at Wymondham

Arcaded 17th Century market cross

A GIANT OF THE FENS

The magnificent swallowtail butterfly, by far the largest species in Britain and unique to the Fens, feeds on the marsh or milk parsley growing among the reeds on the shoreline of the Norfolk Broads. This colourful butterfly adds an impression of tropical luxuriance to a typically English landscape where reeds are still cut for thatching — unfortunately to a lesser extent nowadays than was once the case in an area whose character depends on the old crafts and land usages.

The Norfolk Broads, huge shallow lakes of about 2,600 acres and surrounded by a unique flora have always been mysterious. Recent investigations have shown that they are man-made, the result of peat diggings until about the time of the Black Death in 1349. The inferior peat continued to be cut until the advent of coal and records show that the cathedral priory of Norwich used 400,000 turves a year, consumption which accounts for the size of the Broads. The lakes are surrounded by reed swamps and "alder carr", that is, slightly drier land dominated by the moisture loving alder tree.

In the height of summer the larger sheets of water may well be covered by holiday-makers, but the district is intersected with dykes where the punt can drift through a wilderness of reeds that may seem as remote as the swamps of the Amazon. Heath and marsh orchids are fairly abundant and rare bog orchids may be found. The marsh gentian is also worth a search as well as adder's tongue and moonwort.

39 **NORWICH:** Torn between the greatness of its past, when it was England's third largest city, and the late development of its present, the capital of East Anglia offers a great de to the visitor. Tucked away from the mainstream of the 19th Century, a uncomfortable distance from London and defended from the Midlands by the difficult fenland crossing, the city misse the worst excesses of the Industrial Revolution and is only now growing towards its full potential. A certain amount of painful progress is inevitable and evident. New office building is uniform horrendous. Due to the quiet 19th Century existence which it enjoyed, the city still has the most extraordinarily comple collection of medieval building, bo secular and ecclesiastic. Norwich is no putting to other good uses many interesting church buildings which have remained unused for years: one has become museum, one a community centre, othe are used for similar purposes.

Against this must be recorded the incongruous planning decisions which have led to such eyesores as the National C Parks development near the city wal remains, the insensitivity of the near shopping precinct and the glaring nee shopfront advertisements. The soul, however, finds much that is refreshing: t castle, incongruously clad in Bath sto in the 1830s, is a Norman keep in remarkable state of preservation, whi houses the finest provincial museum in t country. Indeed, it is a long time since t castle was used in any military sen having served as the county gaol for 6 years or so until 1887 when the prese splendid collection was formed.

Religious societies have all built he chapels and churches of 18th and 19 Centuries adding to the richness of t medieval architecture. The Cathedral the glory, set in precincts of outstandi merit. The tremendous length of the na is almost overpowering in its tower

A close in the cathedral

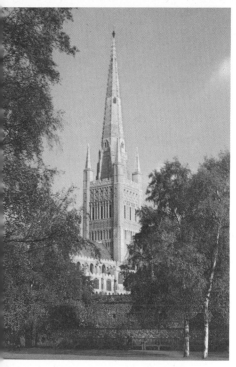

The glory of Norwich — the Cathedral

...lendour and is a splendid example of ...th Norman and Perpendicular English ...chitectural form at its most superb. A ...tal study would fill a large volume but ...ention must be made of the wall paintings ...d, in the chancel, the Bishop's Throne, ...rts of which are thought to be 8th ...ntury, the stall misericords and almost ...ery building outside the main body of ...e Cathedral — a crowd of handsome ...uses and apartments, the cloisters, the ...shop's Palace and Norwich School. ...end time, go slowly and enter and ...ve by the two great gates in the Close. ...e Maddermarket Theatre houses the ...st talent in the amateur theatre, Anglia ... now operate from the Agricultural Hall ...d the great Norwich School of Painting ... well represented in the gallery at the ...stle — Cotman, Crome and others, their ...ndscapes properly dominated by the ...eat natural beauty of this countryside — ...y, sky, sky.

Detail of 14th Century Cathedral panel depicting the Ascension

...omland, from the Saxon for market place

Tudor houses in Elm Street, most picturesque street in Norwich

The glories of Hereward's island

For centuries Ely Cathedral, as G. M. Trevelyan put it, "floated like an ark upon the waters". Until the Fens were drained in the 17th and 18th Centuries, the Isle of Ely was only accessible by boat or by causeways. The Cathedral is totally different from any other great English church. Towering above the level of the surrounding Fenland, the building dominates the countryside for miles around. Instead of the customary two front towers and the square crossing tower, Ely has only one tower and, instead of a crossing tower, there is a unique construction known as the Octagon. The Cathedral has an unforgettable early Norman nave — severe, even grim and gaunt in the discipline of its mood. We show it being built. The Cathedral was founded by St.

Etheldreda in A.D. 673. In the last years of the Saxon power in England, Ely was as great and significant as Canterbury and Glastonbury. After the Norman Conquest of 1066 Simeon, a kinsman of William the Conqueror, was made Abbot and he started rebuilding the Cathedral in 1083.

The Octagon tower was the brain child of one Alan of Walsingham. Our sketch

at the bottom of the page gives some id of the complexity of the structure. T eight massive uprights of oak rise to height of 63 feet, forming the lante Below these are the great timbers whi reach out to rest upon the surroundi stone pillars and support a massive burd of 400 tons of wood and lead.

Perhaps the most splendid chapter the history of Ely was the spirited defen of the island by Hereward the Wake w gathered the Saxon thanes together af Harold's defeat at Hastings and for seve years held out at Ely against the Norm onslaught. Our drawing places Ely in island surroundings of its early days a shows the barges used to carry the hea stones and timbers for the constructi of the cathedral.

Not far from Ely and three quarters of a mile from the ruins of a Benedictine Abbey at Crowland, raised to his memory, St. Guthlac landed his boat at a place still called Anchor Church Fields. Guthlac apparently spent a wild youth until he decided to become a hermit. He built a hut—the abbey was supposedly built on its site — and people came from miles around for his help and advice. Guthlac died in 714. The abbey, built by his relative King Ethelbald of Mercia, was once the wealthiest in the country and its ruins are still magnificent. During the lifetime of St. Guthlac, according to Matthew Paris, writing in the 13th Century, the Crowland area was "a place of horror and solitude". In those days, like much of the Fens, the area was barely accessible "either for man or for beast".

From time immemorial the Fens have been famous for their abundance of fish — especially eels. William of Malmesbury wrote in 1125: "Here is such a quantity of fish as to cause astonishment in strangers while the natives laugh at their surprise".

Eels, indeed, actually became currency in early times. Debts were often settled by payments in eels, and rents and tithes were also fixed in the same way.

Some of the implements used in eel catching are shown on the Right. The broad bladed "spear" is called a glaive, a Saxon word which indicates the weapon's ancient origin. We also show two types of eel trap and a bownet.

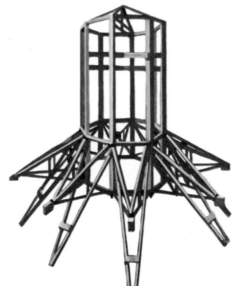

Similarly, the sale of reeds, rushes and p formed a staple part of the economy of the Fe Even in medieval times the principles of nat conservancy seem to have been appreciated in most manorial areas the rules were t rushes and reeds were only to be cut at speci times. Bird life among the Fens was alw remarkable both for variety and quantity.

Thomas of Ely, writing in the 12th C declared: "There are numberous geese, co dabchicks, water crows, herons and ducks'

ABOVE: The Prior's Door at Ely. This door opened onto the cloisters and the Prior's lodgings were at the far side of the cloisters. The door is late Norman and the typmpanum and pilasters are richly carved. The quality of these 12th Century carvings — and they are in a splendid state of preservation — makes this doorway among the most important specimens of Norman architectural design. Foliage scrolls, animals and human figures form part of the decoration. This richness of carving is an important indication of date. Early Norman work was much simpler in treatment. Early engravings show that the columns originally stood on human figures mounted on the backs of lions. These have been worn away over the centuries.

There is a nice touch of humour in some of the carvings — little figures of men in a boat, acrobats and similar scenes from everyday life.

Above we show some of the special tools used for cutting peat and reeds — the sickle-shaped sedge-knife, the curious implement known as a turf "becket" and the special sharply pointed spade, also for cutting turf.

In the later Middle Ages the keeping of swans became a typical Fenland occupation.

The Midland Shires – heartland of England

EDWIN PACKER

From Cromwell's tiny, flat-as-a-pancake county of Huntingdon to the dramatic Shropshire borderlands, the English middle shires flaunt a bewildering pattern of sharply-contrasted landscapes, each teeming with its own vivid contributions to the island character and story.

So varied are they, that it is often difficult to recognise them as parts of a single country, let alone a single region. The fens of Huntingdonshire, with their vast skies and horizons and rises of ground never exceeding 300 ft, relate more to a Cuyp painting of Flanders than, perhaps, to the great moorlands, deep green valleys incised with sparkling waters and the rough stone crags that compose the dales of Derbyshire. The good ploughlands and broad acres of Leicestershire and Rutlandshire, home of the Quorn and Belvoir hunts, with their wooded fox-coverts and thickly brambled hedgerows that severely challenge the courage of both horse and rider, scarcely seem to share a common heritage with the fantastic rock formations of Charnwood Forest — rock, say the geologists, 570 million years old and among the most ancient in Europe.

IN GOOD COMPANY

Much of this, no doubt, is what J. B. Priestley had in mind when he talked about "the magic element" of rural Britain. The magic comes with a glimpse through the trees of some half-forgotten mansion, the sun sparkling on a lake hidden deep in the shires, the grandeur of hills that sweep suddenly into view. And then the staggering variety of experience and visual delight.

It is a journey made in company with the Romans — their ancient Ermine and Watling Streets, now labelled A1 and A5, bisect these counties — with the Normans and with some of the great names of English history. Cromwell, of course — not only because he was born in the second smallest of shires, where we begin our journey, but because we visit Naseby, site of the decisive battle of the Civil War. There are, too, the shades of Henry VIII's poor, forsaken Spanish Queen, Catherine of Aragon; and of Clive of India; above all, perhaps, that embodiment of the English romantic imagination — dauntless Robin Hood flitting through the oaks and birches of Sherwood Forest. But we find ourselves, too, in the company of Byron and D. H. Lawrence and Arnold Bennett and Housman; of men who helped turn England into an industrial giant — Richard Arkwright, Abraham Darby, Josiah Wedgwood.

It is a bitter-sweet journey, of course, for the middle shires, more than any other, have known the scars of trade, commerce and industry and, more lately, the insatiable thirst of our masters to provide more and more concrete paths for articulated juggernauts. In Leicestershire, too, the red-brick villages remind one that much of the Victorian dynamic was concerned with getting things done rather than with the profitless pursuit of beauty.

What would Cobbett have made of the changes wrought by social revolution? He thought the River Ouse scenery "by far the most beautiful I ever saw in my life". The traveller can now judge for himself whether time's hand has wrought kindly.

The route starts at St. Neots but Cromwell's county, unlike the man, betrays no touch of the theatrical. The landscape grows more dramatic in neighbouring Northamptonshire—that shire of "squires and spires". They have built graceful broach spires in this county — spires forming a single unit with their towers, devoid of any dividing parapet. They used local stone, too — and a good stone at that. A belt of limestone stretches from Dorset to the Wash. In

places, it becomes mingled with iron to produce a rich, dark colou In sunshine, the hue lightens, the pure limestone making fi contrast to the ironstone.

There is much of this in and around Northampton. The Saxo church at Earls Barton is built of it, as are many of the houses the town. One sees it again at Higham Ferrers, where both chur and houses are made of it. It marks the route all the way up in Leicestershire.

Northants, Leicestershire, and Rutland despite the industri scarrings, still remain predominantly agricultural counties counties of "good manors, of solid barns, of great houses in the parks, and ruins far across the field". Northamptonshire, particular, is full of manorial estates. Sheep graze everywhere the uplands. Foxes break covert, pursued by baying hounds. The is still a great smack of rural England, as tradition would like about it all.

These shires, of course, form part of that "cockpit of Englan that extends down to the Vale of Gloucester. Here Roses batt were fought; here the merciless Cromwell slaughtered the Royal women camp followers after he had won Naseby. Not that t Cavaliers had much to boast of, either. Leicester still remember its fate. Prince Rupert of Bavaria, following Continental custo demanded £2,000 from the besieged town as the price of immuni from looting, rape or slaughter after it had fallen. The burghe raised £500 and sent it direct to Charles. The astonished Kin unaccustomed to such a practice, admonished Rupert — but ke the money. And when Leicester fell, it was spared nothing.

Around Northampton, the limestone throws up several hi plateaux. Naseby itself stands on the ridge of such a plateau, wi the source of the Avon on one side and that of the river Wella on the other. It is cold and windy on these, as the village nam show — Cold Ashby, Cold Overton, Cold Newton. It is said loca that people in these parts talk more loudly than anywhere el because they have to overcome the wind. An American once cal Northants and Leicester, "the Garden of Eden". He was a fo hunting man, of course, which probably biased his view. Althou one has to pan harder for gold these days — in terms of unsulli scenery — he might well have been taking into account t gastronomic fame of these counties. This is the home of t noble Stilton (which isn't actually *produced* at Stilton), of the dele able red Leicestershire cheeses and of Melton Mowbray pork pie

PRESS ON TO THE WOLDS

Yet as one presses northwards into the heart of the Leicestersh wolds and England's smallest county, Rutland, — which did n become a county until the reign of King John — the land becon a region of undulating hills where sheep graze and where en mous vistas are opened up of a timeless looking countryside full drystone walls and low hedges.

The route passes through such picture-postcard villages Rockingham or sleepy Uppingham with its great public scho There are magnificent reconstructions of medieval castles, such that at Belvoir Castle in the lovely Vale of Belvoir, to be visite noble parks which have been turned into showplaces, such as t at Stapleford Park; or lost little villages with a charming windm such as Waltham-on-the-Wolds.

The River Trent itself winds 170 miles from one side of Engla to the other, conveniently dividing north from south. It

114

e 17th Century mill at Duddington, Northants

rthplace of the poet John Clare (1793-1864) at Helpston

owered invasion, settlement and industry. The Danes sailed up it conquer, squat and intermarry; earlier the Romans had dotted southern banks with their fortress-camps. Today, the glass wers of the industrial barons hover arrogantly over its waters. A ndred years ago, 3,000 salmon were caught annually in the Trent; day there are none. But its tributaries, the Dove, Manifold, erwent and Noe, have trout.

Of Robin's Sherwood, whose spreading birch and oak once vered a fifth of the county, only a parsimonious remnant now mains. There are two reasonable stretches of woodland at Birk-nds and Bilhaagh but the main concentrations today are in the ukeries.

Nor has much survived of that castle in which his old enemy,

the Sheriff, lodged. The Cromwellians destroyed it in 1651 as a reprisal against a county which had mainly supported the King. The first Duke of Newcastle built a town mansion on the spot, but this was burned down during the Reform Bill riots in 1831. Today, the renovated ruins house the municipal art gallery and museum. The site on which it stands is now called Standard Hill, for it was on this spot that Charles raised his Royal Standard to launch the Civil War. A few days later, the wind blew it down.

Eastwards lies Southwell and its glorious Minster. Thence to Newstead Abbey, home of Byron (which he describes in the 13th canto of *Don Juan*), and across the hard D. H. Lawrence country to the southern tip of the glorious Peak District.

Much of the Peak District, of course, is also rugged moorland country where the hill farms have their milk churns returned filled with water because pure supplies have run off the bare hills; of stone walls; of land that has never known the plough. Yet the high ridges are broken constantly by some of the loveliest river valleys in England and the country, particularly around the Matlocks, has its own wealth of ancient castles and solid manor houses.

For a brief passage, after this there is nothing for it but to take the plunge and negotiate the outliers of the Potteries, consoled, perhaps, with the recollection that these parts provided Arnold Bennett with the inspiration for many of his earliest and finest novels, most of them still extremely readable. The objective is a worthy one, Shropshire. A natural glory of England, this, made famous by A. E. Housman, yet neglected by tourists.

It is a fat agricultural land of stock-rearing and dairy-farming, scattered with apple and plum orchards. Its south-east edge is dominated by the dramatic limestone ridge called Wenlock Edge. North of the Severn lies a broad arable plain, dotted with charming black-and-white villages whose somnolence reflects the quiet prosperity of centuries. There are lanes so narrow hereabouts that they just about take a car.

Flat though the overall landscape might be, the plain is broken continually by eminences that seem as grand as mountains. Of these, the most spectacular is the Wrekin, a strange volcanic out-crop of rock which rises in a spectacular and isolated mass to 1,335ft. On a clear day, it is claimed, one can see across 17 counties from its summit.

It is border country, a land which can easily fool the traveller who may never be sure whether he is still in England or whether he has not strayed into Wales. It is hard, too, as one passes the fat manor houses and old farmhouses near Bridgnorth, to think of these peaceful acres as steeped in bloody history. But centuries ago, Saxons sailed up the Severn, sacking and plundering what remained of Roman culture; later, when these same Saxons had sought to erect their own structures, the Welsh went a-plundering them, burning Shrewsbury town.

In the 18th Century, the river became a great trade route, carry-ing raw materials from the south-west. Bridgnorth, where our journey ends, grew to importance as a river port. Today, with its High Town and Low Town, it seems more like an Italian hill-town than an ancient English market and river port. Even its parish church, built by Telford, was designed in the Italianate manner. Nor, even there, does that end the matter, for the tower of its Norman keep leans at 17 degrees from the perpendicular — three times the inclination of the Leaning Tower of Pisa.

22 MATLOCK

PEAK DISTRICT

DOVEDALE

25 MANIFOLD VALLEY

23 TISSINGT

24 THORPE

26 ALTON TOWERS

29 MARKET DRAYTON

27 BARLASTON

28 TRENTHAM

CANNOCK CHASE

30 HODNET HALL

31 THE WREKIN

32 BUILDWAS ABBEY

33 COALBROOKDALE

34 MUCH WENLOCK

WAYFARER'S GUIDE
6

37 ASTLEY ABBOTS

36 SHIPTON

35 WENLOCK EDGE

39 BRIDGNORTH

RIVER SEVERN

Photos: H. J. Alcock / W. E. Brown / B.T.A. / Camera Press / Col Lib Int / Conway / C. M. Dixon / H. F. Dodson / Bob Hardy / D. R. Hooper / A. F. Kersting /
Leicester Planning Dept / Nat Port Gallery / Newstead Abbey / R. A. Palgrave / Pictor / Picturepoint / Pix / Michael St Maur Sheil / Kenneth Scowan / Shropshire Planning Dept /
Spectrum / Tramway Mus Soc / Transglobe / Wedgwood Mus / Woodmansterne / G. N. Wright

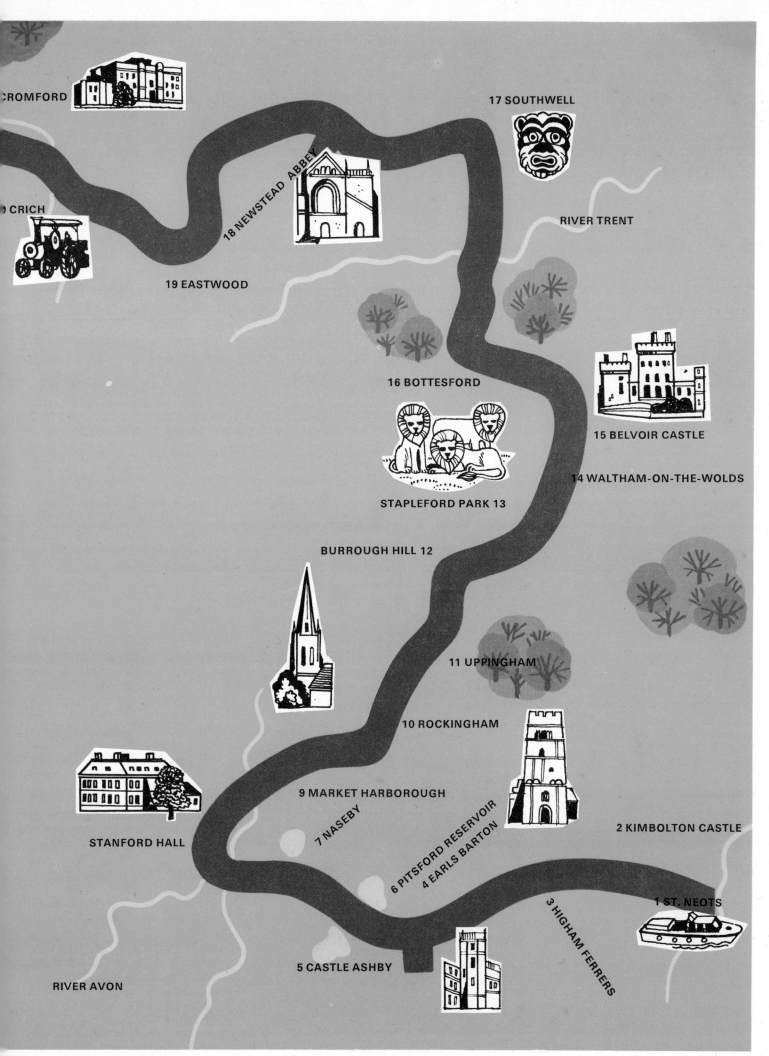

CROMFORD

17 SOUTHWELL

18 NEWSTEAD ABBEY

9 CRICH

RIVER TRENT

19 EASTWOOD

16 BOTTESFORD

15 BELVOIR CASTLE

14 WALTHAM-ON-THE-WOLDS

STAPLEFORD PARK 13

BURROUGH HILL 12

11 UPPINGHAM

10 ROCKINGHAM

9 MARKET HARBOROUGH

7 NASEBY

6 PITSFORD RESERVOIR

4 EARLS BARTON

2 KIMBOLTON CASTLE

STANFORD HALL

1 ST. NEOTS

3 HIGHAM FERRERS

5 CASTLE ASHBY

RIVER AVON

Illustrations: Elsie Wrigley / Richard Hook   Plant Notes: Geoffrey Gilbert   Animals & Birds: Jeremy Johns

117

1 **ST. NEOTS** is an ancient market town, in some danger of losing its distinctive character through modernisation. But there are glimpses of the past around the fine old church of St. Mary and the huge square, one of the largest in England, where some 17th and 18th Century houses still stand. The 15th Century Perpendicular tower of the church rises above the market square, and is a landmark. Particularly impressive in the rich interior are the roof beams, adorned with heraldic animals, harts, griffins, wyverns and non-heraldic hares, camels and rams.

The town has several good historic inn notably the Cross Keys, the Falcon and t Bridge Hotel. Old oak beams still supp the bar at the Bridge, relics of the coachi days. There used to be a heronry across t river and herons are still seen occasiona soaring over the Ouse.

A peaceful scene on the River Ouse in the ancient market town of St. Neots. Herons are still seen soaring over the river

Kimbolton Castle where the first wife of Henry VIII, Catherine of Aragon, died a prisoner

2 **KIMBOLTON CASTLE**: "God praised!" cried Henry VIII in Janua 1536 when told that Catherine of Arago his first wife, had died in this castle. savage revenge for her refusal to admit th he had divorced her — or even had t right to — Henry kept her a prisoner he for the last two years of her life, allowh her to see neither friends nor her sm daughter, Mary. In a final act of petty insu he withdrew her servants. The castle, bu in 1525, stands at the end of the Hi Street, which is lined with 17th and 18 Century houses.

It has been considerably redesigned a added to since Tudor times. In the ea part of the 18th Century, Sir John Vanbru partly rebuilt and partly refaced the exter and in 1763 Robert Adam added t beautiful iron gates on the road from Neots and the gatehouse. There are ma fine paintings, chiefly by Giovanni Pellegr who came from Venice several tim between 1708 and 1719. Queen Catherin dower chest is on loan from the Duke Manchester, whose family formerly own the castle.

At the other end of the High Stre stands the 13th Century St. Andre Church. Among the impressive tombs a monuments is one to the 1st Earl Manchester who bought the castle (now school) and who as Henry Montagu, Lo Chief Justice, was responsible for senter ing Sir Walter Raleigh to execution.

Lady Chapel in Higham Ferrers church

3 **HIGHAM FERRERS,** which is mentioned in Domesday, is a splendid example of what a town looks like when good local stone is used. Ignore the modern outskirts, for the heart of the town is delightful. The houses along the lengthy High Street are often raised above street level and look extremely picturesque. The Market Square has several fine buildings — principally an Elizabethan manor house, the 17th Century Ivy House, the Regency Town Hall and the Green Dragon. An old thatched cottage on one corner now serves as a barber's shop. In the centre of the square is a fascinating 13th Century cross, carved with oak leaves and flowers. On one side is a Crucifixion and on the other a Madonna. St. Mary's Church has a marvellous 170ft. spire and a richly crocketed steeple with a pierced parapet. The tower is 13th Century with a finely carved doorway. The interior of the church is also very fine, with no fewer than seven screens. The stalls are magnificently carved with animals, birds, kings and grotesqueries.

4 **EARLS BARTON** celebrated in 1970 the 1,000th birthday of its church tower, one of the finest examples of Anglo-Saxon craftsmanship in Britain. Today the tower stands as a reminder of those turbulent days that preceded the Conquest, for, solid and square, it was clearly meant as a defensive strongpoint. Doorways high up in the south and east faces gave entrance to the tower, probably by way of a ladder which could be pulled up in time of danger. Probably, too, it was used as a strongroom for church treasures.

Little evidence of Earls Barton's long history now remains, apart from the church and the mound directly behind it which was once a fortified earthwork. The Romanised Britons often lit beacons on the mound when Scots and Picts came raiding down the Nene and later when the Angles and Saxons savaged the area before settling and intermarrying. They in turn were forced to fight when Vikings pillaged their wattle huts and burnt their wooden tower. Earls Barton, indeed, has gone up in flames several times, the last in 1793.

Doorway at Earls Barton's Saxon church

The solid, square tower stands as a reminder of turbulent pre-Conquest days

Ornamental well at Castle Ashby

5 **CASTLE ASHBY,** just over three miles south of our route, is one of the great showplaces of the Midlands, with a setting superbly in keeping with its magnificence. The Marchioness of Northampton, who lives there, has said: "We all walk miles in a house like this, not only along passages but up and down three storeys. There's one advantage — it keeps you fit".

Visitors will appreciate the point. On the ground floor there are 30 rooms which are shuttered, barred and locked after visitors have left, so that the treasures of this Elizabethan and Jacobean mansion are kept safe. These include beautifully moulded ceilings, panelling and staircases dating from late Elizabethan and early Jacobean times and some fine furniture from the second half of the 17th Century.

The best approach to the castle is from Grendon when it is seen nestling in a great sweep of land. The grounds were laid out by "Capability" Brown. In the foreground is a lake, with pike, perch, bream, tench and roach. The wide south avenue from the house is most impressive, extending 3 miles over rolling countryside to great ornamental iron gates. Near the house are Italian-style gardens and the parish church of St. Mary Magdalene. The church has many interesting monuments, particularly a brass of William de Eyremyn, an early rector, made in 1401, a year after his death.

A magnificent castle in a superb setting

One of 30 rooms on view

7 **NASEBY:** Hereabouts the land begins to roll in graceful low hills and the hills form ridges which break to reveal patient grazing cattle. Straddling one of these long ridges is the battlefield of Naseby, a conflict which marked the end of the first phase of the Civil War. The ridge on which King Charles I's army was drawn up is the highest in the county and forms a watershed for two rivers (the Avon, which flows through Leicestershire to the Severn, and the Welland, which goes south to join the Nene). The Cromwellians outnumbered the Royalists by two to one when the two sides met in June, 1645. Although the man who subsequently made himself dictator had moulded a fine army, the battle itself was largely a matter of unco-ordinated fighting. There were a great many small, localised struggles which had no real bearing on the result. As it was, the King lost most of his army, although he succeeded in escaping. Two memorials mark the event. An obelisk, dated 1823, is off the site. The battlefield has been enclosed, but a dip in the ground can be seen where most of the fighting took place. Another monument, just inside a field, is believed to mark the spot where Cromwell's troopers made the decisive charge that carried the day.

Battlefield of Naseby

REYNARD REMAINS

The fox has been in Britain for about 1,500,000 years and while such a contemporary as the wolf is long since dead the fox population remains both stable and strong.

Foxes measure two feet from head to the base of the brush. Ears and legs tend towards black, the muzzle, belly and tail tip are white and the rest of the coat varies from dark russet to sandy-grey.

PITSFORD RESERVOIR is a large man-made lake for boating and angling. Nearby Brixworth, in the centre of the Pychley Hunt country, has the remarkable Saxon church of All Saints, portions of which date from the 7th Century, shortly after the district had been converted to Christianity. Tiles dating from the Roman period have been found built into the church arches. The stair turret outside the tower is 10th or early 11th Century, although the top of the tower, together with the spire, is medieval. There is an Anglo-Saxon carving of an eagle beside the south door. There are many other interesting artefacts in this large, impressive structure, which stands high on a hill, overlooking the village. In the south chapel there is a 13th Century tomb of Sir John de Verdun, with his effigy in chain mail and surcoat.

Stained glass in Brixworth church

Grand staircase, Stanford Hall

One family's home for 500 years

8 **STANFORD HALL** has been in the possession of the Cave family for more than 500 years. Now the home of Lord and Lady Braye, it was built in 1690 on the Leicester side of the Avon. Erected by Sir Roger Cave, it replaced an old manor house on the Northants side of the river which had been the family home since 1430. The old house was demolished but most of its contents were taken into the new Hall and can still be seen among the collection of antique furniture, fine pictures and rare manuscripts which are on show. A unique exhibition at the Hall is a collection of veteran motor cycles and cars, including the twin-cylinder Norton which won the first TT race in the Isle of Man in 1907. Percy Pilcher, an aviation pioneer, worked and tested flying machines at Stanford Hall with the late Adrian, Lord Braye. Pilcher was killed in a flying accident in 1899 at Stanford and there is a statue to him in the grounds. Photographs of the machines he helped to design and build are on show together with a replica of his 1898 "flying" machine.

There is a splendid church at the gates of the Hall, which has recently received a gift of £1,500 from the Pilgrim Trust to restore its fine stained glass, which has representations of the Cave family and also Henry VII and his Queen, Elizabeth of York.

Saints', Brixworth: part of the church dates from the 7th Century

9 **MARKET HARBOROUGH** was first created a market town in the reign of Henry II. It is still a small, attractive town with an especially pleasing square dominated by the splendid broached tower of St. Dionysius's. The town has some excellent Georgian architecture. The most picturesque building, however, is the former grammar school, built in 1614 by Robert Smythe, the founder. It is timbered and stands on wooden pillars which allow pedestrians to walk below.

An 18th Century wrought-iron inn sign, one of the most famous and beautiful in England, decorates the exterior of the town's largest inn, the Three Swans.

The school arches at Market Harborough

Turf maze at Wing. Place for penance?

11 **UPPINGHAM** owes its fame to th public school, founded in 158 The town is sleepy, old-fashioned, wi picturesque bow-fronted windows ar good ironstone buildings which give it pleasant 18th Century air.

A market has been held here since 128 Uppingham was thriving and prosperou but declined after the Elizabethan ag About three miles NE lies the village Wing, which has an ancient turf maz similar to many in France. It is believed have been designed for sinners to penance.

Picture-postcard view of Rockingham

10 **ROCKINGHAM** is a picture-postcard village on a steep hill, with thatched cottages and houses of flint-stone. The church and the former royal castle dominate the village and afford magnificent views over the Welland valley. The castle, built in the Conqueror's time, was in use as a fortress throughout the Middle Ages. Today the site of the keep is a rose garden, but part of the Norman foundation remains. The present building is mainly Elizabethan. Charles Dickens was a frequent visitor and not only dedicated *David Copperfield* to its owners, but based Chesney Wold, his castle in *Bleak House*, on it. The house has a fine collection of pictures and furniture.

Dickens relics at Rockingham Castle, with a portrait of his host, Richard Watson

Iron Age fort with a view at Burrough Hill

12 **BURROUGH HILL** is an Iron A fort covering some 12 acres a sitting dramatically on top of a steep sp There are marvellous views over Leicester and Rutland countrysides.

The tower of Stapleford church seen through the trees in the park

Stapleford's miniature railway

Lion reserve in the Park

3 STAPLEFORD PARK estate was offered for sale on February 24, 1885 as "a valuable freehold manorial domain with a spacious and interesting mansion and park....". This included a model village "occupied by retainers of the family" and "large takes of eels and pike and other fish" from artificial fishponds. Other delights were a small herd of deer, orangeries and peach houses, five lodge entrances and a heronry. It was bought by the Gretton family who have turned it into a showplace. Architecturally, the mansion is a mixture of styles dating from 1402 to Victorian, but all blending harmoniously. The rooms are handsomely furnished with Ipplewhite, Sheraton and Adam pieces and with Aubusson carpets. There are also tapestries and trophies of the chase. From each window there is a view of fine lawns and flowers and the sweeping parkland beyond. The Gothic church, "handled with remarkable restraint and without fancies", says Pevsner, contains monuments and memorials to the Sherards, the family who

owned the house and church for 500 years. The sixth and last Earl Sherard won the nickname "The Naughty Earl". In 1844 he took issue with the Midland Railway which wanted to take a new line through Stapleford Park. After 12 months of bitter argument, an Act of Parliament finally decreed that the proposed railway should take a sharp bend, thereby missing the estate. This became known as Lord Harborough's Curve.

Another time the Earl quarrelled with the Belvoir and Cottesmore hunts and stopped them from hunting over the estate by planting dog spears in the coverts. He also stopped people using his Cottage Plantation by letting loose bears he had obtained from a travelling circus. This was a strange foretaste of what was to come, for today wild life wanders at will in the Park — part of the 50 acres have been made into a lion reserve. There is also a zoo called Animal Land and for the children a miniature railway which links up with two model liners on the lake.

14 WALTHAM-ON-THE-WOLDS is a pretty village in the heart of the Wolds country and a good touring centre. Its main point of interest, probably, is its Black Smock Windmill — now without sails. It is so called because its shape resembles the smocks once worn by rural workers. Waltham is one of the oldest inhabited villages in Leicestershire — the remains of Roman pavements and Saxon coffin lids have been unearthed. Its houses are built in an attractive silver-grey limestone and the fine, early 14th Century Church of St. Mary Magdalene has many gay and grotesque carvings.

Artist's view of Waltham-on-the-Wolds

CATTLE IN CLOVER

The East Midlands have some of the finest pastures in Britain. White or Dutch Clover is a common feature of the fields. Red clover is seen less often, but both types provide food. The work of the grazier is extremely skilled. He has to know the different values and characteristics of grasses which to the outsider look exactly alike. The results of his work depend on timing the grazing correctly. Good pasturage should be served up fresh, ideally within 24 hours of attaining the correct height — short for sheep because they nibble the grass, long for cattle because they tear it with their tongues.

The magnificent vaulted ceiling and the castle ballroom

15 BELVOIR CASTLE dates from the Conqueror's time, but most of what remains today is 19th Century Romantic Gothic. The first Castle was built by Robert de Todeni, the Conqueror's standard bearer, who named it Belvedere (both spelling and pronunciation have been corrupted through the centuries — the accepted pronunciation today is "Beever"). It has been owned by the family of the present Duke of Rutland since the reign of Henry VIII. The medieval castle was destroyed and rebuilt several times but finally, in 1800, the 5th Duke commissioned James Wyatt to convert the existing mansion into a romantic, medieval-looking castle. Wyatt reconstructed many of the private apartments, added a new range to the south-west with a large round tower and rebuilt the existing south-east range. Much of his work was destroyed in a fire in 1816 and the Duchess, who fancied herself as an architect, took over, aided by Sir John Thornton, the Duke's cousin. The general effect was what a professional architect would describe as "unfortunate". Nonetheless, with the later help of Wyatt's two sons, some spectacular results were achieved, notably the Elizabethan salon, decorated in rococo style. The castle is also noted for its fine *objets d'art*, its Gobelin tapestries and pictures by Holbein, Reynolds and Gainsborough. The famous Belvoir fox-hound was named after the castle.

The castle is mostly 19th Century

16 BOTTESFORD has close lin with Belvoir Castle, eight Earls Rutland lying in great splendour in th village church. One of the most impressiv tombs is that of the first Earl which surrounded by the effigies of his mournin wife and nine daughters and six sons, on of whom, John, married the famo Dorothy Vernon of Haddon Hall. contrast, in the market place, stand th ancient stocks and whipping post, ne the stump of the old cross.

17 SOUTHWELL lies at the foot a rolling ridge of farmland, a sm town dwarfed by its Minster. The tw pepperpot towers were added in 1880 b they belie the true age of the churc Traces of Roman paving dating from A. 200 have been found. By 700, the Saxo had built a chapel here and the Norma added a nave and transept in the 12 Century. From then until 1841, t Minster was a collegiate church, a pla of worship for a college of 16 canons, a in 1884 it had its first Bishop when t diocese of Southwell was created. T chapter house has some remarkable a delightful 14th Century carvings. The ea lectern, now standing in the choir, has h a rough time. At the Dissolution of t Monasteries the monks threw the lecte into a lake at Newstead Abbey. It was recovered until 1750.

The Saracen's Head, opposite Minster, is 14th Century. Charles I sl here before giving himself up to

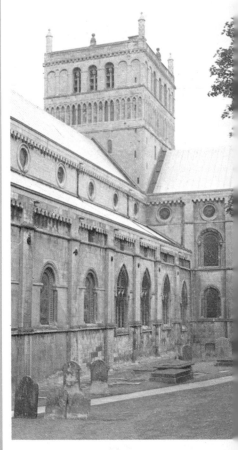

Southwell Minster: chapel since A.D. 700

quiet corner at Bottesford

ottish Commissioners in May 1646, who
turn handed him over to the Parlia-
entarians for £400,000. King and com-
issioner dined together at the inn before
e King made his formal surrender. The
aching era brought new life to the
aracen's Head. The "Champion", from
ncoln via Newark, stopped here to pick
passengers and change horses before
ing on to Mansfield, Chesterfield and
entually Manchester. At least four other
es of coaches called here, some daily,
me three times a week, during the 18th
entury.

On Burgage Green is Burgage Manor,
here Lord Byron once lived. His auto-
aph can still be seen on a wall in the hall.
one end of the town — and still on view
is Bramley Tree Cottage. About 1805, a
nous pip was planted in a pot in the
all garden here. In 1857 Mr. Bramley,
owner, began allowing graftings to be
en from the tree, on condition that his
me was attached to the apple.

Former home of the poet Lord Byron, who sold it to pay off family debts

4th Century choir screen

Memories of Byron abound

Portrait of the poet at Newstead Abbey

18 **NEWSTEAD ABBEY:** Nine
miles north of Nottingham, set in
the restful greenery, lies Newstead Abbey,
former home of the poet Lord Byron. The
Abbey, founded between 1163 and 1173
by Henry II as an Augustinian priory,
passed into the Byron family when Henry
VIII dissolved the monasteries. The museum
here contains many of the poet's personal
effects, including a lock of his hair, items
of clothing and his Adam and Hepplewhite
furniture. There are also engravings, portraits, relics of the Crimea, and letters. The
grounds are extensive and well-kept. In
what is known as the Eagle Pond, a
container was found in 1750 with valuable
documents thrown in by the Augustinian
monks in an attempt to foil Henry VIII's
minions. From this lake, too, was recovered
the lectern now in Southwell Minster.
Byron found the cost of the upkeep of the
Abbey, saddled as he was by the oppres-
sive debts of his predecessor, the fifth
baron, too much and he sold the Abbey
and its grounds. Next to a small Spanish
garden is Boatswain's monument, the
tomb the poet erected for his favourite
Newfoundland dog, inscribed with the
well-known lines:

*To mark a friend's remains, these
stones arise;
I never knew but one — and here
he lies.*

Portrait of D. H. Lawrence by Jan Juta. Lawrence made Eastwood the scene of "Sons and Lovers."

19 **EASTWOOD:** "This town raised only £5 for the Winston Churchill appeal — for a man who really did something for us. So how much do you expect people to give to a memorial for a man we don't wish to remember. We are trying to forget him".

Thus an Eastwood miner's opinion of his town's most famous son — D. H. Lawrence, probably the most significant English novelist of the 20th Century. Fortunately, visitors will not allow Eastwood to forget. This drab mining town has little else to commend it.

Lawrence was born at 8A Victoria Street. Then the family moved to 57 The Breach, then to 8 Walker Street, where they stayed for 10 years before ending up at 97 Lynncroft. It was here that Lawrence's mother died — a death which has been described in Sons and Lovers. The local council, sensitive to Lawrence's standing, has twice tried to raise enthusiasm for a Lawrence memorial, but the only signs are a plaque on the wall at Victoria Street and a phoenix design, taken from the headstone of Lawrence's grave at Vence in France, in the council chamber. East-

wood is on the itinerary of most tourists to this region and it is fairly obvious that it is not because of the beauty of the place. It is because people want to see Lawrence's home and to compare the town with the descriptions he has given in his novels. The Bestwood of *Sons and Lovers* is a straightforward description of Eastwood. Lawrence was not an imaginative writer in the conventional romantic sense. He peopled his novels with characters and scenes based on real life, as did Shakespeare. He never used Victoria Street because he was too young when the family moved to remember it. The house at The Breach is the first one he describes — he called it "Bottoms". He disliked this house intensely. He called the Walker Street house "Bleak House" — because it is high up and catches the wind — but the view from the front windows here pleased him. "Go to Walker Street", he wrote to a friend in 1926, "and look across to Crich on the left, Underwood in front, High Park woods and Annesley to the right. I lived in that house from 8 to 18 and I know that view better than any in the world".

20 **CRICH** stands on an uplan plateau whipped by harsh wind in winter. In summer, it provides the visit with fine views of the surrounding countr side. One of the best observation poin is the Beacon Light memorial to 11,00 Sherwood Foresters who were killed the First World War. Standing 950ft abov a disused quarry, its lantern light can seen 20 miles away at night. Engraved the tower's front are the words of Horace Smith-Dorrien before the battle Le Cateau where so many Foresters die "Gentlemen, we will stand and fight".

Lower down the slopes, in the shel of the quarry, stands the Crich Tra Museum. It contains 40 trams of the la 19th and early 20th Centuries. Few b cities are unrepresented in this nostalg museum. Those who remember the trar of their youth can once again hear t screech of flange wheels against tramlin and take a ride on a tram, including horse-drawn Sheffield tram of the 187(

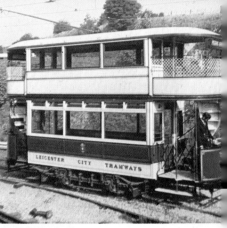

The Tram Museum at Crich gives a nostalgic glimpse of city transport of former days and an opportunity to take a tram ride

Cromford: set in delightful country

The first mechanised textile mill

21 CROMFORD is a sturdy, stone-built village of tremendous significance in English history — for it was here that Richard Arkwright built the first mechanised textile factory in the world. His original, forbidding mill still stands by the roadside. Visitors can still see some of the old cottages he built for his workpeople. Arkwright's grave is at St. Mary's Church, which he built in 1792. Another monument is Willersley Castle, now a hotel. Arkwright started this and lived here for a while, but it was left to his son to complete the castle in medieval style with turrets and narrow windows.

Worth looking at is the bridge across the Derwent — its arches are pointed on one side, rounded on the other. Cromford is set in delightful country. Nearby are the famous Black Rocks, a spectacularly-eroded mass of gritstone which pose an exciting challenge to rock climbers. The view from the summit is worthwhile, stretching across the valley in which the Matlocks lie to Riber Castle. The wooded ravine between Cromford and Grangemill has a beautiful stretch of road, called the *Via Gellia* (built during the 19th Century) and is a particularly pleasing place to visit in bluebell time.

From the Black Rocks near Cromford there is a magnificent view across the valley of the Matlocks to Riber Castle

22 MATLOCK now consists of Matlock itself, Matlock Bath and Matlock Bank — three towns in one stretching along the picturesque Derwent Valley. Once famous as spas, the combined towns are still a holiday resort for visitors wishing to climb limestone cliffs and explore underground caverns. Matlock is dominated by two heights — the formidable peak of High Tor, rising 380ft above the tumbling Derwent, and the Heights of Abraham, 750ft, said to have been named by an officer who fought under General Wolfe at Quebec and who claimed that they resemble the cliffs along the St.

Lawrence. The Heights form a prominence on the south-eastern flank of Masson Hill which the Romans apparently opened in search of lead. The workings are mentioned in Domesday. Convicts in the 13th and 14th Centuries worked in the two caverns here — Great Rutland and Great Masson. Then, with the increasing popularity of the Matlocks as spas, the lead workings were opened to tourists. Grand Duke Michael of Russia was a visitor in 1818 and is reported to have sat facing his pony's tail as he made the ascent so that he could study the ladies in his entourage following behind him.

From High Tor, 380ft. peak at Matlock

23 **TISSINGTON:** This village in the foothills of the Pennines is famous for the old custom of Well Dressing that takes place on Ascension Day. It is a religious ceremony dating from 1350. There are five wells in the village — Hall well, Town well, Yew Tree well, Hands well and Coffin well (from the shape of its catch trough). During the well dressing ceremony, flowers, berries and mosses are embedded in a foundation of salted clay, the design followed depicting either a pattern or a picture. Church services accompany the ceremonies.

The church of St. Mary at Tissington, chiefly Early Norman, is worth visiting. It contains many memorials to the Fitzherbert family, including an unusual one of kneeling angels which reaches almost to the roof, and an interesting Norman font.

The beautiful village of Tissington is famous for the old custom of Well Dressing

The mill at Wetton, one of several attractive villages in the Manifold Valley

25 **MANIFOLD VALLEY:** This beautiful stretch is barely a mile from Dovedale. Here can be seen, just above the treeline and some 250 ft. up, a gaping hole in the side of the valley slope. This is Thor's Cave where archaeological finds indicate that men once lived here. Near the village of Ilam, the river disappears underground. Unless there has been continuous rain, the upper bed remains dry.

Dr. Johnson once visited here and conducted an experiment with corks to satisfy himself that the river was the same one that emerged further downstream.

Yet another landmark is Beeston Tor, a limestone mass which rises 200ft. near to the junction of the Manifold with its tributary, the Hamps. A small cave at the foot of this crag, called St. Bertram's Cave, has also yielded prehistoric remains.

24 **THORPE:** Dovedale and Thorpe Cloud together make one of the most beautiful spots in England. The crystal-clear Dove, home of trout and grayling, flows swiftly through a 2½-mile limestone gorge, richly wooded, after passing the massive shoulder of Thorpe Cloud, an abrupt height at the entrance to the dale. There are other prominences as the river rushes under rocky overhangs. Ilam Rock is a tall limestone pinnacle facing Pickering Tor, a similar pinnacle on the opposite bank. Sharplow Point, also known as Lover's Leap because a young girl suffering from unrequited love is said to have thrown herself from it, also provides excellent views. Further downstream are the Stepping Stones, leading across to Dovedale Castle, while there are also caves in the limestone cliffs at other points.

It is ideal country for the naturalist who will find unusual ferns, mosses, wild flowers and berries. The keen walker can continue for another six miles upstream past Beresford Dale to Hartington. Charles Cotton, friend and assistant of Izaak Walton, author of The Compleat Angler, was born at Beresford Hall, which is now in ruins. Walton, who often fished the Dove, was a frequent visitor to the Hall.

26 **ALTON TOWERS:** Charles, 15th Earl of Shrewsbury began building Alton Towers in 1812, when he was aged 60, by transforming 600 acres of barren hillside into a series of beautiful parklands. The Earl became a fanatical earth mover, landscape gardener and builder, planning and supervising every

The Screw Fountain at Alton Towers

This is Dovedale, ideal country for walker, angler and naturalist

tail of the work. In 1814 he made the lodge his personal residence so that he could oversee the work. Exotic flowers, rare trees and shrubs were planted; lakes, Roman fountains, conservatories and a Chinese pagoda were added. Water was channelled from two miles away to fill the lakes and provide the fountains. Charles died in 1827 and his nephew John enlarged the modest lodge into a turretted and castellated Gothic style mansion. This is now little more than a shell. Alton Towers has now been converted into a vast pleasure park, with boating lakes and a miniature railway, but there are plenty of solitary places to be found.

...ton's Pagoda and Dolphin Lake. The water for the Lake comes from a source two miles away

27 BARLASTON is now the home of the factory producing the famous Wedgwood pottery. The growth of this pottery firm is among the great romances of British industry. Josiah Wedgwood, now acknowledged the greatest of English potters, entered into partnership with Thomas Whieldon of Fenton, then the finest of the 18th Century potters, and discovered a new process for green glaze. Later, he set up at Burslem on his own, bringing to perfection a cream-coloured earthenware. This was greatly liked by Queen Charlotte and became known as "Queen's Ware". In 1762 Wedgwood went into partnership with a merchant called Thomas Bentley and together they produced red-figure vases in the Greek style and cameos known as Jasper ware. A factory was opened at Hanley, called Etruria, for this type of ware. In 1940 the firm moved to the grime-free region of Barlaston. Today visitors can see the pottery-making processes and there is also a Long Gallery Museum with examples of Wedgwood's finest work.

A vase in the Wedgwood Museum

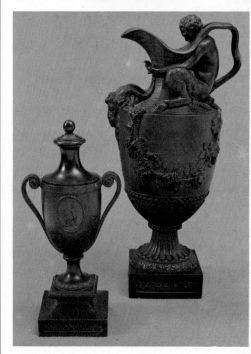

Black basalt vase and a 1778 wine ewer

28 **TRENTHAM** consists of an ancient village and a well-known pleasure park with Italian gardens. Trentham Hall, described in Disraeli's novel *Lothair* as Brentham, was once the home of the Dukes of Sutherland. Today, only the Great Hall and Ballroom remain of the 17th Century mansion, but the park has been made into a pleasure ground of lawns and woods alongside the winding Trent. A burial mound was excavated in the village in 1859 and relics dated around 1,000 B.C. were found. The village church, which has Norman pillars, was the site of a nunnery, founded about A.D. 670 by the daughter of Wulf, first Christian King of Mercia.

Trentham Hall, featured in a novel by Disraeli

Only the Great Hall and Ballroom of the 17th Century mansion remain

Market Drayton has some fine old houses

29 **MARKET DRAYTON** is a attractive old town whose Wednesday market has been held for 700 year It was the birthplace in 1725 of Robe Clive (of India). The 16th Century gramm school where he was educated still stanc and visitors can see the desk on which carved his initials. The 14th Century pari church has Norman remnants and a sturc tower which the boy Clive is said to ha once climbed on the outside. There a several fine Jacobean houses in the tow Ford Hall, a farm at nearby Turn Hill, is t centre of experiments in organic farming 150 acres have been planted with different varieties of grasses and herbs ar the cattle are left to graze on the land all t year round. This method produces health cattle, with milk containing a high butte fat content, and examination of the soil aft several years of this type of farming revea no soil deterioration.

31 **THE WREKIN,** compounded volcanic ash and lava and 1,335 high, rises dramatically from the Seve valley and is said to be the oldest mounta in England. A mile long footpath leads the top from which there is a breathtaki view of the glorious border country.

The Wrekin is really a small range of thr hills, the main peak preceded in the no east by foothills called Ercall and Lawren Hill. There is a footpath between Ercall a the lower slopes of the main hill which ru through gaps known quaintly as Hell Ga and Heaven Gate. From the summit can seen the Needle's Eye on the southe slope. Legend says that this great cleft w made by a warring giant who threw I spade at another — and missed, the spa chipping out the Eye. The legend adds th the two giants then rushed at each oth and while they were fighting, an enormo raven swooped down and pecked out th eyes. The great tears that fell wore away saucer-like depression called the Rave Bowl. Centuries before the Romans, Iron Age hill fort stood on the Wrekin a 400 years ago roaring beacons on its cro lit up the night, warning that the Spani Armada was on its way.

30 HODNET HALL is a 19th Century Tudor-style mansion surrounded by 60 acres of beautifully landscaped gardens. Once a shrub-entangled marsh, fed by underground springs, the area was transformed over 30 years by the late Brigadier A. G. W. Heber-Percy into a place of great beauty. The gardens can be divided into three areas — ornamental formations and plantings; a stretch of natural, rather than cultivated, beauty; and finally the wooded area of the valley. In the early spring, the gardens are a mass of daffodils, then later rhododendrons, laburnum, lilac and azalea followed by primula, roses and peonies, come into flower. The autumn brings berries and the brilliant colours of several varieties of tree and shrub. A special feature is the presence of candelabra primula, iris and bog plants.

The village church has a Nuremberg Bible printed in 1479. A tile commemorates the 19th Century rector, Reginald Heber, who wrote, *From Greenland's Icy Mountains.*

Hodnet Hall's beautiful gardens

This England's oldest mountain?

Norman arches at Buildwas Abbey

32 BUILDWAS ABBEY stands in a meadow beside the Severn, its lovely ruins in stark contrast with the Ironbridge power station and its giant cooling towers, on the far side of the river. Founded in 1135 by Roger de Clinton, Bishop of Coventry and Lichfield, the surprising thing about the Abbey is that so much of it still remains. There are 14 Norman arches and the great pillars in the nave, each 14ft. in circumference, convey something of the majesty of the Abbey when it was first built. A carved seat and other pieces of stone date from the reign of Henry II. Parts of the sacristy, the chapter house, the crypt and the tower still stand. The Department of the Environment has been responsible for saving much of the Abbey. Cleaning pillars and walls has revealed ancient tiles.

Ironbridge over the Severn was cast at Coalbrookdale

33 COALBROOKDALE is a place every Englishman, perhaps, should visit at least once. Here, more than in any other place, lies the cradle of the Industrial Revolution. What it was like before the great ironmasters arrived can only be imagined today. Probably much of the country around had been already despoiled, for even in Stuart times there was a forge here for obtaining iron from ore and for shaping the iron itself. Until Abraham Darby managed to smelt iron successfully with coke, English ironmasters had used charcoal in their furnaces. As supplies of timber dwindled, furnaces had to be built in hitherto inaccessible parts of the country such as the Scottish Highlands, where there was plenty of wood. Darby's discovery changed this pattern. The careful siting of his works gave this man of energy and vision an added advantage — he chose one of the very few areas where supplies of coal and iron were convenient to a great river, the Severn, which would allow cheap transport.

Coalbrookdale gained a succession of historic "firsts" in industry. In 1723 it produced the first large iron steam-engine cylinders. In 1767 it laid the first iron rails in the world and in 1779 cast the ribs of the first iron bridge in the world — Ironbridge still spans the Severn and with a single arc of 100ft. is a proud memorial of this great English age. It was within sight of this bridge, indeed, that Darby's friend, John Wilkinson, launched the first iron ship in 1787, the assembled crowd certain it would sink (it didn't!). Darby's famous iron bridge was designed by Thomas Pritchard who did not live to see it built.

Black and white cottages in the old market town of Much Wenlock

The Guildhall, part-timber, part-stone, is redolent with history

35 WENLOCK EDGE

WENLOCK EDGE is a green, wooded ridge stretching 1 miles across the Shropshire hill country from Much Wenlock to Craven Arms like giant plume on a warrior's helmet. At i highest point it rises 950ft and from i crest can be seen the outline of the Wels mountains. It is an excellent place fro which to contemplate Britain as it wa before the appearance of man, for th limestone ridge was once part of a gre prehistoric sea. It is full of coral fossil formed under the same conditions that our present geological age have produce the Great Barrier Reef of Australia. At period when the crust of the earth was violent motion, the immense pressure opposing forces squeezed the ocean floo producing a concertina effect — th Wenlock Edge. Eventually the sea recede to leave the ridge dramatically above th surrounding land.

West and north of the Edge lie th Shropshire whalebacks — hills in masse or solitary, or in leaning lines, below whic burbling brooks wind through densel wooded dingles. These are known loca as 'hopes', a word that has found its wa into many Shropshire place names, usua in the form of 'hope' or 'hoptun'. Man ha beautified the ridge by building many qu villages. At Easthope, little remains of th 13th Century church ruined by fire in 192 but the new structure has a Jacobean hou glass, traditionally hung near the pulpit remind the preacher how long he had be speaking. On the new door is hung sanctuary ring — which once meant pr tection for any hunted man who grasped Just outside the village is Plaish Hall, impressive Tudor mansion, and on the edg of Mogg Forest an early British encam ment, protected by double ramparts.

34 MUCH WENLOCK

MUCH WENLOCK, an old market town at the end of Wenlock Edge, looks much as it probably did towards the end of the Middle Ages. The ruined priory stands on the site of a 7th Century settlement by St. Milburga, which was destroyed by the Danes in A.D. 874. A century and a half later, the Earl of Mercia and his wife, the notorious Lady Godiva, founded another abbey here which in due course was replaced by a Cluniac monastery established by Roger de Montgomery. There is much to appreciate in the present ruins. The Prior's lodging remains intact, but is not open to the public because it is still used. Pevsner has described it as "one of the finest examples of domestic architecture in England about the year 1500".

The Guildhall, too, is redolent with history. Half-timber, half-stone, it carries on one wooden pillar an iron fastener in which a prisoner's wrists were locked, so that he could be kept upright while being whipped. Upstairs there is a fine panelled council chamber and courtroom and a set of stocks on wheels, which were used to push the prisoner around the town so that all could jeer and pelt him. Sometimes rocks were thrown and people are known to have died while confined in stocks.

Wenlock Edge: green, wooded ridge

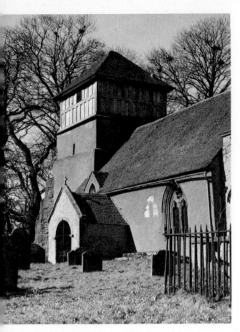

Tower of Shipton parish church

36 SHIPTON: There is evidence that the tiny church here had its origins in Anglo-Saxon times. It probably served a small sheep-farming community, from which the village derived the name Scipetune as recorded in Domesday. The simply-designed chancel and the font are both Norman. One of the windows dates from the 14th Century. The church's hey-day, however, arrived in Elizabeth's reign when considerable parts were "re-edified and builded of newe from the foundation" by John, youngest son of Richard Lutwych. This Richard built Shipton Hall. Using limestone quarried on Wenlock Edge, the same stone used in all the great houses and religious buildings in the area, Lutwych has left us a lovely Elizabethan mansion with mullioned windows, tower and tall chimneys. In the grounds are a stone dovecote and an old bowling green and not far away, along the roadside, the arched entrance to a mysterious tunnel.

JACK'S IN FOLKLORE

The jackdaw's habit of stealing has earned him a permanent place in folklore. He can be readily distinguished from other member's of the crow family by the white-grey nape.

The jackdaw's numbers have increased considerably in recent years.

37 ASTLEY ABBOTS, near Bridgnorth on the road from Ironbridge, first mentioned in an old charter of 1150. The church is almost entirely Stuart being extensively rebuilt in 1633 on the site of an earlier church founded in 1138. Two of its bells were cast at Worcester in 1455 and the church register goes back to 1561. Pulpit, panelling and roof are all Stuart. In the church is a memorial tablet to Colonel Billingsley, a King's man killed in the siege of Bridgnorth in 1646. On the north wall, facing the main door, hangs a Maiden's Garland, slowly decaying — the gloves, ribbon and bouquet of Hannah Phillips who was drowned in the Severn on the way to her wedding on May 10, 1707. The church itself is dedicated to St. Calixtus, an unusual name in England. He was an early Pope who was martyred in A.D. 223. In the churchyard stands an iron sundial — yet another product of the ingenuity of Abraham Darby. An excellent Elizabethan black and white house overlooks the church.

The Maiden's Garland at Astley Abbots

High Town looms 200ft. above the River Severn

38 BRIDGNORTH has a faintly Continental air and is divided into Low Town and High Town. Low Town grew up as a river port on the Severn before the coming of the railways. High Town looms 200ft. above the river, built on the top of a wooded valley. If most of the town's work was done in Low Town, then its administration was carried on at the higher level. The town hall, the castle and the principal churches are all here. During the Civil War, the Cromwellians besieged the castle. While waiting for it to fall, they burned down the town hall — which was later replaced by a barn brought from Much Wenlock, now in High Street. They also damaged the parish church, which had to be rebuilt. After bitter hand to hand fighting, the 12th Century castle, which had withstood the attacks of Henry I and Henry II, surrendered when the Cromwellians tunnelled under the powder magazine and threatened to blow the place up. Little remains of the castle today except its famous leaning tower, — standing some 17 degrees from the perpendicular. The most striking church is St. Mary Magdalene's, built in white stone with Tuscan columns and a tower topped with a lead dome. Thomas Telford, the great engineer, designed it, exhibiting yet again another facet of his genius. The cliff railway takes one from Low Town to High Town, blessed by all who have to face this steep gradient.

'Tallyho' in Merry England

Jorrocks — a hard riding, hard drinking prototype squire — typical of the lusty exuberance of 18th Century England.

The foxhunting squires of the 18th Century have become part of that legend of a Merry England which most of us cherish so fondly. And, indeed, this side of English life is not just a pleasant myth. From the earliest times in England the joys of the chase have been part of a peculiarly English experience. In the early decades of the 18th Century stag hunts were closing down. The destruction of the great forests and the gradual yielding of wasteland to the plough cut down the herds of wild deer. Throughout the middle and end of the 18th Century, foxhunting became the pre-eminent sport of England's country gentlemen and many of the famous hunts of today had their origins in those decades. Although keeping a pack of foxhounds was the accolade of the rich, country-based aristocracy — even in those times it was a pretty expensive business with its panoply of stables, kennels, hunt servants, uniforms and the rest — foxhunting was in many ways an essentially democratic pastime in which local lord or squire rubbed shoulders with the full-time huntsmen, farmers, tenant farmers and the humbler village folk. Regional accents were proudly used by squire and villager alike. And there was nothing namby-pamby about these hunting heroes. Hunting songs were happily bellowed out in ale houses and manor houses. Only the mean-spirited held back from the general jollity. Any lad with a musical voice, a way with hounds and a talent for the saddle could hope to mix with the great aristocracy of England on equal terms on the hunting field and could, indeed, found one of the famous dynasties of hunting families who formed the professional core of the sport. One of the greatest names in foxhunting was that of Hugo Meynell (shown astride his horse), M.F.H. of the Quorn from 1753-1799. A man of wit and fashion in London society, he turned the Quorn Hunt into a prototype for all the great hunts that were to follow. One of the most famous dynasties of huntsmen were the Treadwells. James (Jem) Treadwell (1800-1870) hunted in South Wiltshire for many years and then moved to Dorset

A tankard holding three pints of wine, "exceedingly chaste piece of workmanship" with a design showing hounds breaking cover "with Reynard just in sight". This tankard was presented to James Treadwell as an heirloom for his family when he retired from the Dorsetshire Hunt.

where he built up a tremendous reputation with the great James John Farquharson, who was to become known in hunting lore as "the Meynell of the West". Jem's two sons, Charles and John, both became famous huntsmen — Charles was one of the most scientific hound breeders of his day. After a season with the Quorn he built up the reputation of the famous Bramham Moor pack.

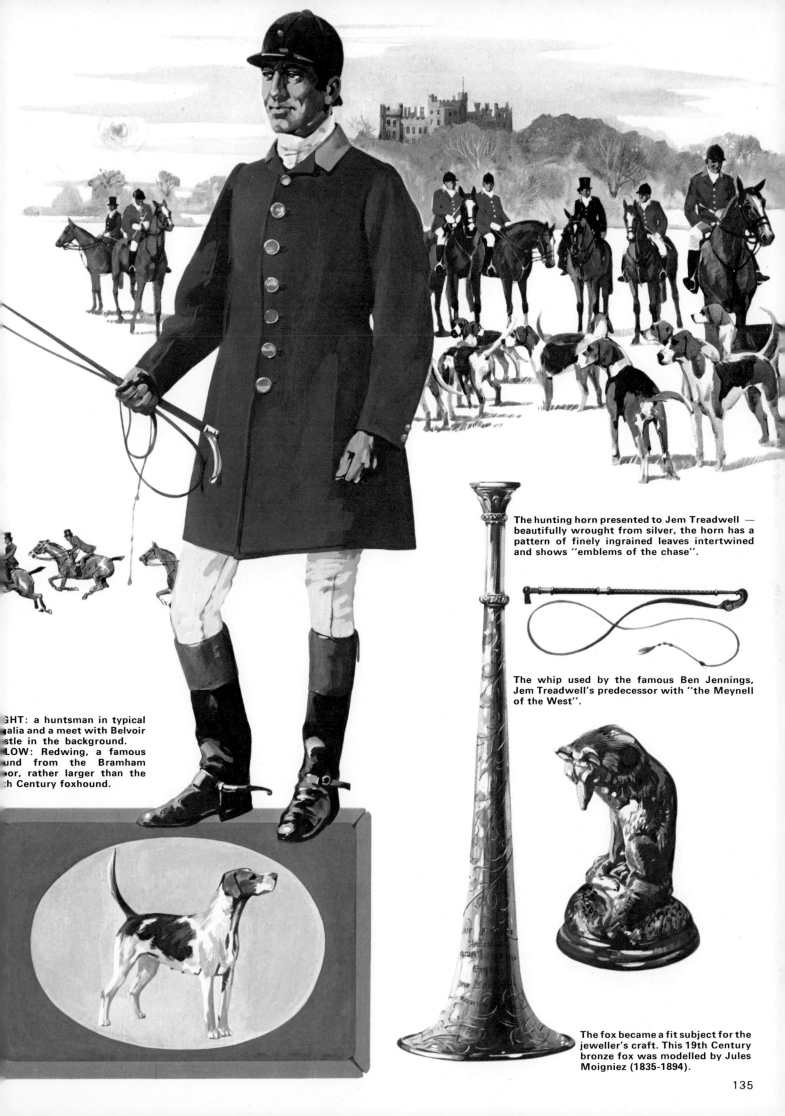

The hunting horn presented to Jem Treadwell — beautifully wrought from silver, the horn has a pattern of finely ingrained leaves intertwined and shows "emblems of the chase".

The whip used by the famous Ben Jennings, Jem Treadwell's predecessor with "the Meynell of the West".

GHT: a huntsman in typical alia and a meet with Belvoir stle in the background. LOW: Redwing, a famous und from the Bramham or, rather larger than the th Century foxhound.

The fox became a fit subject for the jeweller's craft. This 19th Century bronze fox was modelled by Jules Moigniez (1835-1894).

135

The West Midlands – from Oxford to the Wye

MAX CAULFIELD

There are few more lustrous triangles of landscape anywhere than the one based on the jewelled points of Oxford, Stratford-upon-Avon and marcher Chepstow, theatrically bestriding that loveliest of border rivers, the Wye.

Here, spread across five counties, is countryside where even the stone cottages take on a honeyed hue; a land piled heavily with the English glories — rose-red pinnacles and Wren cupolas, tumbling Tudor houses, Shakespearean black-and-white timbered farmsteads, great abbeys, orchards bursting with apples, plums, cherries, lovely winding rivers, in whose lea plum-coloured Hereford heifers rub themselves against the slender hedgerow elm. Villages, grown rich on medieval wool, snooze like stony Rip Van Winkles; lovely wolds hump on each other like damasked pillows giving way, in the drive west towards Wales, to edges bearing the fossil remains of prehistoric seas, to spurs and promontories supporting Celtic forts, to gorges and dramatic wooded heights. It is, nonetheless, a gentle journey, embroidered overall with a *motif* of ancient manuscripts, chambered barrows where prehistoric man mourned his dead, stone manors lit with mullioned windows, deerparks that yield to coloured gardens.

Modern Oxford is an extraordinary antithesis. The Colleges, in masonry and spirit among the great European heritages, ought to have been left to dream in solitary grandeur. Instead, they are bespattered by a utilitarian sprawl of streets and dwellings to the south-east which all but draw off the magic. Fortunately, the heart remains unsullied. Within a square mile of the Carfax is an area of breathtaking loveliness where 653 buildings are listed as being of historic or architectural merit.

The place should not be hurried; it is made for a gentle stroll or reflective thought. Time is essential to yield to the harmonious gardens of St. John's, Trinity, Worcester, New College or Wadham; to enjoy the treasures of the Ashmolean Museum or glance at the 7th Century *Codex Laudianus* used by Bede and the *Anglo-Saxon Chronicle* in the Bodleian.

CHURCHILL'S GRAVE

Across flat, fat, lush, sylvan-streamed, well-farmed land now towards the Cotswolds. Bladon is unremarkable save for the grave of Sir Winston Churchill. Woodstock, overshadowed by Blenheim Palace, merits a look for its stocks and timbered houses.

Great Tew has resisted even one 20th Century building and is a tumbling riot of scalloped thatch and mullioned windows opening on to laurel hedges and the sounds of sheep and pigeons.

England has a splendid habit of thrusting different centuries rather dramatically upon the eye. Almost round the corner lie the Rollright Stones, high on a windy plateau but sheltered by whispering trees, melancholy relics of that Bronze Age, when men were god-haunted. South-westwards and we are suddenly stalking through the Jacobean treasure of Chastleton House before riding into Chipping Norton, at 700 ft. the highest town in Oxfordshire.

So on to Burford through knolled-countryside and the once great royal hunting forest of Wychwood; through tiny villages bearing charming names — Shipton-under-Wychwood, Milton-under-Wychwood, Ascott-under-Wychwood. In medieval times the forest was as large and important as the New Forest and in the Tudor dusk hunting parties used to clatter up for a night's carousal in Burford, among the most beautiful of Cotswold towns, with its main street sloping in a melody of honeyed stone to a

The River Avon, near Pershore

picturesque bridge over the Windrush.

Northleach has a glorious Perpendicular church and a ra grotesque of a cat fiddling to three rats. Thence north-eastwar through dream-ridden countryside to Bourton-on-the-Water whe the Windrush meanders through the town. Far more somnolent, le popularised and reached by back roads, is Lower Slaughter who beauty almost arrests the heart.

Stow-on-the-Wold is a meeting place of eight roads. Chippi Campden is lazy and lovely with oriel, dormer and mullion windows; one flavours the 14th Century here.

Yet oddly, one of the glories of the region belongs to the 2(Century proving, perhaps, that all is not yet lost. Hidcote Man Gardens were created by Lawrence Johnston, an American, w bought this estate in 1907 and, defying an inhospitable site, crea one of the most ingeniously lovely gardens in Britain.

The imagination has to work overtime to recall the somnoler

its delicate lacery of ironworked balconies.

Tewkesbury is heavy with the memory of romantic England. The abbey church, as large and solid as a cathedral, dominates the town, its great tower casting an eternal blessing upon Bloody Meadow itself. In this sunken, waterlogged spot on the town edge, one can still imagine the clash of armoured knights, the cries of wounded and dying men in coats of mail. The town lives up to its reputation — heavily picturesque with priest's holes, its tumbling House of the Golden Key and its quaintly-named Tudor house The Ancient Grudge.

The road grows in drama now as we face north. To the right, the Cotswolds roll gently; leftwards, the Malvern Hills rise to a stature just short of mountainous. The horizons grow wider; there is more space and light. Bredon Hill, 991 ft., dominates the scene. The village is one of the loveliest in a lovely valley.

By way of rich little Overbury, Ashton-under-Hill and picturesque Elmley Castle (which doesn't have a castle any more) to Pershore, capital of the plum. Among the things to see are the abbey, once a glory of England, and a six-arched bridge of largely medieval construction.

MARCHER COUNTRY

Upton-upon-Severn, a great centre for river cruising, is dominated by the red sandstone tower of its old church. The White Lion Inn was the setting for Fielding's novel, *Tom Jones*.

The road now climbs to the spa town of Great Malvern, set steeply into the sides of the Malvern Hills.

We are almost into the marcher country now; it is still a land of picturesque villages, of cattle grazing in lush pastures, but the border hills loom rich and wooded. Buried somewhere, the leaves of the wild woad plant which the ancient Britons used to dye their bodies blue.

Ross-on-Wye is a graceful town, the river remains a winding, tinkling marvel lined with lush pastures and thick woodlands, burgeoning with salmon and trout.

We leave the main route again to visit the twin villages of Symonds Yat, East and West. A steep ascent leads to the Yat rock, as spectacular a sight as there is in England; and a starting point for a 30-mile scenic drive through the Forest of Dean, one of the great primeval forests of Britain with over 20 million oaks, ash trees, hollies, birches and conifers, abundant with wild life and wild flowers. In the heart of this massive Royal woodland one stumbles on old iron mines which provided the weaponry for the Crusades and here and there charcoal-burners still practising their craft.

And then, at last, we are into what all Welshmen insist is Wales (and, indeed, a large sign declares "Welcome to Wales", in case you have any doubts). Nonetheless, the town of Monmouth seems to insist stubbornly that it is English. Its main square is named Agincourt and Henry V's statue is in its Shire Hall. Surely nothing can be more uncompromisingly English than the Nelson Museum (he once stayed at a local inn) which boasts many mementoes of the great Englishman. Don't leave the town without viewing the fine 13th Century fortified tower gatehouse on the Monnow Bridge.

We are now running through breathtaking country — Offa's Dyke, built by Saxons to keep off marauding Celts out of sight on the far side of the Wye, and then to Chepstow, whose massive Castle, in splendid ruin, sits profanely in counterpoint to those lovely, slender and graceful arches of Tintern Abbey miles upstream.

t must have once near-drowned Shakespeare's Stratford. One s in touch with the poet, perhaps, by stroking the mulberry tree wn from the one he originally planted in the garden of New ce or by going to glorious Charlecote Park, home of those cys who had the stripling bard arrested for poaching.

At Broadway, "The Painted Lady of the Cotswolds", stop for stnut cream; or better, tramp to the top of Broadway Hill ere Beacon Tower, a folly, was built by Lady Coventry in 1797. At Winchcombe, Sudeley Castle stands splendid, its Tudor aqueting hall a stark ruin, but still preserving the doll's-sized lroom in which died Henry VIII's last Queen, Katherine Parr. Abruptly, a far more ancient Britain obtrudes. At Cleeve Cloud, Celtic fort sits on a spur of land high above the Vale of Severn; Belas Knap, a chambered barrow recalls the grief of some rude esman. And thus to Cheltenham, a glory of Regency grace with lovely Promenade, its Rotunda dome based on Rome's Pantheon,

26 MALVERN

27 WORCESTER BEACON

MALVERN HILLS

25 UPTON-ON-SEVERN

24 PERSHOR

RIVER WYE

BREDON H

23 BREDON

28 LEDBURY

22 MYTHE

30 MUCH MARCLE

29 EASTNOR CASTLE

21 TEWKESBURY

15 WINCHCOMBE

18 CLEEVE CLOUD

31 ROSS-ON-WYE

1 SUD CAS

32 GOODRICH CASTLE

19 CHELTENHAM

33 SYMONDS YAT

20 LECKHAMPTON HILL

34 MONMOUTH

FOREST OF DEAN

35 TINTERN ABBEY

WAYFARER'S GUIDE
7

36 CHEPSTOW

RIVER SEVERN

11 STRATFORD-ON-AVON

12 HIDCOTE MANOR GARDENS

13 CHIPPING CAMPDEN

14 BROADWAY

COTSWOLD HILLS

10 MORETON-IN-MARSH

3 GREAT TEW

17 BELAS KNAP

9 STOW-ON-THE-WOLD

4 THE ROLLRIGHT STONES

BOURTON-ON-THE-WATER

5 CHIPPING NORTON

RIVER CHERWELL

2 BLENHEIM PALACE

6 BURFORD

ORTHLEACH

1 OXFORD

RIVER THAMES

h Scowan / Peyto Slatter / Spectrum / Patrick Ward   Illustrations: Elsie Wrigley / Richard Hook   Plant Notes: Geoffrey Gilbert   Animals and Birds: Jeremy Johns

Ben Manchip

1 OXFORD: Most of the older Colleges lie within an easy ramble of the High Street. The most ancient is University, closely pressed by Balliol, Merton and St. Edmund Hall. The richest, largest and noblest is Christ Church (Charles I's headquarters during the Civil War) while the most beautiful is Magdalen (pronounced "Maudalayne" in medieval times but now shortened to "Maudlen"). Merton has the oldest surviving stonework; the gardens of St. John's, Trinity, Worcester, New College and Wadham a[re] considered the most beautiful.

All Souls, of which Sir Christoph[er] Wren was a Fellow, was built as [a] memorial for the dead of Agincourt. [The] Codrington Library houses 300,000 book[s]. Brasenose gets its name from a 14th Century knocker shaped like a nose — t[he] Brazen Nose; you can see this over t[he] College's High Table. Christ Church [is] always called "The House". It was found[ed] by Cardinal Wolsey and the main qua[d]

Punting on the Cherwell

St. Edmund Hall, one of the oldest university foundations

The City of Oxford, 20th Century traffic amid the Colleges

Three pictures from MSS in the Bodleian

ngle, which we owe to him, is called "Tom Quadrangle", taking its name from e great bell in Tom Tower (built by ren) and dedicated to St. Thomas of anterbury. The square tower of Magdalen, erlooking the Cherwell (pronounced "Charwell") has a peal of ten bells; at nrise every May Day the college choir ngs a Latin hymn from the tower top. niversity, which legend says was founded Alfred the Great, has a memorial to elley who was sent down for distributing

dcliffe Camera, store for 600,000 books

pamphlet, *The Necessity of Atheism*. e Muniment Room in Merton houses 000 rare documents and the library the met of Sir Thomas Bodley, founder of e Bodleian Library. The chapel has 14 ndows with 13th and 14th Century ss. The Sheldonian was designed by en like a Roman theatre. In the 17th ntury the university printed its books re, but the theatre is now used for nferring degrees and other university nctions. The spectacular Radcliffe mera is the main reading room of the dleian, with an underground store of 0,000 books.

The Bodleian, which receives a copy of ery new book published in Britain, uses 2,500,000 books and is one of the orld's most important libraries. The most cient part of the Library and the old vinity School, the university's antique ture room, are open to the public.

The Ashmolean Museum, founded in 77, contains among its many treasures a d, enamel and rock crystal jewel said have belonged to Alfred the Great, and y Fawkes' lantern.

Near Godstow are the ruins of a nunnery ere the body of Henry II's wanton stress, the Fair Rosamund of Tennyson's em, was once buried. When the spot probably became a shrine for pilgrims, outraged bishop had her body exhumed d reburied outside the walls.

Blenheim Palace, Queen Anne's gift to the Churchill family for Marlborough's victories

2 BLENHEIM PALACE, a grandiose mansion designed by Sir John Vanbrugh, was built at Queen Anne's order as a gift to John Churchill, 1st Duke of Marlborough (son of a Dorset squire called Winston Churchill) for his victories in the War of the Spanish Succession. The first Duke died before the work could be completed. His widow, Sarah, constantly argued with Vanbrugh over the cost and in the end the architect was sent away and forbidden to return to see the completed work. Many fine artists helped in its ornamentation. The stone lions savaging the cocks of France at the main entrance gate were carved by Grinling Gibbons, who also did the stone door-cases of the great hall. Sir John Thornhill painted the ceiling showing Marlborough at Blenheim. Possibly the most impressive room is the long library with a statue of Queen Anne by Michael Rysbrack, who also executed the monument to Marlborough and his wife in the chapel.

Most people nowadays would agree with the poet, Alexander Pope:

*"Thanks, sir" cried I, "tis very fine,
But where do you sleep or where
d'ye dine?
I find by all you have been telling
That 'tis a house and not a dwelling."*

Modern interest centres on the small ground-floor room where Sir Winston Churchill was born on November 30, 1874.

This overbearing mansion, covering three acres, remains one of the largest private houses in Europe. Its fine gardens and park embracing 2,500 acres, were laid out by Queen Anne's gardener, Herbert Wise, but remade in the 18th Century by

"Capability" Brown, who dammed the River Glyme to create an ornamental lake. This had the effect of flooding several rooms which Vanbrugh had built into the bridge over the lake — a bridge severely criticised by Sarah as a "useless expense".

Early in this century, the 9th Duke (rightly) ordered some of Brown's work to be undone and the French designer, Duchene, to create beautiful formal gardens with ponds, fountains and parterre — one of the major delights of Blenheim and reminiscent of Versailles.

Rysbrack's monument to Marlborough

3 **GREAT TEW** with its satellite villages of Duns Tew and Little Tew, is the heart of what is locally called Tewland. No one seems to know exactly what Tew means. Most of the cottages in Great Tew are 17th Century built in honey-coloured stone and are incomparably set amid a bower of woods. Much of the effect is due to the creative vision of John Loudon, an early 19th Century landscape gardener. Lord Falkland lived here in the 17th Century (the local pub is named after him) when his now-destroyed house was a centre for the brightest intellects of London and Oxford. The church, which stands away from Great Tew up a slight hill, is worth a visit for the local carvings on some tombstones.

The main village is now the centre of an interesting experiment undertaken by the present incumbent of Tew Park, Major Eustace Robb. He refuses to allow commuters to move into this village. His aim is to modernise the picturesque but ruined cottages without destroying their antique look and to lease them to permanent residents rather than sacrifice the pretty village to week-enders.

Great Tew, a 17th Century village of honey-coloured stone in a bower of woods

4 **THE ROLLRIGHT STONES** are less awesome than Stonehenge or Avebury. But they show that this upland ridge separating Oxfordshire and Warwickshire was an important place in the Bronze Age. They consist of a stone circle called the King's Men; the King's Stone, standing alone on the other side of the road in Warwickshire, bends in the middle like an old man about to crumple; the Whispering Knights some 400 yards away are a closely packed group of stones bending over a fallen one. Medieval legend has it that the King left his army (the circle of stones) to reconnoitre a valley while a group of knights went into a huddle to plot treason and were at once petrified. The stones are almost 4,000 years old. The circle is about 100 ft. across and the stones vary in height from a few inches to 8/9 ft.

5 **CHIPPING NORTON** owes its prosperity mainly to the medieval wool trade, when its church, St. Mary, one of the largest in Oxfordshire, was beautified, and is now mostly 18th Century. The wide main street is a harmonious blend of buildings in a medley of periods. The classical market hall was designed by George Repton and dates from 1842. Although the front of the Fox Hotel is 18th Century, a fireplace inside is two centuries older. The White Hart is 17th Century.

St. Mary's itself is worth a good look. The Perpendicular clerestory is almost continuous glass. The polygonal porch with a room above has its ceiling vaulted with bosses of strange heads — one is of a sheep-faced monkey holding its head in its arms.

Morris dancing at Chipping Norton

6 **BURFORD** is one of the mo[st] beautiful of Cotswold towns, risi[ng] up from the River Windrush, here cross[ed] by a narrow three-arched bridge. A syn[od] called here in A.D. 683, attended by t[he] King of Mercia, decided to follow the le[ad] taken by the Kingdom of Northumbria [at] Whitby 19 years earlier which had reject[ed] the Celtic Church's computation of Eas[ter] Day in favour of that used by Rome.

Burford thrived on trades associat[ed] with wool during the Middle Ages [—] clothiers, weavers, shearmen, drape[rs,] tailors, dyers and fullers. Some of [the] buildings, dating from the 15th Centu[ry,] remain unaltered. The Bear Inn, the Cro[wn] Inn and the grammar school all date fro[m] this period. Although the Bull is equa[lly] old, its facade is 17th Century. The Georg[e,] the finest of all Burford's coaching in[ns,] has archways and stone fireplaces dati[ng] from 1500. Falkland Hall, which dates fro[m] 1533, is another picturesque buildin[g.] Burford's pride, however, is its Tols[ey,] where the local merchants used to ho[ld] town meetings and where tolls were pa[id.] It now houses a fascinating museum. T[he] fine stone vaulted medieval cellar und[er] London House is worth visiting. T[he] Lamb Inn has medieval masonry. T[he] Priory is one of the most impress[ive] buildings in the town, but althou[gh] originally Elizabethan and with bits [of] Tudor masonry still in it, it dates alm[ost] wholly from only 1800. William Lenth[all,] Speaker of the Long Parliament, on[ce] owned the place (now run by Anglic[an] nuns) and his coat of arms can be seen o[ver] the doorway.

The impressive church at the bottom [of] the High Street has a lovely slen[der] steeple. For many, the most poign[ant] thing about this church is its 14th Cent[ury] font. Carved on the font is the lege[nd] "Antony Sedley prisner, 1649". This reca[lls] the rising by the Levellers against Cro[m]well, who caught up with them at Burf[ord] and shot their leaders. Worth looking a[t in] the church too, is the Harman monum[ent] of 1569. It has Red Indians on it.

Miniature bridge at Bourton (left) and a water[...]

7 NORTHLEACH suffers from the anything-but-dreamy traffic flow along the arterial A40, but it is a town with a lovely Perpendicular church, a fine green-swarded market place and many quaint old houses.

Worth noting are some timber-framed dwellings with overhangs; a group of 16th Century almshouses, a good manor house and the grammar school.

The town's pride, however, is its 15th Century parish church. Worth looking at is the buttressed arch whose apex consists of a carving of the Trinity. There are many fine brasses which reveal the rich clothing worn by the wealthy burghers of this town during the Middle Ages. A brass under the north arcade commemorates John Fortey, who built the nave with its great clerestory and who died in 1458; it shows him, fittingly enough, with his feet resting on a woolsack.

ringtime in Burford (above) and the River Windrush (below)

Northleach's 15th Century parish church

er Slaughter

8 BOURTON-ON-THE-WATER has been somewhat spoiled by the modern houses on its outskirts but it still remains staggeringly beautiful, with the Windrush ambling through, banked by lawns and lovely Cotswold houses and arched by low, miniature bridges. Behind the New Inn is a stone model of the village which is a magnetic attraction for all children. If you can successfully negotiate the tangle of cars that tend to clutter the main street, you will find a picturesque old mill at the far end of the village. There is also a witchcraft museum.

Parts of the church date from the 14th Century but most of it is restored work done at the turn of the 20th.

An unclassified road will take you to the enchanting villages of Lower and Upper Slaughter (never mind the names, the places themselves are lovely) and the villages of Lower and Upper Swell.

Lower Slaughter is as lovely a village as there is in the Cotswolds, with a tributary of the Windrush running under the same miniature bridges one has already seen at Bourton. On a rise above Upper Slaughter is one of the best Elizabethan manor houses in the country, while the church has a 14th Century bellcote.

A tour of the area should be conducted on foot and take in the Swells. The tiny River Dikler flows through both. Finds of Roman coins and jewels have been made in the church at Lower Swell. The great millwheel by the bridge at Upper Swell no longer turns but the pool has become a haven for wildfowl.

THE PILGRIM'S MAZE.

St. Laurence's Church at Wyck Rissington has a dream growing in a garden. In the church is a series of carvings, believed to be Flemish work of the early 16th Century and illustrating the life of Christ. In 1950 the parish priest dreamt he saw the carvings hanging like signposts in a maze. He built such a maze in the rectory garden according to instructions in his dream. The maze represents a pilgrimage through life. Wrong turnings are sins or mistakes. The right path leads to Heaven. A great pine in the centre symbolizes eternity. Signposts connect the maze with the church carvings.

9 **STOW-ON-THE-WOLD:** When Daniel Defoe visited Stow Fair here he recorded that 20,000 sheep were sold. Today it is still a busy and prosperous town. The old market place is a fine square with many picturesque old houses and inns and with an excellent market cross. There has been a Thursday market here since 1107 when King Henry I first made the town a borough and it changed its name from Edwardstow. It is the highest of the Cotswold towns and a local saying goes: "Stow-on-the-Wold where the wind blows cold".

The town hall contains many paintings connected with the Civil War. The last major battle of that war was fought near here when Astley, with an army of 3,000 on his way to join the King at Oxford, met a Cromwellian force. The Royalists were defeated and Cromwell locked up more than 1,000 Royalists in the church. One local farmer, however, made good his escape, but was followed by the Roundheads. Realising that his sweating horse would give him away, he killed it immediately he reached home and buried it. Then he charged upstairs and, fully clad, dived into bed beside his startled wife. When the Roundheads burst into the room he was snoring loudly and his wife indignantly sent the Roundheads packing.

The church has a fine 15th Century tower.

The stocks at Stow-on-the-Wold

10 **MORETON-IN-MARSH:** This a prosperous town with a wid grass-verged main street, which w originally part of the Roman Fosse W and still forms the cross-roads for fo adjacent counties.

The church was originally 13th Centu but was almost entirely restored in the 19 Century. It has fine Elizabethan plate a has the distinction, rare in England, of bei dedicated to St. David.

The town, in mellowed Cotswold sto has many fine 17th and 18th Cent buildings and many interesting inns. Ki Charles I slept at the White Hart Inn July 2, 1644. Moreton-in-Marsh had lo connections with the Redesdale family a the Redesdale Arms is a fine old coachi inn.

The old curfew bell still hangs in its tov overlooking the Fosse Way. The tov itself was once used as the town's lock and has a 17th Century clock.

A few miles west lies Bourton-on-th Hill. On the summit of the steep hill sits Lawrence's Church. The south arcade h is Norman with excellent scalloped capita Down the hill lies Bourton House, which 18th Century. Nearby is one of the fin tithe barns in Gloucestershire. It was b in the 16th Century with very stro buttresses and has a tall, gabled porch. village itself has attractive houses w bow windows.

Once part of the Roman Fosse Way, now the wide, grass-verged main street of Moreton-in-Marsh

144

1 STRATFORD-ON-AVON: The great forest of Arden of Shakespeare's day has largely disappeared now, but the countryside around Stratford still seems centuries removed from the industrial complexes of Coventry and Birmingham lying a few miles north. Shakespeare's supposed birthplace in Henley Street was originally two houses which have been joined together and much restored. Other places which must be visited are the site of New Place, Shakespeare's home after he retired, wealthy and distinguished, from his successes in London; the grammar school just a step or two away, where he was taught a little Latin and less Greek; the church where he lies buried and the 15th Century thatched cottage at Shottery where his wife, Anne Hathaway, was born and where the poet used to go courting. New Place was knocked down in the 18th century by its then owner who got into an argument with the local council over the payment of rates and carried out his threat to demolish the place if they were not reduced. The house next door has been well preserved, however, and gives a good indication of what Shakespeare's house must have looked like. In the garden of New Place is a giant mulberry tree, grown from a cutting taken from the tree planted by the poet himself.

Near Shakespeare's burial place in Holy Trinity Church is Hall's Croft, a fine Tudor house where the poet's daughter, Susanna, lived after her marriage to Dr. John Hall. The town of Stratford with its Memorial Theatre remains charming in spite of the crowds and has many houses and inns dating from Shakespeare's time. The River Avon gives it character and the view from Clopton Bridge is deservedly one of the best-known in Britain. There are many fine walks and picnic spots along the river bank near the town.

Five miles to the north-east lies Charlecote Park, a massive stone mansion dating from 1558. Here, according to tradition, Shakespeare was caught poaching and punished by the irate owner, Sir Thomas

Royal Shakespeare Theatre, Stratford

Lucy. In revenge Shakespeare wrote some lampoons about Lucy and when his authorship was discovered, so the story goes, he fled to London — and fame.

Charlecote was much altered and restored in the 19th Century but the interesting gate-house was left untouched and is still as Shakespeare knew it. The house is now approached by an avenue of limes set in open parkland where deer roam. The grounds were laid out by "Capability" Brown. Both house and grounds are now owned by the National Trust and open to the public at selected times.

Some of the farm buildings opposite the front gate have been made into a restaurant where waterfowl, budgerigars and other birds are housed in a walled garden.

Anne Hathaway's 15th Century thatched cottage at Shottery

Shakespeare's birthroom and relics

Shakespeare by Soest
the German painter

Shakespearian stars: Tom Fleming (left) and Sir Michael Redgrave

12 HIDCOTE MANOR GARDENS, near Chipping Campden, have been called the most beautiful of the 20th Century. The manor was bought by Lawrence Johnston, an American officer of English descent, and in 1907 he began his great work. Rarely can any man have chosen a more unsuitable site. The limestone soil limited his choice of plants and a fierce wind swept the Cotswold scarp and its little stream. He started with a Cedar of Lebanon, some fine beeches, a few barren fields and the stream. He began by creating broad terraces from the scarp. He then planted hedges, creating compartments, all linked by a central vista. These hedges were unorthodox.

Each compartment was given its own special quality, not only in lay-out but in the variety of different and usually exotic blooms and plants sown there. Lime-hating rhododendrons, camellias and magnolias have all been enticed to grow by being planted in beds of sawdust. The stream has been cunningly used to create lovely pools and a whole series of tinkling cascades. This, by any standards, is an achievement, transporting one into a magic world.

In Hidcote Manor, called the most beautiful garden created in the 20th Century

13 CHIPPING CAMPDEN is a typical old Cotswold town nestling among gentle rises. Little appears to have changed in centuries except that today, inevitably, it suffers from too many motor-cars. Perhaps the finest building in the town is the arched Jacobean market hall. The church has a fine 120 ft. 15th Century pinnacled tower.

The prominent window above the chancel arch depicting the Last Judgment is, in fact, a 19th Century addition, but has been so well done that it does not disturb the superb proportions. The church also contains a unique collection of English embroidery, some dating back to Richard II. A side chapel leased perpetually to the Noel family recalls a certain Sir Baptist Hicks who was linked by marriage with them. Sir Baptist, who later became 1st Viscount Campden, built a lovely hou called Campden House. A close friend Charles 1, Sir Baptist burned the pla down rather than allow it to fall into hands of the hated Roundheads. ruins can still be seen a short distance fr the church. Inside the church an orn medieval cope, preserved under glass the west wall, is worth looking at.

The Cotswold Games are held he

The pinnacled tower of the parish church at Chipping Campden (left) and the village seen through the arches of the Jacobean market hall

Cottages in one of England's loveliest villages, Broadway, and (right) the Beacon Tower, built as a folly outside the village

4 BROADWAY remains one of the best known and loveliest of English villages. Its honey-coloured stone buildings, perfectly set off amid green lawns, grassy verges and a profusion of flowers, have been drawing visitors for almost a century. Today, it has 13 antique shops and among local delicacies are its old English honey and chestnut cream.

The main street has been beautifully preserved, a harmonious line of "quaint" shops, embowered cottages and fine gabled houses. One of the best is Abbot's Grange, a 14th Century building that once belonged to the Abbots of Evesham. Additions were made in Elizabethan times but it retains its original chapel, abbot's study, hall and solar. The Broadway Hotel, oddly enough, is nearly all timber, only one wing being built of stone. The most impressive building in the village is the Lygon Arms, originally the local manor house. During the Civil War it housed Charles I and — although not at the same time — Cromwell. Another house, almost as beautiful and well worth studying, is the Tudor House. One of the prominent buildings in the main street is the fine old gabled house now called St. Patrick's Tea Rooms, almost opposite the Lygon Arms.

The Beacon Tower, sometimes called Fish Inn Tower, built by Lady Coventry as a folly, stands on the hill outside the village and on a clear day gives a magnificent view over several counties and it is possible to see Tewkesbury Abbey, Worcester Cathedral and Warwick Castle from it. Now National Trust property, it is open to the public.

Motorists may briefly see a badger's mask in their headlights. At dusk they may see only a grey ghost gliding away. The skylark's clear, liquid notes sound like a hymn to summer. It nests and hides in grass or scrub.

15 WINCHCOMBE: The run south from Broadway takes us along the Cotswold Edge overlooking what was once part of a great prehistoric sea covering the low lying valleys right up to Worcester. Half way down Winchcombe Hill is a track leading to St. Kenelm's Well. Above the church doorway is a seated figure of the saint and the date A.D. 819, the period when he lived. He was a Mercian prince, aged seven, murdered by his ambitious eldest sister, Quendrida. The historian William of Malmesbury records that a heavenly dove delivered news of this dreadful deed to the Pope who then reported it to the Saxon kings of the other regions which made up England at this time. In due course, "God's vengeance" was visited on Quendrida — her eyes were torn from their sockets! The body of the boy saint was found and carried back to Winchcombe. On the way the bearers stopped to rest and at the spot where they laid down the body a spring burst forth.

Near the river is a place called the Ducking Pool where local scolds were ducked for nagging.

The town itself was extremely important and prosperous in the early Middle Ages and was capital of its own shire.

Seated figure of St. Kenelm at Winchcombe

147

16 **SUDELEY CASTLE** lies in splendid grounds a mile from Winchcombe, a beautiful amalgam of ruins and fine rooms and apartments still used by the owners. The original manor house dates from Ethelred the Unready.

Much of it was built in the 15th Century by the first Baron Sudeley, an Admiral of the Fleet under Henry V and Henry VI. A supporter of the House of Lancaster, he lost Sudeley when the Yorkists came to power and the house passed into the hands of Richard III (Crookback). It remained Crown property until the accession of Henry VIII who visited the castle with Anne Boleyn in 1532. On Edward VI's accession, the castle was given to the Lord High Admiral of England, Sir Thomas Seymour, the boy-king's uncle, who married Katherine Parr, Henry VIII's last wife, within weeks of Henry's death.

She arrived at Sudeley with Lady Jane Grey, executed a year later for plotting to seize the throne. Special quarters were built for Katherine within the 12th Century tower. On August 30, 1548, she gave birth to a daughter, Mary, but died a few days later and was buried in the castle chapel.

The infant Mary was never heard of again. Her father was charged with treason by his brother a few months later and beheaded in the Tower. The child, it is believed, died in infancy.

The castle remained in the possession of the Barons Chandos for the next century and was thrice visited by Queen Elizabeth I.

During the Civil War, the 6th Baron was a staunch supporter of the King and Sudeley frequently came under Roundhead attack. On January 27, 1643, the castle surrendered and was sacked.

At the end of the Civil War, hoping to save his estates, Chandos defected to the Cromwellians. They ordered the castle "slighted", that is, rendered untenable as a military post. So Sudeley had its roof removed. Today, the once magnificent banqueting hall is a melancholy ruin, much as it looked at the end of 1649.

For two centuries the place was left to moulder but was finally rescued by two brothers, John and William Dent, successful glove makers who, under the direction of Sir Gilbert Scott, made it habitable again by 1840. Further restoration was carried out by Mrs. Emma Dent, daughter of a Cheshire MP called Brocklehurst, whose descendant, Mark Dent-Brocklehurst, is the present owner. She devoted her life to the castle, seeking to restore in it the spirit of its first owners.

Today it stands as the epitome of a Cotswold castle, with mellowed walls, smooth lawns and cooing doves. Among its treasures are paintings by Rubens, Van Dyck and Turner; a Holbein portrait of Jane Seymour; a portrait of Thomas Seymour; portraits of Mary and Elizabeth Tudor as young princesses; of Anne of Cleves, Henry VIII's fourth wife; and Katherine Parr. There are also some religious books written by Katherine, one bearing an inscription by Henry; a letter written by her accepting Seymour's offer of marriage; and a lock of her hair. One can also see Elizabeth I's christening robe, Charles I's waistcoat and the tapestry bed-hangings of the tragic French Queen, Marie Antoinette, who was executed during the Revolution.

Queen Katherine's garden is famous for its 15 ft. double yew hedges with terraces of clipped trees, herbaceous borders, and rose garden. Nearby are the enchanting ruins of a medieval tithe barn. A lily pond on the site of the ancient moat contains a collection of exotic wildfowl and there is an ornamental pheasantry with rare and beautiful birds, and free-flying budgerigars.

A splendid entertainment is a son-et lumiere bringing to life the exciting history of Sudeley and including a masque given for Elizabeth on her third visit to the castle.

17 **BELAS KNAP:** Just outsid[e] Winchcombe on the A46 [to] Cheltenham a left fork leads to th[e] chambered barrow. Drive up a windin[g] road to a small lay-by. Do the rest of th[e] journey on foot up a further rise, the[n] across two fields to the barrow. In 186[3] when this was excavated 38 skeleto[ns] were found. It is believed they were burie[d] about 1400 B.C.

Relics taken from the barrow are no[w] kept in the church museum in Winchcomb[e].

Chambered barrow excavated in 1863

18 **CLEEVE CLOUD:** Also ne[ar] Winchcombe, but this time lyi[ng] to the right of the Cheltenham road. [An] Iron Age fort built on a Cotswold promo[n]tory, in a picturesque setting above t[he] vale of Severn, it is scarcely more than t[wo] acres in extent. The steep slopes in fro[nt] were considered sufficient protection, [so] there are no discernible earthworks.

The view from Cleeve Hill is one of t[he] finest panoramas in England, consisting [of] the great western spur of the Cotswol[ds]. Right and left are other dramatic spurs. [In] front the land dips sharply to the wid[e] flowing Severn. On the far side lie meado[ws] and orchards, and in the distance t[he] gentle eminences of the Malvern Hills.

Sudeley Castle, home of Katherine Parr, last wife of King Henry VIII

The magnificent view from Cleeve Hill

The Neptune fountain in glorious Cheltenham

19 CHELTENHAM, set on a sheltered ridge between the rise of the Cotswolds and the Vale of Severn, owes its prosperity to its local pigeons which, in 1715, revealed the presence of mineral waters with curative powers. So grateful were the townspeople that they incorporated a pigeon in the town crest.

Today, although its elegance is fading, Cheltenham remains one of the most glorious of English towns.

By 1738 it had been discovered that Cheltenham's waters were beneficial to army officers and administrators who were able to contract liver complaints while serving in outposts of the Empire. The town authorities, conscious that only people of taste, with ample funds to spend in their retirement, were being attracted to the spa, set out to provide a town worthy of them. In the first 40 years of the 19th century they rebuilt Cheltenham into a place of wide streets and tree-lined open spaces bordered by glorious buildings mainly in the classical Grecian style. Squares, crescents, avenues were beauti-fully set out. The architect Papworth was responsible for some of the happiest scenes, including the Rotunda (based on the Pantheon) and Montpellier Walk with its classical caryatids. The climax of all this glorious energy was the Promenade, one of the finest streets in England, which was completed in 1825, the same year that Forbes completed the Pittville Pump Room set in parkland.

Although Cheltenham has attracted industry in recent years, its heart remains unsullied. Today it is more of a festival town than anything else. Every October it holds a Literary Festival, attended by leading writers. In July it stages a Music Festival, one of the most important in the British Isles. Although principally intended to provide a platform for modern British composers, there are also performances of classical music, folk-music, jazz and "pop".

The racecourse is at Prestbury Park just to the north of the town and is the scene of one of the most notable events in the English racing calendar — the Cheltenham Gold Cup.

20 LECKHAMPTON HILL, lying south of Cheltenham, is one of the most dramatic places in Gloucestershire. It is the site of one of the finest of the Cotswold Iron Age promontory forts and well worth visiting.

Nearby is a slender, peculiarly shaped limestone rock, 50 ft. high, known as the Devil's Chimney. According to local superstition it rises straight from Hell. Its slim, dramatic shape, in fact, is not a natural feature — but the result of centuries of quarrying around it.

Devil's Chimney — 'rises from Hell'

21 TEWKESBURY, a gracious old town with many fine timbered houses and good coaching inns, is beautifully sited at the confluence of the Severn and Avon rivers.

Some of the timbers of the Bell Inn are 13th Century, and the dining room has wall paintings done by the Benedictine monks of that period. The Royal Hop Pole Inn has stood on its present site since the 14th Century. The Tudor House was built in 1540 and there is a priest's hole beside the fireplace in what is now a coffee room. The Black Bear, which claims to date from 1308, is a half-timbered building in the High Street near King John's Bridge, and contains pieces of the bridge that stood here in 1200.

Tewkesbury Abbey, one of the largest abbey churches to survive the Dissolution, dates from the early 12th Century and was originally part of a Benedictine monastery which replaced an older monastery dating from 715. The townspeople redeemed it from Henry VIII for £400. The magnificent 132ft. tower mostly dates from 1150; and from its top one enjoys a panorama over the valleys of the Severn and Avon to the Malvern Hills and, on a clear day, to the Welsh mountains. There is a number of fine tombs in the church, and the glorious Warwick Chantry, endowed by the family of Warwick the Kingmaker. In a side chapel is a Raphael painting which once hung in Versailles. The abbey has no fewer than three organs. One, called the Milton Organ, was played by John Milton, the poet, while he was secretary to Cromwell.

Bloody Meadow, near the Abbey, was the scene of one of the bloodiest battles of the Wars of the Roses on May 4, 1471. The Lancastrian army, under the Duke of Somerset, took up positions on Lincoln Green, Gunhill Manor and the site now known as Queen Margaret's Camp. Edward IV led the Yorkists to victory.

The interior of Tewkesbury Abbey

22 MYTHE is the junction of the Severn and Avon — the name Mythe is derived from the Old English *gemythe*, meaning "waters meet". Just about here, the river flows under a bridge built by that remarkable man Thomas Telford.

Telford, born in Dumfriesshire in 1757, the son of a shepherd, was one of that rare body of souls who helped to create Scotland's Golden Age of the intellect, invention and industry that so astonishingly burst forth in a hitherto poor and slothful nation (or so the English considered it) towards the end of the 18th Century — an age which was to produce such great names as Rabbie Burns, David Hume, Adam Smith (who published his *Wealth of Nations* in 1776), James Boswell, biographer of Dr Johnson, explorers such as Mungo Park in Africa and Alexander Mackenzie in north-west Canada.

Telford, like many men of creative genius, lacked formal education. Between 1801 and 1823, he built Scotland's great Caledonian Canal as well as 1,000 miles of road and 1,200 bridges. He was in his 70th year when he built Mythe Bridge. He was an avid reader of poetry and always carried a book of poems. He built several other Severn bridges. He died aged 77 and is buried in Westminster Abbey.

A feature of the river here is an unpredictable tide known locally as "a quarry", said to be an unnerving experience for any oarsman caught in it.

The red sandstone banks along the river are famous for their growths of *isatoris tinctoria*, better known as woad.

The 14th Century tithe barn at Bredon

Mythe, where Severn and Avon meet

One of Thomas Telford's famous bridges

23 BREDON: Drive now through the rich, lush pastures of the lower Avon towards the great apple and plum orchard country of Worcestershire and into what the poet A. E. Housman has called "the coloured counties". Bredon village on the Avon lies in the centre of cider country; it is made up of weathered old timber houses and cottages and has a fine National Trust property, a 14th Century tithe barn 132 ft. long, with five porches, over one of which is an unusual stone cowling. Other buildings worth stopping for are the 17th Century Reed Almshouses and the church. Here there are some fine 14th Century stained glass and unusual medieval heraldic tiles on the altar steps. There is also an Early English chapel.

The Avon winds and meanders lazily around the great landmark of Bredon Hill, at 961 ft. taking on the stature almost of a mountain in this gentle countryside. The view from Bredon Hill, about which Housman wrote:

> Here of a Sunday morning
> My love and I would lie
> And see the coloured counties
> And hear the larks so high
> About us in the sky

takes in no fewer than eight of the coloured counties on a clear day, although some claim they can count 14.

Apart from its associations with the poet and the knowledge that we are in landscape dear to the heart of Sir Edward Elgar, we are also made aware how ancient is the history that lies on this eminence. On top stands one of the great landmarks of south Worcestershire, an impressive Iron Age encampment whose inner ramparts alo[ne] enclose 11 acres. This seems to have bee[n] built or reinforced to hold off the Roma[n] occupation of this region. The bodies of [50] British victims, brutally hacked to piece[s]

Bredon Hill overlooks eight counties

have been excavated from the spot whe[re] they fell in a last desperate stand after t[he] fort's entrance had been breached. Rath[er] incongruously, an 18th Century fol[ly] called Parson's Folly, sits in the middle. T[his] raises Bredon Hill to exactly 1,000 ft.

Elmley Castle lies at the foot of Bred[on] Hill. It is a modest and out of the way lit[tle] village with a street of attractive ha[lf] timbered cottages. The castle itself h[as] long since disappeared. But the park h[as] some fallow deer and the local chur[ch] some fine medieval sculpture.

24 PERSHORE: "A land rich in corn, productive of fruit in some parts by the sole favour of nature, in others by the art of cultivation, enticing even the lazy to industry by the prospect of a hundredfold return," wrote William of Malmesbury, the 13th Century chronicler, describing the rich country around Pershore, capital of the plum.

By the end of the Middle Ages most of Worcestershire had become the greatest stronghold of monasticism in England and this area was one of the last to surrender the Roman Catholic faith at the time of the Reformation; indeed, the Gunpowder Plot was hatched not all that far away.

The town itself began with St. Oswald's religious foundation here in 689. Later, after the Conquest, the Benedictines built one of the largest of all English abbeys; much bigger, apparently, than Worcester Cathedral. Clearly its destruction at the time of the Dissolution must rank as a major disaster. As at Tewkesbury, however, the locals managed to preserve the last remnants by buying them themselves and these are now incorporated in the parish church. The magnificent lantern tower was built in 1350.

Today the town looks pleasant and prosperous, with mainly Georgian buildings. Worth looking at is the Three Tuns Inn, which has an elaborately worked iron veranda; an old house at the end of Broad Street which has finely proportioned bay windows; and the Angel Hotel which has a 16th Century inlaid overmantel. Pershore is approached from the east by a six-arched medieval bridge over the Avon. The central larger arch is restoration work following considerable damage done during the Civil War.

A good place for messing about in boats

25 UPTON-ON-SEVERN: We have now left the glorious Cotswolds countryside well behind us. Once all this land in the lee of the Malverns was the floor of a great sea.

Upton itself is a mixture of old beauty and modern ugliness. Its 14th Century church tower stands conspicuously above the river with an extraordinary white cupola on its top. The original steeple was pulled down in 1745 by the villagers using horses hauling on ropes.

There are several good inns, the most famous being The White Lion, mentioned in Henry Fielding's *Tom Jones*. Upton is now a holiday centre for people exploring the river in cabin cruisers.

John Dee, a rector who dabbled in alchemy and astrology, was imprisoned in 1554 for casting a horoscope of the King and Queen and the Princess Elizabeth. He proposed a Royal Navy — his suggestion being a fleet of "Sixty ships — a little Navy Royall".

SUMMER RAIN LOVER
Presence of the little fern Maidenhair Spleenwort indicates plenty of summer rain. It forms rosettes of two or three inch fronds, each made up of a double row of circular leaflets on a thin, black, wiry stalk which gives the plant its name.

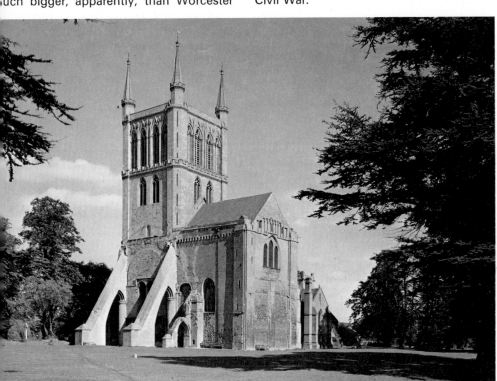

Pershore Abbey (top picture) and the font (below left) and interior

151

26 MALVERN: The area includes Great Malvern, Malvern Link, North Malvern, Malvern Wells and Little Malvern and occupies the site of an ancient Royal Forest called Malvern Chase (Malvern itself is derived from a Celtic word meaning "bare hill".)

Great Malvern, the "capital", is a beautifully-sited town, clinging to the Worcestershire slopes of the hills and rising, in a style reminiscent of Portofino or Amalfi from 350 ft. to 850 ft. It has an air about it and the overall effect is delightful. The road leading up to the hills has easily climbed footpaths.

The practice of hydropathy was begun at Malvern towards the end of the 18th Century and many famous people, among them Queen Victoria and Lord Tennyson, have taken the waters here.

The Foley Arms dates from the earliest period of the town's history as a spa and has splendid iron verandas and original furnishing.

The great glory of the town, however, is its massive Norman Priory Church of Saints Mary and Michael, dating from just after the Norman Conquest, although largely reconstructed in the 15th Century. The church tiles are famous, having been all hand-made in the monastery — over 1,000 being used in the decoration, centring on 100 different designs. From the 15th Century too, date the 40 vast windows containing stained glass rivalling that at York Minster. In nearby Priory Park, which has fine trees and ornamental flowerbeds, is a pool once used by the Benedictine monks, a pool full, then as now, of huge golden carp.

Little Malvern, set against a background of hills, possesses the lovely little church of St. Giles, all that remains of an immense priory dating from 1171. Nearby is Little Malvern Court, which incorporates part of the 12th Century edifice. Mass has been said there for 800 years. It contains a priest's hiding hole.

SIR EDWARD ELGAR

One of the greatest musicians Englar has produced lies in the churchyard of S Wulfstan's, Malvern. Elgar's spirit w always be associated with the Malve Hills. Born in a Worcester cottage, son a local church organist, Elgar taug himself the violin. In time he went London where he existed on "two bags nuts a day" and eked out a livelihood teaching the violin. He married one of h pupils, Caroline, daughter of Sir Hen Gee Roberts — and the bride's paren disowned them. Their life together becam the story of a great love. It was for Caroli that he composed the music which wo him fame and honour. His great mar *Pomp and Circumstance* has almo achieved the status of a National Anthei He received the Order of Merit, becan Master of the King's Musick and Baronet. But with his wife's death i spiration withered. They are buried togeth in the lee of his hills.

Looking towards Malvern from the Cotswolds and (right) Malvern Priory

Sir Edward Elgar

27 WORCESTER BEACON rises to 1,395 ft. and from it can be seen 15 counties — extending, it is claimed, to the borders of Exmoor. North Hill, at 1,326 ft. stands to the north of Worcester Beacon and can be reached by the Ivy Scar rock. Most of the Hills are now National Trust property — one such stretch, comprising 1,287 acres, runs from Little Malvern to Chase End Hill and includes most of the ridge of land and the 1,370 ft. Herefordshire Beacon. On this Beacon stands British Camp, probably the most famous example of a hill fortress in Britain, so large that it is said to have held 20,000 men. It has been claimed that this was where the great Celtic chieftain, Caractacus, was captured by the Romans before being taken to Rome in chains.

It was here that William Langland is said to have composed *The Vision of Piers Plowman* one of the earliest English poems.

Summit of Worcester Beacon, nearly 1,400 ft

Church Lane, Ledbury, lined with Tudor and Jacobean timbered houses

28 **LEDBURY** is one of the prettiest of English market towns and has strong literary associations. Besides being the birthplace of John Masefield, it was the favourite resort of the Brownings and Wordsworth — indeed, Elizabeth Barrett was brought up at nearby Hope End. Her father, the domestic tyrant, Mr. Barrett of Wimpole Street, is buried in the local church.

Almost equidistant from Gloucester, Worcester and Hereford, it is a fine strategic point from which to explore the glorious English countryside. Ledbury itself has a delightful market house, timbered in herringbone pattern and standing on 16 wood columns, dominating the market place. St. Katherine's Hospital opposite dates from the 14th Century, although most of it was rebuilt by Sir Robert Smirke in the 19th Century. There are fine inns such as the Feathers and the Talbot. One of the most picturesque parts of the town is Church Lane, which is cobbled and lined with lovely Tudor and Jacobean timbered houses. The finest house in town, however, is Ledbury Park, built by Lord Biddulph in 1590.

Ledbury church is considered pre-eminent among all Herefordshire's churches. The interior contains many interesting monuments. One of the most fascinating is the Skynner tomb, which shows five sons and five daughters kneeling beside their beruffed parents.

29 **EASTNOR CASTLE,** two miles east of Ledbury, is a startling spectacle of towers and battlements. It dates from only 1812 and the architect was Sir Robert Smirke, who designed the British Museum and the Covent Garden Theatre. The stones were carried by mules from the Forest of Dean.

The great hall is most impressive, being 60 ft. long and 55 ft. high. It is decorated with standing suits of armour, three-quarter suits hanging on the walls and an enormous collection of arms — swords, maces, shields, daggers, pistols — covering several centuries in Europe as well as items from India, Persia and Africa. The inner hall contains fine armour, looted from the Elector of Bohemia by Napoleon. The dining room has paintings by Van Dyck, Lely and Kneller.

The Gothic Drawing Room was designed by Pugin (the architect responsible for the interior of the Houses of Parliament) and is a flamboyant re-creation of the romantic dream with elaborate fan tracery as well as gilding and heraldry. There are also Gobelin tapestries and an Aubusson carpet. Other rooms open to the public include the Octagon Saloon, the Long Library and the State Bedroom.

From the house there is an impressive view of the Malvern Hills, particularly the area around British Camp.

spectacle of towers and battlements

Hellens House in Much Marcle

30 **MUCH MARCLE** is a pretty village, with substantial black and white timbered farmhouses in the area, lying just off the road to Ross-on-Wye. One of the most remarkable houses here is called Hellens — after the family of Helions who once owned it. The house is a typical Jacobean red-brick house with a picturesque courtyard, built on much earlier foundations. The original house dates from the 13th Century and the Black Prince once stayed here — he was a close friend of the owner, James Audley, who fought with him at the Battle of Poitiers. A table in the dining room is called the Black Prince's table, but the present tenants doubt its authenticity.

153

31 **ROSS-ON-WYE** is a town of steep streets, with fine Georgian houses, sitting prettily on a wide sweep of the river and within sight of the Welsh mountains. It is the main touring centre for the beautiful Wye Valley. Much of the town's charm is due to the philanthropy of John Kyrle, the "Man of Ross", who inspired The Prospect, a fine walled public garden giving magnificent views of the river. He created the glorious avenue of elms in the churchyard; the raised causeway carrying the Wilton Road above flood level; he also restored the church spire and installed the fine tenor bell in the tower, and gave the town its first water supply. A monument to him is the country walk known as "John Kyrle's Walk". This is a $3\frac{1}{2}$ mile amble which includes a fine view of the countryside from Chase Hill. On top of Chase Hill itself is an Iron Age camp, reached by an Iron Age road. Just south of the town and helping to create another lovely walk are Penyard Woods, near the site of the Roman settlement of Ariconium, once an important forge.

Ross-on-Wye, sitting prettily on a wide sweep of the river

32 **GOODRICH** stands on a high spur of land on the right bank of the Wye, commanding an old crossing of the river. Probably this was the route followed by the Roman road from Gloucester to Caerleon. The Castle is first mentioned in a document of 1101 and was then called Godric's Castle — probably named for Godric Mappestone mentioned in Domesday. It became Crown property in the 17th Century before being given to the Earl of Pembroke who made his fortune by his skill in winning prize money in medieval tournaments. For many years, the Castle was the seat of the Talbot family, who were created Earls of Shewsbury.

The oldest part of the castle is the square

Norman keep on the south side which dates from the mid 12th Century. A square enclosing wall with angle towers, gatehouse and the buildings of the inner yard all date from the extensive reconstruction carried out at the end of the 13th Century.

The gatehouse has an enormous semi-circular tower which once housed a chapel; it is vaulted and had a portcullis. In the west range are the remains of the great hall which is 65ft. long. In the west wall one can still see a fireplace with its corbelled hood.

The local parish church has associations with Dean Swift — his grandfather, Thomas, was Vicar here. The Dean himself recovered a silver chalice belonging to the church which had been looted by the Roundheads and Swift gave it back to the church in 1726.

Goodrich and its castle also recall Wordsworth's poem *We Are Seven*. The poet loved this place and it was here he met the little girl who provided the inspiration for the poem.

The Wye, from Symonds Yat

33 **SYMONDS YAT** ("yat" mea "gate"): The Wye flows throu a narrow gorge when it takes a gre five-mile loop around Huntsham H before settling back only a quarter of a m away from its original course. The Yat, 475 ft. crag jutting out from steep a magnificently wooded slopes, provic one of the most dramatic and beauti river views in Britain. As one walks bene leafy boughs, it is difficult to recall tha was the scene of bloody battles in Sax and Norman times when the native Brito fought to stem the encroaching tide armed immigrants.

A scenic route, some 30 miles lo starts from the Yat. This goes through Forest of Dean, that beautiful sylv primeval area which has played such important part in English history. Forme one of William the Conqueror's hunti preserves, it is now a wild, lovely tract woodland, 20,000 acres in extent a remarkable for its thousands of holly tre

The village of Symonds Yat is divic into East and West, separated by smooth-flowing Wye.

At King Arthur's Cave in the Dow Hills, some three miles downstream, re have been found of cave dwellers w lived there 20,000 years ago.

Goodrich Castle from the gatehouse

A general view of the castle

34 MONMOUTH: According to the locals, you are not in Monmouthshire, but in Gwent — which is Welsh for a cantred or portion of Morganwg and Wentllwg. The town has fine Tudor and Georgian houses and many narrow quaint old streets.

In a niche in the Shire Hall stands a statue of Henry V, the victor of Agincourt, who was born at the 11th Century castle nearby, now a ruin.

Two rivers, the Monnow and the Trothy, flow into the Wye at Monmouth. One of the town's main attractions is the Norman fortified gatehouse on the Monnow bridge, the only one in Britain.

A fine view of the magnificent countryside awaits those who climb the 800 ft. Kymin Hill, east of the town.

The Norman gatehouse on Monnow bridge

35 TINTERN ABBEY: This beautiful shell looks so delicate that it seems a breath of wind might bring it down, giving the impression of stone lace-work miraculously upheld by paper-thin walls.

The Abbey was founded in 1131 by Cistercian monks from France. This order had embraced the principles of a stricter and simpler life which had sprung from the ideas of St. Benedict in the 11th Century and seeking greater seclusion, simplicity and manual labour, they settled here, in what must have seemed a wild and remote place, on land given them by Walter FitzRichard, Lord of Chepstow.

Little is left of the original abbey; what now stands dates almost entirely from the 13th Century when the abbey was rebuilt under the patronage of Roger Bigod, Earl of Norfolk, to whom we owe the great nave. The Abbey was at its zenith in the 14th Century and once provided refuge for Edward II. It was suppressed in 1536 by Henry VIII. Far from being a wealthy monastery, battening on the poor people, the abbey's income at the time of the dissolution was a mere £192 per year.

shell of Tintern Abbey in the Wye valley

36 CHEPSTOW ("chep" means "market" or "merchant" as in Cheapside), dominated by its great grey castle, is remarkable for its twisting, narrow, hilly main street which has to squeeze itself through the Town Gate like a tube of toothpaste.

Chepstow Castle is an immense and impressive place. It was founded by William Fitz-Osborn, who fought at Hastings, and was considerably strengthened by the De Clare family into whose hands it passed in the 12th Century. Although built primarily as a marcher

Chepstow Castle, peaceful at last

Rennie's iron bridge at Chepstow

castle, its most stirring days occurred during the Civil War, when under Sir Nicholas Kemeys it held out in a memorable siege until the Cromwellians finally broke in and massacred the garrison.

The castle has four great courtyards, the first and largest containing the state apartments, kitchens and domestic quarters. The garrison was always able to gain access to the river, from which it was supplied during sieges, by way of a deep cellar. Beyond the second courtyard lies the Great Tower, which was the castle keep.

Worth looking at are the Town Gate, dating from the 16th Century, the bow-windowed houses in Bridge Street, and the 18th Century almshouses; the well-preserved town walls and John Rennie's bridge over the Wye — one of the earliest iron bridges in England.

The Welsh Borders – through Marcher country

MAX CAULFIELD

Stretching from the rich red loam pastures of the Herefordshire cider country, studded with cosy, half-timbered cottages, Jacobean manor houses and lazy, cherry-coloured cattle, to the majestic volcanic upheaval of Cader Idris ('the chair of Idris'), most romantic of all Welsh mountains, lies some of the most astonishingly vivid and legendary landscape in Britain.

Here is an incomparable kaleidoscope of stark mountain grandeur; hushed-lovely river estuaries where even the sands yield gold and precious metals; wildly beautiful moorlands amidst which buzzards, black grouse, kestrels and ring ouzels fly and the almost extinct red kite occasionally shows itself; great forests of oak and conifer resting like fleecy green eiderdowns upon the cragged hills, shading rare Arctic plants and flowers and luxuriant mosses and lichens; rushing, tumbling cataracts carving astonishing bowls out of solid rock; and defiant Celtic forts or broken medieval castles speaking of a violent and bloody history.

A COUNTRYSIDE TO ENVY

Eastwards it is rich English agricultural land, probably unsurpassed anywhere in Europe; a countryside of soft fruits, tossing corn, apple-heavy orchards and sweet meadow where yeomen farmers and country squires live in comfortable homes, gazing out at soft-grey dovecotes or Norman churches, interiors rich with carved tombs, and counting their famous breed of Hereford cattle, raised on the wooded slopes to the west. Other Englishmen have long been envious of these chaps who speak the South Saxon dialect – an accent pleasantly free of northern awkwardness or southern stridency and characterised by an underlying lilt of Welsh – for they boast here of their six Ws, water, wool, wood, wheat, wine and women. A. E. Housman, the poet of these coloured counties, has described Shropshire as "the country for easy livers" – a lush land where men happily ignore the rat race and in their lazy old market towns and nurtured countryside often reach astonishing age. Old Parr, who lived from 1483 till 1635, was a Shropshire lad – and it is believed locally that, if Charles I had not insisted on bringing him to London and there fêting him uproariously, the odds are that he would be living yet.

It is bold marcher country, of course, and real blood has often stained these lands an even redder hue than its red sandstone rocks. At Chapel Lawn, high on a strategic hillside, looms one of the most melancholy Celtic forts in all Britain – an enormous spread of earthworks which many authorities hold to be the proper site of Caractacus's stand against the Romans. Here in these now-somnolent counties, too, the Saxon tide was at last held firm by Britons fighting with their backs to that mountain wall known to the Romans as Britannia Secundus. Dane and Norseman followed, looting, burning and raping – and all the time the British kept raiding down from their mountain strongholds and leaping Offa's Dyke (built by a forgotten King of Mercia to keep them out) plundered and burned Saxon settlements and later, the prosperous Normanised villages.

> The mountain sheep are sweeter,
> But the valley sheep are fatter;
> We therefore deem it meeter
> To carry off the latter

sang the Welsh and several times they sent towns like Leominster up in flames while they carried off their booty.

As one turns west, geological time grows older. Great domes of mountain, formed out of arid volcanic heat, rise. Their actual bu[...] and line were first formed by crinkling when earth movemen[...] pressed molten lava up against the hardest and oldest rocks [...] earth, the pre-Cambrian rocks around Anglesey; then glaciers a[...] erosion finally moulded them to their present fantastic shap[...] There is little need to hear Welsh spoken or read the "foreig[...] road signs to realise that this is a different country. It is an u[...] English area of great fold upon mountainy fold, towering, aw[...] some chunks of land where only sheep or mad mountaineers mig[...] walk. The Welsh themselves huddle in their lovely breathtaki[...] valleys where cascades tumble down riotously and gurgling wa[...] runs sweetly. History bears a different aspect here. It seems [...] reach back farther and yet be still relevant; it concerns a co[...] tinuing struggle for survival, independence, separate identi[...] Myths, legends, tales, stories, history thus roll themselves int[...] mystical Welsh entertainment. One stops to read an old tale [...] the *Black Book of Carmarthen* or a version of the Celtic epic [...] *Mabinogion*, both first cast in medieval scriptoria by the wh[...] Cistercian monks who have left soft memories on this land.

The hills, however, still reverberate to the shouts of last galla[...] desperate stands – at the foot of Cader Idris, Welshmen under [...] first (and last) native Prince of Wales lost their independen[...] then rebel Owain Glyndwyr (Shakespeare's Owen Glendow[...] raised a fire that has never been properly put out. We are l[...] among witches' pools, fairy lakes, drowned cities of marble, gia[...] who sit like Father Zeus atop staggering mountains and little gr[...] men, lurking in dark lakes, who cast spells on climbers. We are [...] lovely Wales. A land where men still, as they do along [...] Maddawch estuary, dig for gold.

A TOWN OF COSY COMFORT

Leominster grew rich on wool in the Middle Ages; the coun[...] around supporting a species of Ryeland sheep, first bred by [...] local monks, whose wool proved so valuable that it became kno[...] as "Lemster ore". Cross-breeding, alas, has all but wiped out [...] breed, although a few sheep can still be seen – hornless, wi[...] backed, with woolly forelocks. The town, whose chief export [...] is its famed Hereford cattle, sits in cosy comfort on three tr[...] waters, a straggle of half-timbered houses, some with overhang[...] 15th Century gables, interlarded with Georgian or mellow[...] Victorian Italianate buildings, stout inns and narrow streets. I[...] full of curiosities, such as a ducking stool in the Priory used[...] deter nagging women. The nagging, it seems, stopped abruptl[...] 1809 – anyway, the stool has not been used since.

Between here and Ludlow lies a land of wooded beauty, [...] veloping such stately homes as Croft Castle or Berrington Hal[...] such minor marvels as Eye Manor. Ludlow is an antique gem[...] enormous border castle; a church massive as a small cathedral [...] a jumble of ancient buildings, which together make up a to[...] boasting itself "superior to that of any inland town in the countr[...] A few miles past Ludlow is what is possibly the most roma[...] fortified manor-house in England, lovely Stokesay Castle.

Running west, we find the character of countryside alm[...] imperceptibly changing. The hills grow higher, denser and [...] road sign says "Welcome to Wales". The road to Newtow[...] either bleak or majestically lovely depending on one's pers[...] reaction to wilderness. This is untamed countryside. Ye[...] provides an exhilaration of the spirit only too rare for those [...]

At its foot, a shining beauty of a still lake, Tal-y-llyn. At Tywyn one reaches the coast; not the most enchanted part of the Welsh littoral – not, at least, until one comes to Aberdovey. Then great spreading sea-strands, golden and lovely, bend into the estuary of the Dovey – the second of those enchanted river mouths that rival the best there is.

Machynlleth is the noblest of Welsh towns. Glendower made it the capital of Wales and called a Parliament here in 1404 at which he was declared monarch. His Parliament House, on Maen Gwyn Street, is now called the Owen Glendower Institute and houses an arts centre. Although from the 17th to the 19th Century Cardiganshire was famous for its lead, zinc, and silver mines and its seafaring and woollen industries, it is now predominantly a grassland country and its main source of income is derived from milk and livestock products. It is a lovely, spacious, rolling county, softer in its contours than the stark volcanic rocks further north. Aberystwyth is reached along a lovely road, off which shoot such happy inland glens as Artists Valley or quiet seaside towns like Borth. The crescent-shaped front is all that a Victorian watering place might be expected to be, brought to a stop at its southern extremity by a great Norman castle. The hill fort of Pen Dinas, perched 400ft. above the town, is the best in the county, but the town's glory is its university. In the National Library nearby are some of Britain's most precious manuscripts – the *Book of Taliesin* and the *White Book of Rhydderch* and the *Bangor Missal*, the latter beautifully illuminated after the Irish fashion.

On the road to Devil's Bridge lies Nanteos house, a rare and disturbing example of a Welsh Georgian country house which has no fewer than five ghosts and a cache of lost treasure in its grounds. The waterfall at Devil's Bridge is deservedly one of the sights of Wales, tumbling some 500ft. through a rocky chasm and under three separate bridges, one on top of the other, the lowest dating from the 12th Century.

Left of the road to Llangurig lie the glorious humps of the Plynlimmon range, their sides scarred with the courses of falling water. Two great English rivers have their birthplace in these Welsh hills – the Wye and the Severn. Llangurig is quiet and undistinguished except for the fact that here the Wye finally becomes a river instead of a stream. From here to Rhayader, we are circling around the vast open moorland region of Cardiganshire known as the Great Desert – a wild and almost virtually uninhabited country. The rare nesting birds of these moors are peregrine, merlin, teal, golden plover, dunlin and short-eared owl while there are several fine moths such as emperor, fox, northern eggar, drinker, ruby tiger and wood tiger.

Rhayader has the tang of a Wild West town, lost as it is amid this great wilderness. It is a good centre for walkers, geologists, botanists. Three miles west begins the great Elan Valley dam system, where the marvel lies not only in the sheer technology of the achievement, but in the way the water has been cunningly used to enhance the splendour of wild scenery. By way of Cross Gates to journey's end at Llandrindod Wells, the finest of Welsh spa towns. Few now come to take the waters but treatment can still be had in the Rock Park for those who wish it. The town is well-stocked with good hotels and is a strategic touring centre with the lure of trout, salmon and other fresh-water fish in the nearby River Ithon.

e harbour at Aberayron, on the Cardiganshire coast

k themselves up in towns or cities. Wales is dramatic scenery – untain, valley, river and waterfall – rather than the quiet ries of England which usually resolve themselves into sweet t pastures and architectural wonders. By way of oddly-named aylittle, across a moorland road, to Cemaes Road we reach allwyd and the beginnings of Snowdonia National Park. One usts now to mountains folds never much less than 2,000ft. and en rising to near-3,000ft.; to scenic wonder piling on scenic nder.

Dolgellau sits at the head of the Mawddach estuary amid fabled untryside. It is the county town of Merionethshire (named for eirion, the son of a British chief called Cunedda who, after pelling the Irish from North Wales in the 6th Century, founded present Welsh nation). A picturesque, brooding town, built of local dark slate, it is hemmed in by mountains and gorges ept to the west, where the land opens out into what is possibly most glorious sea estuary in Europe. Dolgellau is a hospitable vn, and incurably Welsh, still remembering that Glendower d a native Welsh Parliament here. People come to walk on ecipitous hillsides, pony-trek, fish or study the rare plants, sses and ferns that shelter in the lovely glens, running down m the Forest of the King.

From here to Tywyn, this is Wales at its wildest and most utiful. A great pass brings one down towards sea level with that st beautiful mountain, Cader Idris, lost in cloud, to the right.

18 MAWDDACH

17 DOLGELLAU

BARMOUTH BAY

19 CADER IDRIS
2927

DINAS MAWDDWY 16

20 TAL-Y-LLYN

DOVEY FOREST

15 MALLWYD

DYSYNNI 21

14 CEMAES

TYWYN 22

RIVER DOVEY

24 MACHYNLLETH

23 ABERDOVEY

LLANWNO

FAN HILL
1580

25 ELLENNITH

32 PLYNLIMON FAWR
2468

13 LLANIDL

PONTERWYD 31

26 ABERYSTWYTH
27 NATIONAL LIBRARY

33 LLANGURIG

NANTEOS HOUSE 28

BRYN GARW
2005

RIVER WYE

DEVIL'S BRIDGE 29

34 RHAYA

30 TEIFI POOLS

LLYN GWYN

ELAN VALLEY 35

RIVER SEVERN

11 NEWTOWN

10 KERRY

9 CLUN

HOPTON CASTLE 8

STOKESAY CASTLE 7

6 LUDLOW

BEACON HILL
1796

RICHARD'S CASTLE 5

4 CROFT CASTLE

EYE MANOR 3

BERRINGTON HALL 2

LEOMINSTER

37 LLANDRINDOD WELLS

Ben Manchip

...tions: Elsie Wrigley/Richard Hook   Plant Notes: Geoffrey Gilbert   Animals & Birds: Jeremy Johns

1 **LEOMINSTER** (pronounced Lemster) is thick with early English domestic architecture — No 29, Bridge Street, for example, dates from 1400. The narrow High Street and the even narrower Drapers Row have picturesque medieval and Tudor houses. One of the loveliest timber-framed buildings in all Herefordshire is Grange Court, a Jacobean masterpiece which served as town hall until mid-Victorian times. Until it was moved in 1855 to its present site near the ancient priory church, its ground floor, with colonnade of oaken Ionic columns, was used as the local butter market. The ground floor, alas, was filled in with masonry when re-erected, but the rest has been beautifully preserved. Worth noting are the unusual carvings of male and female busts on the upper windows.

Leominster, once one of England's greatest woollen markets, is today a tranquil country town, exporting Hereford

Leominster's pride — the Priory Church

cattle all over the world and providing anglers with good trout fishing in either the Lugg, the Pinsley or the Arrow, the three streams which water it. It seems to have been always a centre for fine architecture — the landlord of the Royal Oak Hotel, for example, is only too delighted to show you his unique minstrel gallery which flushes to the wall when not required or pulls out for a ball. The town's great pride, however, is its red stone Priory Church, beautifully positioned on open green swards. Originally a Saxon foundation — its donor was Lady Godiva's husband, Earl Leofric — the present priory was built by the Benedictines and has some notable features. The north aisle, for example, has been so designed as to give an impression of height unequalled in any other Norman church in England. The earliest remaining part of the present church has no fewer than three naves. A beautifully-traceried 15th Century west window ennobles the central nave while the 14th Century aisle is remarkable for Decorated windows. Among the other treasures of the church is a 15th Century chalice, one of the finest left in England. And, of course, the ducking stool.

The area south and west of Leominster is lush stock-rearing countryside, studded with orchards and hop-kilns. There are good stone houses, half-timbered farmhouses and Georgian country homes. Wharton Court is built of Jacobean stone and has an elaborate staircase dating from 1603 which is certainly worth seeing. A half-mile away on Brierley Hill lies one of the most interesting prehistoric camps in Herefordshire. It is an Iron Age fort.

Berrington Hall's impressive interior

2 **BERRINGTON HALL,** three mi[les] north of Leominster, is a fine sandstone late 18th Century house b[uilt] by Henry Holland, the younger, a fashio[n]able Whig architect of the period a[nd] son-in-law of the famed landscape g[ar]dener "Capability "Brown. It was built [by] Thomas Harley, third son of the Earl [of] Oxford, who made a fortune supplyi[ng] clothing to the British army fighting American colonial rebels and who beca[me] Lord Mayor of London at the impressiv[e] youthful age of 37. Holland charg[ed] £14,500 to design and construct [the] house and Brown, who laid out the garde[n] got £1,600. The reddish ashlar sandsto[ne] quarried from Shuttocks Hill, a mile aw[ay] was carted to Berrington by a ho[rse] tramway specially built for the purpose[.]

4 **CROFT CASTLE:** The four rou[nd] towers and ancient walls of C[roft] Castle, northwest of Yarpole, date fr[om] the 14th Century, though almost certa[inly] built on the site of a much earlier buildi[ng] for the de Croft family are mentioned [in] Domesday as owning a castle here. [In] what was originally a Welsh bor[der] stronghold the castle now looks m[uch] more a residential, than a military pla[ce]. This is due to the fact that its pink-sto[ne] castellated front and much of the inte[rior] were "modernised" during the 16th a[nd] 17th Centuries and that the castle is [still] lived in. The great Gothic staircase a[nd] beautiful ceilings were actually add[ed] during the 18th Century and the porch [as] late as 1914. Nonetheless, it is a hig[hly] impressive and spacious mansion and [has] much interesting decoration and g[ood] pictures.

The park is one of the most gloriou[s in] the country, with a long avenue of Spa[nish] chestnuts, oak and beech. The chu[rch] next to the house should be visited [it] possesses a marvellous tomb of [Sir] Richard Croft and his wife. Sir Richar[d is] figured wearing the armour he wore at [the]

Grange Court, a Jacobean masterpiece, once used as the town hall

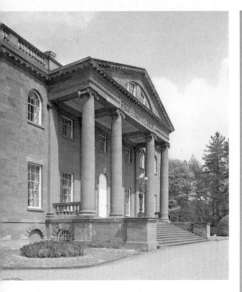
e mansion's red sandstone front

The house is much as Holland left it, th an impressive front hall, library and awing room — all with beautiful plaster ilings and excellent furniture. The site as actually chosen by Brown and the mi-circle of horizon visible from the use embraces Bush Bank and Burton ll (963 ft) eleven miles away; the rthern ridge of the Black Mountains 300 ft) 25 miles away (and marking e boundary between England and ales); the Brecon Beacons (2,906 ft) miles away; and Radnor Forest (2,166 20 miles away. The immediate parkland nsists of 455 acres, scattered with rare es, shrubs and plants and includes a nous 14-acre pool with a four-acre and, laid out by "Capability" Brown. e house is National Trust property.

3 EYE MANOR: Flanked by its Early English church, lovely Eye Manor looks out over lawn and meadow to gentle, wooded hills. It gets its name from the Norman family of de Eye who built the first hall here in the reign of Henry III. The present manor house is,

Ceiling decoration at Eye Manor

startlingly enough, a product of the Negro slave trade. A rich Barbados merchant called Ferdinando Gorges bought the estate in 1673. Gorges bore the nickname "King of the Black Market" because of his part in the slave traffic. On retirement he built the manor house, of simple exterior but marvellously decorated inside. The ceilings in nine of the rooms are master-pieces of the Italian plasterers' art. On display are magnificent books produced by the present owner, Mr. Christopher Sandford's, famous "Golden Cockerel" Press and a unique collection of corn dollies and other decorative straw-work done by Mrs. Sandford. The famous Beck collection of costume dolls, showing fashions over 800 years is also here.

The manor house at Eye, built by a man who made a fortune in the slave trade

ttle of Tewkesbury, and the effigies of th himself and his wife look uncannily l. Just to the north of the house lies oft Ambrey, a 24-acre Celtic hilltop mp which was occupied from 400 B.C. A.D. 50. From the summit on a clear day, s said, one can see more than a dozen glish and Welsh counties.

oft Castle and its glorious park

In the church is this magnificent tomb of Sir Richard Croft and his wife

5 **RICHARD'S CASTLE,** to the left of the road to Ludlow, is one of only three pre-Conquest Norman castles in England and owes its foundations to Richard le Scrob, one of the Norman aristocrats on whom Edward the Confessor, more Norman than English himself, lavished grants of land. It is now little more than a heap of earthworks with the remains of one wall standing.

St. Bartholomew's Church nearby is a delightful country church mainly of the 14th Century. But the north wall is Norman, with two small circular headed Norman windows. There are many memorials in the church to the Salwey family, the present owners, one of the most ancient families listed in Debrett. A 13th Century coffin lid, with a beautiful raised foliated cross, stands against the west wall of the aisle. Outside the church are two notable monuments. The first is the detached bell tower which was once used also for military purposes. East of the south wall of the church lies the second — the remains of a chamber called St. Anthony's Bower, named for a 4th Century hermit who lived here.

A quarter-mile nearer the village lies The Court House, a black-and-white Jacobean farmhouse which has an old cider mill in its grounds and a dovecot, believed to date from the 14th Century, which has 1,000 nesting holes.

Inside the old church at Richard's Castle

The 14th Century church's unusual exterior

Medieval Ludford Bridge over the Teme leads into the historic town of Ludlow

6 **LUDLOW** is a beautiful old town which has marvellously preserved evidences of its long history. Approached from the west, over Mary Knoll, a 900 ft rise, it lies spectacularly below in mellowed beauty. Its streets create a lovely pattern of overhanging half-timbered Tudor and Jacobean houses and stately town Georgian mansions, all intertwined with fascinating alleyways.

The massive red sandstone castle dates from 1085, when it was built by Roger de Montgomery, Earl of Shrewsbury. It has played a notable part in English history. The two little "Princes in the Tower", the sons of Edward IV were kept here before being removed to London and death. More significantly, Prince Arthur brought his bride, Catherine of Aragon to Ludlow and even laid out the walk around the castle for her. His death here a few months later meant that Henry VIII duly inherited the throne, paving the way for the English Reformation. In 1634, the poet Milt[on] attended the first production of his masq[ue] *Comus* in the castle hall.

The Church of St. Lawrence is almost [as] large as a cathedral and the large e[ast] window is brilliantly coloured. The ash[es] of Housman, the poet, lie in the churc[h] yard. Here also is the Reader's Hou[se] part-medieval, part-Tudor.

Broad Street has many half-timbe[r] buildings, some said to date from the 1[5th] Century. It climbs steeply from the medie[val] Ludford Bridge, through Broad Gate, [the] only surviving gateway in the ancient to[wn] walls, past the Angel Hotel, where L[ord] Nelson once stayed, and ends at the Bu[tter] Cross, a fine Georgian building. The to[wn] is justly notable for its ancient inns. [The] Rose and Crown was first licensed in [the] 16th Century, but pride of place goes [to] The Feathers, one of the best example[s of] Jacobean half-timbered work in Engla[nd]. Ludlow is a first-class centre for touri[ng]

In massive Ludlow Castle, built by the Normans, the "Princes in the Tower" were kept before being taken to London and death

The Feathers Hotel, a fine Jacobean half-timbered building

Castle walls overlooking the River Teme

One of Ludlow Museum's fossils

An ivory carving found in the castle

Romantic-looking Stokesay Castle is in reality a fortified manor house. The main buildings were completed by the 14th Century

7 **STOKESAY CASTLE,** despite its name, is in fact a fortified manor-house, and one of the most attractive in the country. Its fortifications, however, are so minimal that clearly it could never have withstood a serious siege. The visitor enters through a picturesque timber-framed gatehouse and finds himself in a walled courtyard, once surrounded by a moat. Across the courtyard are the main buildings of the castle, all completed by the early 14th Century, parts of which are surmounted by a half-timbered storey, which is extremely picturesque. Other buildings are believed to have existed in the courtyard for towards the end of its occupied life — in 1672 — Stokesay was taxed on seventeen hearths — and most of these no longer exist.

The property first belonged to the de Lacys, but it was granted sometime before 1115 to Theodoric de Say, of a family which took its name from Sai, near Argentan in Normandy. Originally the property was simply called Stoke, meaning dairy farm. About 1281, it was bought by Lawrence of Ludlow, the greatest wool merchant of his day whose descendants held it until 1497 when it passed to the Craven family. Today, it is a most romantic looking place with its half-timbered upper storey and its splendid Great Hall.

Close-up showing the half-timbered storey

8 **HOPTON CASTLE** which lies to the left of the route a few miles before Clun is probably one of the most beautiful, if melancholy ruins in England. This is partly because of its lovely situation — it is set in a typically tranquil English meadow — which appears so oddly at variance with its bloody history. It was, in fact, the site of one of the most brutal minor encounters of the Civil War. The Roundheads, under Colonel Samuel More shut themselves up inside it — 31 men holding it against 500 Cavaliers for three weeks. When the Cromwellians were eventually forced to surrender, the incensed Royalists took revenge by shooting all the garrison, except their leader, and flinging their bodies into a nearby pool.

This engraving shows the death of the Earl of Northampton at Hopton in the Civil War

CLUN, a small but ancient town, remains, as in A. E. Housman's day, "one of the quietest places under the sun". [Wa]lter Scott clearly knew what he was [ab]out when he sought tranquillity here to [wri]te his novel, *The Betrothed.* There are [fas]cinating historic sites nearby. St. [Ge]orge's Church has an unusual pyramid [ro]of set on a Norman tower but the [gre]ater part of the building was heavily [res]tored in the 19th Century. The pulpit [an]d reredos are Jacobean, however, and [the] lychgate dates from 1723. The castle, [wh]ich sits dramatically on a hill above the [riv]er, has a Norman keep.

Also worth visiting are Trinity Hospital, a one-storeyed building dating from 1618, and the 18th Century Court House. The saddleback bridge is medieval, with five arches. Two miles to the northeast lies part of Offa's Dyke, the great earth wall built by an 8th Century King of Mercia to keep out the Welsh. But easily the most dramatic site lies three miles to the south, at Chapel Lawn, where there is a magnificently situated Celtic hill fort. The great Celtic chieftain, Caractacus, is known to have fought the Romans in the vicinity and many authorities believe this was the site where he made his last heroic stand.

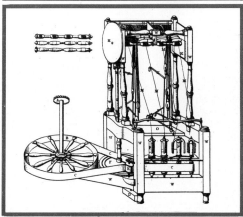

Richard Arkwright and his spinning machine

[Th]e bridge at Clun, an ancient town said to be "one of the quietest places under the sun"

11 **NEWTOWN,** which lies at the junction of the Mule and the Severn, was given its name as a means of distinguishing it from Caersws, an ancient settlement six miles up river. In one sense, the town stands as a memorial to lost Welsh independence. Llewellyn, the first and last native Prince of Wales (for although Glendower later declared Wales independent, he called himself King) recognised its strategic position, and built a fortress. Edward I, also aware of its strategic importance, ordered the castle to be razed. In the resulting disturbances, Llewellyn lost his life and Wales her independence. In 1279, Edward granted a charter a little further east at a ford over the Severn for the creation of a new town. This took shape on a right-angled grid which, by the 16th Century, was being cited as the ideal pattern for a new town.

Today, however, the place belongs mainly to the 18th Century, although the impressive High Street has several black and white timbered houses. Most of the ancient wool factories have been converted into shops.

The Midland Bank houses a museum dedicated to Newtown's most famous son, Robert Owen, the Socialist. Born in 1771, Owen was a pioneer with Richard Arkwright of the new machine-spinning and weaving industry. The condition of the weaving workers stirred him to a life-long and passionate devotion to education for the masses and the reform of society.

10 **KERRY:** This remote border village just before Newtown is set [am]ong magnificent, if uninhabited, hillsides [tha]t have bred two things: sheep and [riv]ers. The Teme and Clun have the Ithon, [Mu]le and Lugg as their companions. The [she]ep are a famously hardy breed — a [cro]ss between fat Shropshires and Welsh [mo]untain sheep, and they roam these vast [em]pty hills from the Forest of Clun to [Ker]ry Hill, Radnorshire and parts of [Mo]ntgomeryshire.

[T]he church — Norman and Early English, [bu]t heavily restored — was once the scene [of] a famous 12th Century quarrel between [the] Bishop of St. Asaph, who accepted the [aut]hority of Canterbury and Gerald de [Ba]rri, Archdeacon of Brecon, who hoped [to] establish a Welsh church, under the [ae]gis of the ancient see of St. David's. [Le]arning that the bishop was travelling to [sei]ze Kerry with a party of armed men, [Ge]rald raised his own forces and, riding [har]d, arrived first.

[E]ntering the church, he formally said [M]ass and ordered the bells to be rung so [tha]t the bishop should know he was beaten. [Un]deterred, the latter advanced right up [to] the church door. Gerald, escorted by a [pro]cession with candles and crosses came [ou]t of the church and began excom[mu]nicating the bishop who had already

begun a ceremony of excommunication against Gerald. Gerald's ceremony, however, was considered the more effective because, as a master of bells, he was able to have them rung in triplets. The baffled bishop thereupon withdrew, leaving Gerald apparently victorious. However, although Gerald retained mastery of the church, he failed in his efforts to remove Wales from the jurisdiction of Canterbury and 750 years elapsed before a separate Church of Wales was officially recognised.

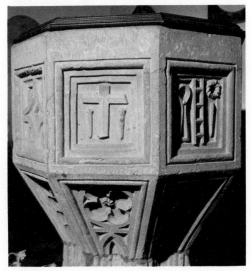

The ancient font in Kerry church

12 **LLANWNOG:** The road from Newtown to Llanidloes follows the winding course of the infant Severn which rises in the Plynlimon Hills visible at this point on the horizon. A few miles off the main road and worth a visit is the hamlet of Llanwnog, where John Hughes, the so-called Welsh Robbie Burns is buried. Few people outside Wales know much about this man who was once stationmaster at Llanidloes. In fact, he wrote the words of those famous songs, *Men of Harlech* and *God Bless the Prince of Wales*, and his memory is held in great esteem.

The Severn — and the road alongside it — wend their way through a valley of great beauty, with the hills growing ever steeper. Near a small bridge at Llandinam stands a statue to David Davies who was born nearby and became the first native Welsh millionaire. He had a flair for finance and engineering and helped build the Barry Docks in South Wales. He also spent part of his fortune helping to found the University at Aberystwyth. The hills and valleys here are famous for harpists who play the three-stringed *telyn* or Welsh harp which was invented in the 14th Century and was in common use throughout the country until the Industrial Revolution broke up the simple life.

Detail of the late 15th Century rood screen in Llanwnog church.

CALL OF THE WILD

The buzzard is Britain's most comm bird of prey and Mid-Wales provides huge sweep of rough territory it needs hunt. The buzzard is easily recognised its silhouette. Its call is also distinctive, high, mewing notes carrying far over op land. Its prey is limited by its size to noth much larger than a rabbit.

13 **LLANIDLOES** is near the source of the Severn and one of the loveliest towns in Wales — despite the factories and housing estates on its outskirts. The hub of the town is the excellent half-timbered Tudor Market Hall, raised on oaken arches, where John Wesley once preached. The word Llanidloes means the Church of St. Idloes. The saint was a 6th Century missionary. The church is impressively spacious and incorporates some of the stones and timbers from nearby Cwm Hir Abbey which was destroyed at the Dissolution.

Out of season Llanidloes is a leisurely town through which sheep are lazily driven and where Welsh is mainly spoken.

In 1839 the town was seized by local Chartists who held it for several days. A short, if sharp scuffle with constables and militia ended the affair — 'the mayor signalling the end of the fight by emerging from underneath his bed where he had hidden. Many of the rioters were subsequently sentenced to transportation.

Our route now runs northwards towards the oddly-named hillside village of Staylittle. A few miles out from Llanidloes, it passes Fan Hill, which rises almost 1,500 ft above the Severn Valley and overlooks the great Clywedog Reservoir. Near here are the famous Fan lead mines which were worked until the end of the 19th Century.

Stained-glass windows at Llanidloes. The church incorporates stones from an abbey

The Dovey valley near Cemaes, haunt of anglers after salmon

15 MALLWYD stands on the edge of the Snowdonia National Park, amid some of the most glorious scenery in Britain. It is a small, unpretentious place, but of long-standing importance as a staging point. Today it is a favourite spot for anglers and has some picturesque cottages built of the local dark stone.

Mallwyd church, on the edge of Snowdonia

4 CEMAES: As the route runs towards Snowdonia, it traverses some of the wildest and most desolate moorland in Wales — although these once bare and bleak hills are gradually becoming mellowed due to extensive afforestation, mostly with conifers. In this beautiful, if harsh countryside, many wild birds such as the buzzard and heron, nest. Cemaes is a sleepy village which first grew to importance as a coach staging-post. Today it is mainly a centre for anglers fishing the Dovey river for salmon. From the local inn, once visited by George Borrow, a path can be taken up the mountainside to the great plateau of Mynydd y Cemaes from which there is a marvellous view of the valley of the Dovey, as it reaches towards its mouth.

6 DINAS MAWDDWY is a fine angling centre, situated in the south-east corner of Merioneth and at a spot where the swift-flowing River Dyfi, as it not Anglicised into "Dovey", receives tributaries, the Cerist and the Cowarch. Several footpaths above the village give access to tributary streams where there are fine waterfalls, particularly at Nant-y-Aigwen and Pistyll Gwyn. It is tremendous climbing or walking country. It is, in fact the main starting point for climbers attempting the Aran range — Aran Mawddwy, 2,970 ft high, lying just eight miles north of the village. But there is good upland rambling for the energetic. The angler will find salmon, sewin and trout in the enchanting Dyfi.

For many centuries Dinas was inhabited "The Red Robbers of Dinas" who preyed on the surrounding countryside and resisted all attempts at suppression. They were named for their copper-coloured hair which is highly unusual in Wales, and were indeed regarded as a race apart. There are several "explanations" of their origin, but they were most likely descendants of those Irish who colonised

The peaceful village of Dinas was for centuries the headquarters of the Red Robbers

large parts of Wales from the 3rd to the 7th Centuries, but were finally forced to withdraw, except for such pockets as this and a well-established "kingdom" in Breconshire. By 1555, they had become so daring that they killed a judge who had been sent to the area as part of an effort to suppress them. As a result, the district was swept by troops and the Red Robbers finally dispersed. But to this day, many of the inhabitants of Dinas possess a distinctive copper-blond hair.

17 **DOLGELLAU,** the county town of Merionethshire, is a fine old comfortable grey town, built of stones quarried from the rocks of the majestic mountains that rise steeply all around it. It is a busy social and commercial centre, standing on the River Wnion, two miles from its confluence with the Mawddach, whose estuary is as beautiful and magical as anything in Europe. It is a town of squares. The largest of these is Eldon Square and from it lead narrow streets where there are cosy inns, catering for tourists and the local mountain farmers and shepherds. The town boasts a pure mountain water supply.

Curfew is rung every night at 9 o' clock from the tower of St. Mary's Church which has a fine 13th Century effigy of a member of the ancient Vaughan family who have lived in the area for centuries. The town's finest architectural work, however, is probably its seven-arched bridge, built in 1638.

The name Dolgellau (pronounced Doll-gethley) seems to mean Meadow of the Slaves. Gold is still mined in small quantities on the hillsides overlooking the Mawddach estuary and it seems certa that the Romans, using native slave worked these, for coins bearing the nam and title of the Emperor Trajan have bee found in the vicinity. Dolgellau is als immensely proud of its associations wi the great Welsh hero Owen Glendower, f he held his last Parliament here. Th building itself, however, was taken dow in 1882 and re-erected in a park Newtown in 1883. A fascinating tale als connects him with Nannau Park, $1\frac{1}{2}$ mil from the town, which is the seat of t Vaughan family (open to the public appointment only). An earlier house on t site was razed by Owen, after an episo with his traitorous cousin, Howel Se Howel invited Owen to hunt with him, b treacherously turned his spear on him wh Owen was off-guard. Saved by his armou Owen took revenge by razing the hou and removing Howel from the sight of me Some years later, Howel's skeleton w found in the trunk of an ancient oak. T oak itself was struck by lightning in 18 and the spot is now marked by a sundi Both Sir Walter Scott and Bulwer Lytt have used the episode in their novels.

Dolgellau, where curfew is rung at 9 p.m.

18 **MAWDDACH:** The road from Dolgellau to Barmouth alongside the Mawddach is one of the wonders of Wales and should not be missed. Near Llanelltyd, two miles seawards from Dolgellau, lies the Clogau gold mine from which has come gold for recent royal wedding rings. Nearby are the ruins of a Cistercian foundation, Cymmer Abbey, set in soft meadowland against a magnificent background of mountains.

There are several beautiful rambles in the vicinity of the Maddwach. Precipice Walk circles a high ridge two miles north of Dolgellau and gives fine views of the Aran peaks, rising to almost 3,000 ft and the massive north escarpment of Cader Idris, nine miles long. To do the six miles walk, which runs through enchanting meadow and woodland, start from a sign-posted track beginning from Nannau, which lies on the Llanfachreth road.

A marvellous view of the five peaks of Cader Idris can be obtained more easily by walking up the lane leading from the north side of Dolgellau bridge to the golf course near Hengwrt. Looking back from here, the whole range is visible in great majesty. Another enchanting walk in the vicinity is Torrent Walk. The entrance to this lies about two miles east of Dolgellau, near the village of Brithdir. One walks up the cascading torrent created by the river Clywedog, a tributary of the Wnion. The total length of the walk is less than a mile. From Dolgellau, there are also two good starting points for the climb to Pen-y-Gader, the main summit of Cader Idris. These lead up either the Foxes' Path, $4\frac{1}{2}$ miles or the Bridle Path, 6 miles.

The Mawddach estuary near Bontddu on the way from Dolgellau to Barmouth

THE WEDDING-GIFT TOWER

On the coast at Garreg, just to the north of Aberystwyth, are the sturdy ruins of an ancient castle, which blend into the landscape as if they had grown out of the rocky outcrop on which they stand. Which is exactly what they are meant to do. But the castle is not ancient, not a ruin. It is, in fact, a wedding present.

In 1915, when the architect Clough Williams-Ellis was a junior officer in the Welsh Guards, he met and fell in love with Annabel Strachey. His commanding officer suggested that a suitable wedding present might be a silver salver, engraved with the signatures of his fellow officers. Williams-Ellis explained that, while he appreciated the thought, he had quite a bit of family silver stacked away, and what he really lacked was a ruin. There was a rocky eminence in the grounds of Plas Brondanw which cried out for a ruined castle. The Guards were surprised but not dismayed, and the result is the outlook tower which is known locally as Castle Brondanw.

FOLLY AFTER FOLLY

It is interesting not just because it is a classic Folly — useless, extravagant and romantic — but because it was the forerunner of a fantastic Folly on an even greater scale. Clough Williams-Ellis (who received a knighthood for his services to architecture and the environment) went on to create his fantasy village at Portmeirion, near Portmadoc.

This man of vision wanted to show the possibilities of developing an ancient landscape without ruining it. He began his extraordinary exercise in architectural imagination on a rocky peninsula between the estuaries of the Glaswyn and the Dwyryd in 1926. He ended by transforming a wild part of Wales into a showplace with many of the characteristics of Portofino in Italy. But what a mixture! By the sea he converted a 19th Century mansion into a hotel with a great Renaissance fireplace. On a hill he erected an Italian campanile — near a cluster of 19th Century English houses. Everywhere there are vistas and flights of steps to viewpoints overlooking sea and mountain. It is one of the sights of Wales and, not surprisingly, the setting for many films. It must be the only fantasy under Government protection. It is scheduled as "of architectural and historic importance" and cannot be altered without Ministerial approval.

From Cader Idris there are superb views over vast areas of north and mid-Wales

19 **CADER IDRIS,** after Snowdon, is unquestionably the most famous of all Welsh mountain ranges although at 2,927 ft. its highest peak is relatively low and is, indeed, topped by its nearest neighbour, Aran Fawddwy. However, it possesses a marvellous brooding majesty of its own and its great length of almost nine miles makes it a notable landmark.

Although its name is popularly supposed to mean the Chair of Arthur or Idris, a mythical giant, it is more likely that "Cader" is derived from the Welsh for "a settlement" and that Idris was a local chieftain. Certainly there is no justification for connecting the mountain with the shadowy King Arthur of the fables. The mountain remains an area of myth and legend, however. One legend has it that anyone unfortunate enough to sleep a night on Cader Idris awakens either blind, mad or a poet (but not necessarily all three). Across the valley, too, is said to lurk a Little Hairy Green Man who casts a magic mist over the mountain whenever he spies any climbers trying to scale the slopes.

The easiest route to the top is from Llanfihangel-y-pennant, three and a half miles to the southwest. The toughest route, which should not be attempted by the inexperienced, is from near Tal-y-llyn, which takes the climber past the legendary Llyn Cau, said to be a bottomless lake with a Loch Ness type monster. In the 18th Century, it is said a boy attempting to swim the lake was caught by the legs by the monster. Cader Idris is undoubtedly worth the effort needed to climb it. From its crest, there are superb views over vast areas of north and mid-Wales — to the west, the whole Mawddach estuary as far as Barmouth; to the north, the peaks of Snowdonia, and even Bardsey Island lying off the Lleyn Peninsula; and, looking southwards, to St. David's Head in Pembrokeshire. The precipitous slopes are often as much as 900 ft deep on the north side. All over the range are springs and tarns and there is ample free trout fishing, especially for the energetic.

20 **TAL-Y-LLYN** is at one and the same time the name of a small hamlet and of the beautiful lake that lies at the western foot of Cader Idris. Although just over a mile long, with its northern end fading away into reeds and shallows, the lake is perhaps the loveliest in Wales. A track running along its northern shore gives the walker a splendid chance to enjoy its beauties without interruption from motor traffic.

All around lie magnificent aspects of Cader Idris and the great Tarens range opposite, which is sometimes called the Little Brother of Cader Idris. The Tarens themselves offer fine walking and climbing country and their valleys are the home of the pinemarten, foxes and the insect-eating sundew. In these hills, too, one often sees a death-duel between a buzzard and a seagull. The hamlet itself consists of two cosy little fishing hotels and a small church with a chancel roof painted over with red and white roses.

Tal-y-llyn, at the foot of Cader Idris, is perhaps the loveliest lake in Wales

SAUCE FOR THE TURKEY COMES FROM THIS BERRY

The great raised bog of Tregaron w originally a glacial lake which gradua filled with vegetation. It forms a little wor of its own, desolate and at times eerie. first glance the vegetation looks like wilderness of grass and sedge but a clos look shows that the bog is still growing d to the sponge-like qualities of its mc which keeps the surface soaking althou it is considerably above the old water lev Here can be seen the pink star-like flowe of the cranberry which are followed berries so large that the little shrub usua rests them neatly on the green moss. Th of course, is the berry so beloved Americans as the traditional flavouring their Thanksgiving Day turkey.

21 **DYSYNNI:** Southwestward the landscape opens out in the narrow Dysynni valley, which seems softly beautiful after the rugged and bare grandeur of Cader Idris. Most of the roads in the Dysynni valley are narrow and winding and the hillsides splendidly steep and teeming with wildlife. Buzzard and hawk hover constantly in the sky. The area is rich in historic and prehistoric sites. At Castell y Bere once stood the most important castle in Wales. After the almost casual death of Llewellyn, Prince of Wales near Builth when his party was surprised by English troops, his brother Dafydd held out here for a time against Edward I's forces. Eventually Dafydd was forced to surrender the castle and fled northwards where he was betrayed to the English and brought to London and executed after public humiliation, thus ending the existence of Wales as an independent nation. Near the village of Bryn-crug stands Bird Rock, (Craig yr Aderyn) the only inland nesting place for the cormorants that are such a feature of these coasts.

The softly beautiful Dysynni valley where the hillsides teem with wildlife

22 TYWYN is a pleasant seaside town which can be a more than satisfactory alternative to Dolgellau as a centre for touring the area around Tal-y-llyn and Cader Idris and the Dysynni valley. Many will consider its principal attraction its fine beach, which stretches nearly six miles from the mouth of the river Dysynni in the north to the estuary of the Dovey in the south. The sands are fine, firm, and white, and safe for walking and bathing.

A mile or so north lies the tidal Broadwater through which the Dysynni river flows before reaching the sea. The Dysynni itself offers the angler many attractions. Free fishing for salmon and sea trout is available on the north bank from Ferry Farm to the sea and on the south from the junction with the River Fathew to the sea. The Broadwater itself is a large open stretch of sand covered by the sea at high tide, when it becomes a good fishing ground for those in search of bass.

Tywyn parish church, although retaining much of its original Norman stonework has been considerably restored. Its great treasure, however, is "St. Cadfan's Stone", said to be the most ancient monument in the Welsh language. Legend has it that Cadfan was a 6th Century French missionary who came to Christianise this wild region. One translation of the stone, however, suggests that it is a monument to three ladies of the 6th Century who were carried off by Irish invaders and whose departure left "grief and loss" behind. The church also contains notable effigies of a knight in 14th Century armour and a priest of Edward III's reign.

The intriguing narrow-gauge Tal-y-llyn railway runs from Tywyn to Abergynolwyn during the summer months. Originally built in 1865 for the transport of slate. This survivor of the steam age is now maintained by a preservation society. There is a halt at Dolgoch where the beautiful Dolgoch Falls drop a spectacular 125 ft.

the seaside and tourist town of Tywyn

erdovey harbour, an attractive little port and holiday centre

23 ABERDOVEY lies at the mouth of the Dovey estuary — an estuary which closely challenges the Mawddach for the title of Britain's loveliest river mouth. It is an attractive little port and holiday centre, and offers miles of magnificent beaches, sand dunes, excellent golf and sea-fishing. At low tide, it is sometimes just possible to discern the remains of sunken tree trunks — relics of a time, 7,000 years ago, when much of what is now Cardigan Bay was still land. Their presence has given rise to the legend of "The Bells of Aberdovey" which are said to sound from beneath the waves, from a sunken city, whenever trouble threatens the region. A stiff climb from Aberdovey leads to a ridge about a mile north where there are marvellous panoramic views across Happy Valley.

24 MACHYNLLETH: The road from Aberdovey runs along the
th side of the Dovey estuary and ends at
chynlleth, one of the most charming
lsh towns, and historically of great
tegic importance. An Iron Age en
npment nearby was clearly built to repel
borne invaders who might threaten to
b at the heart of the country through the
fi valley. Later the Romans built roads
th and south of it. When Owen
ndower proclaimed Wales an indepen
t kingdom in the early 15th Century he
de Machynlleth his capital. The site of
present Owen Glendower Institute is,
ording to tradition, the building where
held his Parliament and where he was
claimed King of Wales.

t is now a clean, smart town, with
eral points of great interest. The
ndower Institute on Maen Gwyn Street
must visit. Plas Machynlleth, once the

home of the Marquess of Londonderry but now used to house some of the council offices and a permanent exhibition of Welsh textiles, has some fine 16th and 17th Century work. Four good inns still cluster round the tower. The Royal House is said to be the inn where the future Henry VII stayed on his way from Milford Haven to Bosworth Field. The White Lion and the Wynnstay Arms are other good 18th Century inns nearby. Maen Gwyn Street has some charming houses dating from the 17th, 18th and early 19th Centuries and a pre-Roman direction sign, called The Maen Gwyn, set into a house wall.

At certain times of the year the town becomes a very lively and colourful place. The Plas Machynlleth Hunt, a foot pack of hounds, meets by the Clock Tower every New Year's Day. Twice a year, in May and September there are vivid huckster fairs, which specialise in exciting Dutch auctions.

Lake scenery near Machynlleth

25 **ELLENNITH:** The road from Machynlleth to Aberystwyth is probably as pleasant as any in Wales with the great sweep of Cardigan Bay lying to the right and the mountains inland rising in a series of step-like plateaux to the heights of Plynlimon Fawr in the northwest corner of Cardiganshire. There are several small and insignificant hamlets along the road which, nevertheless, offer a variety of sport and scenic delights. Near Tre'rddol, a narrow winding road leads into the lovely glen called Artists' Valley. The reputed grave of the 6th Century Celtic story-teller, Taliesin, lies in a little valley beyond the first ridge of hills above the hamlet of Tre-Taliesin. Tal-y-bont, once the site of an important silver mine is now of primary interest to the motorist as a starting point for a memorable drive. The Ellennith, one of the inland moor-barriers of Wales, is now being broken into by roads, by-products of new reservoirs and conifer plantations. Tal-y-bont stands at the neck of roads leading towards Elerch from which the motorist can plunge deep into the hitherto unknown Ellennith and then make a circuit of the magnificent new Rheidol reservoirs and the forest-plantations rising alongside them.

When one has completed the circuit, it is still possible to reach the sea at Borth, which although a straggly undistinguished place built on a pebbly storm-beach, lies just behind a splendid three-mile stretch of firm, and level golden sand.

A mountain road near Tal-y-bont

THE TINY TRAINS OF WALES
Within easy visiting distance of Dolgella are six miniature steam railways which provide an entrancing method of reachi mountains, valleys and rivers inaccessib to cars. These little beauties are the wor of pioneers, handed down, restored and cherished as in their brass-polished, gleaming heyday. Two lines are directly on this route: the Tal-y-llyn Railway, starting at Tywyn, and the line between Aberystwyth and Devil's Bridge. A little to the north of the route is the Welshpo and Llanfair Railway and a few miles south-west along the coast from Dolgel runs the tiny Fairbourne line with a gauge of only 15in. To the north is the Festiniog Railway of Portmadoc and beyond that the Snowdon-Llanberis lin with the widest gauge of the six — still only 2 ft. 8½ in. — and a mountain clim of 4⅝ miles at a steady 5 mph. Most of the lines are open from late March to early October.

27 **NATIONAL LIBRARY** of Wales is an imposing Edwardian building, plumped down among the main University of Wales buildings on Penglais Hill (today the old college buildings along the seafront are largely used only as a museum). The Library boasts the most complete collection of Welsh books and manuscripts in the world and altogether possesses more than two million printed works and about 30,000 MSS. During the summer months, many of its greatest treasures are on exhibition. These include the 13th Century *Black Book of Carmarthen*, the earliest MS in the Welsh language.

One of its finest treasures is the earliest complete text of the *Mabinogion*, the national epic. This is the earliest prose literature known in Wales, although the tales themselves are derived mainly from the Irish who invaded and settled north-west and south-west Wales from the 3rd to the early 7th Century. Later portions probably relate to genuine Welsh historical incidents, albeit many are concerned with the Y Gogledd, or 'men of the north' who spoke Gaelic rather than Welsh. Another manuscript is the Hengwrt Chaucer text of the *Canterbury Tales*. The basis for the collection was assembled by Sir John Williams, a Royal physician, who died in 1926. The printed book department contains copies of the earliest books printed in Welsh. There is also an extensive collection of maps, prints and drawings.

Print showing guests bringing wedding gifts

"Black Book of Carmarthen", oldest Welsh MS

Library copy of "The Songs of Ceiriog"

28 **NANTEOS HOUSE,** perha the most perfect example Georgian domestic architecture in Wa lies just two and a half miles southeast Aberystwyth. The name Nanteos its means Valley of the Nightingale. present house was built between 17 and 1757 for the Powell family on the s of an older one. The myrtle bushes grow against the facade are reminders of various ladies of Nanteos — for each br to come here planted a sprig from wedding bouquet, from each of wh grew a tree.

The library contains many interest 17th Century books and also a letter Lord Byron who once stayed here. main showpiece of the house, howeve the Music Room, a symphony of colc in soft pink, white and gold. The plast work is exquisite, and there are panels the ceiling depicting four arts — mu painting, sport and wine-making. Ther also a superb marble fireplace, the cen piece of which depicts cne of Aeso fables. It was in this room that Rich Wagner wrote part of his opera, *Pars* The kitchen is another intriguing feat of the house. It has a vast scrubbed ta

The harbour at Aberystwyth, a good centre for both motoring and walking

26 ABERYSTWYTH: Two rivers — the Rheidol and the Ystwyth which, for most of their length, flow through some of the wildest and most sparsely inhabited moorlands in Britain, enter the sea at the resort and university town of Aberystwyth. Apart from the normal holiday amenities, the town has plenty of places of interest and is a good centre for some magnificent motoring or walking. There is a Celtic fort, one of the largest in Wales, on the summit of Pen Dinas, a hill that rises just south of the town. The ruins of the town castle, built by Edward I, sit on a small promontory on the sea front amid pleasantly laid out gardens. During the reign of Charles I, it became, rather curiously, a mint. Thomas Bushell, who then owned the concession to the Plynlimon lead-mines nearby, discovered a new process for refining silver ore and was given royal permission to mint coins. The Civil War, however, ruined Bushell.

Just north of the castle lies a complex of buildings that is of great significance to the Welsh people. The heart of the complex is a Victorian Gothic hotel built about 1860 by a railway engineer called Thomas Savin who dreamed of popularising Aberystwyth by building his own railway line from London and offering anyone who bought a return ticket to Euston a week's free board in the town. His scheme failed after he had spent £80,000 on the hotel. Out of his ruin however came a greater good fortune for the Welsh. A patriotic committee paid £10,000 for the building and set up the first constituent college of what was to grow into the University of Wales. The then Prince of Wales (later King Edward VII) was installed here as first Chancellor and the great statesman William Ewart Gladstone made his last appearance in public here. Behind Alexandra Hall, a funicular cliff railway hauls passengers to the top of the 485 ft high Constitution Hill, from which it is possible to walk two miles to the fine beach at Clarach.

The Rheidol and Ystwyth valleys are both easily accessible from Aberystwyth. The Rheidol Valley is usually approached by way of Llanbadarn Fawr, a village on the site of a 6th Century religious settlement. The present 13th Century church contains two Celtic crosses. Just beyond Capel Bangor, it is worth descending into the Rheidol Valley to see the main power station and the Civic Award winning bridge, weir and dam of the hydro-electric scheme just above Aberffrwd. The Ystwyth Valley, for its part, begins rather bleakly, but eventually moves into enchantingly beautiful wooded country.

One of the minor delights of Aberystwyth for most people, is the 12-mile journey through the Vale of Rheidol by narrow gauge railway to Devil's Bridge.

Entry to stables at Nanteos House

and benches, with copper and pewter dishes lining the wall and a roasting spit beside a huge oven — all preserved as they were when used two centuries ago.

The house is reputedly haunted. A grey lady dressed in a crinoline has been often seen in one of the bedrooms, and a black lady whose appearance inevitably foreshadows the death of a member of the Powell family has been seen on the staircase (her picture hangs in the house).

Treasure worth millions of pounds is believed to be buried in the grounds.

For years, the most precious object in the house was the famous Nanteos Cup (it has now been removed elsewhere). This was said to be the Holy Grail, the cup used by Christ at the Last Supper. The origin of this belief lay in the legend that St. Joseph of Arimathea once visited Britain. The relic, according to tradition, was originally kept at Glastonbury, but was hurried away to nearby Strata Florida at the time of Henry VIII's Dissolution. When Strata Florida in turn was destroyed, seven monks fled the 17 miles across the mountains to Nanteos, bringing the cup which was entrusted to the Powells. For years, the cup was believed to have healing properties.

29 DEVIL'S BRIDGE: Either of two beautiful roads, the A44 or the A4120, lead from Aberystwyth to the glorious falls of the Mynach river at Devil's Bridge, one of the most famous beauty spots in Wales. The falls are startlingly lovely, dropping almost 500 ft through boulder-strewn, wooded gorges, creating several deep pools on the way. Across the falls are built no fewer than three bridges, one on top of the other. The earliest and lowest dates from the 12th Century and was built by monks from Strata Florida.

Falls of the Mynach at Devil's Bridge

Reservoir waterlife — a tufted duck

31 PONTERWYD: The road from Devil's Bridge to Ponterwyd leads through a spectacular valley and offers motorists who have preferred to stick to the coastal strip from Machynlleth to Aberystwyth, a second chance of driving into the Ellennith and viewing the spectacular Nant-y-Moch reservoir, lying over 1,000 ft above sea level.

A new road from Ponterwyd leads up to the reservoir and into the heart of this hitherto inaccessible part of the Plynlimon range. It is marvellous country for any who do not mind leaving their cars for a while and stretching their legs. The highest summit is about mid-way between the reservoir and Eisteddfa Gurig on the Rhayader road. One may also stumble across the sources of the Wye and Severn.

Rhayader offers opportunities for anglers

32 PLYNLIMON FAWR: For those who prefer to walk up to Plynlimon Fawr, the highest mountain (2,368 ft) in Cardiganshire and the summit of the Plynlimon range, the recommended easy route is to start at the inn at Dyffryn Castell.

There are signposts set at convenie intervals across these moorlands, whi to a stranger may easily appear rath featureless. There are said to be mo beautiful approaches to the mountain, b these are much longer and more demandir

The Plynlimon range near Ponterwyd

Teifi Pools — the trout are fine

30 TEIFI POOLS: South-west of Devil's Bridge, but only accessible along sheep tracks which are not passable to motorists, lies wild and austere countryside leading to the collection of lakes known as the Teifi Pools. The trout here are of a particularly fine quality and are said to have been first introduced into the lakes by the Cistercian monks of Strata Florida.

This is extremely desolate countryside and the haunt usually of only wildfowl and such birds as the coot, heron and hawk. A less delightful denizen of these wastes is said to be the black adder, although some maintain it is confined mainly to the nature reserve known as the Cors Goch Glanteifi, or Bog of Tregaron. One should, however, also watch out for the red adder.

33 LLANGURIG is a rather featureless town, but it does mark the spot where the infant Wye turns from a mere stream into a proper river. Yet Llangurig is an ancient place, for the nearby Fan lead mines were worked since Roman times and the church, although restored, dates from the 12th Century.

Although the lead and silver mining was carried on in a small way for centuries, it was not until the 18th Century that the town's fortunes were really made when lead-mining was given a new impetus by a remarkable Welshman called Lewis Morris who modestly described himself as "master of all arts and sciences". The heyday of the mines was reached in the 19th Century, but today the mines have been taken over by the Institute of Industrial Archaeology who intend that the shafts, levels and workings should be preserved for public viewing.

One of the ancient lead mines

34 RHAYADER is a small sheep market town on the Wye, lying in the midst of bleak moorland country — in fact, between Plynlimon and Radnor Forest, and between the Ellennith and the Melienydd, the latter areas known as "the great moorland desert" of Wales. To the tired traveller, reaching Rhayader at dusk is not unlike coming into a town in the Wild West just as the saloons are about to get busy.

The town, despite its isolation, has a long history, being associated in its early days with Rhys, prince of South Wales. The castle he once built here was destroyed during the Norman-Welsh wars. In Tudor times, Rhayader was savagely raided by a notorious band of Cardiganshire robbers called the Plant Matt (Children of Matt)

who not only rescued a member of their gang from the town jail but murdered a judge who had been sent to try him. In the mid-19th Century, Rhayader became the headquarters of Rebecca's Daughters, the tollgate breakers.

Today it is a peaceful if sometimes deserted looking town with one or two good inns and ample opportunity for anglers or walkers to enjoy themselves in the miles of uninhabited countryside stretching out in all directions. where there is nothing but streams and moorlands and wild life. The name Rhayader derives from what were once the great Wye rapids nearby — rapids which are now sadly diminished owing to the building of the great Elan Valley dams and reservoirs two and a half miles to the west.

Vortigern makes a treaty with the Saxons

36 LLYN GWYN: The area between Rhayader and Llandrindod Wells has been probably as much trampled upon by history as other regions in Wales, but although the ruins are many, few of them are really impressive. The Romans, for instance, had a camp at Castell Collen, on the west bank of the River Ithon, about one and a half miles from Llandrindod Wells, but only some unimpressive earthworks now remain. One, in fact, can gain a better impression of what existed there from the artefacts found on the site which are now in the county museum in Llandrindod.

There are other earthworks — prehistoric this time — on the shores of Llyn Gwyn, near Nantmel — where there is a persistent legend of a drowned city. What is real enough, however, is a find of Romano-British jewellery nearby. Experts believe this jewellery may have belonged to one of the several wives of Vortigern, the traitorous British chieftain whom history says invited the Anglo-Saxons into Britain. Certainly many traditions surrounding Vortigern continue to exist in this area.

Romantic Elan Valley — a successful partnership of man and nature

35 ELAN VALLEY: Immediately west of Rhayader lies the romantic Elan Valley, much beloved by Shelley who once toyed with the idea of setting up a permanent house at Nantgwyllt. This was after he had brought his girl-wife Harriet Westbrook to a mansion in the valley and had startled the natives with his unconventional behaviour — such as sailing paper boats on the river, sometimes using a note as a sail and a cat as a passenger. Today the spots Shelley knew in this once wild and romantic valley, are now submerged under a great series of dammed lakes that supply the city of Birmingham with its water supply. These reservoirs — there are five in all, with another one to come — were created by damming the river Elan which, after uniting with the Claerwen, joins the Wye at Rhayader. Work began on the Elan reservoirs in 1892 and they were formally opened by King Edward VII in 1904, although they were not completed until 1907. Following the

Second World War, the branch valley of the Claerwen was also dammed. This was formally opened by the Queen and, occupying some 600 acres, is the largest of the dams.

The drive round these lovely lakes can be easily accomplished within the hour, except during the height of the holiday season. One should first follow the signpost to the Claerwen dam, then retrace the route to the viaduct separating Caban-Coch, the lowest of the Elan dams, from Garreg-ddu. Drivers should then fork left and follow the road to the head of Craig-Coch, the highest reservoir, returning to Rhayader by a mountain road.

Although most reservoirs seem lifeless, unnatural places, this can certainly not be said of the Elan Valley works which supply Birmingham with over 60,000,000 gallons daily. In a subtle way, the work of man here has been marvellously made to complement that of nature and the drive proves an exhilarating and rewarding experience.

Lake at Llandrindod Wells

37 LLANDRINDOD WELLS is the largest and most popular of Welsh spas, although to be objective, it does not possess the elegance of Bath or Tunbridge Wells. Its history as a spa, however, dates back to Roman times and its modern popularity began under Charles II. At the height of its fame in the mid-19th Century, it drew as many as 80,000 people annually. Modern spa treatment is still available at a centre in the well laid-out Rock Park. A few yards from this centre stands a free chalybeate waters fountain.

The Celtic dream

The Mabinogion is a collection of eleven British Celtic stories reflecting an ancient culture that still inspires the Welsh people. They were first written down in two 14th Century manuscripts, The White Book of Rhydderch and The Red Book of Hergest, now preserved in the Welsh National Library and Oxford University respectively. The word 'Mabinogi' itself means a story and a Branch simply means "a part or portion of the story". The Four Branches are easily the most interesting. The characters are mythological, representing divine or semi-divine figures. Although not *written down* until medieval times, the material itself obviously dates from the Celtic dawn and was handed down orally, as in Ireland, from generation to generation by the bardic order. The shadowy figure of Arthur appears in the later tales. He bears little resemblance to today's accepted figure. His followers are slay hags, witches, monsters, and he himself is a giant, ridding Britain of other giants, witches, monsters and undertaking journeys to the Otherworld to carry off treasure.

(1.) Olwen of the White Track. Olwen, daughter of Hawthorn, King of the Giants, was a maiden of great beauty, such that "whoso beheld her was filled with love". Wherever she trod "four white trefoils sprang up" — hence her name Olwen, meaning She of the White Track.
The hero Eilhwch, despite a warning that "none ever returned from this quest alive" goes in search of her as his wife and is set a series of almost impossible tasks by her monstrous father.

(2.) Prince Pwyll and his meeting with Rhiannon. Pwyll, Prince of Dyfed, decided one day to sit on an enchanted mound at Narberth (North Pembrokeshire) of which it was said "whoever sat upon it would have a strange adventure". Presently he saw a lady clad in gold clothes approaching on a milk-white horse and immediately sent his servants to fetch her. Yet however fast they rode, she kept the same distance away. Finally, Pwyll himself decided to pursue her only to find her still mysteriously flitting away until suddenly he cried out his love. At once the Lady Rhiannon stopped, declaring that "it were better for thy horse" had he called out sooner. Her family, she said, were trying to force her to marry someone else, but if Pwyll rejected her she would marry no one. Eventually they were wed, but not before other adventures.

(3.) Branwen and the invasion of Ireland. Branwen, sister of Bran, the King of Britain and "one of the three chief ladies of the island and fairest damsel in the world" was married to the King of Ireland so that "Ireland and Britain might be leagued together and both become more powerful". The

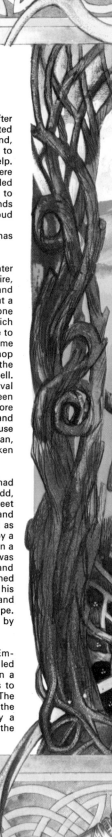

wedding was held at Aberffraw (in Anglesey) after which the bride's brother, angry at not being consulted about the wedding, insulted the Irish. Once in Ireland, the Irish took revenge on Branwen who managed to send a starling to her brother with a message for help. This resulted in a British invasion of Ireland where almost all the warriors on both sides were killed including her brother the King, causing Branwen to lament: "Woe is me that I was ever born; two islands have been destroyed because of me" and with a loud groan, her heart broke.
Bran's castle was said to be at Harlech, also at Dinas Bran Castle, near Llangollen.

(4.) Manawyddan and the mouse. An enchanter having cast a spell over North Pembrokeshire, Prince Manawyddan found the land desolate and uninhabited. After several misfortunes, he found that a host of mice were eating his wheat. So he sat up one night to kill them, but managed to catch only one which he decided to hang as a thief. Many strangers came to his house offering him money for the mouse. Each time Manawyddan refused until finally a pretended Bishop asked him to name "whatever price thou wilt" for the mouse. Manawyddan's price was the end of the spell. The "Bishop" agreed, revealed that he was a rival Prince called Llwyd whose friend had once been insulted by Manawyddan's friends and that therefore he had cast a spell. The mice, in fact, were lords and ladies of his court. And touching the reprieved mouse with a wand, he changed her into a fair young woman, explaining that she was his wife, who had also taken part in the act of vengeance.

(5.) Gwydion and Llew. The hero Gwydion had a son Llew who had a beautiful wife, Blodeuwedd, fashioned for him by magic from oak, meadow-sweet and broom blossoms. Alas, she proved unfaithful and she and her lover Gronw decided to slay him. But as Llew was the son of a god, he could only be slain by a special spear and then only when he had one foot on a dead buck and the other in a cauldron. Llew was tricked into showing Blodeuwedd the position and immediately Gronw threw the spear, which turned Llew into an eagle. Gwydion, after a long search for his son, found him in Nantlle (in Caernarvonshire) and with a magic wand restored him to human shape. Blodeuwedd, for her treachery, was punished by Gwydion by being changed into an owl.

(6.) The Emperor of Rome. Maxen Wledig, Emperor of Rome, had a dream in which he was led into a strange country where a fair maiden sat on a golden throne. On wakening, he sent messengers to seek out the maiden and they found her in Britain. The Emperor went to Caernarvon to woo and wed the maid. In his absence, his empire was seized by a usurper, but he succeeded in reconquering it with the help of his wife's British friends.

North Wales – the Celtic homeland

BILL GRUNDY

Multum in parvo — a lot in a little. The Romans were all over this part of the country, so they may very well have thought up the phrase especially to describe our route. There's some of the lushest meadowland in Britain, rolling green across Cheshire and Shropshire. The fields seem freshly scrubbed, the cattle look contented. In the sheltering arm of a wood is a half-timbered farmhouse or a mellow Georgian manor. This is England, and England at her best.

Then suddenly you're in another country altogether, a country where they speak a different language, one far older than English, one they spoke "before the Romans came to Rye and out to Severn strode." This is Wales, a land where mountains as wild as any in Britain tower above you, where the raven, not the skylark, is king of the air. But also a land with wonderful golden beaches and little rock-bound coves, modern holiday resorts and watering places some as unspoilt as when Victoria was on her throne. A land where earthworks and burial mounds and castles and churches plot the long march of man up to the present day, when his nuclear cathedrals tower over Trawsfynydd and crouch on the cliffs of Anglesey.

Our starting point is Nantwich in Cheshire. Its very name says what a good choice it is. It means, and has meant for 1,300 years, "the famous place of buildings." There aren't so many left now, but what there are are fine; Churche's Mansion, for example.

From Nantwich the route rambles through the richness of Cheshire. The River Weaver staggers tipsily across the meadows and every now and then humpbacked bridges mark the course of the Llangollen Canal. In doing so they mark the work of one of the finest engineers this country ever produced — Thomas Telford. It was he who cut the road through the Welsh mountains we shall be following. It was he who built the bridge across the Menai Strait that we shall be crossing, so give Telford a salute each time you encounter his canal.

AT THE GATEWAY TO WALES

From Cheshire into Shropshire, and more miles of rolling grassland, soft-eyed Jerseys, and a feeling that man and Nature are working well together. But English as the country is, the road to Oswestry, old King Oswald's town, is the road to Wales, as names like Welsh Frankton and Maesterfyn would suggest even to the word-blind. And those blue hills ahead are the mountains of Wales. So race on into Oswestry, the gateway to the Principality. But don't miss Whittington. Here on the very border of Wales is everything English. A castle, a moat, a village green, a duckpond, and a pub, and all within a couple of acres. So much in so little.

Oswestry may be in Shropshire, but there's no doubt it's near Wales. Lloyd Mansion is splendid English black-and-white, but its real name is Llwyd Mansion; that border isn't far away.

Chirk, to the north, has a harsh-sounding name, but plenty to offer. For we are in Wales at last and in the grounds of Chirk Castle you can see what remains of Offa's Dyke, the wall built to keep the Welsh out (or was it to keep the English in?). And further west a far more lasting wall is visible, the Welsh hills, not yet fierce and forbidding, but the valleys are deeper now, and their sides are steeper. Which is why Thomas Telford had to carry his canal across them by magnificent aqueducts, like the one ahead, the Pontycysyllte, soaring high above the silver Dee.

Quite suddenly you're in Llangollen. If it is International Eisteddfod time (July), you may be short of somewhere to stay, but you won't be short of something to do. And when you've samp-led all the treasures of the town, set off again along the A5 to Bala through what Ruskin called "some of the loveliest brook and glen scenery in the world." Down below the river sparkles, and across the valley the hillsides are golden with bracken, and green with oak and ash and the spreading Christmas trees planted by the Forestry Commission.

The road from Bala to Festiniog climbs up beside the scurrying Tryweryn, designed surely for the trout's delight. But the land is getting harsher, and across the cold, menacing waters of Llyn Celyn are the twin peaks of Arenig Fawr and Arenig Fach, bare bony mountains both. And beyond them miles of waste, brown with bracken, ruled across by the black peat lines of the drainage ditches.

Then, all at once, straight ahead, are the mountains of Snowdonia, rising rank on rank. From now on, it's all downhill through slate-grey Festiniog, through Maentwrog with its distinctly Tyrolean flavour, along the flat meanderings of the Dwyryd to Penrhyndeudraeth, where Bertrand Russell thought his last thoughts, and on to Portmeirion, a dream made real, an Italian village on a North Wales peninsula, impossible but true.

Once you've crossed the tollroad over the Glaslyn estuary — but please do look back at the view of the mountains — there's the whole of the south coast of the Lleyn Peninsula in front of you; Portmadoc and nearby unspoilt Borth-y-Gest; Criccieth with its castle and its memories of David Lloyd George; Pwllheli with its beaches and its holiday camp; Abersoch and its boats; and the iron-bound coast of Hell's Mouth round to Aberdaron, which is Lleyn's Land's End.

There is no way now but to turn up the northern coast of the peninsula, so reminiscent of Pembroke, a plateau from which conical hills stand up without warning. Ahead are the triple peaks of Yr Eifl, more familiarly, the Rivals. One of them, Tre'r Ceiri, is the site of the finest prehistoric village in Wales.

Fifteen miles of glorious coast road bring us to the county town of Caernarvon with the finest castle in the country, where Princes of Wales are invested, where pennants flutter in the breeze, and where trumpets sound a dying fall in the evening air. This is your base camp, your springboard for the assault on the Snowdon massif lying just to the south-east, so rest awhile and take your fill of the castle and the town that was founded by the Romans, who called it Segontium, and from its quays shipped Anglesey copper and gold, lead and pearls from the mountains and rivers you are soon about to cross.

Three passes strike through Snowdonia, all running north-west to south-east. Aim first for Beddgelert, with Llyn Cwellyn on the right and the huge mass of Snowdon on the left. All the way along the crags loom dangerously over the valley.

At Beddgelert, reputed site of the grave of the faithful hound Gelert, a left turn takes you past Llyn Dinas and Llyn Gwynant, and another takes you back towards Caernarvon via Llanberis. With Snowdon now on your left and Glyder Fawr on the right, the route runs through a magnificent example of a pass shaped by the glaciers of the Ice Ages — steep-sided, U-shaped, with hanging valleys from which streams drop in white ribbons, to the main valley below. Above you the crescent-shaped hawk hovers and the raven grunts his deep-throated croak as he flaps his slow way from one crag to another. At Llanberis itself those tired of driving

Further south lies Rhosneigr, and beyond that still, almost at the Strait again, is the incredible Sahara-like stretch of Newborough Warren, a paradise for naturalists and the best place on the island for views of the whole majestic skyscape of Snowdonia, land of the Princes of Gwynedd.

So back across the bridge, through Bangor, a university town with some style, to Betws-y-Coed by way of the Nant Frangcon Pass, the third and last way through the mountains. The scenery is much the same as before — stupendous. Through grey slate Bethesda, the road climbs towards the forbidding pile of Glyder Fawr, with 3,000 ft. peaks all around. As you drop down into Capel Curig, look to the right. There, queening it over them all, is the summit of Snowdon itself, often scarfed in cloud, but sometimes heart-stoppingly golden in the sun.

The road to Betws is thickly wooded, real squirrel country. The Swallow Falls, whose Welsh name means Foaming Cataract, a much more accurate description, are truly beautiful. So is Betws itself, despite the traffic and the summer crowds.

The route north is along the Conwy Valley, flat-bottomed, wide, and as Conwy comes nearer, wider and wider still. The sun begins to sparkle off the water, producing that special light known only in estuaries. When Conwy itself is reached, it is time to stop and stare again, for here be marvels — yet another of Telford's suspension bridges, with its modern replacement; the Smallest House in Wales; and a huge castle, which has stood there for nearly 900 years.

When you've had your fill, turn east for the last leg of our route. Within a mile or so you'll see the truth of the old saying; "God made Llandudno Bay but man made Llandudno Junction". There is no doubt who was the better architect. The Junction is a mess, but the Bay is a miracle, an arc of well-washed sand, hemmed in by the limestone headlands of the Great and Little Ormes.

The route to Chester is now a seductive one. A55 has been much improved. You can speed along it where delays were once inevitable. But if you do you'll miss a lot. Towns like St. Asaph, crouched in its gentle valley, dominated by the smallest cathedral in England and Wales; Holywell, where the pilgrims still come to the sacred spring, hoping to leave their crutches behind them; Ruthin with its castle and its "Breeches Bible" in Llanfwrog Church; and many other gems.

But even if you stick to A55, there's still Ewloe Castle and there's always Hawarden, the home of Mr. Gladstone, where the writer once had the privilege of being taken round by a distinguished old gentleman, descendant of the Grand Old Man himself ("I vote Tory", he said. "So would Grand-dad if he'd been alive today"!).

And then the last flat run across the Saltney marshes to the end of our route — the ancient city of Chester. There can surely be no finer finish. This must be one trip where arriving is as pleasurable as travelling. Roman remains; medieval town walls; the Rows, those unique, undercover, first-floor, shopping arcades that modern architects are just beginning to re-invent; fine inns; famous stores; a river; a racecourse; and a cathedral — within Chester's walls you can find anything.

So we end, fittingly enough, with another, and a final example of *multum in parvo*, a lot in a little, a phrase you will surely agree is a pretty fair description of the route we've taken together.

The view at Llyn Gwynant, Caernarvonshire

Beach and Castle at Criccieth, Lleyn Peninsula

then look at the castle or take the mountain railway to Snowdon's distant summit, at a price of course, and maybe only after a long wait in a queue. And then it's the twisting run back to Caernarvon and a look across the Menai Strait at the next objective — Anglesey. The road leads to the island by way of Telford's suspension bridge. The views from it are marvellous, with the Menai Strait glittering on either side, and woodlands running down to the water's edge. But once you're across you are in Wales no longer, or at least you're in a very different Wales. You are in Mon, the mysterious island of the Druids.

They speak Welsh here, of course; more than in any other county in Wales, or so they say. And yet it doesn't feel like Wales. For one thing, there are no mountains here; even the so-called Holyhead and Parys Mountains would hardly rate as hillocks anywhere else in the Principality. And for another thing, the centre of the island is a bit of an industrial mess.

SEAWEED-COVERED ISLETS

But forget about that. Go anti-clockwise around the coast, for the beauty of the island lies in its bays. The wide sands of Red Wharf, Benllech and Dulas; rocky Moelfre and the ghostly port of Amlwch; the beach at Bull Bay, and Cemaes's splendid semi-circle. Beyond Holyhead — devoutly to be missed — is Trearddur Bay, with seaweed-covered islets punctuating its golden sands.

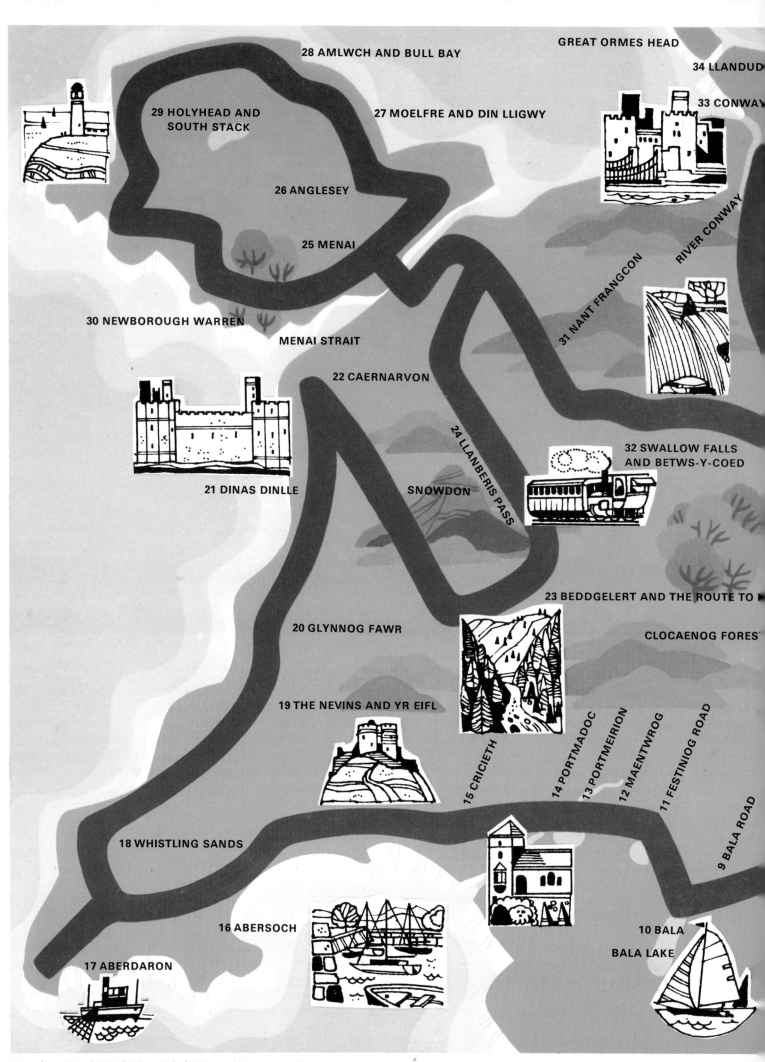

GREAT ORMES HEAD

28 AMLWCH AND BULL BAY

34 LLANDUD

33 CONWAY

29 HOLYHEAD AND
SOUTH STACK

27 MOELFRE AND DIN LLIGWY

26 ANGLESEY

25 MENAI

31 NANT FRANGCON

RIVER CONWAY

30 NEWBOROUGH WARREN

MENAI STRAIT

22 CAERNARVON

24 LLANBERIS PASS

32 SWALLOW FALLS
AND BETWS-Y-COED

21 DINAS DINLLE

SNOWDON

23 BEDDGELERT AND THE ROUTE TO

20 GLYNNOG FAWR

CLOCAENOG FORES

19 THE NEVINS AND YR EIFL

15 CRICIETH

14 PORTMADOC

13 PORTMEIRION

12 MAENTWROG

11 FESTINIOG ROAD

9 BALA ROAD

18 WHISTLING SANDS

16 ABERSOCH

10 BALA

BALA LAKE

17 ABERDARON

Photos: *Peter Baker / B.T.A. / Colour Lib Int / K.N. Done / Noel Habgood / Picturepoint / Bruce Scott / Spectrum*

36 CHESTER

RIVER DEE

35 ST. ASAPH AND
THE CHESTER ROAD

WAYFARER'S GUIDE
9

1 NANTWICH

LLANGOLLEN BRIDGE

8 LLANGOLLEN

7 TREVOR

6 CHIRK (CHIRK CASTLE)

5 OSWESTRY

4 WHITTINGTON

3 ELLESMERE

2 WHITCHURCH

Ben Manchip

Illustrations: Elsie Wrigley / Richard Hock   Plant Notes: Geoffrey Gilbert   Animals and Birds: Jeremy Johns

1 **NANTWICH:** The "wich" in the name indicates a salt town, like nearby Northwich and Middlewich, where brine is dried out to make salt. The brine came from the rocks underlying so much of Cheshire, rocks which were laid down, millions of years ago, when these islands were as hot and dry as any desert.

Today Nantwich is worth looking at for other reasons. Churche's Mansion is now a licensed restaurant, which doesn't stop it being one of the finest black-and-white half-timbered buildings in the county, heavily decorated but not so heavily that it topples over. It's near the centre of the town, so there's no difficulty finding it. And while you're still in the town take a look at Sweet Briar Hall and the "magpie" houses in Welsh Row. The church is 14th Century and has an eight-sided tower and some splendidly-carved stalls. And if all this staring and all that salt makes you thirsty, try the half-timbered Crown Inn.

The altar, St. Mary's Church, and (inset) one of the splendidly carved stalls

Before cars — mounting block at Nantwich

2 **WHITCHURCH:** Do not drive noisily through Whitchurch. You might waken it up. For the over-riding impression it gives is one of sleepiness, which is odd for what is actually a busy Shropshire market town. But see it on non-market days and you'll take the point. This is the heart of "Oh, peaceful England", which is fitting, since the man who wrote that song, Sir Edward German, was born here in 1862. There aren't too many of the old buildings left, but the feeling is still that of a town that has been here half as long as time. The church was largely rebuilt in the 18th Century, but there are some interesting 15th Century monuments, including the tomb of the Talbots. Not the most exciting place in the world, Whitchurch, but taking a break here never did anybody any harm.

3 **ELLESMERE:** You mustn't m[iss] this place — "Little Lakeland". T[he] first lake, or mere, appears in lovely woo[ds] as you approach the town from Wh[it]church. The one you'll see best is by t[he] roadside near the town centre. There['s] parking, picnicking and boating here (b[ut] watch it, because the water is very, ve[ry] deep). When you've had enough of t[he] meres, go up to the old castle mound—no[w] turned into a bowling green—and look o[ut] on England's green and pleasant land.

15th Century monument in Whitchurch parish church

Little lakeland at Ellesmere

WHITTINGTON: Don't miss little Whittington. It is tiny, but its acreage contains most things that go to make up the traditional English village. There's the ruined castle (with a curse on whoever opens an old chest in one of the two towers, all that is left of the ancient [on]e). There's a moat, with a drawbridge and swans; a pond with ducks to go with it; a village green (triangular, like all the best ones); and of course there's a pub, or rather, pubs. You would have to go a long way to find so much tucked into such little space. Add to that the 17th Century Halston Hall, a bit to the north-west, and who could ask for anything more?

Street scene, Oswestry

5 OSWESTRY: The place where once you could see St. Oswald's tree, or cross. You cannot now, but there is still a lot left. This was the town of saintly King Oswald of Northumbria — that would be about the middle of the 7th Century. The fact that the splendid black-and-white house, Lloyd Mansion, is properly called Llwyd Mansion shows just how near the Welsh border is now. So, in its way, does the fact that the town has a Norman castle, or at least the ruins of one. Richard II held a parliament there in 1398, but for nearly 300 years before that the castle had been there for war, not parley. In those days the border was fighting country. Even further back in history Oswestry clearly lived through troubled times. A mile or so up the Gobowen road is Old Oswestry, a large earthwork, some 2,000 years old, and now an Ancient Monument. To the west of the town you pick up traces of Offa's Dyke, that rampart running from the Dee to the Wye, named after the 8th Century King of Mercia, and designed to keep the warring Welsh away from the equally warring English.

[Th]e ruined castle at Whittington — complete with curse

DARK SCAVENGER

The raven is the largest British member of the crow family. Once common in the centres of towns and cities, the raven has gradually been forced north and west, so that it is rare in all England but the Cornish Moors. North Wales offers both seclusion and a suitable diet, for sheep carrion is almost staple food. However, ravens will eat almost anything and those that summer on Snowdon rely upon tourists' scraps for their survival. Perched, the bird is far from beautiful, but in flight it is magnificent.

[Wa]rning to visitors: the water is deeper than it seems

6 **CHIRK:** The road north leads by way of Gobowen, hardly more attractive than its name, to Chirk, far more pleasing than its harsh monosyllable would suggest. Chirk Castle is fine, from the imposing wrought-iron entrance gates right up to the 15th Century house itself. But check the opening hours. The park, which is extensive, contains more remains of Offa's Dyke, and they do say that if the weather's good you can see 17 counties from the castle. There is no real proof that anybody has ever seen them all at the same time, but if you are lucky enough to get a glimpse of half of them, you will not forget it, for the scenery is delightful. And different. For you're in Wales now, and will be for the next 200 miles or so.

Wrought-iron entrance gates at Chirk Castle

7 **TREVOR:** The route now bends westwards towards Llangollen. But keep a lookout for the turning on the right signposted "Trevor" (the name of a place, not a person) which takes you down to the silvery Dee just below the marvellous Pontycysyllte aqueduct. It was built by Thomas Telford in 1805, is 1,007 ft. long and soars 120 ft. above the river. As a change from sitting down by the Dee looking up at the aqueduct — a pleasant enough pastime in itself — make your way up to the towpath and look down on the country-side below. It's delicious. The canal bed is cleaned by a very simple method, built into it by Telford himself. You (or rather British Waterways engineers) simply pull out a plug in the bottom of the cast-iron trough carrying the water of the canal, and it all drains out in a splendid waterfall down to the Dee below. This was done last in late 1971, so the next cleaning isn't due for a long time yet.

Now carry on along the north side of the Dee valley with the river and the canal on your immediate left. The scenery is getting even better now, with steep hillsides, beautifully wooded, and a ruin on almost every summit. Then all at once you find you're in Llangollen.

Thomas Telford's Aqueduct 120 ft. above the Dee

LLANGOLLEN: The International Eisteddfod; the Horseshoe Falls; Valle Crucis Abbey; Plas Newydd; Castle Dinas Brân; the Eglwyseg Rocks; the famous 13th Century bridge over the Dee; the church dedicated to St. Collen, the man with the longest name in Christendom — what more do you want from a place this size? In fact, if it's Eisteddfod time, which is to say July, you'll get much more, for a cross-section of the world will be there as well, from Nigerian dancers to Serbo-Croat singers.

Most of the places mentioned are reachable by car, but there's a real case for parking the vehicle and using your legs. Stand for a while on the bridge over the Dee and see how many salmon you spot. Then have a look at St. Collen's church. It really is his church since he is buried here. He lived in the 7th Century and rejoiced in a name too long for most men to manage—Collen ap Gwynnawg ap Clydwg ap Cowdra ap Caradog Freichfras ap Llyr Merim ap Yrth ap Cunedda Wledig. After which it seems odd to think he might have been a Frenchman, for he was educated in Orleans, and became a hermit in Brittany before settling in this beautiful valley to which he gave his name, Collen having become Gollen.

Not very far from the Bridge over the River Dee is the conical hill called Dinas Brân, wearing the ruins of its castle like a crown. The view is worth the walk. To the west is the Horseshoe Pass. The views from the top are splendid, especially of the Eglwyseg Rocks, great layers of carboniferous limestone, full of fossils about 250 million years old.

On the way back down the Horseshoe Pass, call in at Valle Crucis Abbey. Valle Crucis, the Valley of the Cross, takes its name from the Pillar of Eliseg, put up in memory of Prince Eliseg, killed in battle in A.D. 603. The cross was thrown down by Roundhead soldiers and broken, but was later re-erected. The Abbey was a Cistercian foundation, dating from the end of the 12th Century, and though it is ruined, the ruins are noble.

Nearby are the Horseshoe Falls. They are not natural; they are yet another example of the engineering genius of Thomas Telford, who built them in 1830 to provide a constant supply of water to his canal, and they've been doing it ever since. Before you leave Llangollen, you must look at Plas Newydd, the home of the "Ladies of Llangollen", who were actually Irish, and have been described as genuine English eccentrics! The house is far grander now than when Lady Eleanor Butler and her friend the Honourable Sarah Ponsonby settled there, dressing like men, receiving the famous and the gifts they brought, and devoting their lives to "celibacy and knitting blue stockings". Not the least eccentric thing about them is that the house was bought in 1809, while the Ladies were living in it, by their maid Mary Caryll, who left it to her mistresses when she died, something of a reversal of a more usual pattern of events! All three now sleep in St. Collen's churchyard, together for ever.

The Union Canal at Llangollen

Noble ruins of Valle Crucis Abbey

Plas Newydd — "for blue stockings"

The Dee at Llangollen with its 13th Century bridge in the background

9 **BALA ROAD:** From Llangollen to Bala by way of Corwen takes you through what John Ruskin described as some of the finest brook and glen country in the world. And indeed it must be. Everywhere these days there is evidence of the work of the Forestry Commission, but there are more than enough deciduous trees — the oak, the ash, and the alder — for the colours never for one moment to be monotonous. The river unwinds its silver ribbon below, now racing through a stretch of rapids, now sliding round a gravel reach to form a pool that must be full of salmon and trout. Above the tree line the bracken is golden and the sky is blue — sometimes! Not always, but when it is the road to Bala is like the road to Heaven.

The Bala Road — "finest brook and glen country in the world"

10 **BALA** itself is a straight town strung along a straight street. It is high-ish, fairly wide, and not particularly handsome. But Bala Lake, or Llyn Tegid, to give it its proper Welsh name, is delightful. Five miles or so long by one mile wide, it is the longest natural lake in Wales, and the circuit — down the north-west side along the Dolgellau road, and back up the south-eastern side through the village of Llangower — is well worth doing. And if your interests tend that way you can swim, boat, sail, or fish the lake as well. Fishing is particularly rewarding — trout, pike and perch, and a unique specimen called the gwyniad, unique because it is found nowhere else. Why it hasn't ever swum out of the lake into the wide world by way of the River Dee has never been explained.

Bala Lake, longest natural lake in Wales

11 **FESTINIOG ROAD:** From Bala climb up by the sparkling Tryweryn, a torrent made solely for trout, past Llyn Celyn, now a reservoir for Liverpool Corporation, but none the less menacing for that as it crouches under the shoulders of Arenig Fawr (2,800 ft.) and Arenig Fach (2,200 ft). These are our first real mountains. Once the lake is left behind the road climbs through bare, brown peatlands. Nobody and nothing lives here, except the mountain fox and its prey. Men have tried to, as the occasional ruined cottage proves. But the fact that the cottages are ruined proves they failed. Then quite suddenly there is a building in the distance. It turns out to be a garage. "The highest garage in Wales" it claims. And the loneliest, as well, without any doubt.

The land now falls away sickeningly on the left hand side, but at least it provides a splendid place for a carpark and a viewpoint. And what views! Ahead are the mountains of Central Snowdonia with the top of Snowdon itself just visible. And

then the climb is over and the route dro down through a wooded valley to Fe iniog, splendid only because of its setti Mountains, mountains everywhere, a plenty of drops to drink, for every hillsi has its lake and waterfall, and even predominantly grey slate of the a glistens with all sorts of colours after ra Two waterfalls are worth seeing — Cyn and Rhaiadr Cwm. Both are just before y get into Festiniog itself. Rhaiadr Cwm most impressive, being made up of successive stretches of rapids and falls

12 **MAENTWROG** has been called the prettiest village in Wales, but then so have many others. It has Tyrolean-looking houses; the Raven Falls and the Black Fall, Rhaiadr Du; it is the site of the meeting of the Prysor and the Dwyryd, two attractive rivers; and all around are the mountains with the sea obviously not far away to the west. If you want a legend, this place has got it too; in the churchyard is the stone of Twrog, a giant who gave his name to the village. Or was he not a giant but a saint? Nobody seems to know for sure, which leaves you free to make up your own legend.

But if after that you feel in need of definite guidance, Maentwrog has a milestone that will tell you how far you are from London (226 miles), Dolgellau Caernarvon, Bala, Beddgelert, Harlech and Barmouth.

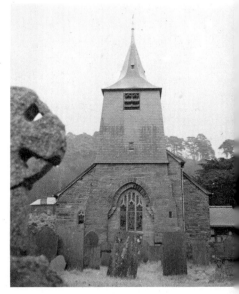

Maentwrog — a Tyrolean look

3 **PORTMEIRION**: Whatever else you have to miss on the route, don't miss this Italian village on a North Wales peninsula, a riot of colour, invention, fantasy, humour, and beauty (it was used as the location for a TV serial some years ago, *The Prisoner*, starring Patrick McGoohan). The owner and architect, Sir Clough Williams-Ellis, having been left a legacy and some land, set about creating some of the beauty he had seen in Italy in his native Wales. He succeeded beyond belief. Portmeirion is a hotel surrounded by the cottages making up the village, but it is open to the public from Easter to October, from 10.00 a.m. to 7.00 p.m. And even if you cannot get there during those months, still try and have a discreet look round. It will stay in your mind forever.

Portmeirion, Italian-style village

Another look at Portmeirion: humour, fantasy and beauty here

Portmadoc harbour — a haven for small yachts

14 **PORTMADOC** is reached by the toll road across the Glaslyn Estuary, where there are magnificent views back up into the mountains. Portmadoc is a tiny little port that once shipped out most of the slate quarried up around Festiniog. Less than 200 years ago the land it stands on did not exist. It was reclaimed from the sea by the efforts of William Alexander Maddocks, after whom the town is named. It was a long struggle against the elements, lasting from 1798 to the 1820's, by which time Maddocks was near the end of his life. Now of course the slate trade has declined almost to nothing and Portmadoc has had to find new sources of income. Tourism is one, for the place is surrounded by beautiful scenery — the mountains already mentioned, beaches like Black Rock Sands to the south-west, and the splendidly unspoilt little seaside resort of Borth-y-Gest, one mile due south, where there is a distinctly restful, Victorian air about the place. But to stand on Portmadoc's little quay-side and look out across the harbour is to feel rested too, for all is quiet and it's clear that here time waits for no man, but only for the tide.

187

15 **CRICIETH:** Spell it with two c's, as the English mainly do, or one, as do the Welsh, it still remains a nice little spot. It faces due south, with a very mild climate, a castle, two beaches, two churches, and Brynawelon, the home of David Lloyd George. Cricieth castle, although ruined, is most impressive. It stands on a conical mount which sticks out to sea — it is almost a peninsula — and which separates the East and West beaches as it stares across Tremadoc Bay to Harlech Castle, only six miles distant.

The Lloyd George house, Brynawelon, stands on a spur just to the north of the High Street. There is a carved bust of the Great Man, or The Goat, as one or two unkinder colleagues called him, in the Memorial Hall near the larger of the two churches, St. Deiniol's. Whatever his critics said, he was the local hero.

The Welsh Wizard's bones, however, do not lie in Cricieth, but in the nearby village of Llanystumdwy, which was his boyhood home (though not his birth-place; he was born in Chorlton-on-Medlock, in Manchester); the grave is quietly impressive, looking down on the little Dwyfor as it runs below.

Sunset over Cricieth Castle

Bust of Lloyd George in Memorial Hall

16 **ABERSOCH:** West of Pwllheli, a beach five miles long runs to Llanbedrog where, round a headland, is Abersoch Bay. Abersoch itself is in the middle of the gentle crescent of the three miles long bay and is in imminent danger of becoming too popular. But go early in the season and you won't regret it. There will be enough yacht sails about to add to the gaiety and colour, the woo will still dip down to the beach, t weather will in all probability be mild, a the bathing will be an eye-open literally, since the water is exception clear in the bay. The islets to the south St. Tudwal's and the lighthouse on then a warning to sailors that just around t headland is Hell's Mouth.

Abersoch . . . plenty of yacht sails to be seen in 3-mile bay

17 **ABERDARON:** If you are looking for the least-spoiled place of the lot, this fishing village will take some beating. Yet a thousand years ago it was probably as busy a place as any in North Wales. For it was here that pilgrims rested as they came to the end of their long trek to Bardsey, the Island of the Saints. Y Gegin Fawr, the Great Kitchen, was the hostel where they stayed waiting for a boat to take them on the last stage of their journey, often the most perilous, to Bardsey, two miles away. The Great Kitchen is still there, although it is now a café. You will get a distinct feeling that not much else has changed in Aberdaron, though. The present church, down on the beach — the graveyard wall is also the sea wall — is mainly 12th Century, although the doorway is Norman and parts date back another 600 years before that. The beach is splendid and safe, the cliffs are impressive, there's river and sea fishing, plenty of fine walks, and a climate so good that in one memorable year the sun said to have shone on 316 days out of 3 Only 2½ miles away is Braich-y-Pw which is Wales' Land's End, or at least Lleyn Peninsula's; many people, and all of them locals, will be found to sw it is more beautiful and far less comm cialised than the Cornish one.

Aberdaron — 12th Century church

Porth Oer sands whistle while you walk

19 THE NEVINS:

Further along the north coast of the Lleyn Peninsula, back up along the Pilgrims' Way from Bardsey Island, are Nevin (or Nefyn) and Morfa Nevin, two attractive beaches. Morfa Nevin's bay is called Porth Dinllaen, and there are fishermen's cottages on the beach, as well as the 18th Century Ty Coch Inn. Both places are great for sailing, and for walking along the cliffs, which are supplied with lots of pleasant paths, which are in their turn supplied with lots of seats for the weary walker. Not that you'll need them, for the turf on the cliff tops is soft and springy.

Just up the coast from the Nevins are three peaks known collectively as Yr Eifl. In Welsh that means The Forks, but Yr Eifl has been anglicised into The Rivals. And indeed they do look to be rivalling one another as they stand up from the lower land of Lleyn. The road to Caernarvon winds between two of them. If you feel energetic, climb up the one on your left, Tre'r Ceiri. On top is the finest prehistoric village site in Wales. And even if you're not much interested in archaeology, the view from the top is superb.

18 WHISTLING SANDS:

Just north of Aberdaron is Porth Oer, a beautiful little bay, where the silvery sand whistles as you walk on it. Well, not exactly whistles; there's something of a squeak in it, too. To get this effect, which enchants children, of course, try sliding each foot forward fractionally as it hits the sand. Once you've mastered it, you won't want to stop, but if you do, the bathing is good and safe, and you can fish off the rocks. Access to the bay is by a private, but clearly signposted, lane where you can park your car for 5p a day. The owners trust you to put the coin in a slot.

Fishermen's cottages on the beach at Porth Dinllaen

20 CLYNNOG FAWR:

This little village, just north of Yr Eifl, has a magnificent little church, dedicated to St. Bueno. The original building, of wattle and daub, was built in the 7th Century. All of that has gone, of course, except for the foundations. Now on the site there stands a beautiful building in the Perpendicular style, all lightness and grace. There is an ancient chest just inside the door, made from a single log of wood. It was carved to hold the money raised by selling calves and lambs born with a notch in their ears — St. Bueno's birthmark it was called. All such animals were set aside, sold on Trinity Sunday in the churchyard, and the cash went into the chest. It must have been a lively place at times, for there was also in the church a pair of "dog tongs", with which dogs were removed from the church during service.

Near the church and connected to it by a cloister, is the old church where the good saint is said to be buried and where miracles of healing were performed at the grave, or rather on it, for you had to sleep on it for the night, usually after bathing in the well, still in existence near the church.

And to take you even further back in time, between the church and the sea is a four-legged cromlech which could date back 3,000 years or more.

Ancient chest at St. Bueno's Church

Four-legged cromlech — 3,000 years old

The encroaching sea at Dinas Dinlle

21 DINAS DINLLE:

DINAS DINLLE: Further north along the Caernarvon road, and just opposite the imposing entrance gates to Glynllifon Park, now a college, is a little lane leading to the sea. The hamlet it leads to is nothing to get excited over, for though it is right down on the beach, the cliffs have almost died away and the sands stretch featureless to the north. But immediately to the south is a large hill. Climb it and you will find yourself in the middle of an Iron Age earthwork. The impression of the past is overpowering here, particularly in the twilight of a summer evening. But even more overpowering is the sense that all man's works, however massive, are doomed to disappear in the end. For the sea is relentlessly eating away at the hill on which the fortress stands, and one day all will have gone, leaving not a wrack behind.

WATCH OUT FOR SEALS
The coast of North Wales offers an excellent opportunity of seeing both species of British seals: the common seal (ABOVE) and the grey seal (BELOW). There are five known breeding-grounds of the grey seal and only one of the common seal yet, despite the unequal ratio, the common is the one more likely to be seen. Although both species are to some extent under attack from man, neither is in any obvious danger of extinction and the interested traveller may still find an opportunity to study the seal in its wild state — but, of course, it is essential to keep a careful watch on the sea-rocks.

22 CAERNARVON:

CAERNARVON: At first sight there can be nothing to say about this town which isn't about the castle, for the one positively overpowers the other. Naturally enough, for it is the finest castle in North Wales and indeed there are very few anywhere in Britain to beat it. But there's a lot more to Caernarvon than the castle. The name, for instance. When the Welsh looked at the Roman fort of Segontium—the ruins of which are still there for you to see 600 yards southeast of the castle, along the Beddgelert road — they called it by their word for camp or fort — Y Gaer. And to distinguish

Aerial view of Caernarvon

it from other forts in the district they add the phrase "yn Arfon" which is to say " the district of Arfon" and Arfon itself w their word for "Opposite to the Isle Anglesey". So the fort became known Y Gaer yn Arfon, which is more or le what it's called today.

Edward I built the present fortress at t end of the 13th Century, on the peninsu lying between the Menai Strait, the Riv Seiont, and the River Cadnant, now cu verted under the town. Simultaneously built the town and the walls which survi today. They can be best seen along Ba Quay which runs along the course of t now-underground river.

The castle is a masterpiece, although more of a ruin than is evident from t (much-restored) outside. But it is too t to be described here. The admirab Ministry guide is essential; it is on sale the castle. And when you've read it a covered as much of the castle as wind a limb will allow — for there's an awful lot climbing if you're going to explore it all go and sit down across the River Seio Look at the castle standing there as it h done for 700 years, and as other forts d before it, and remember that it was dov the river in front of you that Roman galle sailed from their fort of Segontium a fe hundred yards to the right, a fort who ruins you can still see. Then marvel at t continuity of British history. Why, even t mother church of the district, call Llanbeblig, is dedicated to St. Peblig, w seems very likely to have been really call Publius, since he was probably one of t sons of the Emperor Magnus Maxim There is a lot of history at Caernarvon, j waiting to be picked up.

Beddgelert .... the scenery hereabouts is staggering

Caernarvon Castle — the finest in North Wales — spans 700 years of history

23 BEDDGELERT.

There are three main passes through Snowdonia, and all strike from north-west to south-east. First take the Beddgelert road, the one that leads out of Caernarvon past the remains of Segontium. Within miles you are climbing up to the mountains. The scenery is staggering. On your left is the Snowdon massif, of largely volcanic rocks, rising to 3,560 feet. On the right front, after the cold waters of Llyn Cwellyn have been passed, is the dark bulk of Moel Hebog, almost 1,000 ft lower than Snowdon's highest point, but still forbidding. The crags tower above you, black and fantastic in shape, clothed with bracken on the lower slopes, cleft by streams rushing down their slopes, and specked by whitish dots that turn out to be sheep. There are woods, too, on the descent to Beddgelert, and if you are blessed with sunshine the scene is likely never to leave your mind.

Beddgelert attracts crowds — climbers of course, but fishermen, naturalists, painters, walkers, and those who merely crave its quiet beauty. The pass of Aberglaslyn runs south, the Nant Gwynant Pass north-east. Both are almost painfully beautiful. But despite all that, Beddgelert is perhaps best known for the legend that gave it its name — in English, Gelert's Grave. Gelert was a wolf-hound belonging to Prince Llewelyn the Great. The Prince went hunting, leaving Gelert to guard his infant son lying in a cradle. In the Prince's absence, a wolf attacked the child. Gelert came to the rescue and fought and chased the wolf, finally killing it. When the Prince came home he found the cradle overturned, and blood everywhere. At that moment Gelert returned, blood on his jaws. The Prince, thinking Gelert had killed his son, took out his sword and slew the hound. Then he found his son unharmed under the up-turned cradle. The Grave of Gelert, about quarter of a mile south of the village, was erected by the Prince in his remorse.

It is a touching tale, and the only flaw in it is that the grave was actually built in 1810 as a tourist attraction by a local publican, David Pritchard of the Royal Goat Hotel. Never mind; though the sepulchre is spurious, the tale may be true.

191

24 **LLANBERIS PASS:** The return towards the Menai Strait goes through a classic example of a glaciated valley — the Llanberis Pass. Everywhere are hard unyielding crags, Snowdon to the left and Glyder Fawr to the right, carved and gouged and shaped into their present form by nothing harder than ice. During the Ice Age huge glaciers flowed down these Snowdonia valleys, smoothing away all but the hardest rock outcrops. They formed U-shaped valleys and the side streams were left hanging, so that their waters now drop down as ragged white ribbons to the valley below. On the way to Llanberis you

Dolbadarn Castle, Llanberis

will come across one of the outcrops where the road bends round a rock the glacier could not grind away.

Below the village of Nant Peris, the original settlement in the valley, is Llyn Peris, one of this pass's two lovely lakes. Between it and the other — Llyn Padarn — is Llanberis, with hotels and its castle, Dolbadarn; and, of course, its station for the mountain railway ascent of Snowdon. For those who can't climb the mountain unaided, this rack railway, the only one in Britain, is the way to the summit and one of the finest views that you will ever come across. Given no cloud, you can see Ireland, the Isle of Man, the Lake District Hills to the north and those of Pembroke, far to the south. But be reminded that the queue for the train can be long and the wait longer, that it is not the cheapest trip in the world, and that brilliant sunshine in the valley can be accompanied by cold, swirling mist at the summit. Nevertheless, if you have the time, try it. If all goes well it will take your breath away.

From Dolbadarn Castle you can look up and down the valley observing that U-shaped profile if you wish. But one thing you will not be able to ignore is slate. Llanberis is slate. Everything is slate, from the house in which a man is born, to the gravestone that marks where he lies when he is dead. One look up the valley shows where it has all come from; the mountain side has been torn apart and the rubble lies everywhere. It can sparkle in the sunshine, but on a dull day it can be depressing. Nevertheless, people come to these valleys more than ever before, because they know they are the gateways to some of the finest scenery in Britain, and as a gateway the Pass of Llanberis has no superior.

The Menai Suspension Bridge

25 **MENAI:** We now come across another landmark of Thomas Telford. Come across it quite literally, for his suspension bridge is our only way into Anglesey, the mysterious island of Mona, the home of the Druids, about whom so much nonsense has been written. They were, however, real enough to terrify the Romans when they came to conquer, if the historian Tacitus is to be believed. He noted their habit of murdering captives and using their bodies for divination and prophecy. Nobody in Anglesey is likely to do that to you today, so cross Telford's bridge with confidence. It was built in seven years, cost £120,000—about £2,000,000 today—and is 100 ft. above high water mark. For nearly 150 years it was the longest suspension bridge (1,710 ft) in Britain. The bridge is not only beautiful in itself, it makes available beautiful views to the traveller, who has only to look at the Strait on either side as he crosses, to see a broad band of bright water, dotted with craft of all kinds, with wooded spurs sweeping right down to the water's edge, and fine houses peeping through the trees.

26 **ANGLESEY:** Stick to the coa for that is where the island magic lies, in its beaches and bays, many of them that even in the height of t summer season you can usually find o for yourself. Go anti-clockwise round t island and you will come to the village Pentraeth. All sorts of lanes lead down the sea, to the wide sands of Red Wh Bay, where once a tribe of witches lande having arrived in a boat powered neither sails nor oars and without a rudder. Th stayed to terrify the local folk, and wonder, because it seems likely they we outlawed Irish, suffering the usual punis ment of the time, of being cast adrift their crimes.

Next along from Red Wharf is Benllec a popular resort boasting lots of comfo able hotels and miles of golden sand which explain its popularity with touris

Looking towards Lleyn Peninsula from Abe

27 **DIN LLIGWY:** A roundabout signposted Amlwch to the l Moelfre to the right and Din Lligwy straig ahead. Which of the latter two you look first doesn't matter. Moelfre's harbour rocky, pebbly and absolutely unspoilt. H is the famous lifeboat station where crew have saved more than 600 men fr the sea which can lash this rocky coast

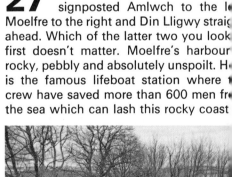

Remains of the ancient village

cient graves at Bryn Celli Ddu, Anglesey

sey

Beaumaris Castle, Anglesey, a fine example of medieval military architecture

iously. If you want to look over the boat, u can count on a welcome, unless the nd's in the wrong quarter, of course. Back to the roundabout and down a rrow winding lane to Din Lligwy. This is cient territory indeed. The first thing that uld catch your eye is Lligwy burial amber, a massive job, probably intended multiple burials and thought to be about 000 years old. Further on are the old apel and the ancient village, with room park in the road. But beware; if it has en wet the path can be muddy. The apel is roofless now, but still with a ugh font, and still looking down over the tant sands of Dulas Bay. About 300 rds away is Din Lligwy, a village about 500 years old, made of square or round uses, roofless, of course, and surrounded a roughly circular stone wall. Look at e thickness of some of the house walls d wonder at the labour involved in a ne when so few tools were available. d across the fields the sands of Dulas y again, where a watch must always have en kept for the Irish and Danish raiders no terrorised these western coasts.

28 **BULL BAY:** It is odd to go to ghostly Amlwch Port today, dark and near derelict, and realise that once its name was on the lips of merchants all over the world. For copper dug out from Parys Mountain (no mountain, really; only 500 ft. high) was shipped from the port. And copper prices were important. Today,

Amlwch is a forgotten port, but the neighbouring beaches are splendid. Bull Bay has attractive coves on its west side, and Cemaes Bay has a fine semi-circle with a sheltered cove on its east. Do not let the ever more frequent signs to Wylfa nuclear power station, crouched on the cliff top, put you off. The coast is delightful.

The forgotten port of Amlwch as it looks today

29

SOUTH STACK: The coast road has swung south now past Church Bay and Llanfachraeth, where the Afon Alaw runs into the sea. Now there is a choice of routes to the real attraction of Holyhead Island — the South Stack, where stupendous cliffs plunge to the sea, and where the rocks composing them are twisted and bent in incredible patterns, and have even been overturned in places. To get there, you can go by Holyhead itself, which can be a traffic nightmare, and is best avoided unless you want to see the harbour. A better way is to aim for Valley and carry on to Trearddur Bay, a lovely beach, attractively punctuated with sea-weed-covered islets, full of rock pools and other fascinating things. From there the road runs to South Stack and its light-house and its suspension bridge.

South Stack lighthouse . . . . "stupendous cliffs plunge to the sea"

30

NEWBOROUGH WARREN In the extreme south-west corn of the island is a place where you cou think yourself anywhere but in the Briti Isles — Newborough Warren. It is a natu reserve now, for in its sandy acres — m after mile of dunes, or so it seems — ra plants are found and visiting birds flock their thousands. The dunes have be fixed, stopping their endless drifting befc the winds, by the planting of Corsic pines, which has changed the character the place without destroying any of charm. It is undoubtedly the best place the island for views of Snowdoni staggering skyscape.

The name Newborough merely mea that it was new when Edward I set up t village to accommodate the natives he h booted out of the town at the far end Menai Strait. There he built a cast making it into an entirely English sett ment and calling it Beaumaris.

Ebeneser Chapel, Newborough Warren

31

NANT FRANGCON: It is time now to go back for the last attack on Snowdonia. Head for Bangor, a university town of some style, with perhaps the oldest cathedral in the British Isles, and certainly the one that has been knocked about most over the centuries. Pass through Bethesda; it has little to offer, but you may be lucky enough to hear some of the singing for which the town is famous. If not, lift your eyes to the hills, for despite the greyness down below there is inspiration in the mass of Carnedd Llewelyn and Carnedd Dafydd ahead and to the left. The road climbs up another of those perfect glaciated valleys — U-shaped, steep sided, with the streams which fall from the hanging valleys streaking the hillsides with foaming white. Ahead the road seems to aiming for the heart of Glyder Fawr, bu the last minute it turns to the left, along chill shore of Llyn Ogwen, seeking easier path through the mountains. It fir it, for soon the bracken and the scree a the overwhelming crags fall away and road begins to drop down the valley of Afon Llugwy towards Capel Curig. Ke your eyes open to the right as you approa the little climbing village. If the weathe kind you may get a glimpse of Snowc towering above the surrounding pea picked out by a shaft of sunshine lanc through the clouds. After Capel Curig valley sides are well-wooded and Llugwy races along beside you. Keep lookout also for The Ugly House on left hand side. It was built in the 1 Century out of huge blocks of stone a may have shocked passers-by then, bu the intervening centuries it seems to ha shed its ugliness and gained some cha On the right, an unclassified road leads to Caer Llugwy, a Roman camp. It is i good strategic position, high above river and commanding the whole vall but what some poor unfortunate La thought of it as he stood on guard in wir has unfortunately not been preserved posterity. Or perhaps fortunately.

Valley of the Afon Llugwy towards Capel Curig

Swallow Falls, Betws-y-Coed

32 **BETWS-Y-COED:** Suddenly the valley of the Llugwy becomes almost gentle. The hills are still high, but they are now all wooded and only the occasional crag breaks through. Then on the left comes the sign "Swallow Falls". These are pure delight. Stretch after stretch of white water leaping over a tumble of rocks or dropping plumb into deep pools, in one of which the ghost of Sir John Wynn of Gwydir is imprisoned as a punishment for the cruel way he dealt with his tenants. These days you have to pay to see the falls, but they're more than worth it, running as they do for hundreds of yards through a thickly-wooded gorge.

Betws-y-Coed, the Chapel in the Woods, is busy but its bridges are beautiful, and the river is almost indescribably lovely, sliding over slabs of rock, and chasing itself round huge boulders. All around are tree-clad hills, and attractive houses, and friendly hotels. If the Swallow Falls are crowded, you can always go to the Fairy Glen, or the Conway Falls, or any of the many beauty spots around.

The Fairy Glen at Betws . . . . one of the many beauty spots around here

THE THEATRE OF 1,000 PUPPETS

In the little Harlequin Puppet Theatre on Rhos-on-Sea promenade overlooking Colwyn Bay, famous puppeteer Eric Bramall presents a company of more than 1,000 puppets in a season of plays, operas, musical comedies and cabaret. Continuing a childhood passion for toy theatres and puppets, this puppet master founded the Eric Bramall Marionettes in 1946, and created a travelling puppet theatre with a company of string puppets. He toured the country, packing and unpacking a ton of scenery and equipment at every theatre. With the building of the Harlequin Puppet Theatre in 1958, his touring days ended. Harlequin productions have appeared on TV, and Eric Bramall has also created many children's puppet shows specially for television. The theatre now has a repertoire of more than 60 productions, including *The Mikado*, *Alice in Wonderland* and *The Nutcracker Suite.* In some sketches the puppeteer is also shown so that the audience can watch his skill. Afternoon shows are for children, evening ones for adults.

195

33 CONWY:

The route drives north from Betws, through Llanrwst, which has been destroyed at least twice in war, and has risen again each time. Soon after Llanrwst, the valley begins to widen and sand banks appear. Wading birds abound and the heron can be seen standing in one-legged thoughtfulness, or pouncing like lightning. The river is approaching its estuary. Sun sparkles on the wet sand, and the pattern of ripples on the water suggests that more than the wind is causing them. The tide is at work now. And there at the river mouth lies Conwy itself. It is a masterpiece of a place with another of Edward's magnificent castles and the Smallest House in Britain, (down by the quay); as well as wonderfully preserved town walls overlooking a harbour almost always rainbowed by the sails of the yachts moored there. If the weather isn't good enough for out of doors there's always Aberconwy, a 14th Century house, and Plas Mawr, now the museum of the Royal Welsh Academy of Art. The children can be set to checking that Plas Mawr has as many doors as there are weeks in the year, and as many windows as there are days.

Conwy . . . "masterpiece of a place with a magnificent castle"

34 LLANDUDNO:

Just over a century ago, Llandudno didn't exist, except for a few cottages and the church of St. Tudno, a 6th Century good man. The church is still there, on the Great Orme Head, but almost everything else has changed. Except for the Great Orme and the Little Orme, which are wonderful limestone headlands, with breathtaking views, caves inviting exploration, and exhilarating walks over the springy turf. And the magnificent arc of Llandudno Bay's golden sands.

The town has a wide Victorian elegance, gracious terraces and some of the best shops in North Wales. The climate is as mild as one could wish. The Happy Valley, on the Great Orme, is a place to spend time looking at the sea, the people, or the botanists who come to collect specimens. There is a frightening cable railway to carry you almost from the centre of the town to the top of the Great Orme, there to look across Conway Bay and the cliffs running westwards towards the sunset. And there are decent hotels to soothe your nerves afterwards with good food and drink. St. Tudno knew a thing or two when he settled here.

Great Orme Railway takes you from centre of Llandudno to cliff panorama

35 ST. ASAPH:

The North Wa[les] coast road has always been [the] easiest route, since there aren't any mou[n]tains to cross. You can speed along for lo[ng] stretches, leaving the coast and its horro[rs]. Yes, horrors. For though the caravan h[as] made cheap holidays available to thousan[ds] who would not otherwise be able to [get] away, nobody can deny that a caravan co[n]urbation is not beautiful; earth hath ma[ny] things to show more fair. So cut inla[nd] from Abergele and aim for St. Asaph. [On] the way, stop at the "Marble Church" [at] Bodelwyddan, a 19th Century woma[n's] memorial to her husband.

Sunny St. Asaph isn't far away, crouch[ing] in its little valley, and dominated, but n[ot] very strongly, by the smallest cathedral [in] England and Wales. The first church he[re] was founded by Kentigern. He had be[en] invited by Cadwallon of Gwynedd to set[tle] anywhere he liked in North Wales. [He] chose a spot where he saw a wild b[oar] rooting the ground with its tusks, which [is] why St. Asaph is in its present delight[ful] spot. The cathedral museum, in the vest[ry] has a fascinating collection of old pra[yer] books and Bibles, including the Breech[es] and Vinegar Bibles (Adam and Eve took [fig] leaves and made themselves "breeche[s]," says the first; and the second talks ab[out] the Parable of the Vinegar, instead [of] the Vineyard.)

But St. Asaph's history goes a long w[ay] further back than that, for the nearby C[efn] Caves, in the limestone hills above [the] town, contain fossil remains that take [you] right back to the Old Stone Age.

The road now runs to Holywell, wh[ere]

CHESTER: The straight road across the Saltney marshes leads [t]o one of the most historic towns in [B]ritain — Chester, Roman Deva. It is [al]most impossible to begin to list the [tre]asures of this town. There are beautifully [ex]cavated Roman remains. There are [m]edieval town walls, nearly two miles long, [an]d walkable-on for most of the way. [T]here is the broad sweep of the Dee, [en]closing in a great meander the Roodee, [sc]ene of revelry and Chester races. The [c]athedral is 14th Century and needs a [g]uide book to itself. There are many lovely [ol]d half-timbered houses. And, most [ch]aracteristic of all, there are the unique [R]ows, which are first-floor undercover [m]edieval shopping arcades, where you can [w]ander in comfort whatever the weather.
 As Chester is a market town and shopping [ce]ntre for Cheshire, North Shropshire and [N]orth Wales, and the gateway to the [h]olidays resorts of the North Wales coast, [tr]affic has always been a problem. Chester [h]as tried to solve it by constructing inner [rin]g roads. But the Chester most people [th]ink of is still as beautiful as it always has [b]een. However, it is a place to explore [be]fore that beauty disappears.

Chester, one of the most historic towns in Britain

[St]. Asaph's, smallest cathedral in England and Wales

[Th]ere is a sacred spring to which the lame [an]d the halt still come for deliverance. The [w]ay it started is interesting, to say the least. [Ap]parently Winifred, a young saintly virgin, [w]as the niece of St. Bueno, who built the [ch]urch in far off Clynnog Fawr. One day a [ge]ntleman attempted to ravish her. She [re]sisted, so he took out his sword and [ch]opped off her head. Whereupon he [dr]opped down dead and the ground [op]ened and swallowed him. The head [ro]lled down the valley and where it [st]opped, a spring started flowing. St. [B]ueno, who was there at the time, was not [un]naturally angered, so he carried the head

back to the corpse, with which it miraculously became united once again. After which unusual experience, St. Winifred went on to live for another fifteen years and St. Bueno went back to Clynnog.
 Further on, as Chester approaches, drop in at the ruins of Ewloe Castle and have a look at Hawarden, the home for many years of the Grand Old Man himself, William Ewart Gladstone. In the grounds are the ruins of the earlier castle, built in the reign of Henry III and destroyed some centuries later. The Library of the present castle contains many interesting mementos of the great Liberal Prime Minister.

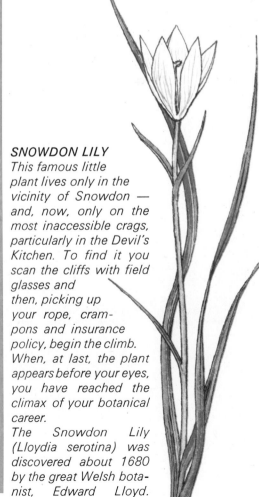

SNOWDON LILY
This famous little plant lives only in the vicinity of Snowdon — and, now, only on the most inaccessible crags, particularly in the Devil's Kitchen. To find it you scan the cliffs with field glasses and then, picking up your rope, crampons and insurance policy, begin the climb. When, at last, the plant appears before your eyes, you have reached the climax of your botanical career.
The Snowdon Lily (Lloydia serotina) was discovered about 1680 by the great Welsh botanist, Edward Lloyd.

The Age of the Manor House

The England of Elizabeth was the England of the manor house, and these manor houses, built in a bewildering variety of styles and from many different materials — local stone, brick, timber and plaster — reflected the sheer exuberance of the Elizabethan love of life. The splendid houses were lovingly draped with elaborate tapestries and given warmth and richness by deep wainscotting.

These fine houses spoke of a new wealth, a new peace in the land and a rapidly developing sense of national style and self-assurance.

Plas Mawr in Conway is one of the finest surviving Elizabethan houses. Built in the 1580s by Robert Wynne who claimed descent from the father of Caractacus, even in those days Plas Mawr was regarded as a "vast house". At that time it would have been set in spacious grounds, reflecting the Elizabethan love of gardening and flowers.

Imagine, when you visit it, the richly ornamented chimney breast in the banqueting hall, which is covered with heraldic devices, shields and crests carved from stone, painted in correct heraldic colours, and you will gain some idea of the general splendour of the rich Elizabethan's life style. The cut-away section in our artist's impression gives some idea of the colour effects so beloved of the Elizabethans. Note too the particularly fine courtyard at Plas Mawr, typical of the period.

Elizabethan manor houses were alive with bustle and activity. Glass had recently been introduced and although the windows were latticed, the general effect of the long "parlours" and galleries was of a richly textured combination of light dappling the ornate woodwork and reflecting from the carved and painted ceilings.

In the drawing below we show the Elizabethan builders at work and some of the implements they used. In the timber framed houses many builders were by no means particular in their choice of timber. Much of the material used was "green" wood and the builders relied on thickness and sheer strength to take care of any warping.

The Elizabethans were great gardeners a many plants and flowers were introduced in England around this time. The selection on t right shows some of the new plants and flowe which have now become a part of Englan gardening heritage. There was an almo pedantic symmetry in the Elizabethan garde Rectangles and squares divided flower garde and there were broad walks flanked with b and lavender, trimmed into low hedges. Orchar and bowers were also popular.

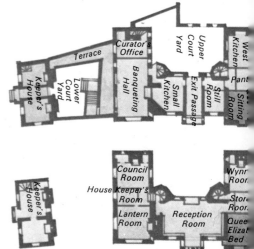

The arms of Robert Wynne, Dorothy Griffith, and of Robert and Dorothy Wynne

A stone and silver gilt jug of the period

An Elizabethan silver gilt tankard, a drinking glass used by Queen Elizabeth and an earthenware bowl

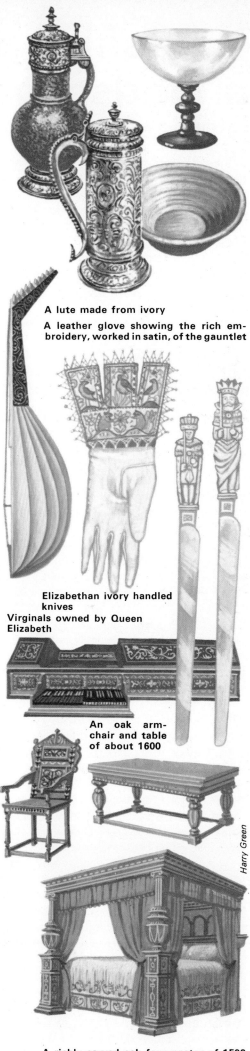

A lute made from ivory

A leather glove showing the rich embroidery, worked in satin, of the gauntlet

Elizabethan ivory handled knives

Virginals owned by Queen Elizabeth

An oak armchair and table of about 1600

Harry Green

A richly carved oak four-poster of 1593

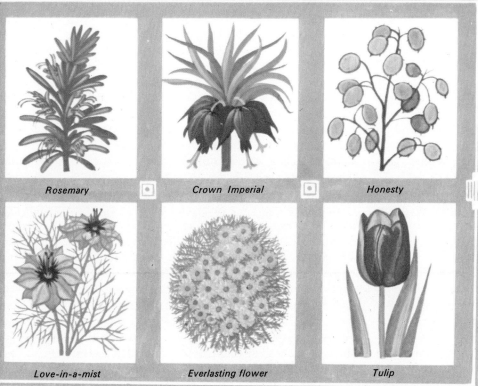

Rosemary

Crown Imperial

Honesty

Love-in-a-mist

Everlasting flower

Tulip

Yorkshire and Lakeland –
a landscape made for poets

VALERIE JENKINS
of the London Evening Standard

This is a journey that becomes something of a literary pilgrimage. From Haworth in Yorkshire, through the Lake District, the associations of the natural scene with famous novels and poems are quite unavoidable. On the moors you might see a Brontë at any moment; at Grasmere you begin to know what Wordsworth was getting at.

It is also a route that takes you through dramatically different scapes. From gloom and desolation on the moors around Haworth (Charlotte Brontë's "lonely moor, silent and still and trackless") to the rocky, bracing Jurassic limestone dales; to the rugged and harsh mountain roads like Honister Pass that can, at any moment, be transformed to dreamy lush valleys like Buttermere.

With the colours and contours, the dialect changes too. You have just got accustomed to the thorpes and garths and strays and gates and thwaites of Scandinavian derivation in Yorkshire, when you come upon all these dodds and ghylls and becks and tarns, fells and crags and cairns of Cumbria, that have such a Gaelic ring to them. Of course, Cumberland became part of England only in 1157. Before that it was part of the Scottish kingdom of Strathclyde, and border warfare carried on until the battle of Clifton Moor near Penrith in 1745. Hence the small square pele towers in the area which often later became houses, and the pure Scots names like Blencathra, Skiddaw, Helvellyn, Glaramara and Pike o' Stickle.

SPECTACULAR LANDSCAPES

It is hardly surprising that such outstandingly spectacular landscapes in these counties should produce strongly regionally-based literature. One would hardly expect the same from, say, Middlesex. The moors and dales of Yorkshire's West Riding, softened with heather and scored by pylons, are as synonymous with the works of the Brontës as Wessex is with Thomas Hardy. It doesn't take much imagination to picture Emily, the most gifted sister, walking over these moors; they are so evocative of what you have read.

Top Withens, a ruined farmhouse, is possibly the site Emily had in mind in *Wuthering Heights* (Wuthering is Pennine dialect for "storming") where "on that bleak hill-top the earth was hard with a black frost, and the air made me shiver through every limb." It is an ideal location for a "perfect misanthropist's heaven." You can also find Wycoller, where Wycoller Hall was the model for Charlotte's Ferndean Manor in *Jane Eyre;* and on the road between Ingleton and Kirkby Lonsdale, at Cowan Bridge, was the Clergy Daughters' School the Brontë girls attended, which became Lowood in *Jane Eyre.*

The Brontë brilliance against this local background continues to present an enigma. Was it because of, or in spite of, these isolated moors, that Emily—a shy and lonely young woman who would wander there in solitude for hours—could produce the most haunting novel in English literature?

"Her native hills," wrote Charlotte Brontë of her sister Emily, "were far more to her than a spectacle; they were what she lived in, and by, as much as the wild birds ... *Wuthering Heights* was hewn in a wild workshop, with simple tools, out of homely materials ... on a solitary moor."

The moors change sharply, in the corner of Lancashire, into the lake-and-mountain pattern of Westmorland. On the main road from Kirkby Lonsdale to Kendal a large sign says simply and boldly "LAKES→". What is there new to say about them? The adjectives of scenic description are so hackneyed, the coinage to long debased. I think the most striking thing about the scenes that, if you take with you, as I did, an 1873 edition of Wordsworth poems engraved with illustrations of Lake views, you find th haven't changed a bit in 100 years. The area is mercifully pr tected from the excesses of progress; the mountains, at least, cann change.

So you will give thanks forever to National Parkhood—th Lake District is Britain's biggest National Park, the Yorkshi Dales one of the biggest—which means that these splendid acr are preserved and protected. It was only in 1951 that 866 squa miles of the Lake District became a National Park. And much the land and buildings are safeguarded by the National Tru whose founding father, Canon Hardwick Rawnsley (vicar Crosthwaite Church near Keswick for 30 years) is rightly ho oured throughout the district. And it isn't just a matter of lak and fells: it's 250 species of birds, other wild life, wild flowe and the great pine forests that are protected and enhanced.

If the spirit of Wordsworth pervades the Lake District, it joined by the spirits of his sister Dorothy, his friend Samu Taylor Coleridge, Robert Southey, Sir Hugh Walpole, Beatr Potter, John Ruskin, Thomas De Quincey, Dr. Arnold of Rugb of Harriet Martineau and her visitors George Eliot and Charlot Brontë; and of holidaymakers Charles Lamb and Shelley. In t Lake District, you are in illustrious company.

As for Thomas Gray of elegiac fame, he is practically credit with discovering the Lake District. He visited in 1769 and pu lished his journal, *A Tour in the Lake District*. Walking by t lakes at nightfall, pondering on the deep serenity of the wate the long shadows of the mountains, the murmur of waterfa in the quietness, he — like the Lake poets after him — "wisb for the Moon, but she was dark to me and silent, hid in her vaca interlunar cave."

POETRY OF NATURE

The Lakes were a magnet to the Romantics; they epitomise the conventional conceptions of the poetic. And indeed the ea Romantic poets were convinced of a correlation between extern nature and the state of man's reflections. Man was in a pysch logical relationship with Nature. And in their surroundings, in t mountains and lakes, the colours of the sky, the woods and strean they found the materials for precise observation through whi states of feeling were identified. John Ruskin called it the pathe fallacy; to the poets it was something approaching pantheism.

Dorothy Wordsworth's journals testify to this inspiratio creation process: "We came into the orchard directly after brea fast," she wrote in a typical entry, "and sate there. The lake w calm, the day cloudy ... William began to write the poem *The Celandine*." A Wordsworth servant, showing a visitor t house, pointed to the study but added that Wordsworth's re study was out of doors. Hence those poem-inscriptions writt at the actual point of inspiration: "Written with a slate upon stone, the largest of a heap lying near a deserted quarry, up one of the islands at Rydal" ... "Written with a pencil upon stone, in the wall of a house on the island at Grasmere" ... "Lin written while sailing in a boat at evening" ... "Lines left upon seat in a Yew-tree."

astoral scene in Newlands Valley, Cumberland

In Wordsworth's case the impressions of his early years formed deep and meaningful layer of his later thought. You get an llic picture of childhood from *The Prelude:* scrambling about shores of the lakes; being alone on the fells at night when he eard among the solitary hills low breathings coming after me;" famous occasion when he was rowing on the lake one night, got the distinct impression that a peak was striding after him ith measured motion, like a living thing." No wonder the untains were an almost mystical experience to him, no wonder y seemed like a vast invisible presence.

It is hard to express better than he did his feelings about the nd between Nature and the mind, his belief in the influence natural objects on the formation of character. He loved the ke dwellers, he said, "not verily for their own sakes but for the ds and hills where was their occupation and abode." No: ddlesex is *not* in the same class.

Coleridge, who came to the Lakes later in life, wrote to a friend cribing Greta Hall, his house at Keswick. Setting the scene, said Skiddaw was at his back, Bassenthwaite on his right, h its majestic case of mountains, all of the simplest outline — *ke a giant's tent.*"

'It is encircled by the most fantastic mountains that ever thquake made in sport," he wrote. "As fantastic as if Nature l *laughed* herself into the convulsion in which they were made." The real geological history of these fantastic shapes is more ndane. What caused them was a combination of volcanic ption, glacial action, and millions of years of frosts, snows and as. The Lakeland mountain range is probably one of the oldest sses in the world, older than the Alps, the Andes or the nalayas.

The climate of the region explains the purity and whiteness

of the light, and the luxuriant freshness of the mountain greenery. It is very wet indeed. It caused Coleridge increasing ill-health and drove him to sunny Malta. Cumberland and Westmorland get the western rain-bearing winds direct from the grey Irish sea, giving the Lake District the heaviest rainfall in England. This has advantages in the gentleness of the air, the clarity of the colours, the fulsomeness of the forestry. Certainly, the weather cannot often spoil the Lakeland scenery. Even the thick mist that I experienced could not completely blot out the beauty.

Travellers in the Lake District should be warned that they face an essentially gastronomic journey. In Cumberland you eat *heartily.* A glance at the distribution maps in any gourmets' guide indicates the cluster of recommended eating-places crowded into the northwest corner — surely the most prodigious selection outside London. You should return about five pounds heavier, unless you fast for a while before setting out, in preparation for meals that last five or six courses — the fish course being obligatory in this area.

You can, of course, counteract such culinary extravagance with outdoor sport and exercise. There are few restrictions on swimming anywhere in the Lakes, and a few organised bathing places like Millerground on Windermere and the Isthmus on Derwentwater. You can go fishing (on application), boating and sailing, climbing and fell-walking. In winter there is skating on Rydal and Derwentwater, and the Cumbrian speciality of fox-hunting on foot over the fells. But you don't have to *do* anything at all. There is, after all, plenty to occupy you if you just observe. Lakeland never repeats itself, never bores. As the hero of Walpole's novel, Rogue Herries, said of the Glaramara fell: "It changes with each moment of the day."

AWAY FROM IT ALL

There is in fact so much to see it can be overwhelming. I'm not quite sure how one should feel after spending time in Lakeland: relaxed? enervated? dissatisfied with one's urban lot? Father West, who published the first Guide to the Lakes in the 18th Century, said: "Such as wish to unbend the mind from anxious cares or fatiguing studies, will meet with agreeable relaxation in making the tour of the Lakes . . . Such as spend their lives in cities, and their time in crowds, will here meet with objects that will enlarge the mind, by contemplation . . ."

But when I read what Charles Lamb wrote after a holiday in Keswick, I tended to agree with him. He waxed ecstatic on the purple colours of the fells in a letter to a friend. "We have clambered up to the top of Skiddaw, and have waded up the bed of Lodore. In fine, I have satisfied myself that there is such a thing as that which tourists call *romantic,* which I had very much suspected before."

Later, however, on returning to London, he pondered on what he had seen, and on the sensation of being free to wander among mountains, and concluded thus:

"Besides, after all, Fleet Street and the Strand are better places to live in for good and all than amidst Skiddaw. I still turn back to those great places where I wandered about, participating in their greatness. But after all I could not *live* in Skiddaw. I could spend two, three years among them, perhaps, but I must have the prospect of seeing Fleet Street at the end of that time or I should mope and pine away, I think."

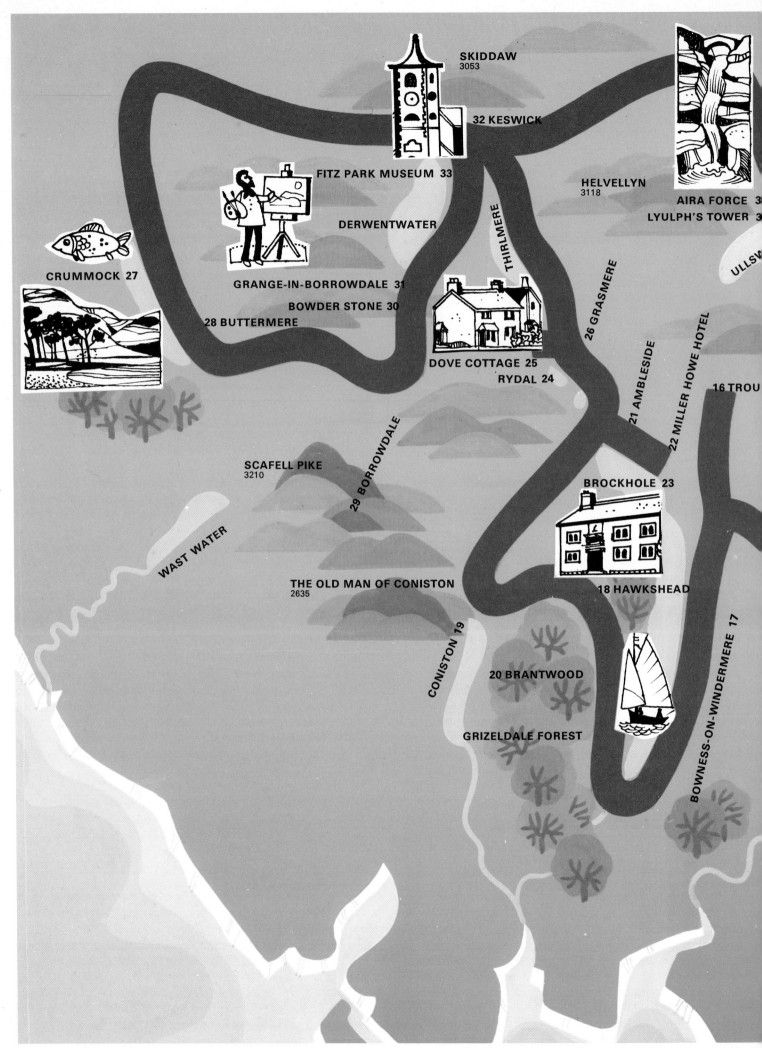

SKIDDAW
3053

32 KESWICK

FITZ PARK MUSEUM 33

DERWENTWATER

HELVELLYN
3118

AIRA FORCE 3

LYULPH'S TOWER 3

THIRLMERE

CRUMMOCK 27

GRANGE-IN-BORROWDALE 31

BOWDER STONE 30

28 BUTTERMERE

26 GRASMERE

ULLSW

DOVE COTTAGE 25

RYDAL 24

21 AMBLESIDE

22 MILLER HOWE HOTEL

16 TROU

SCAFELL PIKE
3210

29 BORROWDALE

BROCKHOLE 23

WAST WATER

THE OLD MAN OF CONISTON
2635

18 HAWKSHEAD

CONISTON 19

20 BRANTWOOD

BOWNESS-ON-WINDERMERE 17

GRIZELDALE FOREST

Photos: B.T.A. / Peter Baker / Col Lib Int / Countryside Com / Mary Evans / V. K. Guy / Noel Habgood / Kildwick Hall / K & J Jelley / Keystone / Judge Photography / Mansel / Col / Pictor / P
point / Pix / Sanderson & Dixon / Walter Scott / Kenneth Scowan / Spectrum / Studio Weeks / Tullythwaite House / Bertram Unne

36 POOLEY BRIDGE

37 SHARROW BAY

HAWES WATER

PEN-Y-GHENT
2231

KENDAL 14

13 KIRKBY LONSDALE

12 INGLETON

ULLYTHWAITE HOUSE

11 CLAPHAM

MALHAM TARN 7

GIGGLESWICK 10

SETTLE 9

8 LANGCLIFFE

6 KIRKBY MALHAM

5 RYLSTONE

KENT

MALLOWDALE FELL

4 SKIPTON

3 KILDWICK HALL

Ben Manchip

2 BRONTE PARSONAGE

1 HAWORTH

tions: *Elsie Wrigley | Richard Hook*   Plant Notes: *Geoffrey Gilbert*   Animals and Birds: *Jeremy Johns*

203

Top Withens which became Wuthering Heights in the novel

glimpse of the graveyard, especia
in a drizzling November twilight,
enough to convince you of its absolu
rightness as an inspiration to the ext
ordinary, precocious, isolated Bror
children, working fantasies into th
particularly imaginative Celtic minds.
Haworth church (St. Michael's), a bra
plate near the chancel screen marks t
place of the Brontë vault, and close by t
church is the Black Bull, where Branw
drank so much.

The parsonage, built in 1779, retains
frugal little rooms preserved as they we
when Mrs. Gaskell visited the house
1853, down to wallpaper and curta
fabric. Here is the Chesterfield upon whi
Emily died, in 1848, never admitting f
illness, refusing to have a doctor. Here
the peat store where the Brontës ke
their two tame geese, a room that Cha
lotte later turned into a study for f

Keeper, watercolour by Emily Brontë

1 HAWORTH: I'm no enthusiast, but
even I enjoyed a short trip up the
valley on the Worth Valley Railway. There
is an undeniable excitement in taking a
steam train journey again, seeing Ladies
Only carriages, hearing that haunting 3.10
to Yuma sound of the whistle. Like other
steam railways, including the famous
Festiniog, it is kept going by volunteers who
have maintained it just for love since 1968,
after the line had been axed by BR some
years earlier. From Haworth you can take a
round trip or just do the last mile of its
journey up a steep hill to Oxenhope —
fare 12p, just to help pay for repairs to
stock and engines. The vista here is pure
Brontë with industrial additions: bleak
open moorland, and cottages making
little black shapes on the brows of hills.
This, of course, is where the film of The
Railway Children was made. In the station
booking-hall there is a mass of literature
about this and other lines for loyal
preservationists, including their magazine
Push and Pull; also souvenirs like honey
and lemon curd which they assure you is
smoke-flavoured. Small museum and workshop in the yard.

Haworth has an extremely steep, cobbled
village street that you must walk up (car
park at bottom), past the predictable Olde
Gifte Shoppes: there is actually one called
that. But a Brontë shuttle for 40p, and a
copy of Wuthering Heights purchased at
the very chemist-shop where Branwell
Brontë used to buy his opium, are a cut
above the commoner souvenirs at such
scenes of literary pilgrimage — Haworth
is second only to Stratford-on-Avon and
receives 112,000 visitors a year. And there
was Haworth, a very mundane, grey stone-
and-slate spinning and weaving village,
ennobled and immortalised by the lives of
those four gifted, sombre Brontë children
up in the parsonage. On the way you pass
the church where, a century before
Patrick Brontë came there, the stern and
relentless William Grimshaw, one of the
leading early Methodists, was incumbent.
It was he who invited John Wesley to
preach there in 1748. The service began at
five in the morning.

father's curate, the man she married n
months before her death. Here are l
bonnet and shawl, tiny laced boots, b
and white print dress; Emily's mug, Au
Branwell's teapot, everything tiny, ne
somehow seeming scaled down. E
nothing tinier than the miniature boc
in which the children wrote their fi
stories together, pinhead handwriting
pages hardly more than an inch square

There are portraits of them all, sampl
that they worked, drawings they did: k
above all, an atmosphere that see
redolent of those days when Mr. Bro
would, each night, lock the door at ni
open the dining-room door and tell
daughters not to stay up late, wind
clock placed halfway up the stair. Dc
lovers go for Emily's drawings of her d
Keeper, who followed her coffin to
vault; walkers can follow nearby wa
to places mentioned in the novels, I
Top Withens which became Wutheri
Heights, or to the waterfall, Charlott
last walk before her death. Hawo
Parsonage will not disappoint you.

3 KILDWICK HALL: Eat dinner, if
you can, at Kildwick Hall, a 17th
Century manor house, now a restaurant,
between Keighley and Skipton. An imposing well-restored stone house, its
windows overlook gardens and the Aire
Valley, and inside it is comfortably furnished, lots of brocade and a restrained log
fire. On our night the table d'hote dinner,
served with a minimum of flourish, consisted of consommé, poussin with cauli-
flower and courgettes, chocolate mousse,
all good. The pleasure is equally in the
eating and in being at Kildwick Hall.

Kildwick Hall, now a restaurant

...worth Parsonage Museum from the garden

Charlotte's painting of Anne

...niature book by Charlotte

...ung girl drawn by Charlotte

The parlour of the parsonage, home of the Brontës

4 SKIPTON, formerly Sheep-town, has an unforgettable, well-proportioned main street. We saw it prettily lined with fairy-lit Christmas trees, on a bustling market day. For the gateway to the Yorkshire Dales it is hardly spoilt (it has a nine-hole golf course, the headquarters of the Craven Pot-Holing Club, an indoor pool and lots of ideal tea-rooms with fresh cream cakes). If you 'pass the Victorian Palladian town hall, the church whose roof dates from Richard III's day, you find to the east of it, high on a rock above its moat, Skipton Castle. It is one of the most complete and best preserved castles in the country. Fundamentally a Norman fortress, it later belonged to the Clifford family, whose coat of arms it bears: their motto, Désormais (Henceforth), forms an imposing balustrade over the gateway tower in great sculptured stone letters. And the yew-tree in the courtyard is 17th Century.

One of the most complete castles

Silhouette of memorial cross

5 RYLSTONE: An insistently English village that centres on its pond, complete with ducks: remembered mostly from Wordsworth's long and fanciful ballad, *The White Doe of Rylstone*, which local people say is more poetic licence than hard fact. As you approach the parish church of St. Peter, pause at the entrance to the churchyard to observe the ridge on the skyline of curving moorland behind you. This, I am sure, is one of Yorkshire's most extraordinary and mysterious panoramas, particularly in early morning light. Eerily, on the brow of the moor, appear a cross, an obelisk, parts of a ruined wall and tower. According to the Rector of Rylstone, the cross is supposed to commemorate the battle of Waterloo, and is made of wood strengthened with iron, set firmly in the rocks at the crest. The obelisk was erected by a local man who camped up there on the moor for two or three days, in memory of the men from the villages of Cracoe, Hetton, Rylstone and Bodley who died in the 1914-18 war.

The jagged ruin is Norton Tower — a watchtower to discourage Clifford poachers from seducing herds of deer over to their territory from the Norton side (the Nortons and the Cliffords being two great historic families in the West Riding).

TAIL WAGGER

The grey wagtail is ill-named, for with a bright yellow belly, slate blue back and white flashes on the tail, wings and cheeks the wagtail is far from being so dull. It feeds on water insects such as dragonfly nymphs, mayflies or even freshwater molluscs and crustaceans. In hilly country it often teams up with the dipper. The Lake District is an ideal spot for grey wagtails which swoop along its rushing streams resting now and then on a boulder or overhanging branch. They measure about eight inches and get their name from the incessantly bobbing tail which is as long as the body. The male in courtship flies in slow motion fanning his tail. The female builds the nest close to water, usually of moss and grass lined with hair, but occasionally takes over a dipper's abandoned nest. It lays in April to June and its eggs are buff and faintly speckled. Often two broods are hatched each year. The shrill call of the wagtail is seldom heard. A cousin to the grey wagtail, the yellow is a summer visitor and can be recognised by its smaller size and less varied colouring.

6 KIRKBY MALHAM: For so tiny village as Kirkby Malham, there i surprisingly large church, and one wh is full of interest. Next door is an early 1 Century vicarage. The main feature of church is its box pews, carved with initials of occupying families. Also unplaned table made by a character cal the Mouse Man of Kilburn, Rot Thompson. He joined his father to w as a carpenter late last century, and wh working in a church one day remark that they would both always be as poor church mice. From then on he carved small mouse somewhere on each pi of furniture: the table here has the mou running up a leg.

Another local man made the churc crib: not exactly Grinling Gibbons, good honest work. Empty niches in pillars remain since the statues w removed in Cromwell's time; but there i 12th Century font, a 14th Century ches church register from 1599 — and a hea slot in the door for barring it to prov secure sanctuary, that reminds you "Bar the door!" in *Murder in the Cathed* A climb up to the bell-tower rewards y with a splendid view of the Dales.

Gordale Scar — a geological fault

7 MALHAM TARN: Three landmar Gordale Scar, Malham Cove a Malham Tarn, are all reached from hamlet of Malham, which has on triangle of the village green an inn da 1723, the Lister Arms, with mullion windows.

Malham Cove and Gordale Scar are bo part of the same geological fault, and bo can be spectacular at certain tim especially after rain. Malham Cove is 240 ft white cliff, with the River A

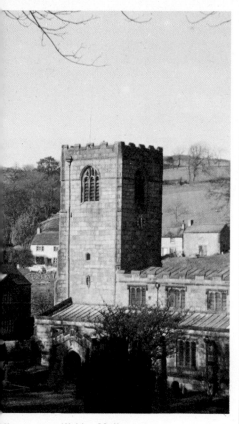

ll tower at Kirkby Malham

The delightful countryside about Langcliffe

8 LANGCLIFFE: Simply to pass through, this village is a delight. It is almost a model village, everything just so: the sort of scene that children draw. A village green, a steepled church, village school, picturesque rows of cottages, and on the village green the obligatory oak tree with bench seat and drinking fountain surmounted by a cross. May it never change.

alham hamlet with 1723 inn

The Cove, spectacular after rain

uing from its base; Gordale Scar is a rge with a series of cascading water-ls. On the surrounding limestone moors, ss-crossed with the characteristic dry ne walls of the area, there are clusters sheep, indistinguishable from the rocks. scarred, rather harsh landscape.

By far the most beautiful place for miles und is Malham Tarn. It's a natural lake 150 acres, formed by a dam of Ice Age bris and fringed by trees. The lake, the e Georgian Tarn House and 2,000 acres all around are National Trust property. Walk past the field centre to get to the tarn itself. Here is absolute peace and calm, utter silence. If you are unfamiliar with the countryside it can seem like another planet: it is possible to spend a long time just standing and staring out at the still water, so clear that there's always a reflection of sky and clouds. You may see the occasional kestrel, wheatear or ring ouzel. It is an intoxicatingly beautiful spot. The easiest descent is down the cove's west side.

9 SETTLE, mentioned in the Domesday Book as Setel, is the tourist centre of the West Riding: an old-world town in the hills, quiet and attractive, with gabled houses, mullioned windows and turrets. The centre of Settle is the market square with its town hall and that remarkable building called The Shambles. The Shambles is 17th Century on the lower floor, late Victorian above, and its six arches, formerly open, are now occupied by shops and cafés. The other notable building in the town is The Folly, up the High Street, a large stone house built by Thomas Preston in 1679, so called because he ran out of money before finishing it; however Nikolaus Pevsner, the architectural authority, says it could be called The Folly anyway because its details are so capricious and wilful. An Italianate column here, a playfully arched Gothic lintel there.

Archaeologists and anthropologists should visit Pig Yard Club Museum, which contains bones and artefacts found in Victoria Cave, some of which date from the Ice Age. Victoria Cave is reached from Langcliffe and was originally a hyena's den. Later it became a Neolithic hunter's cave, which explains the remains of reindeer antler and flint tools found there; later still it was a Romano-British refuge.

Victoria Cave, dates from Ice Age

Attermine Scars, near Settle

10 GIGGLESWICK, which almost joins Settle, is famous for its school, a grey and unprepossessing looking building in the manner of Victorian scholastic architecture, but with a bright green copper dome that you can see for miles. This rather unexciting town need not detain you: it is chiefly a centre for climbing, with Giggleswick Scar, the heights of Ingleborough and Pen-y-Ghent nearby. A mile northwest of the town is the Ebbing and Flowing Well, which does just that, ebbing and flowing eight times a day. On June 29, 1927 hundreds of people climbed Giggleswick Scar to see the total eclipse of the sun.

The parish of Giggleswick, a climbing centre

The village of Clapham — centre for potholers

11 CLAPHAM: In a county abounding in pretty villages, Clapham is one of the most picturesque. It is a centre for walking, climbing and — under supervision and in the right gear — potholing. You follow the line of greystone houses and whitewashed cottages with their fine trees and well-kept gardens, up to St. James's Church which is pleasant enough and has a super rushing waterfall alongside, under a leafy stone arch. Beyond here is the starting point for lakeside walks.

At the National Trust Information Centre you begin for example, the ascent of Ingleborough (2,373 ft) with its cave penetrating 900 yards into the hill, and its surrounding maze of limestone caves crowded with stalagmites and stalactites. Or walk to Trow Ghyll Gorge or Gaping Ghyll, a cathedral-like underground chamber, 378 ft deep. Or failing these ignore the energetic pursuits and just look at aesthetically pleasing Clapham, the reverse of its London namesake.

12 INGLETON: "You must not leave this town," cries a large sign on an overhead bridge in Ingleton, "without seeing the crystal cascades and lakes". This is, in fact, up to you. It is a town devoted to tourism, capitalising on its waterfalls caused by the junction of the Rivers Doe and Twiss, which then become the Greta. A chain of cascades, Thornton Force, Beezley Falls, Snow Falls, Baxenghyll Gorge, plunge down the ravines, and there are more potholing opportunities in the rock chambers of White Scar Caves. There is a caravan site near the starting point for seeing the cascades.

he crystal cascades plunge down the ravines at Ingleton

A view of Ingleborough, 2,373 ft

13 KIRKBY LONSDALE: This is an exceptionally pleasant and enjoyable town, with everywhere you turn in its narrow Georgian streets of grey stone, some little old inn, like the Sun, the King's Arms. You are not the first to be charmed by it: "Here," said John Ruskin, "are moorland, sweet river and English forest at their best.". He was speaking of what is now known as Ruskin's View. This is signposted through the churchyard of St. Mary's, some parts of which date back to 1100, the earliest church in the Lune Valley; and a little raised gazebo with steps has been constructed at the church gates, so that you can ascend to appreciate this fine view from the best vantage point. It is a soft view, of muted gentle lines and colours. "One of the loveliest in England". said Ruskin, "and therefore in the world". In the town, the Devil's Bridge, over the Lune, is considered one of the best old English bridges, and is a registered ancient monument.

he Lune River at Kirkby Lonsdale, "one of the loveliest views in England"

14 **KENDAL:** Westmorland's biggest town, called the "auld grey town" because of its heavy grey limestone buildings, is the gateway to the Lake District. The woollen industry was its staple for 600 years after Edward III granted a letter of protection to a Flemish weaver in 1330, establishing the trade. Nowadays the boot and shoe industry is more important but the town's motto remains: "Wool is my bread". The River Kent, on which Kendal stands, provided ideal water for cleaning and dyeing the once famous Kendal Green wool, a particularly fine and hardwearing cloth. Shakespeare's Falstaff in *Henry IV part 1* refers to "three misbegotten knaves in Kendal Green".

The Abbot Hall Museum of local crafts, opened by Princess Alexandra in 1970, has samples of other Cumbrian tweed colour weaves that supplanted Kendal Green — heather mixes, spring blues and lilacs. Part of the museum is given over to a reconstruction of a Victorian sheep farmer's house, meticulously detailed, down to having an 1889 edition of *Pilgrim's Progress* on the reading stand, a patchwork counterpane and hand-worked linens in the candlelit bedroom, china perfume jars and pin cushions on the dresser. Abbot Hall itself is a Georgian House containing an art gallery. The elegant ground floor rooms keep their 18th Century grace; cool, expansive, perfect proportions everywhere, adorned with Hepplewhite and Sheraton, exquisite plasterwork and silver. The upper storey has three galleries of modern art, one of which is sometimes given over to the work of local schoolchildren.

Kendal has a ruined castle where Catherine Parr, sixth and surviving wife of Henry VIII, was born. Her minute book of devotions is in the Mayor's Parlour, as are seven paintings by George Romney, who died here in 1802 after he had come back from London to forget Emma Hamilton. The town hall, late Victorian, has a fine carillon of bells playing a repertoire of Scots, Welsh and Irish tunes. The parish church of Holy Trinity, next to Abbot Hall, possesses four aisles and is the second widest parish church in England. By it is the Serpentine, a pleasure-ground.

Near Kendal, if you make a detour fro the route, are two stately homes. One Levens Hall, five miles south, an Eliz bethan house that grew from a pele-tow refuge against the Scots — Kendal w once rife with border warfare. Here a carved oak fireplaces, Old Masters, topia gardens with fine trees and shady foo paths, the winding River Kent, and a he of fallow deer. Three miles south of Kend is Sizergh Castle, 15th-18th Centur which also grew from a 14th Centu pele-tower, built for defence again raiders. It has good panelling, Jacobi relics, and a Tudor Great Hall.

The obvious souvenir from Kendal Kendal Mint Cake which actually is mac here. It was carried to the summit of Mou Everest by Sir Edmund Hilary and Sherp Tensing on May 29, 1953. "We sat on t snow and looked at the country far belo us . . . we nibbled Kendal Mint Cake," member of the expedition wrote. "It w easily the most popular item on our hig altitude ration. Our only criticism was th we did not have enough of it".

Stop here for good food

15 **TULLYTHWAITE HOUSE:** While in the neighbourhood of Kendal you should try to eat lunch or dinner at Tullythwaite House. This is a modest little farmhouse, the real McCoy, at Underbarrow, four miles west of Kendal. It is run by the famous Mrs. Johnson, who though she is getting on in years still cooks divinely, but only to order. It is quite astonishing value. On a Sunday lunchtime we sat by the fire at a beautifully polished mahogany dining-table and ate orange and tomato soup, roast beef with roast potatoes, Yorkshire pudding, carrots, leeks with cheese sauce, followed by blackcurrant pie and stewed damsons (they insist you try two helpings of dessert), Stilton and biscuits, and coffee. Everything fresh, home-baked, delicious too.

16 **TROUTBECK:** This is a short diversion. Townend at Troutbeck is a small, whitewashed stately home. Past the house and past the gnarled tree stumps in the centre of the village of Troutbeck, you reach the Mortal Man Hotel, established 1689, which has this splendid verse on its inn-sign:

> "Oh Mortal Man that liv'st by bread,
> What is it makes thy nose so red?"
> "Thou silly fool, that look'st so pale,
> 'Tis drinking Sally Birkett's ale."

Turning here down the hill, you con to the Jesus Chapel whose immediate noticeable east window is by Willia Morris and friends. It bears these artis familiar grape and sunflower motifs, unusually predominantly green windo The story is that Edward Burne-Jones w commissioned to design the windo While he was engaged on it, Morris a Ford Madox Brown came to Troutbe for a fishing holiday and offered to he Hence the communal effort.

Down the hill into Troutbeck — watch for the Mortal Man

Kendal parish church from the Serpentine

Sizergh Castle, grew up from a 14th Century pele tower

KILLER IN THE MOSS

We take it for granted that animals eat plants, but we are impressed when a plant catches and kills an animal for food. One of our native species is the sundew, which abounds in the Lake District. The plant forms a red rosette about two inches across which shows against the bog moss, where it grows. Its leaves are covered with hairs which form globules of sticky liquid to trap flies. As the fly struggles other hairs turn slowly towards it and digestive fluids are released till only a dry husk remains. A handful of moss with sundew left in a saucer of rain water under glass will thrive if fed on fragments of meat. The plant produces white flowers in summer. There are two species to be found, the common sundew and the great sundew, which predominates in the far north.

17 **BOWNESS-ON-WINDER-MERE,** a mid-19th Century town of the Italianate villa type, headquarters of the Royal Windermere Yacht Club, blends with the town of Windermere itself. To pass between the two you drive right by the lakeside. Windermere, $10\frac{1}{2}$ miles long, is the largest lake in England and very popular for steamer and boating trips. It has one island — Belle Isle, privately-owned with a mansion built in 1774.

In the 15th Century St. Martin's Church at Bowness-on-Windermere there is a wooden equestrian statue which the church lost for 45 years and rediscovered in 1912. It shows St. Martin cutting his cloak in two with a sword, to give half to a starving beggar. There are some exceptional stained glass windows, especially the east window, the Crucifixion; and delicate mural inscriptions uncovered when the plaster was restored in 1870. Bowness has a clock tower, built by subscription in 1907 to the memory of M. J. B. Baddeley, author of the most famous ever guide to the Lake District.

Windermere, largest lake in England, from Bowness

Hawkshead village

Ann Tyson's cottage

19 CONISTON: The road from Hawkshead to Coniston is a joy. The view over the five-mile Coniston Water at the north-west tip gets better and better, finally rounding upon the row of grey cottages with the hills beyond. The Old Man of Coniston (2,635 ft) can be climbed from the village in less than two hours; an alternative walk takes you to the lakelet of Tarn Hows, well signposted.

In the village of Coniston, a modern memorial slab in local green Cumberland slate on the village lawn pays tribute to Donald Campbell, who was killed making an attempt to break his own water speed record — doing, it is said, 310 mph — in Bluebird on Coniston Water in 1967.

A view of Coniston Old Man

Autumn tints bedeck the shores of Coniston Water

18 HAWKSHEAD: To enjoy the rolling, curving, fir-lined lakeside road, take the long route around Windermere to Hawkshead (there is a ferry from Bowness) and glimpse the occasional pheasant. This road takes you down to the southern tip of Windermere, via Newby Bridge (a quaint old bridge with five low arches and sharply-pointed buttresses), then up again to the tip of Esthwaite.

At Hawkshead, once a county town, now a village, the schoolboy Wordsworth lodged at Ann Tyson's cottage, still to be seen. He was educated at the old grammar school founded by Edwin Sandys, Archbishop of York in 1585. Behind the school, which has a desk carved with Wordsworth's name, you can walk up into the hilly graveyard where the Sandys family vault is. The church, St. Michael and All Angels, used to be whitewashed. Wordsworth described it in *The Prelude* when he returned to Hawkshead from Cambridge:

I saw the snow-white church upon her hill
Sit like a throned lady sending out
A gracious look all over her domain.

It had been whitewashed by two local men three years earlier at a cost of six guineas. While at school he often went up to the churchyard on summer evenings to sit and talk with the old men on the benches. Inside the church the white walls have some beautifully restored murals and decorated texts, a happy discovery of the late 19th Century.

20 BRANTWOOD: By 1871, when he came to live at Brantwood, on the east side of Coniston Water, John Ruskin was one of the most eminent of Victorians, a powerful influence on English art. He was 52, and had already published his most famous works, *Modern Painters, Stones of Venice* and his autobiography *Praeterita.* In the summer of 1871, when he was recovering from a serious illness, Ruskin heard that Brantwood was for sale and immediately paid £1,500 for it, without even going to see it. He was, characteristically, more concerned with the view than with the house — and the views are, in fact, almost too perfectly ordered: of field, lake, fells. When he saw the house he pronounced it "a mere shed of rotten timber and loose stone". His first addition was the tiny little turret room jutting from the southern corner of the house, leading from his bedroom. You stand in the windowed turret for supreme views north, south and west.

The house was bought in 1932 by J. Howard Whitehouse who collected the Ruskiniana that is on view in the hou... today. The study is most impressiv... much as it was, with many of Ruskin... own drawings and paintings, his des... armchairs, bookcases, picture cabin... books, globes and even his inkwell a... blotting-cover. In the coachhouse is o... of his carriages, his boat the Jumpi... Jenny built in 1879, his bathchair and ... travelling bath. And if you visit t... bathroom in the house you will s... Ruskin's bath, the high boxed-in varie... In the grounds, Nature Trails lead visito... all over the 200-acre estate up to the t... of the fells behind the house, through t... profusion of daffodils, by the waterfall a... Ruskin's stone chair. The house is us... by students on field courses, but the cura... makes literary pilgrims very welcome.

Ruskin died in 1900, and is buried ... Coniston churchyard. Over his grave is ... tall, beautifully carved cross of grey-gre... slate-stone, quarried nearby, with t... simple inscription "John Ruskin 181... 1900". The carvings speak for what ... cared for, and illustrate his chief works.

Bridge House, Ambleside

21 AMBLESIDE:

"The little town of grey slate houses with grey slate roofs has no architecture of distinction", says the book; but Ambleside is surprisingly lively and unspoilt, for the holiday centre of the southern part of Lakeland. If you are cunning enough to arrive in Ambleside on the last weekend in July, you catch the rush-bearing ceremony, when children carry fresh rushes to be strewn over St. Mary's Church floor. This is something of a field day in the town. The Armitt museum has Roman pottery, shoes, buttons, and tools found between Clappersgate Bridge and Waterhead, formerly the site of a Roman camp. Waterhead is a good bay for swimming, and from the car park there are guided walks for visitors led by voluntary wardens during summer weekends.

Coming out of Ambleside, you cross by the Bridge House, an odd little structure, on a small bridge over Stock Beck. The little house was built in 1650 apparently as a garden house by the Braithwaites of Ambleside Hall, lords of the manor. It used

Stock Ghyll Falls

to be surrounded by orchards. The last person to live in it was Chairy Rigg, a man who repaired chairs and sold ferns; he died in 1901. Bridge House was the first National Trust centre in the country.

22 MILLER HOWE HOTEL:

While at Ambleside you can do no better than spend a night at the Miller Howe Hotel, which is getting to rival the famed Sharrow Bay as the gastronomic centre of the Lake District. It overlooks Lake Windermere and Langdale Pikes, a brightly lit hideaway between the foot of the Kirkstone Pass Road and Bowness. Here is the set menu the night I was there: Savoury cheese peach with asparagus and bacon; chicken broth; fish egg and mushroom custard; pork cutlet in tomato mustard and cream sauce, accompanied by buttered courgettes with toasted almonds, diced carrots, brussels sprouts with egg and lemon, creamed parsnips, minted garden peas, mushrooms and button onions, Parisian potatoes, sweet salad; then cherry frangipan with cream; Stilton and biscuits; coffee and mints.

The scene from the hotel

THE TINY NATIVE SURVIVES

The Lake District is one of the few areas where the native red squirrel has not yet been threatened by the American grey. The red is only a little over seven inches from head to the base of its tail, which is almost as long again. Squirrels do not hibernate and so can be seen at almost any time in their favourite woodland haunts. You can tell where red squirrels can be found because broken nutshells or chewed pine cones are indications of their presence.

John Ruskin lived at Brantwood because the views were so perfectly ordered

National Park centre

23 **BROCKHOLE:** Roughly half-way between Ambleside and Windermere, on the lake side of the A591, is the mansion of Brockhole, the first National Park Centre in Britain, and a beautiful house with 32 acres of well-landscaped grounds overlooking Windermere. Inside there are models and diagrams of Lakeland, relief maps and slide shows. You can learn about Lakeland industries, history and geology of the lakes, rock climbing, wild life, fishing and fell-walking.

24 **RYDAL:** On the roadside by the shores of Rydal Water (the smallest, three-quarters of a mile by a quarter and one of the most appealing lakes, usually the first to be skatable in winter) are some steps leading to a mound known as Wordsworth's Seat. It seems he used to sit and ponder here, observe and compose. The place is about 200 yards beyond the last house on the Keswick side of Rydal Village. Going from Rydal to Grasmere, it is impossible to avoid Wordsworthian connections. Rydal Mount, sign-posted, off the road, is the house where he went to live in 1813 and where he died in 1850. A whitewashed house directly under a peak, on the steep slope beyond St. Mary's Church, it is open to the public. Through the churchyard just below is Dora's Field, which was planted with daffodils by Wordsworth for his daughter.

A note here about the Rydal-Grasmere road. It is uncommonly good, curving round the head of the lake and through the woods in an almost tritely picturesque fashion. Always there are thick banks of fir trees at the right, and the road is never more than a few yards from the lake, rising and dipping, so you get glimpses of Rydal and then Grasmere, small and calm and gloriously wooded. Near Grasmere is Nab Cottage at the roadside on the right, where De Quincey and later Hartley Coleridge (Samuel Coleridge's son) lived.

Rydal Water

Wordsworth and his sister Dorothy lived here

25 **DOVE COTTAGE:** At the turning to Grasmere village, a lane opposite leads to Dove Cottage where Wordsworth and his sister Dorothy, and later his wife and children, lived a life of "plain living and high thinking" as he put it. In this quite humble place they lived chiefly on an appallingly carbohydrate diet of bread, porridge, potatoes and milk paying £8 a year rent and 1s a year window tax. All the upper rooms are As They Were, so is the well in the garden which Wordsworth himself dug, still fed by the same stream. The fireplaces and panelling are original (the building was formerly a pub called The Dove and Olive Bough) and there are manuscripts, first editions, the family bible, and Wordsworth's hat and walking-stick and the cape he always wore up to his death. But the garden was his delight, and the doting Dorothy's too:

"Sweet garden-orchard, eminently fair,
The loveliest spot that man hath ever found".

Together they stocked it with roots, wild flowers, ferns and mosses brought back from their rambles. They built a little stone stairway to the terrace, and a moss-covered hut and seat where the poet often wrote his "Lines composed upon . . . His eye, he said, was "made quiet by the power of harmony and the deep power of joy" at Dove Cottage.

Another view of Rydal Water, smallest of the Lakes

LITERARY INN

The Swan Hotel at Grasmere is probably the only inn whose sign was written by William Wordsworth. He used to call here with his literary friends on their walks about the surrounding lakes and mountains. Their host was a jovial man, Anthony Wilson. On one September morning in 1805, a Dr. Davy, Sir Walter Scott and Wordsworth called at the Swan to borrow the inn's old white pony. Their host, on seeing Scott, is said to have greeted him with: "Why, Sir, you've coom seun for your glass today!" So the simple, abstemious Wordsworth learned that Scott had been making up for the deficiency of whisky in the Wordsworth household by calling for a daily glass at the Swan.

26 **GRASMERE:** Broad fine meadows stretch away from Grasmere towards the village, home of Michael the sad shepherd in the Wordsworth poem. In fact you can eat at Michael's Nook, a restaurant right in front of Greenhead Ghyll.

A simple slate slab in Grasmere churchyard says that Wordsworth and his wife were buried there. Wordsworth was devoted to Grasmere; he first saw it as a schoolboy when he came alone from Hawkshead, looked down and felt that

Here must be his home,
This valley be his world.

In the churchyard lie buried many more of the Wordsworth family, (the poet himself planted eight of the existing yew trees, near the river) including Dora their daughter, two other children, Dora's husband Edward Quillinan, Dorothy Wordsworth and Hartley Coleridge. This church, like the one at Ambleside, has a rush-bearing ceremony, on the Saturday nearest August 5. It is a thanksgiving and merry-making day when the church floor is strewn with new rushes — a custom once necessary to keep the feet off the cold floor. There are also sheepdog trials held in August at Rydal Park. And Grasmere Sports, on the Thursday nearest August 20, includes Cumberland-Westmorland wrestling, hound trailing, pole leaping and fell racing.

The village and lake at Grasmere

27 **CRUMMOCK:** Pass Thirlmere, with the steep tree-masked flanks of Helvellyn on the right. This is the lake which became a reservoir for Manchester's water supply in 1895, connected by a series of huge aqueducts across the 95 miles — a development which directly caused the formation of the National Trust by the heroic Canon Rawnsley of Keswick. At Keswick, the route now starts a large loop, taking the Braithwaite road out of the town.

A possible extension of the route here could take in Cockermouth if you are mad keen to see Wordsworth's birthplace, a mid-18th century house nine windows wide, at the west end of the main street. It was saved by subscription by the National Trust when in danger of being pulled down in 1938. There is also at Cockermouth the school where Wordsworth and Fletcher Christian (of the Bounty) attended. But Cockermouth is an optional extra — I find it unengaging.

The loop from Keswick circles round the foot of the Whinlatter Pass at High Lorton, giving a constant vista of mountains all round, and leading to the exquisite and wholly un-urbanised Crummock Water. It lies in a noble setting, within the folds of the Buttermere Valley, and is one of the most unspoiled parts of all Lakeland. There is fishing by permission (trout and char) — obtain fishing licences and hire rods and boats from the local representative of the National Trust which owns both Crummock and Buttermere. You might see here the dark little Herdwick sheep, a very tough local breed, grazing close to the road, very surefooted on the slopes of Grasmoor (2,791 ft); from them came the famous hardwearing Hodder grey (as in John Peel's coat so grey). Today they have been largely replaced by the heavier Swaledales.

Crummock Water, one of the most unspoiled parts of Lakeland

The pines at Buttermere, "the gem of the Lakes"

28 **BUTTERMERE:** If too captivated by the beauty, stillness and tranquillity of the scene between Crummock and Buttermere — they were probably once joined together, now separated by meadows, woods and hedgerows — there is a convenient map of footpaths by the stream on a notice-board to direct your path should you wish to linger. Most people do; this is, as they say, the gem of the Lakes, and people are forever painting the reflections in the water. Across the water you can see High Stile, Chapel Crags, and the well-named Sour Milk Ghyll which really does tumble down the sheer fellside from Bleaberry Tarn in a milky froth, just as the guidebooks testify. And there is a series of becks and ghylls, every few yards, glimpsed between the Scotch fir and larch trees. Close by Scale Force, the highest waterfall England with its drop of 100 ft between perpendicular walls of syenite.

Watendlath, best explored on foot from Borrowdale

29 **BORROWDALE** is one of several contenders — and a favourite — for the title of most beautiful Lakeland valley. Wordsworth waxed enthusiastic in *The Yew Trees.* To get to the hamlets in this valley you go through the dramatic Honister Pass, an excellent motoring road though until 1934 the surface and gradient were so bad that a toll road ran from Seatoller to the slate quarry. For in Honister Pass are the rocky formations of the isolated Buttermere and Westmorland Green Slate Quarry: it is probably the most famous pass in the Lake District, with its enormous green boulders. It also has the reputation of being the windiest — a wind so strong you can see they say. When the wind from the southwest is split by the fells, forming two torrents, you can hear the roar for half a mile. Primeval volcanoes and Ice Age glaciers carved out the sweep of Honister

Crag (1,190 ft) and there is a superb view over Borrowdale to distant Helvellyn.

The pleasant green valley of Borrowdale begins at Seatoller where in summer you can have tea at the Yew Tree (dated 1628). A village of distinct charm, with little slate-roofed cottages; very close to Borrowdale with its dainty whitewashed late Georgian church. Seathwaite is merely a farm and some cottages but lies in wild country and is said to be one of the wettest places in England. Graphite used to be mined there for making Keswick pencils. Rosthwaite, another hamlet, perhaps typifies Borrowdale: situated where the valley divides, it's tiny, neat, with a couple of inns, a farm, cottages and church, and footpaths up to the climbing huts; for this is prime walking country, e.g. to Great Gable, the seventh highest Lake mountain, whose summit can be approached by a route made by the Honister quarrymen.

30 **BOWDER STONE:** Between Rosthwaite and Grange-in-Borrowdale, off the road a mile from the famous Grange Bridge that artists are always painting, is the Bowder Stone. It's an enormous boulder that seems to be about to topple over but never does. It cannot be seen from the road so you have to walk up through a slate quarry to find it: a remarkable, bulky rock, poised so precariously you may approach quite warily. Actually it is anchored securely and there is a ladder up to the top for a fine view of Upper Borrowdale. It is 36 ft high, 62 ft long and is said to weigh nearly 2,000 tons. The type of rock is foreign to the area's volcanic material, so it probably came down carried by glaciers from Scotland. There is a local notion that you should join hands underneath it and make a wish.

At the nearby village of Grange, the roads meet and Grange Fell and Scawdel form the Jaws of Borrowdale. Between them there is an ancient British fort on Castle Crag.

The stone, securely anchored

31 **GRANGE-IN-BORROWDALE:** Of all the giftshops and craft studios that inevitably abound in this area, Lakeland Rural Industries workshop and studio at Grange-in-Borrowdale is a personal favourite. Ever since I stopped here to buy a candlestick when I was a hiking sixth-former, and could not raise the necessary 18s, and the kind lady said I could take the candlestick and send her the money when I got home: a rare display of trust. Also, a very serviceable candlestick. They also have rugs and local pottery, rings and objects made from Honister slate, which is considered the finest in the country. They specialise in hammered stainless steel and copper. A sheet of steel is cut to shape, beaten with a heavy hammer, planished over a stake, decorated, trimmed, dimpled, edged and hand polished. Near the studios are Lodore Falls, hymned in Southey's poem of that name.

Weaving mohair cloth on a Lakeland loom

A quiet corner of Derwentwater, near Keswick

32 KESWICK: You come upon Keswick quite suddenly, round the northern shore of Derwentwater. Keswick is splendidly placed, with Skiddaw on the right, and an elegant circle of heights behind Derwentwater: Lorton Fells, Grisedale Pike, the rounded hump of Grasmoor and the beginnings of the Scafell Range, Mecca of Sunday climbers. It is possible to drive round the lake.

Keswick, whose market got its charter in 1276, has a distinctive main street and market place, with Moot Hall, the town hall, on an island site in the centre. It has a black-trimmed whitewashed tower, very pretty, and a one-handed clock. The original building on this site was a courthouse and prison; it was rebuilt in 1695 and 1813. The clock bell and materials come from Lord's Island, one of the three islands on Derwentwater, which was the family seat of the Radcliffes, Earls of Derwentwater, who forfeited their property after the 1715 rebellion. Keswick is the northern hub of Lakeland tourism — there is a good information centre at Moot Hall — and is well provided with shops and hotels and restaurants. There is very good bathing at the Isthmus on the Lake. The obvious souvenirs are local pencils made of cedarwood and mineral blacklead (plumbago) formerly found in the Seathwaite mines.

The town has many literary associations.

Coleridge lived at Greta Hall — now part of Keswick School — on Cowhill at the north end of the town from 1800 to 1809, and Robert Southey from 1803-43. Wordsworth visited them both there and wrote his poem *To the River Greta*. Southey is buried at Crosthwaite Parish Church, St. Kentigern's, a 12th Century church not far from Keswick, and is commemorated by a white marble effigy with an inscription written by Wordsworth. Also buried there is its former vicar, Canon Hardwick D. Rawnsley (1851-1920), who so benefited mankind by ensuring the preservation of just such tracts of land as you are now travelling through: he was a founding father of the National Trust.

There is a memorial to Canon Rawnsley on Friar's Crag, which is owned by the Trust, about 20 minutes' walk from the town above the east shore of Derwentwater. Ruskin said that this crag was one of the earliest memories of his life, and there is a memorial to him there too: it was one of his views. The novelist Hugh Walpole lived near the southwest corner of the lake, and his Rogue Herries saga was set in this district. He is buried in the churchyard of St. John Evangelist in Keswick, whose spire is a prominent landmark. Charles Lamb spent holidays at Keswick, and Shelley, sent down from Oxford, came to live here for some time after his marriage to the ill-fated Harriet.

33 FITZ PARK MUSEUM: After spending a little time browsing in the lattice-windowed public library St. John's Street, Keswick, which houses good collection of old books on the Lake District, illustrated with engravings, visit the Fitz Park Museum. It contains original manuscripts of Wordsworth, Southey Ruskin, Walpole; the manuscript of John Peel, the Cumbrian hunting song; also Flintoft's three-inch-to-a-mile scale model of the Lake District so you can follow your route in 3-D. Butterflies, birds' eggs fossils and local antiquities, geologic specimens, collections of 250 British birds and 150 dolls, and even a 500-year-old cat. Next door is the art gallery which has work by Turner, Brangwyn and Steer. The museum and gallery form part of High and Low Fitz Parks, which have cricket and tennis, putting, bowls, swings, roundabouts, slides, a play corner and pleasant walks by the River Greta.

Another institution to visit in the town is the Keswick School of Industrial Arts High Hill, founded 1883. All kinds of hand-worked art in silver, copper, brass and other metals can be seen and bought

Southey's manuscripts on view

Turner: paintings in art gallery

34 AIRA FORCE: The road down to Aira Force on Ullswater is [de]serted and especially eerie in twilight; [bu]t Aira Force is the most worthwhile [de]stination in any light, any season. From [th]e car park at the bottom you cross a [bridg]e and follow the stream upward, along [we]ll-trodden paths and steps through [tre]es and bushes. The roar of the waterfall [ge]ts greater and greater, until at last you [com]e in sight of the source, where plunging [fro]m a ravine, under a bridge that you can [sta]nd on to look down, is the force itself, [cra]shing with amazing power 60 ft. sheer [do]wn into the still pool below. If you climb [ev]en higher up you can almost, but never [qu]ite, lose the sound. It is a deafening, [me]morable experience, Wordsworth's [''w]ild stream of Aira''. Aira Force is part [of] the Gowbarrow Estate of over 700 [ac]res, now maintained by the National [Tr]ust — Gowbarrow being a beautiful [na]tural pleasure ground, always associated [mo]st closely with Wordsworth's famous *[da]ffodils.* Walkers can ascend Gowbarrow [Fel]l (1,578 ft) for an unparalleled view of [fell]s, parkland and waterfall, embracing [Ski]ddaw and Blencathra, Penrith Beacon, [the] Cross Fell range and Helvellyn.

Ullswater: be sure to take the road to Aira Force

[Ull]swater, with Lyulph's Tower

35 LYULPH'S TOWER: This is the most romantic, the most [pic]turesque, and also the most misleading [mans]ion in all Lakeland. Not far from Aira [Fo]rce, overlooking Ullswater, stands [Ly]ulph's Tower, square, Gothic, ivy-[shr]ouded and forbidding. Driving right up [to] it at dusk, we expected any moment to [ha]ve a bat fly out at us, or to hear the [cla]nking of chains. With its castellated [to]wers and arched windows, a glimmer [of l]ight high up in one window, it seemed [a ti]meless vision: straight out of Tennyson's [*Ma]riana,* moated grange and all. Not a [roma]nce: it is, bizarrely, a hunting-lodge [bel]onging to the Howard family, built in [18]30 by the Duke of Norfolk, and an [exc]ellent example of the Gothic Revival [in p]recisely the ideal setting. The reputed [ori]gin of Lyulph, or Lyulf, is Ulf or L'Ulf, [the] princely baron of Greystoke who [bequ]eathed his name to Ullswater.

The most majestic Lake

36 POOLEY BRIDGE: "In order to see the lower part of Lake Ullswater to advantage", said Wordsworth, "it is necessary to go round by Pooley Bridge, and to ride at least three miles along the Westmorland side of the water, towards Martindale. The views, especially if you ascend from the road into the fields, are magnificent". It is true: Ullswater is the most majestic lake, nine miles long in a Z-shape, and hardly populated at all. Pooley Bridge is little more than a joining of roads and a powerboat starting point at the extremity of the lake (there is no road at the other tip of the lake, only fell walks).

37 SHARROW BAY: Here is the best place to end a journey through the Lake District. A haunting view over the lake; the sound of lapping water right below your bedroom window; the absolute stillness all around — no hotel could have a more relaxing setting. The Sharrow Bay is a delightful 16th Century country house with 12 acres of garden and woodland. Meals are gastronomic marathons, local fowl especially good, and the rooms are sumptuous and well-thought-out in every detail. It has style. For the last night in Lakeland, a stay at the best hotel on the loveliest lake. Why go further?

The hotel at journey's end

The landscape of genius

Probably no equal stretch of miles in Britain is so rich in literary associations as the route that links the Lake Poets of the late 18th and early 19th Centuries with the incredible Brontë family of Haworth Parsonage in Yorkshire's West Riding.

Wordsworth and his friends brought nature back into English poetry. After the polite elegance of the 18th Century's Age of Reason, there was a longing among the Lake Poets to search for deeper meanings — 'a motion and a spirit that impels all thinking things, all objects of all thought, and rolls through all things'.

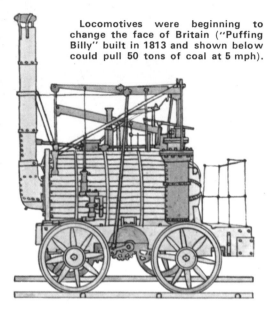

Locomotives were beginning to change the face of Britain ("Puffing Billy" built in 1813 and shown below could pull 50 tons of coal at 5 mph).

"What happy fortune were it to live here", declared Wordsworth when he first saw Grasmere as a boy. He was born at Cockermouth on the northern fringe of the Lakes in 1770. Twenty-nine years later William and his sister Dorothy tramped over the hills from Kendal — where they had paused to buy furniture — and took possession of Dove Cottage on the evening of December 21 1799, just in time to celebrate Dorothy's 28th birthday.

The cottage was formerly an inn on the right of the old coach road from Ambleside to Keswick and for eight years it was home for the Wordsworths. Here, William wrote many of his most famous poems and Dorothy kept that Journal which proved how much the poet owed to the sensitivity and awareness of his sister.

In the frieze of pictures below we see Coleridge, co-author with Wordsworth of 'Lyrical Ballads', a landmark in English literature. Coleridge, brilliant, erratic and — like Thomas de Quincey, on the extreme right — given to opium eating, was a frequent visitor to Dove Cottage. De Quincey, author of 'The Confessions of an English Opium Eater', took over Dove Cottage when the Wordsworths left in 1808.

Grasmere is seen on the left with the kitch of Dove Cottage, still kept as it was in Wor worth's time. Below, we see Rydal Mou Wordsworth's last home — "a modest mansi of sober hue" — where he died in 1850.

Between Wordsworth and the Brontë sist we have Robert Southey, a minor Lake Poet n mainly remembered for his 'Life of Nelson' w lived at Greta Hall overlooking the river Keswick.

From the placidly beautiful Lakes to storm-worn parsonage at Haworth on the ed of the moors near Keighley is not far in mi but in mood and feeling it is a world away.

When the Reverend Patrick Brontë mov into the parsonage in 1825 with his daughte Charlotte 'Jane Eyre', Emily 'Wutheri Heights' and Anne 'Tenant of Wildfell Ha his brilliant son Branwell, an artist who ne fulfilled his early promise, and "Aunt Branwe — his wife had died from cancer four ye earlier — the mills of Bradford and the wool towns were already busily producing Industrial Revolution.

Southerners, it has been said, can ne appreciate the fierce poetry of Emil

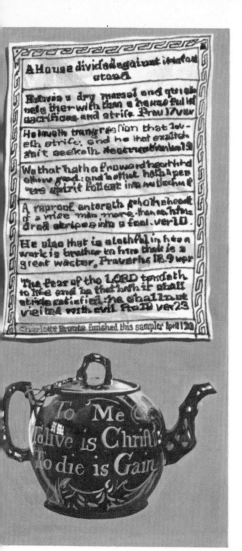

By E. J. B. — Oct 27th 1841.

'Wuthering Heights' until they have visited Haworth. We show here the entrance hall at the parsonage — "the floor and stairs were done with sandstone . . . the walls stained a pretty, dove-coloured tint".

Branwell Brontë, who became the family problem, drank, got into debt, and took opium, is shown in the medallion.

The Duke of Wellington, copied here from Goya's famous portrait painted in 1812 after the Duke's victory at Salamanca, was an early hero of the Brontë children.

On the left is a sampler worked by Charlotte, and "Aunt Branwell's" teapot.

Emily Brontë shared something of her brother's painting talent. This portrait of Hero the hawk — kept as a pet — was painted by her.

The double sofa to the left of Charlotte's sampler is typical of the period — a period which also saw the beginnings of photography in the shape of Fox Talbot's camera of 1835 with which he produced the first photographic negative on paper.

John Beswick

221

The North Country – a cradle of culture

RACHEL AND DAVID POWELL

A couple of miles outside Doncaster there is a motorway sign which reads, quite simply, THE NORTH. Just that, nothing more, simply: THE NORTH. The economy of the thing is devastating for it captures, to the full, the patronising Whitehall notion that God-is-alive-and-well and living at Potter's Bar and that all the rest — **THE NORTH** — is an afterthought of Creation.

Down the years, this myth has become an essential part of Anglo-Saxon sub-culture — a myth based on the notion of taciturn men with roughshod manners and tweedy faces striding across uplands populated solely by sheep and brass bands playing *Jerusalem* while, in windswept houses threatened by subsidence and proletarian anarchy, the womenfolk tat away their hours waiting for the hooters to blow an encore to "There's Trouble t'Mill."

The image, as with all generalisations, is a nonsense. Nonetheless, it is widespread, especially as far as Yorkshire and County Durham are concerned. The whole region (and the West Riding alone is as large as Gloucestershire, Worcestershire and Herefordshire put together) is conveniently typecast as "dour" or "bleak" or, for the more literate, as the epitome of the "dark Satanic mills." The impression is deep-rooted in history and it is now nearly two centuries since William Cobbett, in his *Rural Rides*, wrote: "This county of Yorkshire is a cold and friendless place, a far ride from my own gentle countryside in the south."

The stigma remains but the locals don't give a damn. The hill farmers of the Dales; the miners of the Durham field; the trawlermen of Whitby are chauvinist to the point of indecency which, depending upon one's attitude, is the damnation or salvation of the region as a whole — damnation as far as genteel, suburban conventions are concerned; salvation as far as some of Britain's finest countryside goes.

UNSPOILT BEAUTY

For Durham and Yorkshire have some of the last undiscovered regions of Britain. In the post-war stampede for leisure, the Lakes and the Welsh coast and the Southwest have become an extension of the candy-floss culture, by-products of a society on the run from its own life style. Not so Durham and Yorkshire. The raw and undistilled beauty of the lakes and moorland and sea coast are still, largely, unspoilt: a last frontier of sanity at the gut of Britain. And the people themselves are a product of this environment, a people who make a conversational gambit of silence and who can fashion a speech from the monosyllable 'Eh.' The thing, to the off-comer, is disconcerting; a rejection of the values of a society conditioned to believe that God is a white-collared worker and that a long evening with the television is a surrogate for sex.

Yorkshire and Durham folk are too individualistic to fall for such pap. They live too close to reality, in a landscape that toughens, to accept any pre-packaged notion that the "good life" is lived semi-detached on a mortgage and shaped like a win on the pools. But it is not only the environment that has quarried their character. It is also their past. For 20 centuries Durham and Yorkshire, and its peoples, have been at the epicentre of our island's story; since before the Sixth Legion raised the imperial standard at York the region has been a focal point of our history.

It is now more than 10,000 years since Palaeolithic man first hunted across the lowlands of the two counties and, during the long dawn of civilisation, the eastern sea coast was overrun by succeeding waves of European migrants — the Beaker people, who

introduced the cultivation of wheat; the Hallstatt folk, w[ho] settled near Scarborough; and the Marnian tribes who broug[ht] with them their elaborate war chariots in which they drove de[ep] into the Pennine foothills. By the first century B.C. the wh[ole] region had been hammered into a loose tribal confederacy, t[he] Brigantes, whose capital was at Almondbury, near Huddersfie[ld]. This was the advanced culture which the Romans subjugated [on] their march north. During the long peace of the Empire, wh[en] much of southern England turned soft and effete, Yorkshire a[nd] Durham were still shadowed by outlying Celtic tribes who, payi[ng] small tribute to Rome, fought a long rearguard in defence of th[eir] civilisation and culture.

HISTORY OF VIOLENCE

With the withdrawal of the Legions in the early fifth century t[he] imperial peace was shattered and, for the next 500 years, the no[rth] was scourged by Vikings and Danes who haunted the easte[rn] reaches in their longships. The land knew war often, even with [the] coming of William the Conqueror. Edwin and Morcar, the Sax[on] earls, raised their standards against the new king, and he suppress[ed] their pretensions brutally. During the years of the "Harrying [of] the North", the Normans ravaged the whole countryside betwe[en] York and Durham, and 25 years after their passage the area w[as] still described as a "waste" by the Domesday survey.

So the epic has continued: long wars with the Scots — the cha[in] of strongholds reaching through Brancepeth and Whitton [at] Richmond and Bolton Castle stand as monuments to those bit[ter] years; the "Rising of the North," raised at Raby Castle; [the] campaigns of the Civil War; and the apocalypse of the Industr[ial] Revolution. Each event, in its turn, has helped to shape [the] character of the region and its people. Fountains Abbey a[nd] Durham Cathedral, Markenfield Hall and Barden Tower may [all] be touched with the romance of history but, nonetheless, th[ey] still retain a rugged sense of their original purpose: a rough he[wn] and stubborn quality that is a hallmark of the people as we[ll].

J. B. Priestley tells of an old woman from Halifax-or-somepl[ace] out shopping in a local store. When it came to paying the bill, [the] shop assistant quoted the price in the then new-fangled deci[mal] currency. The woman didn't understand and, patiently, the ass[is]tant explained that she was dealing in decimal coinage. After list[en]ing, attentively, to the explanation, she replied: "It don't matt[er] luv, we're moving ter Bradford next week."

The comment is typical of a people who consider that the Vener]able Bede played for Sunderland Town and that winning [the] County Championship is akin to an Act of God. To the off-com[er] the attitudes may seem defensive, even parochial. In fact they [are] only another dimension, cloaked by self-consciousness, of [the] Durham and Yorkshireman's innate pride — pride not only in [the] achievements of their counties but also in the beauty of th[eir] countryside. And they have something to be proud about. T[he] whole region has enormous and varied scenic impact. Withi[n a] 50-mile radius of York, the landscape ranges from the ha[rsh] Pennine uplands to the brutal geometry of the great indust[rial] towns; from the cool of the southern dales through the gentle V[ale] of York to the wilds of the northern moors and some of the m[ost] spectacular seascapes in England.

Not that this is a countryside that it is easy to come to terms w[ith]. Like its people, it is an acquired taste, to be explored and lea[rned]

d slowly appreciated. Although there are showpiece views
specially the man-made grandeur of such places as York Minster
d Raby Castle), it is the cumulative impact of the landscape that
akes Durham and Yorkshire memorable: the switchback ride
cross the northern moors before the plunge into the valley of the
ees; the calm deeps of Wensleydale and Wharfedale; the lime-
one cliffs about Whitby and Scarborough on their march against
e sea. For geographical convenience, the region can be divided
to three zones — the western dales and uplands, the central
ain and the eastern seaboard backed by the North Yorkshire
oors. These in their turn are bisected by the Great North Road.
Once this road may have smacked of romance (the Legions mov-
g north to the Wall, Cromwellian troopers riding south after the
ll of York, Turpin spurring his way through the night) but today
s role is purely functional and, as such, it does small credit to the
gion. If, in fact, first impressions are damning (and, too often,
e motorist's first impressions of Yorkshire and Durham are con-
tioned by this fast, through route) then the A1 is the damnation
the region as a whole. To move north from Ferrybridge, with
obscene cooling towers and thickets of pylons, to Scotch Corner is
drear and monotonous experience—and totally unrepresentative
the beauty of the surrounding countryside. The A1 image does
ve one advantage: it reinforces the existing prejudice that this
rt of THE NORTH is beyond the pale of gentility and, in its way,

has helped to save the region from the blind rape of commercialism.

The times, however, are changing. Yorkshire and Durham are
slowly realising that there is brass to be made from other people's
muck but, the reservation is critical, the present development of
the tourist industry is well controlled. Inevitably there are exceptions, but they are few and far between. York and Durham and
Richmond are fine examples of conservation at work. Pickering and
Barnard Castle are still, essentially, small market towns. The
occasional outcroppings of pop culture are lost against the wide
horizons of moors and dales.

The reasons for this phenomenon, the phenomenon of a region
that has not sold out its birthright, are, obviously, manifold but one
thing is for sure — it is the people of Yorkshire and Durham themselves who have resisted the onslaught. They may be taciturn,
stubborn, many things but, in their own terms, "we likes what we
knows and we keeps what we likes." For more than 2,000 years the
invaders have overrun the Kingdom of Northumbria— Marnians
and Romans, Angles, Saxons, Danes and Normans — and each
has added something to its character. Few, however, have changed
it. The present invasion may be more insidious, more subtle, but it
is unlikely to be more successful than all the rest.

A couple of miles outside Doncaster, there is a motorway sign
which reads, quite simply, THE NORTH. It is well worth seeing,
for yourself.

ats hauled up on the beach in the shadow of Flamborough Head

36 BRANCEP[...]

35 RABY CASTLE

34 STAINDROP CHU[...]

33 BARNARD CASTLE

32 BOWES

31 RICHMOND

30 EAS[...]

THE PENNINES

WAYFARER'S GUIDE
11

6 BEWERLEY

5 STUMP CROSS

7 BRIMHAM ROCKS

4 BURNSALL

3 BARDEN TOWER

2 BOLTON ABBEY

1 ILKLEY

Photos: W. Baxter / B.T.A. / Colour Lib Int / Dept. of Environment / C. M. Dixon / Durham Cathedral / John Edenbrow / Mary Evans / Noel Habgood / A. F. Kersting / Keystone / Mansell Col / Picturepoint / Pix / H Smith / Spectrum / F. Spencer / Bertram Unne / J. Wakerly / Anthony Whelan / Yorkshire Life / Yorks Museum / Yorkshire Post

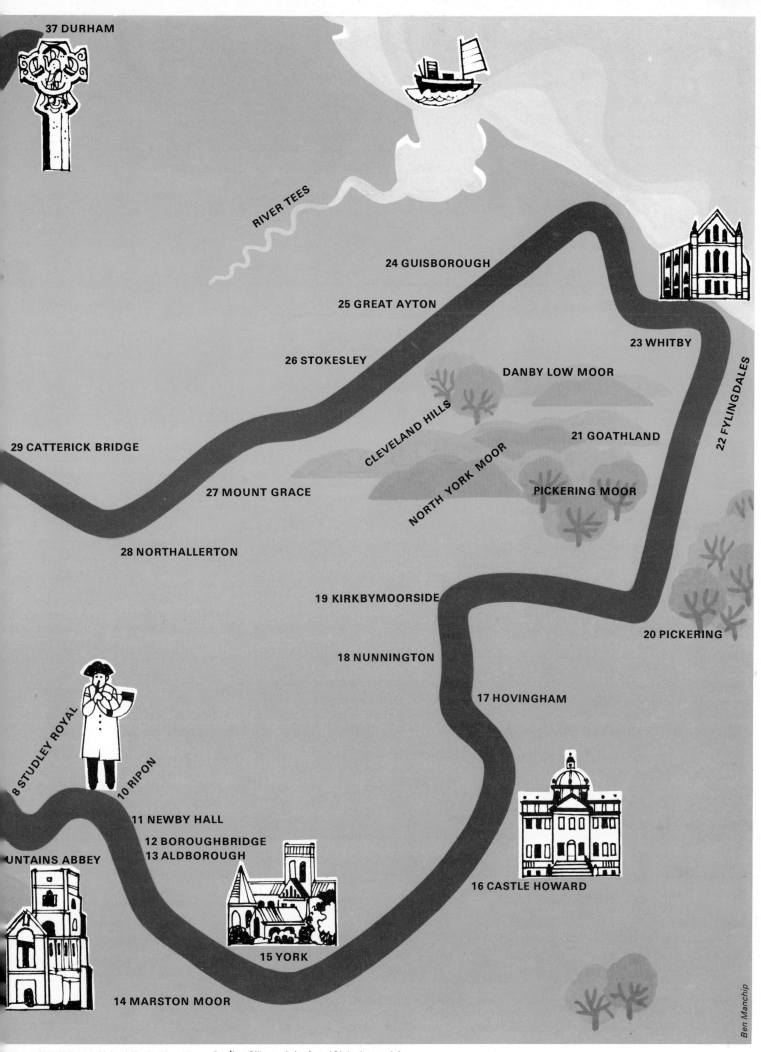

37 DURHAM

RIVER TEES

24 GUISBOROUGH

25 GREAT AYTON

26 STOKESLEY

23 WHITBY

DANBY LOW MOOR

22 FYLINGDALES

CLEVELAND HILLS

21 GOATHLAND

29 CATTERICK BRIDGE

27 MOUNT GRACE

NORTH YORK MOOR

PICKERING MOOR

28 NORTHALLERTON

19 KIRKBYMOORSIDE

20 PICKERING

18 NUNNINGTON

17 HOVINGHAM

8 STUDLEY ROYAL

10 RIPON

11 NEWBY HALL

12 BOROUGHBRIDGE
13 ALDBOROUGH

16 CASTLE HOWARD

UNTAINS ABBEY

15 YORK

14 MARSTON MOOR

Ben Manchip

ations: Elsie Wrigley / Richard Hook   Plant Notes: Geoffrey Gilbert   Animals and Birds: Jeremy Johns

The moor famed in song

1 ILKLEY: There is more to this old town and the surrounding moors than its legend in song. At the gateway to the Yorkshire Dales, Ilkley and the moors which flank it have been settled for 4,000 years. The town, called Olicana by the Romans, became fashionable only in the 18th Century when clear water springs were discovered at White Wells (the remains of the original bath houses built over two round baths hollowed out of the rocks can still be visited) but the moors surrounding the town are rich with traces of Bronze Age culture. The mystery of the cup and ring carvings still baffles archaeologists whilst the mysterious curved swastika, a primitive symbol of fire, is identical to similar carvings found throughout Europe and the East. And the song? It's a warning in dialect to young men not to go courting hatless or, as they have it in Yorkshire, baht 'at!

3 BARDEN TOWER, ruined an roofless, stands above the Riv Wharfe. It was built late in the 15th Century when this part of the Dale was a roy preserve. By the 17th Century the Tow was derelict but it was restored by th powerful Clifford family for use as a hun ing lodge. Besides the tower there is retainers' cottage, now used as a tea roor and a small chapel whose porch is now sheep pen.

Ruined and roofless

A RARE DISPLAY

About the end of March the visitor Yorkshire can see what is perhaps the be display of the sub-Arctic purple saxifra in this country.

This is the home ground of Regina Farrer, the botanist and gardener w. popularised the rock garden. The Crav limestone district of Yorkshire requires short divergence from the route but it tak one into an area that has fascinat botanists since Tudor times. The stone hard, white mountain limestone but bei soluble in rainwater it has been carv out in endless caves and fissures. Flat are divided by deep fissures provide a refu for many plants.

The ruins of the ancient priory in Wharfdale

2 BOLTON ABBEY: The ruins of this great Augustinian priory (Abbey is a misnomer introduced in a railway timetable!) stand in a beauty spot painted by Turner and immortalised by Wordsworth. The Black Canons who inherited the land spent 400 years building it, but most of the monastic buildings were destroyed at the dissolution of the monasteries, the stone being used for nearby Bolton Hall. The nave was spared and is still in use. Close to the Hall, a home of the Dukes of Devonshire, the road is crossed by a three-arched aqueduct which once carried water for the monastery's flour mills.

Two miles upstream from the Priory, the River Wharfe is channelled through a narrow cleft of rocks. This natural curio, The Strid, has been a temptation to weekend athletes for more than a century — and a number have met their death trying to leap the deceptive narrow ravine above the tearing waters below Barden Bridge.

the glorious moorland scene about Burnsall

BEWERLEY: On the west bank of the River Nidd this small village is dominated by Guise Cliff and the towering ruins of Yorke's Folly, built in the 19th Century to provide local employment. A restored Tudor manor house stands where a tributary of the Nidd leaves its glen while nearby a small Chapel of Ease, built by Marmaduke Huby, Abbot of Fountains in the 16th Century, is open to the public. The chapel is small, of monastic simplicity, and its thick stone walls keep it quiet and peaceful.

Nearby Pately Bridge is a short drive from Gouthwaite reservoir, a favourite reserve for bird watchers.

Bewerley from Yorke's Folly

BURNSALL: This moorland village by the River Wharfe is a showplace the Dales. Beside the river is the Green, complete with maypole, and the narrow road curving steeply up the hill passes the parish church of St. Wilfred with its curious swinging lych gate. At the east end of the church is a medieval alabaster carving of the nativity. The church was rebuilt in the 16th Century and in 1612 it was 'repaired and butified' (see the quaint inscription just above the south door) by Sir William Craven, who also founded Burnsall's Grammar School in 1602. The Dale sports are held annually in August on the feast of St. Wilfred.

STUMP CROSS: On a stretch of bleak moorland above Burnsall is a small white hut with the sign "Stump Cross Caverns" the only evidence above ground of a labyrinth of caves extending for 3½ miles. These were discovered in 1860 by lead miners and are now popular with potholers. There is a bizarre display of stalagmites and stalactites, many of them named, like the Jewel Box, the Sentinel.

bizarre display in the underground labyrinth

The Dancing Bear rock

BRIMHAM ROCKS: A majestic outcropping of millstone grit rocks that march against the skyline on the moors above the Plain of York. Many of these sculptures of time are individually named — the Dancing Bear, the Pulpit, the Oyster Shell — while the Idol Rock, weighing 200 tons, balances on a pedestal only 12 ins in diameter.

227

Ornamental birds in Studley Royal park

Fallow deer in the Park

8 STUDLEY ROYAL: A herd of deer now has the freedom of the tree lined park of this 18th Century hall which was burnt down in 1945. The landscaped gardens, with their ornamental waters, temples and statuary, were the work of John Aislabie, who was Chancellor of the Exchequer in 1718. After the South Sea Bubble he retired to his Yorkshire estates where he turned his talents to designing these gardens which are amongst the finest in the North.

10 RIPON: A peaceful little city, one of the smallest in Britain, which still finds the 20th Century an uncomfortable experience. Georgian and Victorian houses crowd above the narrow streets that lead into the market square with its 90ft obelisk built in 1781 in memory of William Aislabie, 60 years MP for Ripon. The town hall, which stands on the south side of the square, carries the gilded frieze: "Except Ye Lord Keep Ye Cittie, Ye Wakeman Waketh in Vain!" From Saxon times till the end of the Elizabethan period, Ripon was governed by a Wakeman. His job was to act as guardian of the city, for which he was paid a premium by every householder on the guarantee that he would make good any losses incurred during the curfew hours. The curfew itself was heralded by the sounding of a horn at sunset an[d] during the night hours, a watch patrolle[d] the streets. Although there is no longer [a] Wakeman, the tradition continues th[at] each evening at nine o'clock the Ci[ty] Hornblower, in his tricorn hat, sound[s] "curfew" at the Mayor's House and th[e] Market Cross. There is now a café in wh[at] was once the Wakeman's House an[d] behind it, there is a small museum.

The outstanding feature of the city is th[e] Cathedral of St. Wilfred, a Saxon sai[nt]. Although at a distance its profile is rath[er] squat (its spire collapsed in 166[0]) architectural historians maintain that it h[as] possibly the finest Early English west fro[nt] in Britain. The interior of the cathed[ral] covers a range of styles, from its Sax[on] crypt of A.D. 670 to the building abo[ve].

Cathedral of St. Wilfred, whose spire collapsed in 1660

9 FOUNTAINS ABBEY: The finest example of medieval, monastic architecture in Britain, the now skeletal remains of the abbey haunt the quiet valley of the River Skell. Fountains was founded in 1132 by 12 Benedictine monks from St. Mary's Abbey, York, who had broken with their parent order to adopt the stricter Cistercian discipline. The first, crude monastery, named De Fontibus after the numerous springs, was soon replaced by a massive stone abbey which was gradually extended until, in early Tudor times, Abbot Huby completed the 168ft tower at the end of the north transept. In the 16th Century the community owned thousands of acres throughout Yorkshire; they were trading in wool, cloth and lead, and eight sister abbeys had been founded from Fountains. In 1539 the monastery was dissolved, the Abbot hanged, the monks dispossessed, the roofs torn down and everything of value seized for the Crown. Down the centuries, Fountains has been savaged many times, but much of the abbey and outbuildings still remains. Abbot Huby's tower still shadows the Chapel of the Nine Altars, the 300ft cellarium with its 19 pillars and vaulted ceiling is cool to the summer days, while the great refectory echoes to a memory of the past. During October, Fountains is floodlit and Son et Lumière is performed among the ruins. The main entrance to the abbey is overlooked by Fountains Hall, built in the early 17th Century by Sir Stephen Proctor, the Collector of Fines on Penal Statutes, with stone from the abbey's outbuildings. The Hall, which is open to the public, is a fine example of Jacobean architecture with its minstrel gallery, cavernous stone fireplaces and panelled rooms.

Floodlights among the arches

round ranging from 12th to 16th Century. The nave is divided from the choir by a delightfully ornate rood screen, featuring highly painted statues of kings and queens surmounted by an angel choir. All the figures are modern, replacing figures which were removed several hundred years ago. An extravaganza of 15th Century imagination, the misericords show a pig playing the bagpipes for piglets to dance to, a mermaid with her looking-glass, Jonah being swallowed by the whale and his providential escape from the Leviathan's belly and other humorous, grotesque, and surprisingly temporal figures. Over the chancel entrance to the choir is a wooden hand which was operated by the organist's foot, and was used to beat time for the benefit of the choristers.

Newby Hall, south-west view

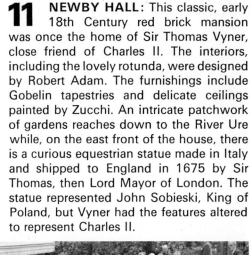

11 NEWBY HALL: This classic, early 18th Century red brick mansion was once the home of Sir Thomas Vyner, close friend of Charles II. The interiors, including the lovely rotunda, were designed by Robert Adam. The furnishings include Gobelin tapestries and delicate ceilings painted by Zucchi. An intricate patchwork of gardens reaches down to the River Ure while, on the east front of the house, there is a curious equestrian statue made in Italy and shipped to England in 1675 by Sir Thomas, then Lord Mayor of London. The statue represented John Sobieski, King of Poland, but Vyner had the features altered to represent Charles II.

The children's railway at Newby Hall

City hornblower sounding "curfew"

Memorial at Boroughbridge

12 BOROUGHBRIDGE was the site of a major battle in 1322; the place where the rebel Earl of Lancaster sought sanctuary from Edward II; and where Prince Rupert rested his horse the night before Marston Moor. Between the modern by-pass and the old road are the enigmatic Three Arrows, prehistoric monoliths believed to mark a Bronze Age burial site. Since the by-pass was completed in 1966 Great North Road traffic has found a new staging post and Boroughbridge has become something of a ghost town.

Reconstruction of a chapel

"The skeletal remains haunt the quiet valley"

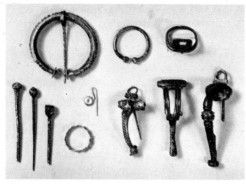
Roman brooches and pins

Tesselated pavement

13 **ALDBOROUGH:** This village with its green and maypole and Tudor style manor house was known to the Romans as Isurium and 1,800 years ago was the headquarters of the Ninth Legion and the home of the Consuls and Governors of York. A few traces remain, including two small tesselated pavements (now roofed over in the middle of a cabbage patch) which show a leopard sitting beneath a palm tree and an eight pointed star. There is a figure of Mercury in the parish church and Aldborough Museum has a collection of objects excavated on the site.

14 **MARSTON MOOR:** The site of Cromwell's defeat of Prince Rupert and the Duke of Newcastle in 1644, which "decided the North for Parliament", is marked by an obelisk set up by the Cromwellian Association.

Cromwell at the battle

The south choir aisle in the Minster

15 **YORK:** The problem of York is a simple one — that it has too much of everything. The city is a chronicle of history punctuated by some of the finest architecture in Europe. But there is more to York than the aesthetics of the past. It is, essentially, a city of today: a city that has come to terms with the facts of modern life. York has not merely survived the vicissitudes of 2,000 years, it has adapted the best of the past to the demands of the present — the medieval Guildhall is still used by the City Council: the Tudor "King's Manor" is now a part of the new University while the gracious Georgian Assembly Rooms are still booked regularly for meetings and conferences.

In the year A.D. 71 the Romans established York (Eboracum) as the headquarters of their Sixth Legion and as capital of their Northern Provinces. For more than 300 years, the city was a centre-point of trade and commerce and it was here that the Emperor Constantius died and that his son, Constantine the Great, was proclaimed Emperor of Western Rome. The Romans withdrew from Britain in the 5th Century and for the next 500 years the story of York is largely unknown.

William the Conqueror was crowned by the Archbishop of York, but the North rebelled against the new regime. The opposition, however, was doomed and The Harrying of the North left scarcely a building standing between York and Durham. By the end of the 11th Century all open resistance had been quashed and the supporters of the King (such as the Percy and the Nevilles) had obtained vast power in the North.

There is much evidence of medieval York still to be found within the walls but as times became more settled, the city began to spread. By the 18th Century York, now an important staging post, was rapidly developing outside its walls in such areas as the Mount and Bootham, where many fine Georgian houses can still be seen. With the coming of the railway in the mid-19th Century, York attained a new dimension of influence for George Hudson "The Railway King" and sometime Lord Mayor of York, made the city the great railway centre of the north.

The Zouche Chapel: a poem in stone

The most important relics of the Roman [er]a are in the Yorkshire Museum. An [oc]tagonal brick bastion still stands in the [M]useum Gardens. In the same Gardens are [th]e 11th to 13th Century ruins of St. Mary's [A]bbey. The medieval walls of York, [ex]cellently preserved and restored, are [n]early three miles long and are pierced by [ga]teways, or "Bars". The great Micklegate [B]ar still dwarfs the road to the south and it [w]as here that the severed heads of traitors [w]ere displayed. Walmgate Bar, to the [no]rth of the city, still has its barbican and [po]rtcullis whilst, above the gateway, is a [ha]lf timbered Elizabethan house. Nothing [no]w remains of the two Norman castles [w]hich were built in York, though on a high [m]ound where one of them stood is the [qu]atrefoil Clifford's Tower built in the 13th [ce]ntury for Henry III and named after its [fir]st Governor. As the shadows of York's [hi]story shorten, the traces of the past [m]ultiply. From the 14th Century there are [th]e exquisite Merchant Taylors' and Mer[ch]ant Adventurers' Halls. The Guildhall [ba]dly damaged in the war, but now [re]stored), St. Anthony's Hall and St.

Clifford's Tower, 13th Century

William's College are all fine examples of 15th Century craftsmanship.

The domestic architecture of the Restoration and Georgian periods dominate the city's centre. The Treasurer's House, now owned by the National Trust, dates mainly from the late 17th and early 18th Centuries; the Mansion House (still the home of York's Lord Mayor) was built between 1725 and 1730 and the classically functional Assize Courts were opened in 1777. This central area of the city is inter-linked by a weft of narrow streets including The Shambles, (one of the finest medieval streets in Europe) and Stonegate (the Via Praetoria of Roman times) which are both closed to traffic.

Much of the history of York and its principal industries are synthesised in the city's two great museums — the Folk Museum besides Clifford's Tower and the Railway Museum beside the station, itself a superb example of 19th Century railway architecture. The Castle Museum is housed in two buildings which were formerly prisons, one for women and the other for "felons and debtors". The Museum offers

The Minster, a bulwark of sculptured granite that crouches protective above the city

a study-in-miniature of the folk culture of Yorkshire; the most memorable section being the cobbled streets complete with a variety of Victorian shop windows, a candle factory, a fire station, a bar-room, and workrooms where craftsmen carried out their trades. A few paces from the museum there is a small watermill which grinds corn to fill miniature sacks of flour for the tourist. In the former Debtors' Prison can be seen the cell which held Dick Turpin before he was hanged on the site of the present Knavesmire Racecourse.

Only two cities in England (London and Norwich) have more churches than York, which has 18 built in medieval times. All, however, are overshadowed by the superlative Minster, the largest Gothic church in England. Building began in 1220, took more than 250 years to complete and it was only in 1480 that the central lantern tower was finished. Although the exterior of the Minster has been refurbished several times since the 15th Century, its overall appearance is much the same as it was nearly five centuries ago — a bulwark of sculpted granite that crouches, protective,

above the surrounding city. The quality of permanence, however, is deceptive, in 1965-1966 a full scale survey of the Minster's fabric showed that "the foundations were over-loaded and failing due to fatigue and old age . . . the Norman walls, used as footings for the two later towers, were grossly overloaded and in poor condition, wide shear cracks had opened and there was evidence of a tendency to burst."

The situation was so critical that in 1967 there were warnings that the Minster might have to be closed. The threat, however never materialised. In mid-1967 a £2,000,000 appeal was launched to "Save the Minster" and a massive rescue operation mounted. Since then the foundations of the central tower have been strengthened with reinforced concrete; the east end has been shored-up; the western front underpinned and much of the stone-work cleaned — all without interrupting the everyday life of the Minster. The restoration work, in fact, has added a sense of urgency to the Gothic interior with its treasure of medieval stained glass. York,

The picturesque Shambles

mside bowl in York Museum

Roman urn

...day, boasts possession of approximately ...ree-quarters of all the old glass in England ...d there are more than 100 windows of ...edieval glass in the Minster.

...During the last war, 80 of the finest of ...ese windows were removed for safety ...d the post-war restoration work, involv-...g reglazing and cleaning, took more than ...years. The result is breathtaking, making ...cavern of shifting light of the Minster's ...aring interior. Behind the high altar rears ...e east window which contains the largest ...ea of stained glass (1,700 square feet) of ...y window in the world. Created in the ...rly 15th Century by John Thornton, the ...ventry glass maker, it features innumer-...le stories from the Old Testament and ...ds with the Apocalypse of St. John the ...vine. In the north transept there is the ...ore subdued five sisters window dating ...m the 13th Century and centre-piece of ...Dickens story, while the south transept ...dominated by a rose window.

...Opposite the Minster's south door ...nds a Roman column, from about A.D. ...0, which was found under the Minster ...ring restoration work.

16 **CASTLE HOWARD:** This massive Vanbrugh palace is a question mark of taste. The fashionable 18th Century writer, Horace Walpole, rhapsodised that it was: "At one view a palace, a town, a fortified city, temples on high places . . . In short, I have seen gigantic palaces before but never a sublimer one."

Macaulay disagreed: "The most perfect specimen of the most vicious style." Castle Howard was the first architectural commission of the 32-year-old Vanbrugh, at that time a captain in the Royal Marines, who went on to design Blenheim in association with Nicholas Hawksmoor. The south side of the house is 292 ft long — a marching colonnade in Palladian style.

A series of galleries house precious china, sculptures, miniatures, tapestries and paintings by Velazquez, Van Dyck, Titian, Canaletto, Reynolds and Gainsborough. The palace also has the largest private collection of 17th to 20th Century fashions in Britain.

A massive Vanbrugh palace

17 **HOVINGHAM** is the home of the Worsley family; the present owner of the 18th Century hall being Sir William Worsley, father of the Duchess of Kent. A week long cricket festival, which has featured many of the game's greatest players, has been held annually on the great lawn of the hall for a century.

Quiet corner at Hovingham

18 **NUNNINGTON** is a village with a strong Royalist history. The church houses the fine stone figure of Sir Walter de Teye, who died fighting for the crown in 1325, and also a marble memorial to Sir Richard Graham, first Viscount Preston, a close friend of Charles II who was condemned to death, but later reprieved, for plotting the restoration of James II in 1690. Nunnington Hall is a fine example of late Jacobean architecture.

Village with a Royalist history

19 **KIRKBYMOORSIDE:** No one has yet established whether the "k" in Kirkby should be included or not. The Ordnance Survey remains historically purist, but locals insist on the abbreviated form. One thing, however, is certain — this small market town, gateway to the North Yorkshire moors, has a "kirk" with a register containing the record of the death of George Villiers, Duke of Buckingham. This 17th Century courtier and rake, a confidant of Charles II, retired to his estate at nearby Helmsley after being tried by the House of Lords for the murder of the Earl of Shrewsbury and "the public debauchery" of Shrewsbury's wife. He was riding near Kirkbymoorside when his horse dropped dead and, being a superstitious man, he took this for an evil omen. He was right. Before he could find another horse, he caught a severe chill and died within hours at a cottage in Kirkbymoorside.

A farm near Kirkbymoorside

20 **PICKERING:** The medieval castle stands etched against the backcloth of the North Yorkshire moors and commands the eastern approaches to the Vale of Pickering. Built in the 12th Century, the castle (now the property of the Duchy of Lancaster) was enlarged in the 14th. The shell keep, built between 1220 and 1230 on a 43ft. artificial hill, was surrounded by three towers — Devil's Tower, Mill Tower and Rosamund's Tower, named after the Fair Rosamund, mistress of Henry II. King John visited the castle frequently and Richard II was brought here, a prisoner, before being taken to his death at Pontefract. Pickering Church, basically early Norman but much restored, has some fine wall paintings from the 15th Century, featuring Biblical scenes, including the martyrdom of the saints.

A quiet corner on the outskirts of Pickering

THE SELF-TAUGHT ARTIST

James Lloyd, self-taught artist, wh specialises in sheep, horses, cows, tre and people, does his painting in a coun house in a village outside York. He paints into the night as if to compensate for r having started serious work as an artist un so late in life. He did not take up paintir till he was past 40, having worked as policeman, postman, lamp-lighter, stok and shepherd, and uses a pointillis technique which he learned by copyir newspaper photographs dot by dot. At or stage he owned a farm high in the Pennir and painted the farm animals with the ri detail of a medieval tapestry. Born Cheshire in 1905, he spent his childho and teens on his father's farm.

Recognition came in the late 1950's. H wife sent some of his paintings to the la Sir Herbert Read, who visited Lloyd, w John Berger, the art critic. Exhibitio followed, the demand for his work gre and he then decided to devote his time painting. Two examples are seen belo

21 **GOATHLAND:** This rugged village is a focal point for archaeologists, naturalists and historians. A Roman road, Wade's Way, once cut across the moors near the village and nearly a mile of is still maintained. Traces have also been found of turf 'mazes' laid out by the Romans and of Anglo-Saxon cairns. There too, a curiosity of more recent history. The North Yorkshire Moors Railway Preservation Society has reopened the railway line through Goathland. This moorland region is covered by a network of streams and waterfalls and near Beck Hole is a small valley noted for its rare wild flowers. During the summer the Sword Dancers, or Plough Stotts, occasionally perform their dances in Goathland village.

On the way to Goathland the Saltergate Inn is worth a visit to see the peat fire that has burned for 170 years "to keep the devil in his place".

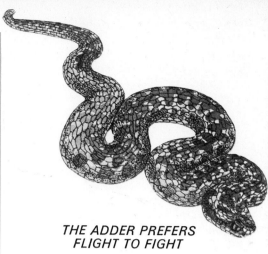

THE ADDER PREFERS FLIGHT TO FIGHT

Compared with other British snakes the adder is short and thick, tapering noticeably towards the tail and seldom stretching more than two feet. It can be recognised by a bright yellow V on its neck but this distinguishing mark cannot be relied on for the harmless and beautiful grass snake has a similar feature. The adder, however, has distinctive zig-zag markings. The scales or shield that cover the adder's body are conspicuous and the diverse patterns are noticeable for their variety. The snake is to be found round and about the Pennines on dry moorland and on sunny slopes. Contrary to popular belief the adder is not aggressive, preferring to hide or escape rather than defend itself. It seldom bites man and when it does happen it is rarely fatal — only seven people have died of adder-bite in the last half-century.

Goathland, a focal point for archaeologists

22 **FYLINGDALES:** To the east, standing futuristically against the skyline, are the giant globes of the Fylingdales Early Warning System. Built in the early 1960's these three, space age domes, 140 feet in diameter, provide Britain with radar 'cover' against ballistic and aircraft attack.

In contrast is the Saxon cross known as Lilla Cross, possibly the earliest Christian monument in the country. The Cross, which stands on Lilla Howe on Fylingdales Moors, cannot be reached by road.

Mallyan Spout, one of a network of waterfalls around Goathland

Roadway to the space age

23 **WHITBY:** The fishing port crouched on the hillsides about the small harbour, is shadowed by a headland crowned by the ruins of St Hilda's Abbey. Here, in A.D. 664, the Celtic and Roman churches agreed the date of Easter. Here, in the late 7th Century, the Saxon historian, Bede, received his early training and here, 1,300 years ago, Caedmon, the swineherd-turned-poet, sang to the Abbess Hilda his transcendent "Song of Creation":

Here first shaped
The Lord Eternal
Chief of all creatures,
Heaven and Earth . . . . .

A thousand years after Caedmon sang his song, in yards below the ruined Abbey, shipwrights built three small vessels — *Endeavour, Resolution* and *Adventure* — which James Cook commanded on his voyages of discovery to the South Seas. The whole of this region, in fact, is rich in associations with Cook and high on the west cliff of the town there is a bronze statue to the man who claimed Australia for the Crown. But Cook is only one of the many Yorkshiremen who, through the centuries, have sailed from Whitby and the now sightless tombs of the parish church are a wake to their adventures — the adventures of whalers and trawlermen and slavers and of the 12 Whitby lifeboatmen who, watched by thousands of people, were battered to death by towering waves in the great storm of 1861. The church is described by Nikolaus Pevsner as "a wonderful jumble of medieval and Georgian — hard to believe and impossible not to love." The interior is flanked by galleries that overlook a mosaic of box pews, some of which even have their backs to the triple decker pulpit.

A serpentine path of 199 steps leads down from the church to the old town where, in Grape Street, the house where Cook taught himself the principles of mathematics and navigation and seamanship can still be visited.

Captain Cook statue at Whitby

Margaret Tudor, gift to church

24 **GUISBOROUGH:** One of t frontier towns during the Angl Scottish wars of medieval times, with priory founded by Robert de Bruce in A. 1119. All that remains of this gre Augustinian foundation is the Norm gateway and the east end of the Chur built at the end of the 13th Century. monument, known as the Bruce cenotap and probably presented to the Priory Margaret Tudor, a daughter of Henry VII, now in St. Nicholas Church. A great cask of stone, its sides are flanked by fi knights of the Bruce family separated smaller figures of saints.

GREETING IN THE DALES

The mountain pansy with its large yello flowers greets the visitor in late June to t lower slopes of many of Yorkshir dalesides. The trees about are mostly a and animals have been deterred fro grazing by the deep fissures. The result that many rare wild plants have a chance grow and spread.

In Upper Wharfedale and Littond many interesting plants can be fou within a short distance of the road. Lo for screes, pavements and old ash woo This is the traditional ground of our m impressive orchid, the Lady's Slipper. T yellow slipper-shaped flower is unlikely be overlooked.

Fishing port crouched on hillsides about a small harbour

...seberry Topping, near the village where Cook spent his childhood

28 NORTHALLERTON: Although primarily a product of the 19th Century, traces can still be found of a more discriminating past including the Fleece Inn in the market square; the 18th Century Sessions House and the Norman-medieval church with its 15th Century tower. The interior of the church has a small collection of Saxon crosses and some fine monuments. Two miles north of the town, on the Darlington Road, there is an obelisk to the English victory at the Battle of the Standard in 1138. The battle took its name from the enigmatic standard that the English barons carried with them into action against the Scots — the mast of a ship mounted on a four wheeled carriage and having, at its peak, a pyx containing the consecrated Host.

5 GREAT AYTON: The village has grown up on either side of [th]e River Leven and is chiefly known as the [pla]ce where James Cook spent his child[ho]od. The cottage where he lived has been [dis]mantled and re-built in Australia but the site is marked by an obelisk quarried from Hick's Point in New South Wales — Cook's first Australian landfall. The small school which Cook attended now houses a museum in which can be seen the books and equipment he may have used as a boy.

Harvesting near Northallerton

...orgian houses in the High Street

The Carthusian priory ruins

An inn near Catterick

26 STOKESLEY: The tree-lined River Leven is crossed by a cob[web] of small, old bridges. The High Street, [wh]ich is flanked by some fine Georgian [ho]uses, is wide enough to contain islands [of b]uildings and large cobbled areas includ[ing] the market place. Each year, in Sep[tem]ber, the town becomes a hustle of life [wh]en Yorkshiremen gather for the [Sto]kesley Show.

27 MOUNT GRACE: The only Carthusian priory in Yorkshire, Mount Grace is idyllically landscaped amongst the woods to the south of Ingleby Arncliffe. The foundation of Thomas Holland, a Duke of Surrey, executed for conspiracy against Henry IV, the Priory is now only a tracery of ruins beneath the soft hills. The approach road to Mount Grace, completed in 1420, is now sentinelled by a superb Jacobean house built by Thomas Lascelles in 1654 from the west front of the Priory itself.

29 CATTERICK BRIDGE: This area has been an army camp since the days when the Legions, en route for the Scottish border, established a camp at Cataractonium, a site north-west of the present village. Catterick races are, today, one of the great meetings of the North.

237

30 EASBY: The Church and Abbey of Easby, standing south of the main road, are both Norman, but it is probable that the Church was founded before the White Canons established their abbey in 1152. The Church is small and contains many Early English features, having been enlarged and restored in 1424. Of particular interest are the frescoes in the chancel and the copy of the early 8th Century Easby Cross, the original of which is in the Victoria and Albert Museum. The Abbey, although in ruins, is of great architectural interest for its unusual arrangement of buildings. For those with no knowledge of monastic design it is also a pleasing ruin with lovely windows and arches. The Abbey was originally approached by a Gatehouse, rebuilt in 1300, which, though roofless, is otherwise complete.

The Abbey, a pleasing ruin

THE SPECTRAL PREDATOR

The spectral form of the barn owl is all t[...] rarely seen in Yorkshire these days for t[...] predator has been a victim of polluti[...] The bird is not exclusively nocturnal [...] towards winter's end, the barn owl [...] forced to hunt by day when its true col[...] is revealed — golden brown with wh[...] undersides. Its sense of hearing is so ac[...] that it can locate its prey in pitch darkn[...] by this sense alone. It swoops in silence [...] its victims: voles, shrews, mice, small bir[...] beetles, frogs, sometimes even bats a[...] fish. Its cry is blood-chilling — a lo[...] shriek. The barn owl lays its eggs on [...] gorged pellets in barns, hollow trees a[...] ruins and hatches two broods a year.

31 RICHMOND: The Gas Board should be ashamed of themselves: one of the finest views in the north, across the Swale and up the rugged escarpment, is blemished (what a euphemism) by a single gasholder that crouches, rusting, in the valley. But this is the only scar about this North Riding market town, which has a neatness, a compactness, a sense of history that is rare in Britain. In the late 11th Century Alan the Red began work on Richmond Castle and, today, his keep still rises 114 ft from the surrounding moat. The castle has never been tested in war, but it has housed a line of royal prisoners, including William the Lion, King of Scotland, and Constance, Duchess of Brittany. Richmond town, which lives within the shadow of its castle, is compelling for its sense of the past. In the centre of the cobbled market square is Holy Trinity Church, with shops and offices built into the walls. The church, once used by the grammar school, is now being converted into a museum for the Green Howards. A web of cobbled 'wynds' radiates from the square and in Friars Wynd there is a small Georgian theatre built by the actor-manager Samuel Butler in 1788. During its heyday in the late 18th and early 19th Century many of London's stars including Edmund and Charles Kean and Ellen Tree, played at the theatre, but by the 1850's its popularity had so declined that the box office closed. For the next 90 years the theatre was used as an auction room, corn chandler's store, a furniture reposit[...] and, during the Second World War, a[...] salvage depot. In 1943, however, [...] theatre was re-discovered and a play v[...] staged to mark the 950th anniversary [...] Richmond's enfranchisement. Since th[...] the whole of the theatre has been co[...] pletely restored, and today it is one of [...] finest examples of a Georgian playho[...] in Britain. Almost opposite the theatre [...] all that now remains of the Francis[...] monks' ambition to build a Church adjo[...] ing their 13th Century friary — a f[...] arched, oblong tower built in the 1[...] Century. The work was never comple[...] and the Friary itself was dissolved. A s[...] walk from the theatre is St. Mary's Chu[...] in which can be seen the beautifully car[...]

Castle and bridge over Swale

wooden choir stalls removed from Ea[...] Abbey. For tomb hunters there is also [...] memorial to Sir Timothy Hutton, his v[...] and their 12 children, four in swadd[...] clothes and eight kneeling. Beneath e[...] child is an epitaph, one reading:

Into this world, as strangers to
an inn,
This infant came guest-wise, whe[...]
when't had been,
And found no entertainment wor[...]
her stay,
She only broke her fast and went [...]
away.

Richmond: neat, compact, with a sense of history

...tting for Dotheboys Hall

33 **BARNARD CASTLE:** The centre of the *Rokeby* country, immortalised by Scott in his novel. Today Barnard is an easy-going little market town on its cliff above the Tees but once it was the key to Norman control of the Upper Tees valley. The castle, which rises 100 ft above the river, was built in 1150 by Bernard Balliol, hence Bernard or Barnard Castle. His successor, John Balliol, founded the Oxford College of that name while his son, the second John Balliol, became King of Scotland. During the rising of the north of 1569, the castle was held for eleven days by Sir George Bowes for the Queen — a siege which broke the rebel cause. Although the castle was officially "dismantled" in 1629, it still retains the sturdy character described by Leland in Tudor times — "the Castelle of Barnard stondith stately upon Tese." The 14th Century keep, topped by a flattened dome, has walls 10 ft. thick which house a staircase while Brackenbury's Tower has an opening in its vault for lowering provisions to the dungeons below. The architectural anachronism that is Bowes Museum stands only a quarter of a mile from the town centre. This extravagant French château of the renaissance style was built by John Bowes of Streatland Castle. An avid Francophile, Bowes married the Parisian actress Josephine Benoit, later to become Countess Montalbo. The couple planned to build their museum in Calais but, because of the unsettled political climate in France, they transferred their ambitions to Barnard Castle. The building, in ornamental grounds, houses a wide range of English and European art, porcelain, tapestries, objets d'art; a children's collection of dolls and doll's houses and a large section devoted to Teesdale folk history.

The Bowes Museum

32 **BOWES:** Dickensian ghosts still haunt this grey and wind-swept moorland village, the setting of Dotheboys Hall. It was to the remote academies of Bowes that parents farmed-of their children in the early 19th Century. In the 1830's it is estimated that there were over 800 boys boarded in the town. Then Charles Dickens arrived.

At one of the schools he visited, he was turned away from the door by a vulpine character by the name of Shaw, the prototype of the infamous Wackford Squeers. As he left, he passed through the churchyard and: "The first gravestone I first stumbled was of a boy who had died suddenly, I suppose his heart broke. He died in this wretched place, and I think that his ghost put Smike into my mind on the spot." The result of Dickens's exposures in *Nicholas Nickleby* destroyed the academies of Bowes and, within the years, the town's school population dropped to 20 boys.

Bowes's history reaches deep past the nightmare of Dotheboys Hall: back to the second century A.D. when the Legion established a camp on the site. All that remains of this outpost of the Empire is a large Roman bath and a stone in the church commemorating the Arabian campaigns of the Emperor Severus. Six hundred years after the departure of the Legions, the Normans once again fortified the town and the ruin of their massive keep still stands to the south of the main road.

Barnard Castle overlooking the Tees

Fifth Earl of Westmorland

34 **STAINDROP CHURCH:** The tombs to the Neville family in this old Church are some of the finest in Britain. The building itself is a hybrid of style ranging from the Anglo-Saxon foundations to the 15th Century oak roof but it is the medieval monuments that command attention. All are to the owners of nearby Raby Castle and, between them, they trace the evolution of English court fashions over 300 years. The oldest tomb is to Elizabeth Fitzmeldred, who died about 1260; the most outstanding to Ralph Neville, grandfather of Warwick the Kingmaker, who died in 1425; the most remarkable to Henry, the fifth Earl of Westmorland, who died in 1564. The Earl is dressed in full armour with his feet resting on a greyhound while, on either side of him, are two of his wives with long chains hanging from their waists and their feet resting on pet dogs.

35 RABY CASTLE:

This great moated stronghold, set in 270 acres of parkland, is an aggregate of history. For 400 years it was the northern seat of the formidable Neville family and since then it has been the home of the Vanes. Built mostly between 1331 and 1389 by the Lords Ralph and John Neville, Raby still has a sense of latent power; from the 80 ft Cliffords Tower, with its 10 ft thick walls, to the massive Neville gateway with its flanking towers and 60 ft passageway into the inner court. Today these furnishings of war may be an anachronism, but in the years of the Nevilles, Raby was in the front-line of the long wars between England and Scotland. In 1569, however, the family betrayed their loyalty to the English crown by planning the "Rising of the North" at Raby.

The rising cost the Nevilles their royal favours — and Raby Castle. For the next 60 years the stronghold was a Crown possession and then it was purchased, with Barnard Castle, by Sir Henry Vane. Sir Henry's son, Sir Henry Vane the Younger, was a lifelong champion of Parliament, a close friend of Milton and Cromwell and, during the Civil War, was twice besieged in Raby. Although a Commonwealth man, Vane was no regicide but this did not save him at the Restoration. He was executed on Tower Hill for, in the fatal words of Charles II,

he was: "too dangerous a man to live."

More than three centuries have passed since Sir Henry rode to his death from Raby but, except for minor 19th Century alterations, the castle still retains its patina of history, which makes it uniquely worth a visit.

Raby Castle: moated stronghold

37 DURHAM:

The old city h... some of the most superb med... eval architecture in Europe. The drive... from the west is through rolling countrysi... and then, quite suddenly, there it is — th... old city set above the River Wear on i... soaring hillside. The contrast is explosiv... for old Durham is a statement of the pa... and a proof that, for all the pressures... commercialism, preservation can be ma... to work.

The conservationists did start with son... natural advantages which, more than 1,20... years ago, the monks of Dunelm we... quick to exploit for strategic ends. Trac... have been found of both prehistoric ar... Roman remains in the area, but it was t... monks who first recognised the defensi... qualities of Durham. In the 9th and 10... Centuries, with the east coast constant... harried by the Danes, the promontory... which the city now stands provided... natural fortress bounded, as it is, on thre... sides by the Wear and on the fourth by... escarpment.

Here, in 762, an Anglo-Saxon bisho... was consecrated and here, in 995, t... monks brought the body of Saint Cuthbe... The story is now clouded by legend but... is said that the saint's coffin becan... immovable on a nearby hill. The proble... it seems, was insuperable until Cuthbe... himself (though two centuries dea... personally announced his intention of re...

The keep at Durham Castle

Sanctuary knocker, Durham Cathedral

Interior from Brancepeth Church, richly endowed

36 BRANCEPETH:

The castle is not open to the public, but the nearby church is worth visiting. During medieval times the church was richly endowed by the Nevilles and in the 17th Century, John Cosin, a Bishop of Durham,

spent huge sums on furnishing the interior with a treasure of fine woodwork. Two Neville tombs stand in the chancel and a third, to Ralph who "died of grief at the loss of his only son", stands at the foot of the tower.

g at Durham. A century later Bishop William of Calais began to build the cathedral which now houses the saint's tomb and, until the Dissolution of the monasteries, the shrine of St. Cuthbert was a centre of pilgrimage.

During the turbulent, medieval years, Durham served the English Kings well as a buffer-state between themselves and the Scots and, from William the Conqueror onwards, the Crown bestowed riches and increasing powers on the Prince-Bishops of Durham. The seat of their power was the great cathedral which looks, today, much as it did when first completed in 1133. The dominant exterior feature is the 200 ft high, 50 ft wide central tower and the twin-towered west front which rises almost sheer from the banks of the Wear.

The 12th Century north doorway is dominated by a brass sanctuary knocker — an evil head with a giant ring in its mouth. Two monks were always stationed in a room above the north door to admit those seeking sanctuary. Fugitives were allowed to remain in the cathedral for up to 37 days and then, if their affairs were not settled, they were given a safe conduct to the coast, carrying a cross and wearing distinctive clothing. Between 1464 and 1524, 331 fugitives claimed sanctuary in Durham.

The interior of the cathedral is one of the most perfect and unspoilt examples of Norman architecture in Britain; the great arches of the nave supported on massive pillars whose circumference (approximately 23 ft.) is equal to their height. The earliest of the Norman work is in the choir. The 14th Century altar screen, made in London of Caen stone, was brought to Durham by sea and road and took seven masons nearly a year to erect. On the south side of the choir is the bishop's throne which, set in its own small and ornate gallery, is said to be the highest in Christendom — a temporal conceit of spiritual power. Saint Cuthbert's grave lies immediately behind

11th Century illuminated Bible

the high altar, the huge gravestone let into the floor of a shrine that has been hollowed out by the feet of ten centuries of pilgrims. On the north side of the Palace Green, immediately opposite the cathedral and dominating the open escarpment, is the castle. Built on the orders of the Conqueror, the present fortress is a conflict of architectural styles ranging from Norman to the 18th Century work of James Wyatt. Now the home of University College, the 13th Century hall of the castle is one of the finest dining halls in England. Armour and banners range the walls punctuated by portraits of bishops and benefactors, and in a corner of the gallery there are stone seats provided by the 15th Century Bishop Fox for his musicians.

The remainder of the old city spreads, like ripples, in concentric circles about the cathedral and the castle — a study in the slow evolution of all that is best of English architecture from Tudor House with its over-sailing upper storeys, through the old grammar school built in the Restoration period and the cool lines of Abbey House built in the Queen Anne period, to the austerity of modern design in the new University lecture rooms. But it is not only the aesthetics of the place that are captivating; it is the cool elegance of a city that has tamed the on-rush of commercialism and kept faith with a past that, in Durham, is still alive.

Detail from St. Cuthbert's coffin

The three great towers of Durham Cathedral

The Borders – key to two kingdoms

DOUGLAS KEAY AND FRANK WALKER

The important roads of Britain – the get-there-faster roads – mostly run up and down the country. But if you want to see people and places, take a cross-country route, threading a path between the great highways. Our route is like that. Swing off the motorway at Gretna, and soon you will be in the true Border country, with the road cleaving its way by Langholm and surging up the broad shoulders of the Cheviots, sweeping down from the high pastures to the riverside towns of Teviot and Tweed. On to the supranational burgh of Berwick, which gives its name to a Scottish county but – after 13 changes of ownership – is now forever England. Then down the Great North Road to the English bastion of Alnwick, before striking once again across the round-backed Cheviots to the Border of Roman times, the wall that was built to hold back the northern savages.

If you could pick your time in history, you could stop almost anywhere on this 200-mile route within sight or sound of battle. As Andrew Lang put it, "the air is full of ballad notes borne out of long ago". James Hogg, the Ettrick Shepherd, who could dress a ballad as crisply as the better-known Scott, caught it thus:

> Lock the door, Lariston, lion of Liddisdale,
> Lock the door, Lariston, Lowther comes on.
> The Armstrongs are flying, their widows are crying,
> The Castletown's burning, and Oliver's gone.
> Lock the door, Lariston – high on the weather gleam –
> See how the Saxon plumes bob on the sky.
> Yeoman and carbineer, Billman and halberdier;
> Fierce is the foray, and far is the cry.

Not much to sing about you might think. But in these softer times it is easy to sentimentalise. These were the bloody and brutal Borders where, in the space of a fortnight, an English army flattened five market towns and 243 villages, destroyed 14 abbeys and 16 castles and towers. Retribution, it should be said, came quickly at the end of that fortnight, when the English were slaughtered at Ancrum Moor and charitably buried amid the ruins they had created.

RUINS KNOCKED ABOUT

Along our route, particularly on the Scottish side, you will see the topless towers. In towns with mostly Victorian architecture, they stand out like decayed teeth. But they are picturesque too – the "jewels of the Borders" – for they are highly satisfactory ruins – unmistakably knocked about a bit but with enough left standing to show their function and character. The English, of course, came mainly in punitive role, and none the less brutal for that. Flodden is still a black memory after more than 400 years. Not that the Border Scots were angels of mercy. The staple industry was reiving or raiding — for cattle and anything else available. Robbery was the prime purpose, but there was no lack of stomach for killing when called for. And amid all this the Border families – Armstrong, Kerr, Scott, Elliot, Maxwell – were no less troublesome than the Highland clans, interrupting their blood feuds only to fend off the Auld Enemy.

Most borders are prickly places, man-made lines drawn arbitrarily for political or military reasons. Here the line is drawn slanting across the waist of Britain. One could quite sensibly argue it ought to have been rubbed out after the Union of the Crowns in 1603. The idea was that the whole Border area would become the "middle shires" of the new Great Britain. It seeme[d] logical. Look at a topographical map. At the top we have th[e] Highlands, reaching diagonally down into the west. In th[e] middle a completely different terrain, the Forth-Clyde Valley, [or] the Scottish Midlands, if you like. Thirdly the Southern Upland[s] a range of hills, 1,500–2,000ft., rolling down over the Border dee[p] into England, to Derby in fact. Is the Pennine shepherd muc[h] different from the lad of the Lammermuirs? Is the mill work[er] beside the Tweed different from the man on the Tyne?

Before the Union, the two governments got together to for[m] three "Marches" on either side of the Border, each with its ow[n] warden to keep the peace. But in many cases the system seemed [to] exacerbate the feuds. Came 1603 and an idealistic King Jam[es] dismissed the wardens of the Marches, set up a commission f[or] the Borders to achieve "a more perfect union". It was a long tim[e] a-coming, but it did come, and one may wonder why the Bord[er] should still exist today. We make weak jokes about Customs pos[ts] about needing your passport. But the division is there all right.

INTO ANOTHER KINGDOM

Our route takes us back and forth across the line, but even if yo[u] fail to notice the "Scotland" and "England" signs you are usual[ly] aware of entering another kingdom. The scenery is much the sam[e] but the architecture is different, and there are fewer ruins on th[e] English side. More signs of wealth, too, with some exception[s]. And accents can be quite changed in a mile or two.

Even today village housewives tend to do their shopping at th[e] nearest town on their side of the Border rather than cross th[e] line, which they call "ower the Border". When people south of th[e] line talk of "England" they could mean "Britain". But never th[e] Border Scot.

Rugby football is mostly a middle-class sport in England and [in] much of Scotland, but in the Scottish Borders it is the game of th[e] people, as in Wales. There are some soccer teams, true, but rugb[y] is the thing. It's as if eight burly forwards, thundering down th[e] pitch, were emulating a cavalry charge. And, talking of cavalr[y] you will notice this is horse-riding country. There's a lot [of] hunting and horse-racing – on the English side, too – and in th[e] South of Scotland there is the phenomenon of the Commo[n] Ridings, with up to a hundred young men spurring their stee[ds] like their ancestors, the reivers.

Our route starts in the "Batable Lands" of the southwest, b[ut] probably no more debatable than other parts of the no-man's lan[d]. It's a quiet start, even dull – Gretna a dreary place – a successio[n] of squat villages, fairly nondescript, until the land begins [to] undulate, the road winding through trees. Quick-changing scen[e] as we run into the foothills, though still on the valley floor alon[g] side the River Esk. A pleasant road if you are not in a hurry f[or] the A7, the shortest route to Edinburgh, is one of the twistie[st] highways in Scotland.

Langholm is a bustling town of tweedmakers but attracting l[ots] of tourists. The next 23 miles northward are mostly "sporting[",] meaning it's a winding road, at times hemmed in by hillsides [so] you can almost stretch out and touch the grass. You run in[to] Hawick alongside the River Teviot, the low-level approach whi[ch] is less dramatic than swooping down from the surrounding hil[ls]. A dour, grey-looking town, the High Street a hotchpotch

ctoriana – bay-windowed houses upstairs, modernised shops
tted in below. Here, as in most Border towns, you can pick up a
it-length or cardigan at reputedly bargain prices in the shops or
rehouses of the mills.

A few miles beyond Hawick, still beside the Teviot, your eye
ll be caught by that oddity in Scotland, a large village green at
nholm – a squared off village so much more attractive than the
ual ribbon development. A pleasantly undulating run now, rich
mland, plenty of trees, till suddenly, at the foot of a hill, you
d yourself in Jedburgh and at the market cross in the square,
ected by the A68 to Carter Bar ten miles south. Jedburgh is
mmed with history – talk about royal name-dropping! – and
u could spend half a day here, but there's a long way to go.

On the way to Kelso you can divert left about three miles to
at was once the capital of the county, Roxburgh, one of the
ir royal burghs of Scotland. Now a handful of houses and
veral farms. Approaching Kelso we get a full-face view of Floors
stle, seat of the Duke of Roxburghe (he retains the final 'e'),
no is one of the three big landlords of the Borders, the others being
e Dukes of Buccleuch and Northumberland. The Teviot now
rges with and loses its identity in the Tweed. The ruined abbey

is on the right as we run into a great wide cobbled square served
by nine roads, but with space for park benches, and all fringed
with attractive hotels, shops and houses – a bright and busy place.
On into Berwickshire and Coldstream between two rows of 18th
and 19th century buildings and no obvious town centre – more
interesting down towards the river. At the far end a bridge into
England, but we stay on the north bank through pastoral country.
Several points of interest, like the quaintly-named Simprim, then
into Northumberland.

Norham Castle is a truly beautiful ruin, almost theatrical on the
hill above a completely English village, perhaps with less character
than its Scottish counterpart but with more charm. This is a good
approach to Berwick, viewed over the wide estuary of the Tweed.
A workaday place in the centre, cluttered with A1 traffic, but we
skirt it and have to double back to see the interesting back streets,
ramparts and harbour.

Now we head south on the Great North Road, fairly fast over
ridges, with sea views on the crests. At Beal you can divert five
miles to Holy Island, or, just past Fenwick, you can stop at a high
point and get a good view of the fairy-like castle. On a clear day
you can see further out the Farne Islands, of the Grace Darling
rescue, the seal and bird colonies. Through the staging-post of
Belford and on to Alnwick, now bypassed by the Great North
Road, but still a busy market town, dominated by the massive
castle of the Percys. Attractive wide causeway after narrow high-
walled streets, and the local tongue has a touch of "Geordie",
halfway to Newcastle. Quite a climb out of town, following a road
that might have been made by the Romans (but wasn't), straight
over hill and dale, and back into the Cheviots again.

Scenically this is probably the best section of the route – from
woodlands to high pastures, across the moor with heather and
bracken. Up and down the ranges, across the shoulders of hills.
Down through the forest into the lovely little town of Rothbury,
where the road divides on different levels to let you window-shop
on foot, grass alongside. Then on by the north bank of the River
Coquet which, as the dale widens out, idles on in lazy links. But
we're off to the hills again, a bleaker landscape.

By contrast with Rothbury, the ancient and curio-packed
village of Elsdon is an anti-climax, with a vast seven-acre green
that is uneven and unkempt, criss-crossed by muddy paths. High
on the moors, Otterburn is a straggling village, unremarkable
apart from its link with the famous battle. A mile beyond the
village the site is marked by the Percy Cross.

At Elishaw we turn on to the A68 that has come over the tops
from Jedburgh en route for Scotch Corner, breasting the ridges in
long fast straights, an exhilarating drive but for the heavy traffic.
We are now on the last leg. Our finishing point is only a few miles
out of Newcastle at Heddon-on-the-Wall.

Not much to be seen of Hadrian's Wall – a fragment just south
of the village. But there's plenty of it further west, if you have the
time and inclination. For some distance you can drive on top of
the wall, which was used as a foundation for the military road
built after 1745. Here and there the original wall outcrops as a
deviation from the modern road, and you can stop in a lay-by to
make a close inspection, perhaps patrol the wall like a Roman
sentry, looking out for these Border savages.

hing boats in the harbour at St. Abbs

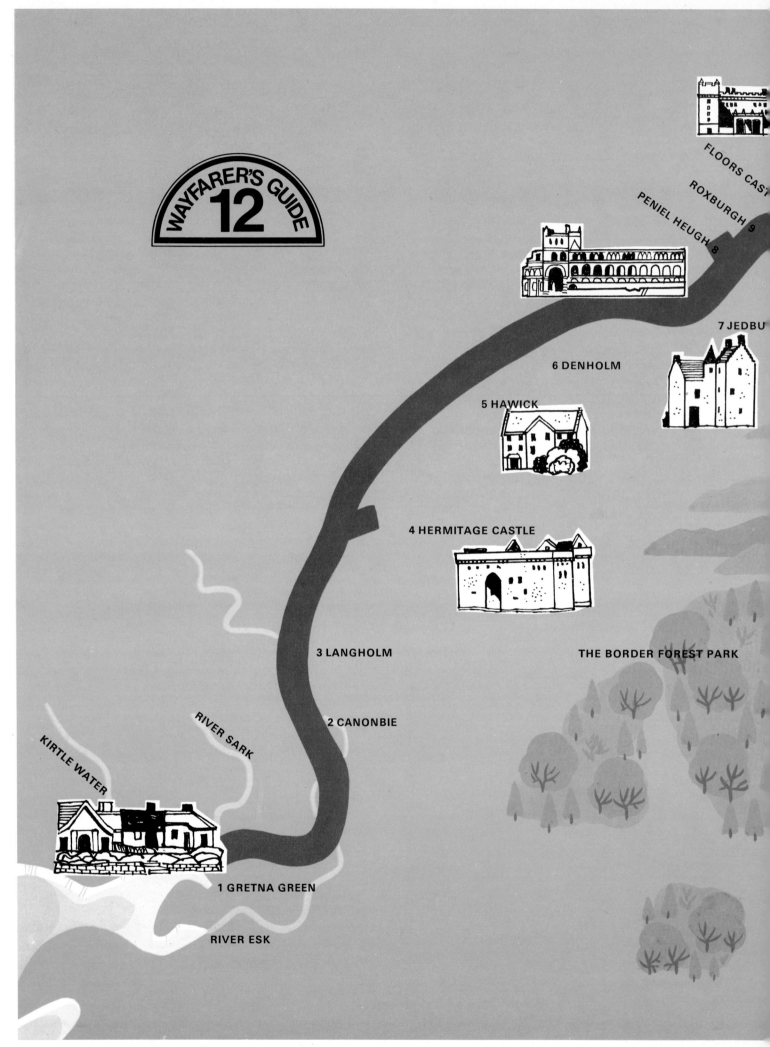

WAYFARER'S GUIDE 12

FLOORS CAST

ROXBURGH 9

PENIEL HEUGH 8

7 JEDBU

6 DENHOLM

5 HAWICK

4 HERMITAGE CASTLE

THE BORDER FOREST PARK

3 LANGHOLM

2 CANONBIE

RIVER SARK

KIRTLE WATER

1 GRETNA GREEN

RIVER ESK

SWINTON 15

SIMPRIM 14

THE HIRSEL 12

18 BERWICK-UPON-TWEED

19 HAGGERSTON

17 NORHAM CASTLE

16 LADYKIRK

20 HOLY ISLAND

13 COLDSTREAM

RIVER TWEED

11 KELSO

21 BELFORD

22 CHILLINGHAM

CHEVIOT HILLS

23 ALNWICK

24 ROTHBURY

ELSDON 25

26 OTTERBURN

Ben Manchip

27 HADRIAN'S WALL

28 HEDDON

Illustrations: Elsie Wrigley / Richard Hook   Plant Notes: Geoffrey Gilbert   Animals & Birds: Jeremy Johns

1 GRETNA GREEN: Target for runaway lovers for two centuries. Interesting registers at Gretna Hall (1710) listing 1,134 irregular marriages 1826-1855, also at the smithy since 1826. Elopers, often penniless and living in tents, still arrive looking for instant marriage over the anvil, though this stopped in 1939. Now they must wait three weeks and be married by registrar or minister — and this can be done anywhere in Scotland. The much-criticised Scots law of "marry at 16" was to discourage illegitimacy. A house near the church is called "Prince Charlie's Cottage" — he is said to have slept there on return from the English campaign in 1745. Nearby the Scots lost the battle of Solway Moss in 1542.

The Blacksmith's Shop

Johnny Armstrong's Tower from an old print (above) and (below) as it looks today

2 CANONBIE: This picturesque village on the River Esk was the centre of the notorious Armstrongs in the Border wars. They occupied Holehouse Tower, still well-preserved on the river bank. The most famous was Johnny Armstrong, who was hanged in 1530 at the command of James V. The whole family was banished and their descendants were threatened with hanging if they ever returned. Neil Armstrong, the American astronaut, is descended from this family, but he has been invited to return at any time. A scrap of sculpture in the churchyard is the only relic of a Middle Ages Augustinian priory.

3 LANGHOLM: Biggest town [of] Eskdale (pop. 2,400) is sometim[es] called the Muckle Toon o' Langhol[m] "muckle" meaning "strong". A we[ll] planned town of the 18th Century, it h[ad] five busy tweed mills with 600 worke[rs.] It started from one mill which wove she[p]herd's tartan trousers in black and whi[te] check. Today there is extensive catt[le] and sheep farming in the surrounding hil[ls.]

In July, Langholm has its main festiv[al,] the Common Riding — a survival of t[he] centuries old practice of riding a tow[n's] boundaries to establish rights. There is [a] pageantry of horse-riding with the u[n]equalled spectacle of the gallop up t[he] Kirk Wynd and the procession of childre[n] carrying heather besoms.

About 200 years ago there was a han[d]fasting fair to the north where Black a[nd] White Esks meet. Couples paired off for [a] trial marriage, giving their decision at ne[xt] year's fair. Just south at Broomholm is si[te] of several Roman forts, and Langhol[m] Castle is the remains of a tower. Obelisk [on] White Hill is to the "Knights of Eskdale[,]" four sons of local minister, Malcolm, w[ho] achieved knighthood. One was warder [to] Napoleon on St. Helena.

Skipper Bridge, Langholm

The castle ruins

4 HERMITAGE CASTLE: (12m[iles] south of Hawick), 13th Century an[d] outwardly, looking as it did when a strong[hold] of the Douglases. In 1342 S[ir] Alexander Ramsay was starved to death i[n] a dungeon. In 1566 Mary Queen of Sco[ts] rode from Jedburgh to see her wounde[d] lover, the Earl of Bothwell. An old balla[d] tells how the wicked Baron Soulis wa[s] boiled to death in a cauldron.

rns Hole in the River Teviot near Hawick

e Horse monument, Hawick

Museum and war memorial in Wilton Park

5 HAWICK is the largest Border town (pop. 16,700). It is known as the gateway to the Scott country — the family name of Scott predominating. Armstrongs, Elliots, Douglases and Turnbulls — names of once-famous Border families — also abound.

It was a settlement of the Early Britons, but most of the buildings today are post-1850, with much modern housing. The Moat is a Norman relic, an earthwork 50ft high, all that remains of an ancient castle or tower. Wilton Lodge Park covers 107 acres, with a fine house as a museum. Fiercely independent, Hawick has its climax in June with the Common Riding, an almost pagan festival, in which the Cornet and his horsemen pay tribute to the Gods of War and Thunder in the town slogan, *Teribus ye Teriodin* (Hawick folk are known as 'Teries.') engraved on the Horse monument in High Street. After placing the town's colours, yellow and blue, on the mounted statue, the cavalcade rides the boundaries, fords the river, and indulges in some headlong gallops, with man-sized drams at intervals.

The name Hawick comes from the Anglo-Saxon *"Hagawick"* (a place or settlement surrounded by hedges). Visitors tend to call it "Hah-wick", whereas locals say "Haw-ick", even "Hoyke".

Obelisk to a poet and scholar

6 **DENHOLM:** Noted for its large village green, on which is an obelisk to John Leyden, poet and scholar (1775-1811) with a verse by Sir Walter Scott. Also born here was Sir James Murray (1837-1915), who edited the New Oxford English Dictionary. At the south corner of the square is Westgate Hall (1663) and, nearby, nine 18th Century houses.

TARGET FOR THE GUNS

Grouse moors are a charming feature of the north east uplands especially the Cheviot country. Roads cross mile upon mile of undulating country covered in late summer with the purple veil of heather. Towards evening you are likely to hear the loud chuckling cry of the red grouse, "Gobak, gobak". It has been argued that grouse shooting is a frivolous use of the land, distinctly archaic, but it provides a cash income, the birds provide food, and with a modest number of sheep these areas can at least pay their way. Also they have great amenity value and will be regretted if, as seems probable, they eventually give place to conifer forests.

7 **JEDBURGH:** Royal burgh and county town of Roxburghshire (pop. 4,000) within 10 miles of the Border and on an important crossroad since Roman times. The name is said to come from the Gadeni tribe, and there are Celtic traces. Lindisfarne annals show a church here in the 9th Century, and fragments of ornamental stone indicate this was on the site of the abbey. The town was part of Northumbria for four centuries till ceded to Scotland in 1018. It remained a cockpit and the castle was one of five strongpoints ceded to England under the Treaty of Falaise in 1174. More than once the castle was a royal residence. Malcolm IV died there in 1195, and Alexander III had his wedding feast in the castle — interrupted by a spectre warning of his death, which came a year later when he and his horse

stumbled over a cliff near Kinghorn, Fife. 1409 the Scottish Parliament decided t castle was of more use to the English a it was demolished. Now the site is occupi by the county jail, still known as the Cast

The Jethart staff, a 7ft shaft with he shaped like an axe, was a terrible weap in Border battles. The Earl of Surrey, ir despatch to Henry VII on the valour of t Jethart men, said "The strength of Tevic dale once destroyed, a small power wou be sufficient to keep the borders Scotland in subjection".

Handba' is played through the streets all fit young men, those above the marl cross being the Uppies, the others t Doonies. This free-for-all dates back befc the Reformation and is said to ha originated not with a ball but the heads slain enemies.

Sheep on the Cheviot Hills near Jedburgh

Jedburgh Abbey ruins, among the most impressive in Scotland

e abbey cloisters

The red-stoned abbey has a commanding site near the River Jed. Repeatedly battered by the English, it was finally burned by the Earl of Surrey in 1523, but the ruins are among the most impressive in Scotland. The Norman Tower has been restored, and the tracery of the rose window is still in the west front. The nave, 130ft. long, with nine bays and three tiers of arches, is one of the best examples of Transitional Norman. The original priory was founded by David I while still a prince in 1118, for the Augustinian Canons and was elevated to abbey in 1147.

About a mile south of the town, by Handalee Mill, stands the Capon tree, believed to be the last survivor of the medieval Jed forest. The tree, preserved by the Marquess of Lothian, is said to be about 1,000 years old.

THE SHOE A QUEEN FORGOT

Even a queen may forget and in Mary Queen of Scots House at Jedburgh the visitor can see a shoe the Queen left behind in 1566. Mary really did stay in this house, just off the present High Street. On October 9, about four months after the birth of her son, the future King James, she arrived to hold a circuit court (in Scots law, a justice eyre) and lodged in a bastel house: a house fortified to repel invaders from across the Border.

While in Jedburgh she heard that the Earl of Bothwell, her Lieutenant of the Marches, was lying at Hermitage Castle seriously wounded after a struggle with a freebooter. Five or six days later Mary, her half-brother the Earl of Moray, with members of the court and a guard of soldiers rode over to Hermitage to express sympathy and returned the same day, a round trip of some 50 miles over rough country. Soon afterwards, the Queen was taken seriously ill and her death was feared. In later life, a prisoner of her cousin Elizabeth of England, she would cry: "Would that I had died at Jedburgh!" But her French doctor saved her life.

During her illness her husband, Darnley, was hunting in the west and did not visit her till October 28, long after the crisis. He stayed a day, then departed. Subsequently the historian Buchanan accused Mary of an adulterous relationship with Bothwell. This was after Darnley's murder and Mary's marriage to Bothwell. Buchanan, who hated Mary, was a kinsman of Darnley. There was nothing unusual about a monarch travelling the country to dispense justice and as for the ride to Hermitage — on the 400th anniversary, in 1966, a party from Jedburgh rode over the Queen's route between seven o'clock in the morning and seven in the evening, spending a midday hour at the castle. The Queen's house remained a dwellinghouse until 1928 when it was bought for the burgh and converted into a museum. Today it is not only a little treasure store of mementoes of Scotland's tragic Queen — her watch, thimble, and tapestry on which she worked—but also of relics of Jedburgh's hectic past as a frontier post of the ancient Kingdom of Scotland.

e red-stoned abbey across the River Jed

8 PENIEL HEUGH: On a by-road half way between Jedburgh and Kelso this monument stands on a hill 777 ft. up, is over 200 ft. high, and can be climbed by the public. It commemorates the Battle of Waterloo. Nearby is the village of Ancrum where a battle was fought in 1545 between the Scots and Henry VIII.

Only stumps of stone remain of a former Royal castle

Distant view of Peniel Heugh

9 ROXBURGH: Drive through country lanes past rich farms to what was once the county town, and in the 13th Century one of four royal burghs in Scotland (the others being Edinburgh, Stirling and Berwick). Roxburgh changed hands repeatedly. It was captured by Sir James Douglas after a siege in 1314, but 20 years later fell to the English, who held it until 1460. King James II was killed when a cannon exploded beside him, but the Scots army regained the castle which w[as] shattered. A new fort was built in 1545, b[ut] survived only a few years. Now it is an ar[ea] of country houses — good pheasant a[nd] grouse shooting, a few farms and hous[es] no shops other than a post office. Roxbur[gh] revived in the last century, becoming a ra[il]way junction, but now the line is clos[ed.] Two miles on, a grassy hill with a few tr[ees] and stumps of stonework is all that rema[ins] of the castle that was a royal residen[ce.]

A CRAFTY HUNTER

The stoat, which is just under a foot long, is a sly and crafty hunter, and is distinguished by a black-tipped tail. Like the weasel it seeks its prey — birds and small mammals, chiefly mice — by day and night in a wide range of habitats.

Its powers of concealment are greatly helped by nature, for while in summer its coat is woody brown, in winter it can turn through moulting to snowy white. This change is produced by a decrease in the amount of daylight and is rare in the south of England; but in the north and in Scotland it comes quickly after a sharp drop in temperature so that in snow the stoat is perfectly camouflaged.

The winter coat, known as ermine, is used commercially in trimming the robes of peers and judges.

The main square, Kelso

The Turret House, Kelso

10 FLOORS CASTLE near Kelso, one of the largest and grandest houses in Scotland, was long thought to have been designed by Sir John Vanbrugh. But recent research has shown that the castle was designed and built by William Adam, father of the famous Robert. It was completed in 1718 for the first Duke of Roxburghe who wanted a fitting residence after being elevated by Queen Anne in 1707. The Ker family (now Innes-Ker) had been at Floors since the 15th Century. The castle was re-modelled by Playfair in 1838-49 adding ornamentation which some experts believe is not an improvement. The castle is encircled by a wall 10ft. high and three miles long built by French prisoners of war. In the parkland between the Tweed and the castle is a solitary holly tree, said to mark the spot where James II was killed by a bursting cannon in the 1460 siege of Roxburgh. The present 9th Duke owns more than 60,000 acres in the Borders and rich salmon beats on the Tweed. In February, 1962, on Junction Beat four rods landed 46 salmon in one day, believed to be a record.

Floors Castle, one of the largest and grandest homes in Scotland

Looking across the bridge designed by John Rennie

11 KELSO: Scott called it the most beautiful village in Scotland. Now a town of 4,500, its growth dates from 1754 when the ford was replaced by a bridge. The present five-arch bridge, designed by John Rennie, was the model for the Waterloo Bridge of 1811. When the bridge in London was demolished in 1934, two of the lamp-posts were given to Kelso.

Fishing attracts visitors, though a salmon beat on the Tweed can cost £600 or £700. Less expensive is a ticket from the local angling club to fish for trout in the Teviot, with an occasional salmon.

There is a sense of timelessness in the great cobbled square, dominated by the handsome town hall and fringed by Georgian houses and hotels. Despite its nine accesses, the square has no traffic lights and very few direction signs. This can be confusing to travellers, but, as most stop in the square, it's easy to ask the way.

Kelso Abbey was founded by David I (in 1128). It was destroyed in 1545 by the Earl of Hertford, and the local people completed the demolition, clearing most of the site and using the stones for house-building. What remains is the western end — now preserved and said to be unrivalled in Scotland as Norman Transitional work. The ruin consists of the transepts, choir and west and central tower.

The Hirsel, family home of the Earls of Home

Rhododendrons at the Hirsel

The Tweed near Coldstream

Sunset at Coldstream

The bridge over the River Tweed

The High Barn's solid stone walls are 3 ft thick

Monument to the last boar at Swinton

4 **SIMPRIM**: Grain was stored here in the 12th Century when the land was feued from the monks of Coldingham, and later it was a cache for the proceeds of Border raids. In the middle of modern farm sheds is a solid stone building (lintel date 1686), the High Barn, with walls 30ft. to the eaves, 3ft. thick. Bullocks were driven up a stairway to a hide-out on the top floor, according to farmer Hugh Russell. Origin of the name is not clear. In the ruined church it is spelt "Simprin" on a plaque to the Rev. Thomas Bostock who, around 1700, founded Bostock Church.

13 **COLDSTREAM**: The Coldstream Guards have their original headquarters in the market square of the small town. The Coldstream Regiment of Foot Guards claims a double distinction, being not only the oldest Corps by continuous existence in the British Army, raised and organised by Oliver Cromwell under the title of the "New Model", but the earliest "campaign" which the regiment can claim was against the Dutch Navy in 1652 when Colonel Monck was one of three admirals who led the British fleet.

Oliver Cromwell died in the autumn of 1658 and at the end of the following year Monck, who was at the time General Commanding the Army in Scotland, moved his headquarters to Coldstream. His troops suffered so much from cold and privation during that winter they were nicknamed the "Coldstreamers" because of the sniffles they caught, according to an apocryphal story which they deny.

On January 1, 1660, General Monck started from Coldstream on an historic march to London where, in the precincts of St. James's Palace, he and his troops suppressed the riots which had characterised the last few months of Parliamentary rule, and helped to secure the restoration of Charles II. The old Colours of the regiment have been laid up in the parish church since 1921.

The Guards parade on home ground

16 **LADYKIRK:** The handsome, red-stoned "Historic Kirk," was founded in 1500 by James IV as a thank-offering for being saved from drowning in the Tweed. He visited it several times during building and is thought to have worshipped there just before he died at the Battle of Flodden in 1513. It has a stone-slabbed roof and a three-storey tower which may have been designed for defence. The belfry tower by William Adam was added in 1743. Here Bothwell, a Scottish warden of the marches, conferred with his English counterparts; the Regent Mary of Lorraine, on arrival from France, received the Scottish nobles; and Tunstall, last Bishop of Durham to acknowledge the Pope, signed a treaty between England and Scotland.

The "Historic Kirk" at Ladykirk, founded in 1500 by James IV

A QUESTION OF BURNING

Though moors give an impression of un trammelled nature, heather is really a cro that has to be managed. Maintenan consists of burning off perhaps once seven years, but this must be dor scientifically with great care. Leas demand that a certain number of men mu be present to control the blaze, which mu not take place after early spring. If too mu woody material is allowed to accumula the heat kills the heather roots, but if th work is properly done neat bushy plan spring up whose fresh foliage is food f grouse and sheep. If burning is neglecte birch trees establish themselves ar bracken invades the area which becom useless.

18 **BERWICK-UPON-TWEED,** believed to be one of the oldest towns in Britain, is first mentioned in A.D. 870. It has changed hands between Scots and English 14 times in its history. Malcolm II, King of Scotland, claimed the River Tweed as the boundary of Scotland after a battle at Carham in 1018. The town was fought over from 1174 to 1482, since when it has been part of England.

In the once magnificent castle, Edward I, in 1292, decided the disputed succession to the Scottish throne between John Balliol and Robert Bruce in favour of Balliol. The only sign of this dramatic decision today is a plaque on the way to a railway station platform. For the castle, in use until 1603, thereafter fell into decay, and in 1846 was demolished to make way for Berwick railway station.

There was a bridge across the Tweed at Berwick as long ago as 1153. It was swept away by floods in 1199. The older of the present two road bridges is the fifth in line. Begun in 1611, it was not completed until 1634. It is still in use and is regarded as one of the finest in England, preserved as an ancient monument. It is 1,164 ft. long, 19 ft. wide at its widest points, has 15 arches, and carried all the traffic on the Great North Road until 1928 when the Royal Tweed Bridge was opened by the Duke of Windsor, then Prince of Wales.

The fortifications surrounding the town were begun in 1558 at the command of Queen Elizabeth and are still in existence. Ruins of an earlier wall, built by Edward I, may still be seen, including the Bell Tower, used to warn of the approach of an enemy, and the Black Tower, near King's Mount. Wide paths on top of the Elizabethan wall make a fine walk around the town and give an excellent view of the sea.

The Guildhall, sometimes called the Town Hall, is the chief landmark of Berwick, having an impressive 150 ft. spire. Designed in 1750 it has been restored in recent years. The butter market on the ground level is in its original state and the council chamber on the floor above has been redecorated. The 18th Century jail, instead of being below ground, as is more usual, is high up and well preserved.

Holy Trinity Church is said to be the only new church built during Cromwell's rule. It stands on the Parade near the site of a medieval church.

The barracks, also on the parade, house a military museum, open to the public.

Stephenson's Royal Border Bridge

Norham Castle features in Scott's "Marmion"

17 NORHAM CASTLE, commanding one of the fords across the Tweed, was built in 1121 and from 1136 onwards had a history of siege and capture or surrender and re-capture. Here in 1209 William the Lion did homage to King John and agreed to pay tribute. Alexander II, who had succeeded to the throne of Scotland in 1214, invaded Northumberland in the following year and besieged Norham for 40 days, but without success. In 1513 James IV battered down the walls and the barbican and the defences of the outer ward were destroyed. The castle surrendered on August 29, but James went on to his death at Flodden Field on September 9.

The castle features in Scott's *Marmion:*
> *Day set on Norham's castle steep,*
> *And Tweed's fair river broad and*
> *deep . . . .*

Scott was fascinated by the story of the Lincolnshire knight Sir William Castle who, to impress his lady love and bring fame on his "helmet with rich crest of gold," rode headlong into the Scottish men-at-arms besieging Norham in 1318-19. He was unseated, and near dead before being pulled out by lancers from the garrison.

In the village the first church was built in 830. The present church has a register dating from 1653, and the pulpit, vicar's stall and organ screen are 17th Century carvings from Durham Cathedral. The village has an unusual pinnacle market cross mounted on six 13th Century steps. At midnight on February 4 each year the vicar of Norham blesses the nets to open the salmon fishing season.

well above ground

The 17th Century bridge, still in use

Edward III from an old print

19 **HAGGERSTON:** In 1345 Edward III granted Robert de Haggerston a licence to crenellate, that is to furnish the castle with battlements or loopholes. In 1618 the castle was destroyed by fire apart from the large square tower, which was retained in a mansion built by Sir Thomas Haggerston. The family were Catholics and supporters of the Stuart kings. Sir Thomas's first son, John, fell fighting for King Charles in the Civil War. The second son, John, was Governor of Berwick Castle. The mansion was burned down in 1911, rebuilt and finally demolished before World War II. Left standing were the tower, doorway of the conservatory, stables and clock tower.

21 **BELFORD** village was a thrivi... posting centre in coaching day... In 1502 Henry VII's daughter, Margar... broke her journey here on her way to ma... James IV of Scotland. In a letter she to... how "Sir Thomas d'Arcy, capittayne of t... said Barrwyk, had maid rady hyr dynner... the said place very well and honestly."... century later, however, a Mr. Rawd... described Belford as a "miserable, be... garly, sodden town. In all the town not... loaf of bread, nor a quart of beer, nor lo... of hay, nor a peck of oats, and little shel... for horse or man." But in 1812 t... magistrates granted Elizabeth Macdonal... licence to open an inn called the Blue B... The licence, and inn, still exist.

Lindisfarne's fairy-like castle perched on a rock

Stone carving in priory museum

St. Aidan's statue

Ilford, church tower

Rare herd at the castle

22 CHILLINGHAM: The rare herd of white cattle, which is the last surviving herd of the wild cattle that roamed the North, can be seen in the grounds of Chillingham Castle.

The cattle still follow the law of the jungle. They will drive out a cow or bull that is sick and, at the sight of a pack of hounds, they will form themselves into a group as if to stampede — yet they will ignore shepherds' dogs. If they do stampede, again they revert to jungle practice. The cows go first, with the calves in the centre of the formation, and the bulls at the rear. They are still extremely wary of humans and will move away if approached downwind.

20 HOLY ISLAND: Study the tide tables before crossing the causeway which is closed 5½ hours each tide, you have to calculate not only getting [ov]er to Holy Island but getting back. A [m]onastery was first founded on the island, [gi]ven by Bernicia to St. Aidan, the [mi]ssionary bishop from Iona, in 634. But [th]e most famous of the bishops of [Lin]disfarne was St. Cuthbert. He was a [sh]epherd boy in the Lammermuir Hills, [wh]o joined the community at Melrose [Ab]bey and became prior of Lindisfarne in [66]4, bishop 20 years later. Much of the [tim]e he spent on the Inner Farne in [co]ntemplation, but he was a great preacher [an]d renowned as a miracle worker.

[S]tarting in 795, the Danes frequently [pl]undered the island, killing many priests, [an]d the place was deserted for two [ce]nturies after 875. St. Cuthbert's con[gr]egation, led by bishop Eardwulf, fled [be]fore the Danes, taking with them the [rel]ics of St. Cuthbert and St. Oswald. For [11]3 years they settled at Chester-le-Street [bu]t, again in fear of the Danes, the [su]ccessors eventually moved on until in [99]5 Aldhum, 24th bishop in succession to [St.] Aidan, settled at Durham. From then [on,] Durham became the permanent see [of] the bishops who followed Aidan and [Cu]thbert. In 1080 monks from Durham set [up] a cell and built the beautiful priory in [th]e image of their mother church. For 450 [ye]ars thereafter — till the Dissolution — [th]e community lived in peace beyond the [ra]nge of the Border wars.

[T]he Lindisfarne Gospels, a beautiful and [v]aluable work of art, preserved in [Lin]disfarne church, were produced about [A.]D. 700 and contain elements of Egyptian, [Ce]ltic and Saxon art. A note at the end [rea]ds, in part: "Eadfrith, Bishop of the [Ch]urch of Lindisfarne, he of the first, wrote [thi]s book . . . a treasure without deceit. [An]d Alfred, a miserable and unworthy [pri]est, with God's help, overglossed it in [En]glish".

[T]he altar carpet in Lindisfarne church is [a r]eproduction of a page from the Gospels. [Fin]ished in 1970, the carpet was stitched by 18 Lindisfarne women and some members of Alnwick Training College. The average age of the women was over 60, and the task — adding up to more than 1,000,000 stitches — took two years. The carpet, worked in tent stitch, is made up in 11 sections. There are about 50 stitches to each square inch, and it measures 9 ft. 3 in. by 11 ft. 6 in.

The fairy-like castle, perched on a rock at one end of Holy Island, was once a lookout point. It dates from 1539 and is now a National Trust property. A notice at the entrance says: "While every effort will be made by the tenant to open to the public . . . domestic arrangements cannot always permit this." Holy Island is visited by about 50,000 people in a year, and is so interesting that you have to make an effort to remember to keep an eye on the tide.

A view of the priory on Holy Island

The Percy family and the Dukes of Northumberland have lived in Alnwick Castle since 1309

23 **ALNWICK:** As you drive up the steep hill under the massive walls of the castle, you half-expect round the next corner to meet a knight on horseback — like Hammond who, in the Border ballad, rode out to meet King Malcolm III of Scotland with the keys of the castle tied to the end of his spear. As Malcolm came forward to lift off the keys, the spear was thrust into his eye. Hardly a knightly act.

John Wesley, the preacher, may have been a little fulsome when he said; "If I didn't believe there was another world, I would spend all my summers here." But it is a place to tarry amid the outcrops of history, in the wide, sloping main street with its trees, hotels and shopping arcades. It is a busy market town as well as a holiday centre (pop. 7,500).

The Hotspur Tower is the only surviving gateway of four in the walled town, built about 1450 by the Earl of Northumberland and named after his father, the famous Henry Hotspur. The Percy Tenantry Column (1816) marks the generosity of the second Duke of Northumberland who, in an agricultural depression, cut the rents of his hard-pressed tenants. In the column is a glass bottle containing the roll of 1,500 Percy Volunteers who, during 15 years of war, were "clothed, paid and in every respect maintained in arms at the sole expense of that princely patriot."

The town hall, with 18th Century tower and dome, was built by the freemen whose corporation dates back to 1160 and consisted of cordwainers, skinners, glovers, weavers and others. The White Swan Hotel has a reception room in Louis XV style, furnished with the woodwork from the steamship *Olympic,* sister of the *Titanic.*

The castle may not dominate the town, but it is the focal point. It has been owned by the Percy family since 1309, but the first owner, of the site at least, was probably William the Conqueror's standard bearer at the Battle of Hastings in 1066. The Lords of Alnwick at the time of the Conquest were the Tysons, followed by the de Vescys, whose gold shield with its black cross is still to be seen on various buildings in the town. Yvo de Vescy built the earliest parts of the present castle. By 1157 it was completed and remains today in design much as it was then, embracing five acres inside its outer walls which are flanked by 16 towers.

The direct male line of the de Vescys was wiped out at Bannockburn in 1314, but the Bishop of Durham, who held the castle in trust, is said to have sold the estate to Henry de Percy in 1309. The Percy family, first Earls and then Dukes of Northumberland, swiftly became one of the most powerful families in the land. Alnwick

Percy's wallet brought news from Waterloo

Castle withstood many sieges and fac many battles during the centuries. In 13 the first Earl of Northumberland led army of 10,000 into Scotland to avenge burning of Roxburgh and besieged Berw Castle. Though defended by only 48 m the castle held out for eight days. Wher was captured the whole garrison was to the sword. It was on this occasion t the earl's son, Henry, only 12 years old, distinguished himself that he was given title of "Hotspur".

The sixth earl was immortalised Shakespeare — in *Henry VIII.* Unfortun all his life, he fell in love with Anne Bole and was forced to renounce her by king, who also insisted on his being the c to arrest Cardinal Wolsey. Henry ev ordered him to be a member of the co mission appointed to try Anne Boleyn though he got out of that by pleadi sickness.

In 1562 the seventh earl complained t he could not entertain Mary Queen Scots because the castle was "utte unfurnished with not so much as one b in it" and he had but £40 in the world. F years later, however, a survey showed castle was well provided for.

A Percy sailed against the Span Armada, a Percy was shot for conspiring the Gunpowder Plot. The tenth earl tc the side of Parliament in the Civil Wars, opposed the execution of the king and v one of the leaders in the movement restore Charles II to the throne. A duked was conferred on the Northumberlands 1766 when the twelfth earl — who came the title through marriage — gained favour of George III for carrying "certain delicate political negotiations."

The first duke — and, more so, his wife did much to restore Alnwick castle a make it more a residence than a fortre The architect was Robert Adam.

Hotspur Tower, the only survivor of Alnwick's four gateways

The coach used by the Percys on State occasions

24 **ROTHBURY:** A busy but charming market town on both banks of the River Coquet, famous for salmon, trout and char. Rothbury's history goes back to the Conquest, and there are several hill forts, the best being Lordenshaws, earthworks at 880 ft., the meeting place of four ancient tracks. Symbols cut on nearby rocks indicate this was a cult centre. There are also standing stones and barrows on the moors at Debdon and Garleigh Craigside Gardens was the home of Lord Armstrong, inventor of the breech-loading gun. The ruins of 14th Century Cartington Castle require a short detour of about three miles. Rothbury is a good centre for riding, walking and rock-climbing. The highest point nearby is Tosson Hill (1,447 ft.).

Rothbury — charming town

NOT FUSSY

The long, mournful note of the curlew, the high "Cur-iii" that lifts as if questioning at the end of the note gives the bird its name. Until fairly recently the curlew was confined to high moorlands but has now extended its breeding range almost all over Britain. The bird is about two feet long with a delicately curved bill used for finding molluscs and worms in mud-flats. The curlew will eat almost anything from grain to small fish. The plumage is grey-brown and speckled. Its rump and belly are white and show conspicuously in flight.

25 **ELSDON** is an ancient village of curiosities, rather than of the picturesque. The 14th Century St. Cuthbert's Church, containing a Roman tombstone, has an interesting bell-turret. Adjacent is the fortified rectory (also 14th Century). When the church was being restored in 1810, more than 100 skulls were found. They are thought to be those of English soldiers killed at Otterburn. The huge village green covers seven acres. On it are a bull-baiting stone, the remains of a cockpit, and a walled circle or cattle pound, still used in bad weather. Elsdon was once the Norman capital and market centre of Redesdale. To the south-east, on the side road to Rothley, 1,040 ft. up, is a superb view — and the remains of a gibbet dating around 1790.

Penfold for stray animals at Elsdon

S.S. TURBINIA

Northumberland has some of the mo beautiful English scenery; and some gri industrial aspects. Among many importa inventions over the last two centurie were the first steam turbine, by Parson Turbinia, the first turbine driven ship, whic is still on show in a Newcastle museur the first dynamo; and Swan's electric lig bulb. For many years, most of Britain's co came from Northumberland and was ca ried by ships. Railways were developed alternative coal carriers. George Stepher son produced his Blucher at Killingwor colliery. His son, Robert, built the Rock and designed the High Level bridge acro. the Tyne at Newcastle.

Hadrian's Wall from Cuddy's Crag

15th Century fortified parsonage at Elsdon

Mithras, a god from Roman times

26 OTTERBURN: This moorland village is noted for its tweed ~~ade~~ in a local mill — with watermill ~~orking~~. It has various earthworks nearby, ~~so~~ Army firing ranges, but its claim to ~~me~~ is proximity to the field of the Battle ~~Otterburn~~ in 1388. Forty miles away ~~ar~~ Newcastle, the famous Hotspur, Earl ~~Northumberland~~, suffered a humiliation ~~unhorsed~~ in personal combat, and his ~~nnant~~ was captured by the Scots. The ~~oilant~~ Scots retired up Redesdale, pur-~~ed~~ by Hotspur, his brother Ralph and 600 ~~ights~~ and squires and 8,000 infantry. ~~otspur~~, against advice, insisted on a night ~~ttle~~ — most hazardous of military opera-~~ns~~. Without rest after the long march, ~~otspur~~ threw his troops into disaster. ~~ough~~ the triumphant Scots lost their ~~ader~~, the Earl of Douglas, Hotspur was ~~ptured~~ and held to ransom. The battle is ~~mmemorated~~ in the *Ballad of Chevy ~~ase~~,* and marked by the Percy Cross in a ~~all~~ walled field a mile beyond the village.

On the road to Otterburn

Bust of Hadrian found in Thames

28 HEDDON: On the edge of the Tyneside urban development, the village has justified its full title of Heddon-on-the-Wall by the preservation of about 110 yards of Hadrian's Wall. The circular construction built into the wall at the west end is of fairly recent date, but Heddon was a mile fort in Roman times.

~~adrian's~~ Wall still winding across the Northumbrian countryside

27 HADRIAN'S WALL: The sign-post at the crossroads says ~~6318~~", otherwise this is the Military ~~ad~~, and it was built largely on top of the ~~mous~~ Roman wall. In the 1745 rebellion, ~~eneral~~ Wade was stranded in Newcastle ~~able~~ to move his heavy artillery along the ~~adequate~~ road to Carlisle, which fell to ~~onnie~~ Prince Charlie. In 1751 Parliament ~~ted~~ money for a new road. Local farmers ~~ld~~ the land on which the wall ran, and ~~g~~ stretches of it were taken as found-ations for the new road. So now for miles there is little sign of Hadrian's work apart from a roadside ditch, occasional collec-tions of stones and sometimes a grassy ridge, over which the modern boundary dykes run. The wall gained its name from the Roman Emperor Hadrian who ordered its construction in A.D. 122. It ran for 73 miles — from Wallsend-on-Tyne in the east to Bowness on the Solway Firth in the west — and took nine years to build.

Its purpose was to keep out the "bar-barians" but it was also a line of com-munication. Seventeen large forts were spaced out about five miles apart along its length, and in between these were smaller forts. On the northern side of the wall was a ditch averaging 27 ft. in width and an average nine feet in depth. The garrisons stationed along Hadrian's Wall were not Roman legions but cohorts of the regular army. The occupation of the wall continued until the end of the 4th Century. The last watch stood down in A.D. 393.

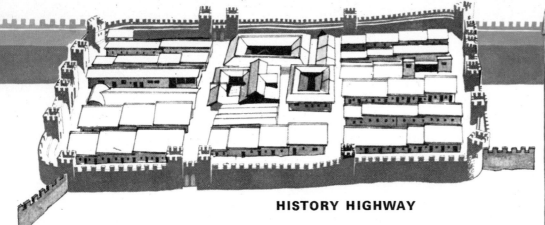

The fort at Housesteads. The building the Wall began in A.D. 122, the year which Hadrian himself visited Britain, a took some nine years to complete.

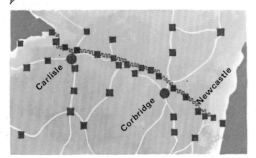

A map of Hadrian's Wall

Dice-pots and dice and an emblem of a legion carved on stone, in this case a capricorn, an imaginary animal half goat and half fish, and the winged horse Pegasus.

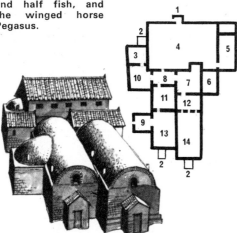

The bath-house at Chester showing elaborate accommodation. 1 porch 2 stoke hole 3 hot dry room 4 changing room 5 latrine 6 early cold bath 7 cold room 8 lobby 9 hot bath 10 ante room 11 third warm room 12 second warm room 13 hot room 14 first warm room

HISTORY HIGHWAY

The edge of an Empire

Hadrian's Wall is one of the most impressive Roman remains in Britain and, with its elaborate system of forts, mile castles and turrets stretching for some 73 English (80 Roman) miles across the narrowest part of Britain, it magnificently demonstrates the organisational power and discipline of the Romans compared with the barbarian world outside the Empire. The Wall, built during the reign · of Emperor Hadrian (A.D.117-138) was constructed to provide a clear division between the Roman and the barbarian world. Throughout their vast empire, wherever no obvious boundaries existed the Romans built one. There were more than 80 mile castles along the Wall. Turrets about 540 yards apart were built between each pair of mile castles. The Wall and its forts were strongly manned by conscripted cohorts, infantry and cavalry battalions, but men from the main Roman legion stationed at York were always on hand to cope with any serious trouble. The Roman cavalry unit could travel 70 miles in 24 hours. The Wall provides a good illustration of the strength of the Roman presence in Britain. A Roman legion consisted of about 6,000 men — and there were three legions in Britain for most of the Roman occupation, the 2nd, 6th and 20th. The great Roman roads criss-crossed the country and the major headquarters of the legions became flourishing towns. All the necessities of civilised living were made available to the Romans in the province. For more than 400 years Britain was part of a vast empire stretching back to Rome and including most of the then civilised world.

A Roman legionaire. Details of his armour based on a reconstruction by H. Rus Robinson. The Roman soldier on the ma carried his baggage on a forked stick. Here

show some of the other implements he wo carry. When Roman soldiers retired t frequently stayed on and settled in the to ships and cities that grew up around the milit centres. If you think of the British in India have some point of comparison.

Roman building and masonry tools. Note surprisingly modern appearance of some these tools.

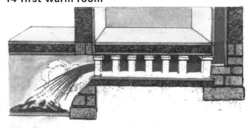

The marvels of Roman central heating showing how the heat was ducted beneath the floor.

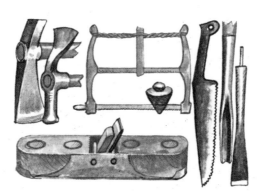

A cross-section showing the outer defence ditch; the Wall itself, usually some 15 ft. high with a 6 ft. parapet on top; the military road and the 'vallum', designed to prevent intruders from entering the fortified zone from the south.

Ditch

Ditch

Wall   *Military road*
Military zone

Vallum

The Emperor Hadrian. He built the Wall to establish the boundary of the Roman world.

Gerry Embleton

Typical Roman mile castle. All these castles, with the usual Roman precision, followed the same pattern. There were more than 80 of these castles along the length of the wall.

A cross-section of the Roman road of Dere Street, near Corbridge, showing the various repair levels over the centuries. Cobbles rather than quarry stones were used on the later surfaces.

Southern Scotland – the romance of the Lowlands

NICOLAS WRIGHT

The moving beauty of Eildon Hill's three peaks roused the dying Sir Walter Scott from semi-coma on his last journey to Abbotsford and took him back to happier days when, standing on the central summit (now known forever as "Scott's View") he could point out "forty-three places famous in war and verse."

Today, 140 years after Scott's death, the Eildons are just as beautiful and still untouched by the hand of man. They form a central, intrinsic part of that Border landscape which figured so largely in Scott's writings and present an ideal backcloth to this, one of the loveliest areas in all Scotland. It is the heartland of the country made immortal by Scotland's greatest romantic writer whose memory follows us along our chosen route.

Scott may well have immortalised the Borders with his pen but there are those who readily feel that these counties stand easy comparison, even without such mighty recommendation, with the best Scotland has to offer elsewhere.

The Highlands are noted for their grandeur — towering mountains and broad horizons where everything seems to have been put together on a grand scale. But, down in the Borders and to the South-West, there is an air of tranquillity about the hills to make up for anything lacking in rugged splendour.

There is countryside of wooded valleys, soft, rolling green hills and winding rivers; of gentle grace and style for although this is a journey through history, legend and local lore, it is also easy on the eye. The traveller should find much to please him.

The journey starts in Edinburgh, "that precipitous city", as Robert Louis Stevenson described it, and passes quickly through the heart of the Lothians, meanders through the Borders, then moves down in a sweeping curve to Galloway and the South-West before wandering back along the coast and inland a little to Dumfries.

It takes one on a route crowded with incident, the picaresque and the portentous; it passes the sites of skirmishes and bloody battles; it is a route of sometimes great and sometimes foolish men; of fairy tales and witchcraft; ruined castles and sprawling estates; Celtic settlements and Roman fortresses; busy townships, idle villages; and above all romance, poetry and song. The ballads sing of the Border reivers or rustlers investing them with a charm they surely never possessed.

RICH IN LITERATURE

From Edinburgh, edged with the serene shape of the Pentlands, we take the road to Penicuik. The hills remain before the eye and exert a majestic influence which far exceeds their height.

The area surrounding Penicuik, the paper-making town, is rich in literary associations and at Ravensneuk Farm on the Peebles road there stands a monument to Allan Ramsay, the poet and founder of the circulating library. Also close at hand is the pleasant little hamlet of Howgate. The Howgate Inn has a reputation stretching far beyond Scotland and Americans depart clutching menus as souvenirs; but the hamlet itself is best known for Dr. John Brown, the author of *Rab and His Friends*, and it was from Howgate that Rab and his master went daily to Edinburgh.

The Pentlands have now fallen behind as we pass through the villages of Leadburn, Cowdenburn, Damside and Romanno Bridge poised prettily at the head of the Lyne Valley. Great houses shelter behind their tree-banked drives and gates and tiny churches nestle in green folds. In another age the Romans marched through here leaving their roads and fortresses.

This is sheep country. Every hillside is dotted with a moving white patchwork and the lithe Border collies move as swiftly among their charges as do any of their Lakeland cousins.

The Border sheep produce the wool which is the basis of a world famous textile industry. The cottage weaving sheds developed into the great mills at Peebles, Innerleithen, Galashiels, Hawick and Walkerburn. But, important as the woollen industry is, it cannot progress fast enough to give jobs to all; in some places the industry is running down and strenuous efforts are being made to attract new employers. Depopulation is a dread word throughout Scotland. Peeblesshire and the surrounding counties of Roxburgh, Selkirk and Berwick are no exception.

The monks first established Border wool as a viable export and laid the beginnings of Border tradition and culture. There were four great abbeys, Jedburgh, Melrose, Dryburgh — where Scott lies buried near Field Marshal Earl Haig — and Kelso. These four abbeys were all founded during the reign of David I (1124-53) and all suffered from the warring forays of the English; each was sacked and burnt time and time again till at last their ruins were allowed to mellow in peace. The ruins are still there with Dryburgh claiming the most beautiful setting, and no visitor can feel he has truly visited the Borders until he has seen the abbeys.

There is much more to interest, ancient ceremony as well as ancient buildings. Typical is the "Riding of the Marches". James was once attracted to such a ceremony at Peebles. The traveller

By the waters of St. Mary's Loch, Selkirkshire: a place of peace and beauty

uld stay for days nay, weeks, in any one spot. Many pause to
h the Tweed, hoping perhaps to emulate the Earl of Home who
1730 caught a salmon which, at 69¾ lbs, was the largest fish ever
ught in a Scottish river.

The River Tweed is much more than a salmon river; its waters
ark the passing of Scotland's history as well as the border between
o countries. One set of laws prevails on the English side of the
er; another on the Scottish bank.

The Tweed passes into Scotland a little west of Coldstream and
om there runs into the Border hills gathering in strength and
gnity as it flows. The transition from a placid, pastoral water is
iftly made. To wander along the winding road which follows the
er through the Tweed Valley is to wander through countryside
ich is beautiful in a country where beauty is no stranger.

We are constantly reminded of Scott, particularly in Rox-
rghshire, where he built Abbotsford, a point now known to the
orld, a short distance from Melrose. Abbotsford was preserved for
sterity by generous subscription and still stands much as he left

Scott's own rooms have remained unchanged and contain his
ecious collection of 20,000 books and various relics associated
th Napoleon and Charles Edward Stuart. Scott described Abbots-
rd as "a Delilah of my imagination" in a letter to the Duke of
ccleuch in January, 1818, yet only five years later, shortly before
financial ruin, Scott had to write "Builders and planners have
ained my purse."

Melrose reminds us, too, of past military honour: the town
suffered much in the 14th and 16th Centuries. The abbey is
believed to contain the heart of Robert the Bruce.

The Borders spread themselves across the county of Selkirk and
down through Dumfries, but the country retains its smiling quality.
Nowhere is this more apparent than by the waters of St. Mary's
Loch. The Loch, cupped by hills, is a place of peace and beauty.
James Hogg, the Ettrick Shepherd, lived and died nearby and his
statue now overlooks the loch not far from Tibbie Shiel's Inn,
itself a literary shrine.

WILD PLACE TO DIE

Approaching Moffat, once a spa and now an important sheep
farming centre, the hills close in and lose some of their softness.
The road is narrow and plunges and turns; isolated cottages tuck
themselves into the hillsides. Along this road we pass the Grey
Mare's Tail, a 200 ft. waterfall, the highest in Scotland, which roars
down the cliffs into the rock-strewn stream. Scott's *Marmion*
describes the foot of the fall as "white as the snowy charger's tail".
This was Covenanter country; when pressed they would seek
refuge from their persecutors in the folds of the hills rising away
from the waterfall — hills like White Coomb, 2,695 ft.

At the head of the Devil's Beef Tub, a curiously sinister hollow,
scooped out of the Dumfriesshire hills five miles north-west from
Moffat, there stands a memorial to a Covenanter, John Hunter,
shot dead by dragoons in 1685. It is a wild and desolate place in
which to die.

As we cross the starkly impressive country which leads us down
into Kirkcudbrightshire and Galloway, the road runs through the
Dalveen Pass, so overshadowed by hills that the sun reaches it for
only a short period each year. Through Thornhill, lying in the
fertile oasis of mid-Nithsdale, the country again takes on a gentler
aspect. The hills are crossed with dry-stone walls and forestry work
can be seen everywhere.

This is an area of contrast — Dumfries and Galloway — bleak
uplands and rich low-lying pasture, picturesque villages and lonely
hill farms. The great historian, Thomas Carlyle (1795-1881) is
reputed to have told Queen Victoria that the road from Creetown
along the edge of Wigtown Bay, to Gatehouse of Fleet was the
finest road in the Kingdom. When asked what he thought was the
second best road he is alleged to have replied, "the road from
Gatehouse to Creetown".

Gatehouse was once a thriving port; it was certainly Galloway's
leading industrial centre and had six cotton mills, a tannery, a
muslin factory and a brewery. Now this pleasantly situated little
town relies on the holidaymaker. Robert Burns thought out the
lines of *Scots Wha Ha'e* on the nearby moors and then wrote them
in the Murray Arms Hotel. He certainly spent much of his time in
the towns and villages scattered around these parts before making
his way to Dumfries in 1791.

Galloway is an artist's lure, particularly Kirkcudbright, capital
of the Stewartry. Each summer potters, painters, and weavers
gather in this ancient Royal burgh on the estuary of the Dee and
seem to interest the passing tourists as much as the town.

So to Dumfries, known to Burns as "Maggie by the banks o'
Nith" and to the world as the poet's last resting-place. It seems
a fitting climax for the traveller who has seen much of what is best
in lowland Scotland.

GLEN TROOL FOREST PARK

MERRICK
2765

21 ELVANFOOT

22 DALVEEN PASS

23 DURISDEER

24 THORNHILL

25 MAXWELTON HOUSE

26 MONIAIVE

27 DALRY

28 NEW GALLOWAY

29 CLATTERINGSHAWS LOCH

LOCH KEN

FOREST OF AE

CAIRN EDWARD FOREST

**30 KIRROUGHTREE
FOREST**

RIVER DEE

**31 NEWTON
STEWART**

32 BARGALY GLEN

33 CARDONESS CASTLE

36 AUCHENCAIRN

37 DALBEATTIE

39 NEW ABBEY

34 KIRKCUDBRIGHT

**35 DUNDRENNAN
ABBEY**

38 KIRKBEAN

WIGTOWN BAY

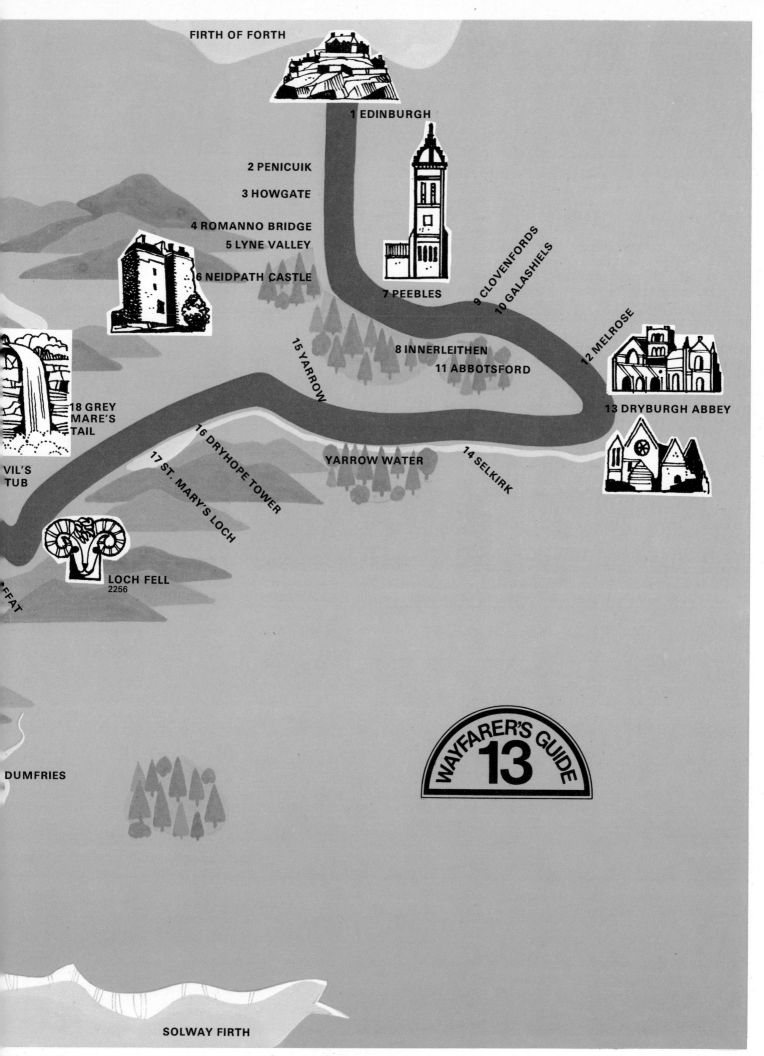

FIRTH OF FORTH

1 EDINBURGH

2 PENICUIK

3 HOWGATE

4 ROMANNO BRIDGE
5 LYNE VALLEY

6 NEIDPATH CASTLE

7 PEEBLES

9 CLOVENFORDS
10 GALASHIELS

12 MELROSE

8 INNERLEITHEN
11 ABBOTSFORD

13 DRYBURGH ABBEY

15 YARROW

18 GREY
MARE'S
TAIL

VIL'S
TUB

16 DRYHOPE TOWER

17 ST. MARY'S LOCH

YARROW WATER

14 SELKIRK

LOCH FELL
2256

FFAT

WAYFARER'S GUIDE
13

DUMFRIES

SOLWAY FIRTH

ations: Elsie Wrigley / Richard Hook Plant Notes: / Geoffrey Gilbert Animals & Birds: / Jeremy Johns

1 **EDINBURGH**: Walk along Princes Street. It is a fantastic thoroughfare like nowhere else on earth and a worthy introduction to this loveliest of cities. On the one hand, an impressive shopping centre. On the other, the breathtaking splendour of the backcloth that never loses its magic: green, flower-decked lawns rolling down a steep slope to railway lines that now serve as a moat defensive to the castle towering over the city atop the sheer crag that rises from what used to be the waters of the Nor'loch. On a sunny day the shimmering steel may help deceive you harmlessly that the water is still there — though the real thing was more marsh than water.

Princes Street is the place, the only place, to begin to see Edinburgh; but see the place on foot for that is the only way to flavour and savour the nuances of the Old Town and the New, the villages still largely unspoiled and, for good measure, the seaside. For Edinburgh is not all history and is never dull — how could it be with that awe-inspiring memorial to Sir Walter Scott (287 steps to the top)? Princes Street has the National Gallery for Scotland at the foot of the Mound, a good place to pause before facing the stiff climb up this man-made ramp of earth that rises to the Castle by way of the Assembly Hall where the ministers and elders of the Church of Scotland meet annually in General Assembly, the Scottish Kirk's Parliament. So to the Castle, whose ramparts are not so impregnable as they at first appear for Cromwell's soldiers captured it and, long before that, the good

Randolph and a band of 30 men scaled the crag and took it for Robert Bruce. Perhaps the watch is closer today, for the Castle houses the Scottish royal jewels, a varied war museum and an unforgettable war memorial erected after the 1914-1918 war. From the parapets you have an aerial view over the Forth to the far hills of Fife and along the Lothian coast; from another corner the Pentland Hills and the route to the Borders.

Leaving the Castle the walk is gently downhill on the famous Royal Mile where every stone is steeped in history. A few years ago much of it was one of the most horrible slums in Europe. Today, the "lands", the high tenement buildings reached by narrow wynds and closes, are so restored that only those who can afford the high rents to cover the cost of restoration can stay there. Thus, for the second time in Edinburgh's story, the teeming masses who peopled the "lands" have moved away. More than two centuries ago, before the New Town came into

Piper in Princes Street gardens

John Knox's house

Palace of Holyroodhouse

Edinburgh Castle, the breathtaking backcloth that never loses its magic

ing, everyone lived in this Old Town. On
e first floor would be a noble; in the flat
ove a judge of the Court of Session who,
his daily journey to court, would rub
oulders with a tailor, a candlemaker or
artisan as they met on their communal
ircase; and in the close he would pass
e time of day with the penniless beggar
o slept on the stones at the back and
dged the price of his brose and ale by
nning errands for the gentry.

As you leave the Castle Esplanade you
ll see Gladstone's Land in Lawnmarket,
ich has been restored inside and out as
was in the 17th Century. A little farther
, the High Kirk of St. Giles; the Parlia-
nt House where the Estates met till
07, now part of the Law Courts; the
ne of the Heart of Midlothian; John
ox's grave; and the City Chambers.
again to John Knox's house and to the
seum of Childhood in Hyndford's
se, where there is a gruesome peep-
ow execution the children love and a
markable doll's house. This is the part of
e Royal Mile known as the Canongate
d at the foot of the hill stands the Palace
Holyroodhouse. It is still used as a royal
ace by the Queen and members of the
al family on official visits to Scotland

e Montrose Panels, 16th Century carved oak,
National Museum of Antiquities

d by the Lord High Commissioner to the
neral Assembly of the Church of
otland. It is also the place where David
ccio, secretary and musician to Mary
een of Scots, was savagely murdered
the Queen's presence.

Down in the valley now, overshadowed
two heights of Edinburgh. Those with
ergy may go into the Queen's Park and
ke their way to the summit of Arthur's
at, lowering over the city and offering
more superb views of the surrounding
untryside. On the other side is Calton
l, with a replica of the Parthenon —
inburgh's disgrace, because the money
out before it was completed. From
lyrood a winding road leads past St.
drew's House, Scotland's Whitehall,
d so back to Princes Street.

Time now to look at the New Town. The
me is a delightful misnomer, for this
w Town began its existence in 1770,
e dream of Lord Provost George Drum-
nd and a young architect, James Craig.

Across the valley of the Nor'loch they
created a town of wide streets, splendid
squares, elegant buildings and sweeping
crescents, a grandiose conception of
town planning that was years, nay centuries, ahead of its time, and a rebirth of
Scottish architecture. But at that time no
one wanted to know. Only as the standards
of living improved did men of wealth and
their families forsake the teeming warrens
of the old "lands" for the gracious living
afforded in George Street, Queen Street,
Charlotte Square, St Andrew Square. It is
still a gracious place and, as more and
more buildings are scoured of their sooty
deposit the New Town is revealed for
what it is: a national heritage.

About the Old and the New Towns have
grown up, inevitably, suburbs. But Edinburgh also nurtures picturesque villages
close by. Try Dean Village, not far from the
West End, and walk by purling waters
through a wooded gully to Stockbridge. Or
go further out to Sighthill, to clean and
pretty Colinton, where Robert Louis
Stevenson's grandfather was a minister,
and walk through the lovely Dell. Or
Swanston, where RLS lived for a time.
And again, to the oddly isolated and intact
village of Duddingston on the far side of
Arthur's Seat and well worth visiting on
foot. Then there is Cramond where at the
end of a steep, narrow street the Firth of
Forth sparkles, giving a splendid view of
the Forth Bridge and a wide pleasant
promenade leading to the old fishing port
of Granton. Edinburgh is indeed a capital
city: Capital of Scotland and a capital
place to enjoy.

Nasmyth portrait of Robert Burns

Allan Ramsay, first library

2 PENICUIK: For centuries this little
town, settled pleasantly in the
south-east folds of the Pentland Hills on
the North Esk, has prided itself on its
paper-making ability, and for centuries
has presented this ability to the world. The
mills are mostly situated along the river
banks and do not encroach on the town's
general air of architectural well-being,
typified by the parish church of St Mungo's,
a severe but not unattractive edifice.

The local lairds are the Clerk family,
whose predecessors were bound by their
tenure to receive the King with three blasts
of the horn at the Bore Stone when he
came to Edinburgh. The motto was *Free
for a Blast.* The family home, Penicuik
House, a fine Augustan building, was
designed by Sir John Clerk (1676-1755),
a well-travelled patron of the arts and a
man of much moment in the community.
He was able to use his breadth of experience
to the benefit of his tenants. The house
itself lasted until 1899, when it was almost
totally destroyed by fire, leaving only a
gutted facade. This still stands while the
present incumbents live in what was
originally the stable block but which has
now been gracefully converted into a
beautiful family home. In the grounds of
the house is an obelisk in memory of the
poet Allan Ramsay (1686-1758) who was
the first man in Britain to start a circulating
library.

About one mile further up the Esk are the
impressive ruins of Brunstane Castle, once
a Crichton stronghold. Much of the
country around has literary associations,
especially with Scott, who greatly loved
the whole area.

269

3 HOWGATE: Literary associations extend into the hamlet of Howgate where Dr John Brown (1754-1832) set his book, *Rab and His Friends*. Several of the characters from this book are buried in St Mungo's Church in Penicuik, where they are commemorated by a plaque set in the wall of a mausoleum and surmounted by a dog's head in relief.

To the north-east lies Auchendinny and Robert Louis Stevenson's beloved Glencorse. When he was far away he wrote a letter home saying: "Do you know where the road crosses the burn under Glencorse Church? Go there and say a prayer for me: *moriturus salutat*. [He who is about to die salutes you]. See that it's a sunny day; I would like it to be a Sunday . . . and stand on the right-hand bank just where the road goes down into the water, and if I don't appear to you! Well, it can't ,be helped". The church is now an ivied ruin.

Four miles south-east of Howgate is the large Gladhouse reservoir, a winter roosting place for flocks of greylag and pink-footed geese. This reservoir, which is situated on the Rosebery estate, is also probably the finest trout fishing water around Edinburgh.

A distant view of Romanno Bridge

4 ROMANNO BRIDGE: A curiou sight meets the motorist just south o Romanno Bridge as the road descends th picturesque Lyne Valley towards Peeble There, set into the hillside, are 14 terrace each having a depth of between six and 1 feet. Some say these terraces are a natur phenomenon, but others claim that the were designed for horticultural or agr cultural purposes by the Romans.

The village of Romanno Bridge was th scene of a battle between rival gipsy ban in 1667, which is recalled by an inscribe dovecote. Romanno Bridge lies in th parish of Newlands, so called when th countryside was first cultivated.

A winter roosting place for pink-footed geese

5 LYNE VALLEY contains a number of tiny parishes. Small though each one is, it still has its remnant of history. Skirling House, soon to be demolished, was built by Lord Carmichael in 1905 round a farmhouse and contains the embroidered cap worn by Charles I on the scaffold in 1649. A little further on, shrouded by overhanging trees, are the ruins of Drochil Castle, built by the Regent Morton in the 16th Century. He had intended to retire there but three years before it was completed, in 1581, he was executed for complicity in the murder of Darnley, second husband of Mary Queen of Scots. Drochil, which had been "designed more for a palace than a castle of defence", was never occupied and its gloomy magnificence now serves only as a shelter for cattle.

Lyne itself, standing on the Lyne Water, a tributary of the Tweed, is one of the smallest parishes in Scotland. The church dates from about 1644 and its size matches its parish — the internal measurements

The tiny church

being only 34 ft. by 11 ft. The pulpit and two of the pews are canopied; tradition says they came from Holland, but they are more likely to have been made in Scotland.

Just west of the church, 100 ft. up a bank on a loop of the river, remain a few traces of a Roman camp, probably once part of a chain of forts guarding communications through the hills.

7 PEEBLES was described by a writ in 1847 as possessing a "singul air of decayed royalty which so strange blends with its perfect simplicity an rurality". The town was once a huntin centre for Scottish kings, and grew u under the shelter of a royal castle, whic has long since vanished. Peebles is th scene of the annual Beltane Quee Festival performed on June 1 on th broad steps of the old parish church befo big crowds. This ceremony arises from th traditional Riding of the Marches whic in turn was a throwback to ancient an primitive times when heathen Celts fires on the hilltops in honour of their god The queen is supported by a court of 30 boys and girls in fancy dress. The festival a week long mixture of song, speech an spectacle — including a horserace.

There is much of interest in Peeble For hundreds of years its main indust

Manor Bridge, near Peebles

6 NEIDPATH CASTLE, one of the most memorable of the Border strongholds, stands in an imposing position above the Tweed, a mile outside Peebles. Neidpath was once held by the Frasers and passed into the hands of the Hays of Yester at the beginning of the 14th Century. After having taken a battering from Cromwell's cannon the castle was purchased by the 1st Duke of Queensberry in 1686. The 4th Duke of Queensberry, known as "Old Q", wantonly laid waste to the surrounding estate towards the end of the 18th Century and was, in fact, denounced in a Wordsworth sonnet as "Degenerate Douglas" for destroying the fine timber standing about the castle. "Old Q" would never allow any replanting and it was 100 years before anyone could try to repair the results of his vandalism.

The castle building is a massive affair and probably would have withstood even the attentions of "Old Q". Parts of the oldest walls are 11 ft. thick and bound together with an ancient cement which, when dry, became as hard and as durable as the stones themselves. One of the few 17th Century lectern-sundials was returned to Neidpath in 1961. Neidpath now belongs to the Earl of Wemyss and March.

as been wool manufacture, and the uality of the local tweeds and knitwear world famous.

Across the Eddleston Water the Chambers rothers, William (1800-83) and Robert 802-71) were born. These publishers d much for Peebles and endowed the orld with their famous encyclopedia. he Chambers Institution, a library and useum, was presented to the town by Villiam Chambers.

The landlady of the 17th Century Cross eys Inn was the original of Sir Walter cott's Meg Dods of *St Ronan's Well*. ungo Park (1771-1806), the explorer so lived in Peebles. So did Professor ohn Veitch (1829-94), the philosopher d poet. No mention of Peebles' literary story should be made without referring John Buchan, later Lord Tweedsmuir, ho throughout his long and distinguished reer kept close contact with Peebles and e upper reaches of the Tweed.

Peebles was occupied by Cromwell's oops when they tried to reduce Neidpath astle and tradition has it that they stabled eir horses in St Andrew's Church. This urch was founded in 1195 and fell into in during the 16th Century. The tower as restored by William Chambers in 1882 his own expense. Another church, oss Kirk, built by Alexander III, later had monastery attached to it, but fell into suse in 1784. The Cross Kirk was so lled because it was built on the site here an old cross was found in 1261. is cross was supposed to have been uried there for 1,000 years. Shortly after-

Peebles "a singular air of decayed royalty"

wards a stone urn containing human ashes and bones was unearthed at the same spot. These were attributed to St. Nicholas the Bishop and many miracles were said to have been wrought at the scene of their discovery.

In the centre of the town stands the Mercat Cross, an octagonal column 12 ft. high, dating back to 1320 and neglected for centuries. In 1859 it was restored by

the town council and placed in the quadrangle of the Chambers Institution. Six years later it was re-erected on its present site.

Peebles is noted for its relaxing climate and pleasant environs, but the tag "Peebles for pleasure" is said to have referred to the quality of the town's liquor — even though it could as easily be applied to the town itself.

Traquair House, the oldest inhabited mansion in Scotland

8 INNERLEITHEN: The earliest mention of Innerleithen was in the 12th Century when Malcolm IV presented the church to the Kelso monks. Here the body of his son rested after being taken from the Tweed where he accidentally drowned. The town did not become widely known until Sir Walter Scott drew attention to its value as a spa in his book *St Ronan's Well,* published in 1824. Its mineral spring on the slopes of Lee Pen was said to have properties similar to the Harrogate waters. In 1827 the Border Games began.

Innerleithen is a noted woollen and knitwear centre. The first mill was established in 1790 by Alexander Brodie, a blacksmith who had made his fortune in London and returned home to provide work for his own people. It was in this mill that the process of dyeing wool in blue with woad was first carried out. However, the mill failed financially and was closed in 1810. Later other mills were opened and these prospered.

Traquair House, a mile south of Innerleithen is believed to be the oldest inhabited mansion in Scotland. William the Lion held court and hunted here in the 12th Century. It was visited by other Scottish monarchs, including Mary Queen of Scots who stayed here with Darnley in 1566. Much of the house, which contains many historical relics, was rebuilt during the 17th Century.

Scott's statue at Clovenfords

9 CLOVENFORDS: As the road approaches Galashiels it runs through the village of Clovenfords which sprang into being from the nucleus of an inn and a smithy serving the carriage and coach traffic. The inn, which still stands, was much frequented by Sir Walter Scott before he moved to Ashiesteel on the opposite bank of the Tweed to spend seven of the happiest years of his life. While at Ashiesteel he wrote *The Lady of the Lake, Marmion* and *The Lay of the Last Minstrel.* John Leyden, the poet, was schoolmaster at Clovenfords in 1792.

In 1869 William Thomson, a noted horticulturist, opened the Tweed Vineries in Clovenfords. Financial troubles forced its closure in 1959 and the grounds are now used as a market garden. The area is known for its bees and during the flowering season the heather-covered hillsides can be seen dotted with hives.

10 GALASHIELS' history, with i woollen mills, is mainly industri but the town clings to the tradition that was once a royal hunting seat. The tow crest, which can be seen on the north-we side of the municipal buildings, shows fox trying to reach some plums hangir from a tree. This commemorates a incident in 1337 when a party of Edwa III's invading soldiers took up the quarters in the town. These soldiers we into the woods to look for wild plums b were caught and slain to the man b armed Scots who swore "they would gi the southern swine sourer plums than ar that had yet set their teeth on edge Hence the motto: *Sour Plums.*

The Mercat Cross, dating from 1695, the scene in midsummer of a gathering the "braw lads", while the war memori is a fine statue of a Border reiver or raide loved so much in Border ballads. A 15 Century mansion, the Old Gala Hous originally the home of the Pringles ar containing some fine ceiling painting now belongs to the Gala Arts Club.

A little north-west of the town la Torwoodlea, a fort, destroyed by th Romans in A.D. 140. To the west lies stretch of the ancient earthwork known a the Picts' Work Ditch or the Catrail. Th dyke, whose purpose has been argue about for years, extended south for mar miles. South of Galashiels are the impres sive remains of the Rink Fort, an ear oval settlement.

Old Gala House, now art club HQ

Flower-lined Bank Street, Gala

Abbotsford House, home of Sir Walter Scott

11 ABBOTSFORD: John Ruskin (1819-1900), the sometimes eccentric writer and art critic, pronounced Abbotsford — the home of Sir Walter Scott from 1812 until his death in 1832 — as "perhaps the most incongruous pile that gentlemanly modernism ever designed". And so it is, an architectural pastiche of turrets and gables, constructed by Scott from the old farmhouse of Clarty Hole, which he bought in 1811. When Scott was overtaken by financial disaster in 1826 a group of his creditors clubbed together and four years later presented the house and library to him. On Scott's death, in 1832, family possession was ensured by generous subscription from his friends.

The house, library and grounds are still very much as Scott left them; he is said to have planted personally nearly every tree on the estate. The library contains some 20,000 books as well as a collection of well-documented historical relics associated with, among others, Napoleon, Robert Burns and Charles Edward Stuart. Scott introduced gaslight to Abbotsford — one of the first country house owners to use it.

A lock of Scott's hair

Scott's study with a collection of relics

Scott: Raeburn's portrait

Legend says the heart of Robert Bruce is buried here

BRITAIN'S BAMBI

The roe is the smallest British dee standing 2ft. high at the shoulder. summer its coat is rusty red which turr pepper-and-salt grey in winter. A buck age can be told from his antlers; in th second year the horns grow but have r points, in the third they become forked wi a single point forward, and in the fourth second, backward point. The roe deer found in Scotland, the Lake Distric Sussex and Surrey.

12 **MELROSE,** famous for its magnificent abbey and the beauty of its surroundings, is the best centre from which to explore "Scott country". The abbey suffered from the English, particularly during the War of Independence in 1322 and from Richard II in 1385. The Earl of Hertford finally reduced it drastically in 1544 but some fine decorative work and figure sculpture has survived. In 1822, at the expense of the Duke of Buccleuch, and under the auspices of Sir Walter Scott, the abbey was greatly restored. It was presented to the nation in 1918. There is a legend that the heart of Robert the Bruce is buried here. This appeared to be confirmed by excavations in the 1920s but the findings were never made public.

Just outside Melrose stands Darnick Tower, dating from the 15th Century. Scott was so anxious to acquire this tower after he moved to Abbotsford that it earned him the sobriquet of "Duke of Darnick".

13 **DRYBURGH ABBEY:** Sir Walter Scott is buried at Dryburgh Abbey close to Newton St Boswells, and shares his last resting place with Field Marshal Earl Haig who died in 1928. Bemersyde, nearby, the seat of the Haigs, has been held by the family since 1162. There is a famous prophecy concerning Bemersyde, coined by Thomas the Rhymer: "Tyde what may, whate'er betyde, Haig shall be Haig of Bemersyde". In the latter half of the 19th Century the house passed to a Clackmannanshire Haig but in 1921 it was purchased by national subscription and presented to the field marshal. The house contains many mementoes from the First World War.

Scott used to visit Bemersyde House and was particularly entranced by a view of the Eildon Hills. This spot is now marked by an indicator pointing out "the forty-three places famous in war and verse" which Scott could see from there. Legend has it that the three Eildon Hills were once one peak but were split into separate cones by a demon held captive by Michael Scott, the great Border wizard. Scott was embarrassed at having to find work for this demon, who completed each task with consummate ease. The demon was finally defeated when Scott put him to work on the endless task of spinning ropes out of sea sand.

The Eildon Tree Stone on the eastern slope marks the spot where Thomas the Rhymer met the Queen of the Faeries and entered the hill to stay in Faeryland for seven years. Dryburgh Abbey, one of the famous group of Border abbeys, was founded in the 12th Century. Like th others it was ransacked and ruined by th English on various occasions. The abbe is set among beautiful trees on a loop the Tweed.

12th Century entrance to Dryburgh Abbey

Memorial to James I of Scotland

4 SELKIRK: Scott's associations are marked in the town by a statue standing in the triangular market place. He was sheriff of the county from 1799 to 1832 and his chair and some of his letters are preserved in the Sheriff Court House. The town museum contains memorials of James Hogg, the Ettrick Shepherd, and the explorer Mungo Park who was born in the village of Foulshiels, four miles to the west. There is an interesting museum featuring old cooking, domestic and rural implements in the 17th Century Halliwell's Close. The town once possessed an abbey and a castle. It was the centre of the Anglo-Scottish wars which ravaged the country for three centuries and after Flodden in 1513 was burnt to the ground. In 1540 James V described Selkirk as "often burned, harried and destroyed".

Two of Selkirk's famous sons, Mungo Park (left) and James Hogg

Newark Castle, scene of Scott's "Lay of the Last Minstrel"

5 YARROW, comprising more than one-third of Selkirkshire, is one of the largest parishes in the south of Scotland. This was once the home of fair maids and bold Border raiders. Many poets, including Wordsworth, have sung its praises. Bowhill, one of several mansions belonging to the Duke of Buccleuch, stands just south of Yarrow on the bank of the Yarrow Water; beyond this is

Newark Castle, once a royal hunting lodge and the scene of Scott's *The Lay of the Last Minstrel*. It was also the scene of a bloody atrocity when General David Leslie, later to become Lord Newark, shot the prisoners he had taken after his victory over Montrose at Philiphaugh.

Each year the Yarrow and Ettrick Pastoral Society holds a well-attended livestock and produce show.

16 DRYHOPE TOWER: Just outside Yarrow, half a mile from the road and overhanging the burn, squats Dryhope Tower, the birthplace in 1550 of Mary Scott — the Flower of Yarrow. In 1592 James VI ordered the tower to be demolished, after its owner, Walter Scott of Harden, was accused of treason. However, only the roof seems to have disappeared. The rest of the building is in rather better order than a great many other Border towers.

Past Dryhope is Altrive, the farm which James Hogg — the Ettrick Shepherd — leased from the Duke of Buccleuch from 1814 until his death there in 1835. Hogg also tried farming at nearby Mount Benger and called it "a grey cauld place". The Gordon Arms, where Sir Walter Scott and Hogg took their last farewell of each other in the autumn of 1830, is a noted inn.

The Yarrow Valley

17 **ST. MARY'S LOCH** is situated in some of the most beautiful country to be encountered on this route. It is surrounded on all sides by steep hills whose slopes tumble into the dancing water. The loch is three miles long and half a mile wide and is separated by a narrow isthmus from the smaller Loch of the Lowes. "There are few spots", an anonymous writer is quoted as saying "where there is so little that is repulsive to man, and yet so few traces of his presence".

Between the two lochs stands Tibbie Shiel's Inn, once the haunt of James Hogg, Christopher North, Thomas De Quincey, William Aytoun, David Brewster, John Lockhart and many other literary worthies of their day. A seated statue of Hogg sits on a patch of green overlooking the area.

The Rodono Hotel set above the loch is named after the ancient barony, granted to the monks of Melrose in 1236. A little further away are the scanty ruins of St. Mary's Chapel in a remote spot "where the shepherds of Yarrow are sleeping". A service of commemoration is held there every August. Hogg's ballad of Mary Scott was set in the chapel.

Dinghies race on St. Mary's Loch

The loch where there are so few traces of man's presence

18 GREY MARE'S TAIL: The road from St. Mary's Loch winds its way through the hills where the Coventers sought refuge from their pursuers. This is a place of wild glens and sparse hillsides; winter gives it a grim aspect. At a spot where the hills seem to crush the road, the waterfall known as Grey Mare's Tail leaps and dashes down 200 ft. from Loch Skeen to Moffat Water. This is the highest waterfall in all Scotland and the whole surrounding area of some 2,000 acres was purchased by the National Trust for Scotland in 1962.

Large numbers of wild flowers grow in profusion here and wild goats can be seen wandering the slopes. A steep path leads to the foot of the fall which was described in Scott's *Marmion* as "white as the snowy charger's tail". A more rigorous climb leads to Loch Skeen at 1,750 feet, and then a path, marked by cairns, runs through Dobbs Lin, a Covenanter hideout, to Birkhill.

Further towards Moffat, Robert Burns' cottage stands on the site of an inn where he wrote the cheerful "O Willie brewed a peck o' maut", and off the road is Craigie-burn House, birthplace of Jean Lorimer.

The highest waterfall in Scotland

Wilson Barrett in stained glass

21 ELVANFOOT stands where the Elvan Water joins the River Clyde and is, in fact, the first place situated on the true Clyde. In 1847, while working on the railway, 37 men died from cholera. They are buried in the graveyard near the Clyde Bridge. Wilson Barrett, the famous actor-manager is commemorated by a stained glass window in the little 19th Century Elvanfoot Church; other theatrical visitors included Ellen Terry and Henry Irving. Opposite the church is a toll-house, said to have been a favourite resting place for Robert Burns between Edinburgh and Dumfries.

The bronze ram in the High Street

19 MOFFAT: Burns often visited Moffat as he wandered restlessly throughout this part of Scotland. It is a clean town, set in the hills, with one of the broadest High Streets in the country. A monument to a ram in the High Street pays tribute to sheep farming, the area's main livelihood. Moffat became a fashionable spa during the 18th Century. The great Hydropathic Hotel, built to cater for the wealthy seeking cures, was destroyed by fire in 1921; but Moffat is still a considerable tourist area.

James Macpherson was staying in the hotel, Moffat House, in 1759 when he published his famous first translation of Ossianic Fragments. John McAdam, the inventor of macadamised roads died in the neighbouring mansion of Dumcrieff and is buried in the churchyard. Moffat is a splendid centre from which to explore the delightful countryside round about.

Monument in the wilderness

20 DEVIL'S BEEF TUB: There are innumerable tales concerning the Devil's Beef Tub, a sinister hollow scooped out of the hills five miles north-west of Moffat, and it is well worth making the short diversion from the main route to go there. It was used as a hiding-place by cattle raiders, and in 1746 a rebel escaped from the Redcoats by wrapping his plaid around him and plunging head over heels into the mist filled tub. This is a barren place and various people have perished here in the winter snows. A monument reads: "Near the head of this burn, on 1st February 1831, James McGeorge, Guard, and John Goodfellow, Driver, of the Dumfries to Edinburgh mail lost their lives in the snow after carrying the bags thus far. Erected 1931". These hills are described as "a wilderness of heather and wet moss", and lonely indeed are the stones commemorating the dead. Another inscription reads: "On the hillside opposite, John Hunter, Covenanter was shot by Douglas's Dragoons in 1685. His grave is in Tweedsmuir Kirkyard".

22 **DALVEEN PASS** running down to Durisdeer is so over-shadowed by the hills that a shepherd's cottage along the way only sees the sun for a short time at midsummer. A castle belonging to the Douglas once stood here, but all that remains of it is a stone built into the wall of a farmhouse, marked with the date 1622 and the Douglas arms.

Approaching the Pass

Hills of Nithsdale above Durisdeer

23 **DURISDEER:** The end of the Dalveen Pass opens out into the welcoming hamlet of Durisdeer, the main part of which lies a little off the road. The church, built at the end of the 17th Century by the Duke of Queensberry, contains a magnificent white marble monument by Van Nost to the second duke and his duchess.

Drumlanrig, a seat of the Duke of Buccleuch, stands on the banks of the Nith, a stately pile of red stone. It was built in 1679-89 by the first Duke Queensberry who was apparently so ho rified by the expense that he spent on one night there and left to brood over th accounts at Sanquhar. In 1745 Drumlanr was occupied by followers of Charl Edward Stuart on their retreat from Derb They caused considerable damage portraits of King William and Queen Ma hanging in the house. Also nearby Morton Castle, an impressive ruin s above a still, sheltered loch.

BLUEBELL OF SCOTLAND

This charming wild flower is the bluebell or wild hyacinth to the Scots and the hare-bell or "witches' thimble" to the English. It spreads all around the north temperate zone and its familiar blue flowers are said to have made early Scottish immigrants to North America feel at home. Bluebell-picking is a favourite family diversion in the woods during the spring.

The winged horse column

24 **THORNHILL** seems to consist mostly of one long, broad street, in the centre of which stands a column surmounted by a winged horse, erected in 1714. A storm reduced the size of the column in 1955. Robert Burns is said to have had his shoes repaired at a shop, the site of which is now covered by the Buccleuch and Queensberry Hotel.

Joseph Thomson, the African explorer was born in Thornhill in 1858.

Bonnie Annie Laurie

25 **MAXWELTON HOUSE,** short distance from Kirkland, the birthplace of Annie Laurie (168. 1761), immortalised in this song:
Maxwellton Braes are bonnie,
Where early fa's the dew,

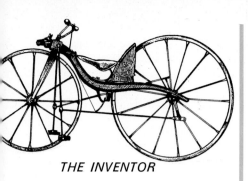

THE INVENTOR

Kirkpatrick Macmillan made sure of his place in cycling history when, in 1829, in the village of Courthill, Dumfriesshire, he invented the bicycle. One of his jobs was to repair hobby horses (two wheels mounted on a wooden frame and propelled by the feet). While working on these he had the brilliant idea of propelling a similar machine with treadles and cranks connected to the rear wheel hub — anticipating the rear-drive safety bicycle by 40 years.

Although his fellow villagers were not impressed with "his daft invention," he had one admirer, a 12-year-old lad called McCall, who saw the bicycle in Thornhill and made a measured drawing of it. In 1845, in his last year as an apprentice wheelwright, McCall produced his own bicycle, based on Macmillan's invention. He later put it into commercial production in Kilmarnock, selling bicycles for £7.10s. each. Macmillan achieved another first in cycling history on an heroic forty-mile cycle ride to Glasgow when he was fined five shillings for knocking down a child — the first cycling offence on record.

The house where she was born

And 'twas there that Annie Laurie,
Gied me her promise true,
Gied me her promise true,
Which ne'er forgot shall be,
And for bonnie Annie Laurie,
I wad lay me doon and dee.

26 MONIAIVE: A mercat cross in the middle of Moniaive commemorates James Renwick, who was executed in 1688, the last Covenanter martyr. James Hogg said of his execution in Edinburgh that when Renwick spoke before he died "few of his hearers' cheeks were dry". Moniaive is a pretty town of coloured cottages, although somewhat marred by prefabricated dwellings.

Crawfordton House, near Moniaive, dates from the 19th Century

27 DALRY: At the top of St. John's Town of Dalry, sheltered by a wall and almost lost under a telegraph pole, is a stone, shaped curiously like a seat. There is a legend that John the Baptist rested here. But the name St. John is supposed to have come from the fact that the land was owned by the Knights Templar, of whom John the Baptist was the patron saint.

Three miles east of Dalry is the loch of Lochinvar which used to contain an island with the ruins of Young Lochinvar's castle. However, in 1968 the level of the water was raised and all that remains of the castle is a small cairn built from stones taken from it before it disappeared beneath the surface of the loch.

Lochinvar, near Dalry

28 NEW GALLOWAY is the smallest of the Scottish royal burghs and stands high above the north end of Loch Ken, just north of Kenmure Castle, once the seat of the Gordons of Lochinvar. This castle appears to have been much altered; indeed, at one time its walls were treated with rough-cast concrete. Now it has fallen into a gaunt ruin, but traces of 16th and 17th Century work still remain. To the north of the burgh in Kells churchyard is the grave of a Covenanter shot in 1685. This churchyard also contains curious carvings and inscriptions. The Glenlee hydro-electric power station, part of the Galloway power scheme, lies to the north-west. New Galloway is popular with anglers and golfers.

Bruce's stone on Raploch Moor

Clatteringshaws Loch

29 CLATTERINGSHAWS LOCH:
From New Galloway to Newton Stewart, the winding road passes through some of southern Scotland's wildest country. This is the Galloway of high hills, sweeping winds and lonely stone-built farmhouses. The strangely-named Clatteringshaws Loch is set by the road, flanked by the trees of the extensive Glen Trool Forest Park and Cairn Edward Forest. One end of the Loch is held back by a great dam which looms high over the road. At the other end, reached after a precarious walk across a marsh on a path made from wooden railway sleepers is Raploch Moor, scene of a battle. The place is marked by an enormous stone inscribed with the words: "It was here that Robert Bruce, King of Scots, defeated an army of the English in 1307. It is said that Bruce rested against this stone whilst his followers gathered up the spoils".

30 KIRROUGHTREE FOREST:
Wild goats and deer dot the hillside through Kirroughtree Forest, and about four miles beyond Clatteringshaws Loch the road passes the foot of a hillock surmounted by an obelisk commemorating Dr Alexander Murray (1775-1813). Dr Murray was born close to this spot and, after working as a shepherd boy, went on to become Professor of Oriental Languages at Edinburgh University and one of the most accomplished linguists of his day. He had little formal education and was largely self-taught, reading voraciously as he watched over his sheep. Near the monument is a waterfall called the Grey Mare's Tail — not to be confused with the one of the same name in Dumfriesshire — and, a little further off, Cairnsmore of Fleet.

Murray's monument

32 BARGALY GLEN, three miles
south-east of Newton Stewart, associated with John Buchan's *Thirty-Nine-Steps*, and Creetown, a little further on, has been identified as the Portanferry of Scott's *Guy Mannering*. This area was also used by Dorothy Sayers as the setting for *The Five Red Herrings*. Thomas Carlyle described the road between Newton Stewart and Gatehouse of Fleet as the finest stretch in Queen Victoria's kingdom. It is indeed beautiful, as it hugs the coast along Wigtown Bay, passing Carsluith and Barholm Castles, once homes of the rival Brown and McCulloch families, but now, like so many other Scottish castles, mere ruins. A narrow road, little more than a track, leads up to Cairn Holy, a mysterious group of standing stones and chambered tombs dating back 4,000 years. It was here Meg Merrilees' gypsies in *Guy Mannering* had their encampment.

A grim legend about this castle

33 CARDONESS CASTLE, stands
in a commanding position overlooking Fleet Bay, a well-preserved 15th Century tower-house, once the home of the McCullochs. There is a grim legend that while celebrating the birth of an heir on the Sabbath the entire family of the Cardines fell through the ice of a frozen loch near the castle, never to be seen again.

Nearby Gatehouse of Fleet has been compared, in part, with Edinburgh's New Town. It was once a thriving port, some say second only to Glasgow, and many industries flourished. Now, however, it is a sleepy little holiday town surrounded by magnificent scenery and an ideal centre from which to explore Galloway. It has become noted as an artists' colony, though not quite so much yet as Kirkcudbright. Robert Burns is said to have composed the words of *Scots Wha Ha'e* on the nearby moors and then written them out in the Murray Arms Hotel. This is an area rich in archaeological discovery; Anworth Church possesses a late Dark Ages cross and there are many groups of cairns and stone circles. Half a mile above Gatehouse are the remains of a Roman fort.

River Cree at Newton Stewart, an old smuggling centre

31 NEWTON STEWART, although
a pleasant enough little town, is noted rather more for its surroundings than its own attractions. It is the educational and agricultural centre of the district and set in hilly and wooded country. During the 18th Century there was a great deal of local smuggling, and the town also began to develop a spinning and weaving industry; unfortunately this failed, although there is a certain amount of hand-weaving carried out now. Much of the area has been reclaimed from bogland and this has created expanses of fertile farmland. Newton Stewart is named after William Stewart, the third son of the Earl of Galloway, who established the town as a burgh of barony.

the land of "The Thirty-Nine Steps"

THE WILD GOOSE

The shrill, noisy pink-footed goose mostly assembles in large flocks. His dark head and neck distinguish him from other grey geese and he is the only one of the species to have his beak and legs pink. He can be seen inland feeding on grain crops and roots, then he returns to roost on estuaries. He arrives in Scotland in September and leaves again in April for Greenland and Iceland which are his breeding grounds. The grey-lag is the only goose to breed in Britain, preferring the North of Scotland. An extraordinary feature of this goose is his fidelity to his mate. Indeed, together they renew their "marriage vows" in an elaborate ceremony each year. The common farmyard goose is clearly descended from the greylag, inheriting its nervous cackling which makes it such an invaluable farm sentinel with its early warning noises.

84 KIRKCUDBRIGHT, in the 16th Century, was the home of onard Robertson, a troublesome pirate. e once captured a rich English merchant p and sold off the proceeds to the lairds the district. On receiving a complaint m Queen Elizabeth I, a commission was pointed by James VI to look into the tter; the twist being that the commssion consisted of those self-same ds!

The town is famous for its summer schools in painting, weaving, pottery and other types of artistic pursuits, despite one or two rather ugly industrial buildings near the centre. The harbour is usually crowded with brightly-coloured fishing boats, and the whole scene is overlooked by the massive 16th Century McLellan's Castle. Robert Burns stayed in the historic Selkirk Arms Hotel, and his famous grace, written for Lord Selkirk while being entertained by him in 1794, is carved on a piece of wood in the hotel dining room.

Some Hae Meat — canna Eat;
and some wad eat that want it;
But we hae meat — we can eat,
Sae let the Lord be thankit.

A little distance from Kirkcudbright is the site of Tongland Abbey, whose most noted abbot, John Damian, also an alchemist, tried to fly from the ramparts of Stirling Castle.

quiet corner of Kirkcudbright's usually crowded harbour

Effigy of abbot in abbey wall

35 DUNDRENNAN ABBEY: Mary, Queen of Scots is reputed to have spent her last night in Scotland in Dundrennan Abbey, a magnificent Cistercian edifice founded by David I in 1142 and colonised by monks from Rievaulx, Yorkshire. Perhaps the most interesting item left among the graceful ruins is the effigy of an abbot in the west wall. He has a twisted expression on his face and a dagger protrudes from just below his neck. At his feet lies the disembowelled figure of a man, suggesting that he, too, died while assassinating the abbot. The abbot is unknown, but in the same recess there is a grave-slab belonging to a Dundrennan cellarman, Patrick Douglas, 1480. Possibly he was the murderer. During the 18th Century the abbey fell into disuse, and many of its stones were used for houses in the village.

38 KIRKBEAN: In the little churc at Kirkbean stands a memori font presented by the American Navy memory of the gardener's son, John Pa Jones, who became its founder. Jon was born in a cottage on the nearl Abigland estate in 1747, and, when I was 13 years old, joined the mercha navy. He eventually made his way America where he became the dashir commander of the U.S.S. *Ranger*, a sh which made many daring raids on Briti shores, including a famous foray Selkirk Mansion in 1778. Jones later sa service with Catherine the Great. He di in Paris in 1792. He has become to t Americans what Nelson is to the Britis

John Paul Jones, memorial in Kirkbean

36 AUCHENCAIRN, on a bay in the Solway, is a popular bathing place, with rows of pretty white-washed cottages marching down to the sea. In the 1690s a famous poltergeist plagued the village and a group of ministers gathered to report in detail on the phenomenon. The hills around are spread with ancient forts and the district is rich in minerals — including haematite. Off the road, is Orchardton Tower from the 12th Century, the only round tower in Galloway.

Orchardton, the only round tower in Galloway

Sweetheart Abbey church

37 DALBEATTIE, is a town of granite. The town's prosperity, as well as its houses, was built from the grey stone. In the late 19th Century Dalbeattie granite was world famous. But the quarry which once produced proud blocks of stone to be shipped to Liverpool for export to distant lands, now produces only granite chips for road surfacing. A mile west of the town lie the ruins of Buittle Castle, where John Balliol, 1249-1315, was born and where his mother, Devorguilla, signed the charter of Balliol College, Oxford in 1282. Two and a half miles to the north is the impressive Mote of Urr, an 80 ft high mound surrounded by a deep trench. This is one of the finest examples in Britain of this type of early Norman and Saxon fortification.

King John Balliol

39 NEW ABBEY: This pleasi village is dominated by the stone of Sweetheart Abbey, so cal because when the previously mentior Devorguilla, who founded the abbey, d in 1289 she was buried there with heart of her husband. which she had k embalmed in a silver casket. The grave v desecrated at some time in the 15th 16th Century, but fragments were corporated in a reconstructed tomb, mark by a memorial slab from Balliol Colle There is an 18th Century water mill at c end of the village while the 60 ft. Water tower, erected "To Our Gallant Pruss Allies, Under Marshal Blücher" looks do from a steep hillock.

The house where Rabbie Burns died

40 DUMFRIES: There is much that can be written about the historic Dumfries, the chief town of the south-west border counties. Robert Burns, to whom it owes much of its fame, described Dumfries as "Maggie by the Banks o'Nith". There are many marks of Burns: the house where he died in 1796, a monument in the town centre, a mausoleum in St Michael's churchyard. This same churchyard contains the grave of 420 people who died in 1832 when cholera raged through Dumfries for two months. Dumfries is a bustling, colourful place, and in 1964 it became the first town in Scotland to clear all its slums. William the Lion made Dumfries a royal burgh and its oldest existing charter was granted in 1395 by Robert II. In 1280, Devorguilla built the dignified, old bridge across the Nith. During the Second World War Dumfries was the headquarters of the Norwegians in Britain, a fact commemorated by a plaque in St Michael's Church. If you wish to make an excursion beyond Dumfries, the 12th Century Lincluden Abbey lies only a short distance away.

The Observatory, Dumfries

The Burns statue

Bridge over the River Nith at Dumfries

Freedom's sword

BANNOCKBURN, the name that stirs the blood of every Scot. This was the scene of the greatest battle ever fought on Scottish soil, the greatest victory for Scottish arms; and the establishment of the freedom and independence of an oppressed nation. The English occupied the country from end to end when, in 1306, Robert Bruce was crowned at Scone. By the midsummer of 1314 they had been driven out everywhere except from Stirling Castle. And on high, dry ground before the castle, Bruce drew up his army of 5,500, poorly armed and as poorly mounted, to face at least 20,000 led by the pusillanimous Edward II, who had vowed to destroy Scotland to avenge the humiliations piled on him by Bruce. The Scot's king had so far succeeded by guerilla tactics. He had no wish for a clash of arms such as Bannockburn, where he was out-armed, out-armoured and out-numbered. But he came to that trial and triumphed with a display of generalship that is still outstanding in the art of warfare.

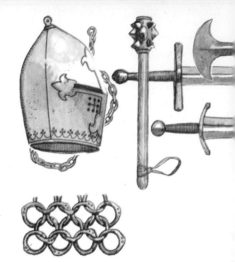

14th Century weapons of war and chain armo[ur]

Sunday skirmish: English force (red) is repulsed on two fronts, Gloucester's Great Van against the main body of Scots and Clifford's horse trying to cut off approach to Stirling Castle.

Three Scottish divisions under Edward Bru[ce] Moray and Douglas met and withstood [the] English cavalry attack. Keith's light horse rou[ted] England's archers and the Scottish spearm[en] pressed on.

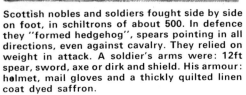

Scottish nobles and soldiers fought side by side on foot, in schiltrons of about 500. In defence they "formed hedgehog", spears pointing in all directions, even against cavalry. They relied on weight in attack. A soldier's arms were: 12ft spear, sword, axe or dirk and shield. His armour: helmet, mail gloves and a thickly quilted linen coat dyed saffron.

Sir Henry de Bohun, a knight in armour, set his lance, spurred his warhorse and charged on the Scottish king, unarmoured, astride a pony. Bruce turned his mount aside and with his battleaxe "cleaved de Bohun to the chine". His generals reproved Bruce for taking risks. The king just shook his head sadly and said "Look, I have broke my good battleaxe".

The Monymusk Casket, always borne before [the] Scottish army in battle, contained relics of [St.] Columba. Before Bannockburn the Scots kn[elt] to be blessed with the sacred relics by the Ab[bot] of Inchaffray. Edward said: "Ha, they kneel [for] mercy!" One of his staff said: "Sire, they kn[eel] for mercy, but not from you. These men mean [to] attack."

On Sunday, June 23, he repulsed 3,000 horse and foot on his main front, 800 horse on his flank. The next day he swung his forces round to face, repulse, attack and destroy one of the greatest armies ever to march out of England. Nearly all the English foot and archers were killed or captured; 00 cavalry, mostly knights or nobles, lay dead. And the booty shared by practically very Scottish town was valued at 200,000, a huge sum in the 14th Century. cottish casualties are not known, but must ave been heavy when the schiltrons stood rm against the English cavalry charge. dward, his vow to destroy Scotland nfulfilled, rode swiftly to Dunbar and scaped to Berwick-upon-Tweed in a wing boat.

The Great Seal of Robert Bruce. It was the custom of Scottish kings to be depicted both as warriors and enthroned. Bruce was crowned on March 26, 1306, at Scone by the Countess of Buchan and had to flee three months later. He returned in 1307 and began his campaign that made him a national hero for all time.

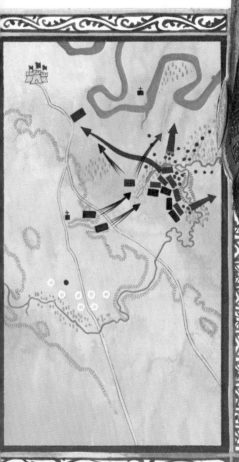

e rout: King Edward flees to Stirling Castle. uce sent in his Highlanders. Their rush forced e English line to give, it fell back in confusion d the whole army disintegrated.

is sword given by Bruce to Douglas is a token the king's last request: "Take my heart to the ly Land". After Bruce died in 1329, Douglas rled the heart among the Saracens and died erwhelmed. A cast of Bruce's skull is the only r likeness of him existing today.

Scottish craftsmen are famed designers of jewellery. These are Celtic brooches which were worn by men and women. The Cairngorm brooch is still in use today with the dress kilt.

Gerry Embleton

Accoutrements of a knight ready for battle: lance, sword, shield and suit of mail with helmet. At Bannockburn the knights on both sides were probably dressed like this. It was, however, a time of changes and experiments. Certainly the English cavalry would be thus armed and armoured — Bruce did not have such heavy cavalry as Edward, so the Scots armour would be lighter. The weight of armour eventually contributed to the English defeat. When horses plunged into the pits or stumbled on calthrops, the rider was thrown and, unable to rise because of his heavy weight, was easy prey for the eager Scottish spearmen. Knights wore iron helmets over the mail coif and some idea of the enormous weight they had to carry can be guessed from the fact that each link in the mail shirt was rivetted and a shirt could have as many as 20,000 links.

Central Scotland – the lonely Highland glens

JAMES LAING

Travel this route and you clasp Scotland around her waist. The land itself has changed little since it was riven by the Ice Age which pushed the rich, loamy soil to the east and created the mountains and lochs of the west with the slow march of its glaciers. It is a deep swathe of country running from Perth, just above the Scotch terrier's head of Fife, across the trailing skirts of the Highlands to the west coast and Oban. It is a land steeped in history, garlanded with heather and flowers, jewelled by mountain, loch and stream, with a splendour hard to match. The route begins in Perth, a city which couches itself comfortably at the navel of the country, a centre point and focus of rail and road. There is a motor-rail terminal in the city which allows a tourist from the south to drive into the yard in the early morning. If it is a Sunday morning all the better, because the Scottish Sabbath still allows a city to be seen at its best. The traffic is minimal and the people leisured enough to talk to enquiring strangers. Perth is a curious amalgam of the recent and the ancient — and by recent in this place it must be understood that 100 years ago was practically yesterday. And Perth has survived so much history and change that it tucks it away in museums and on wall plaques. Here and there are architectural gems but they must be assiduously sought among the stern grey stone.

The city's Kirk was first consecrated in the 13th Century and is now restored. Inside there is a priceless collection of pewter and sacramental silver and there is a 35-bell carillon which was cast and hung in 1936. The grey-clad citizens still hurry to their worship by its tolling, red rimmed Bibles adding a splash of colour to the throng. There is a lot to linger over in Perth, a great deal a casual look can miss, like the room in the Salutation Hotel where Bonnie Prince Charlie established a headquarters during the second attempt to restore the Stuarts to the British throne, an effort which almost succeeded. Alas the hotel itself, with its magnificent Adam window into the dining-room, has succumbed to the 20th Century and music from a weekend discotheque shakes the aged floor.

Driving north of Perth takes the visitor into the rich agricultural depths of the county where the furrows are deep and in the carse (plain) the raspberry canes stand in regimented rows. There's more than a whiff of history in Old Scone, the coronation place of Scottish kings and the seat of the Earls of Mansfield. Scone Palace where Queen Victoria was initiated into the mysteries of the Scottish game of curling, is now owned by Viscount Stormont, an Eton schoolboy, who inherited direct from his grandfather to avoid death duties. From there the route switches the historical interest to Glamis through the gentle towns of Coupar Angus and Meigle.

CASTLE RICH IN RELICS

In Meigle a stroll in the kirkyard will remind visitors of the essential character of the Scot. The graves mark the resting place of farmers and merchants, labourers and lawyers. And, in one sheltered corner, a granite slab marks the grave of Sir Henry Campbell Bannerman, Prime Minister of Britain until a few days before his death in 1908. This is no Arlington or Westminster Abbey. The Scots do not make a fetish of their leaders — only their artists and poets. Glamis Castle is rich in relics. The library shows volumes which date from the time of Cromwell with a curious watermark on each sheet. The story goes that, when the paper

Loch Rannoch with Schiehallion in the middle distance

akers went to the Protector to ask which mark to use, he told
em to carry on using "the old fool's cap", meaning the king's
own. The papermakers misunderstood and marked each sheet
ith a jester's cap and bells. Hence "foolscap" paper.

From Glamis, that joyous château, the country begins to deepen
to darker earth, more bosky than before, through the fruit fields
Kirriemuir, birthplace and now almost a shrine to Sir James
rrie, the creator of Peter Pan. Now comes the moment of
amatic change from the richly textured fields to a gentle roll of
ll and then the mountains lifting their crowns to a changing sky
hich can thrust a shawl of cloud around their shoulders within
inutes. Here the traveller can meet unexpected road hazards — a
rut of pheasant, a herd of deer, or sheep managed by panting
ack and white dogs. Over a field a blunt-headed hawk may be
en hovering. A flash of bright tail will give away a red squirrel
vorting through a dry stone dyke. Occasionally, alone in a tilled
·ld, a standing stone can be seen thrusting its pagan head up-
ards, a monument to the men who placed it there thousands of
ars before.

There is the village of Moulin, reached across the broad shoulder
Ben Vrackie, where Robert Louis Stevenson wrote and where a
uncil of lairds hanged sheepstealers from an ash tree which still
inds in the kirkyard. And Pitlochry where the hand of man has
en gentle. It is here, the centre of the huge Tummel Valley hydro-
ectric scheme, where the land, unchanged for aeons, could have
en scarred. But the men who built here have hidden their handi-
ork in a magnificent blending of the practical with nature. A new

loch was created to the north of the town and its beauty is now a
local boast.

This is, indeed, the highlands. Every step of the route brings a
new view of a mountain. Laid across their flanks like a newly-
woven blanket are the young vigorous forests planted by the
Forestry Commission. Across miles of sweet heather moors march
arrow-straight dry stone walls, fashioned by men whose skill lay in
their hands and eyes. Hidden in the cool dimness of a fold in the
hill are cottages, many now a rubble of old stones. Glowering over
every vantage-point or unassailable island in the many lochs are the
crumbles of old castles and keeps, tendrils of the country's bloody
past. Real peace did not come to this country until the last years
of the 18th Century.

HEART STOPPING DRIVE

Kenmore and Killin have their legends of the giant Celtic hero
Fingal, the embroidered adventures of the outlaw Rob Roy Mac-
Gregor, and their natural beauties. But there is humour, too. A
local will point out with a sardonic smile *one* of the places where
Rob Roy is buried.

Along Loch Lomondside the road leads to a new vista at every
bend, so famed in song and story yet still heart-stopping when
seen for the thousandth time. The two-mile drive across the narrow
head of the loch to Arrochar was the very route taken by the Viking
king, Haakon, when he dragged his long boats to pillage the islands
of land-locked Lomond. The road starts to mount the great height
along the side of Loch Long up the new road, which was once the
nerve-wracking Rest and Be Thankful, into the sombre Glen Croe
and down to the squarish huddle of Inveraray. Up and over and
through the Pass of Brander to Connel with its iron bridges to
Oban and the screeching of gulls sheltered by a screen of islands
which keeps the fury of the sea from its front door.

From Roman times this ample waist of Scotland has been embraced and hailed by thousands of travellers. Some merely come to
look and remember. Many more settled and adopted it as their own
land like the Clan Menzies who came from France and are now one
of Scotland's proudest families. Flemish refugees from the Hugue-
not Wars settled in the east and added their weaving skills. Irish
saints brought Christianity. Pedlars from Europe brought trade.
There is a legend that the west was first settled by survivors of
Atlantis who carved great serpent-like monuments in the hills
above Oban. It has been fought over, bloodied by sectarian and
secular battles, lyricised by generations of authors, used and
abused by modern man, subdued, roused and subdued again
through the centuries when Scotsmen died for causes passionately
held. And the look of the land has hardly changed. There are raging
waterfalls which appear only after rainstorms and which subside
again to become scars on mountainsides when the sun shines.
There are sombre, dark corries where the snow lies year in and
year out forever untrodden by man. There are fields which have
been tilled for centuries and have yielded their bounty grudgingly,
and rivers so abundant in salmon that indentured farm labourers
made it a condition that they should eat it only three times a week.

It is a land where history was only yesterday and where every
town and village has a story. Man has had little to do with the way
the land looks. It is as if it made up its mind æons ago that we'll
be here for only a few thousand years. So grasp the waist firmly.
It is a rich and joyful experience.

uds gather over Glen Croe

WAYFARER'S GUIDE
14

FIRTH OF LORNE

LOCH ETIVE

BEN LAW
3984

BEN CRUACHAN
3695

GRAMPIAN MOUNTAINS

FALLS OF LOCHY

25 OBAN

24 CONNEL

23 TAYNUILT

22 LOCH AWE

15 KILLIN
BEN MORE
3852

BEN IME
3319

16 LOCH LOMOND

19 GLEN CROE

LOCH KAT

21 INVERARAY CASTLE

BEN LOMOND
3194

20 INVERARAY

18 ARROCHAR

LOCH FYNE

LOCH GOIL

LOCH LONG

LOCH LOMOND

17 LUSS

Photos: Aberdeen Inf Bureau / Ardea / Peter Baker / B.T.A. / Camera Press / C.L.I. / Mary Evans / Noel Habgood / Inverness Mus / Sean Jennett / J. Keggie / Picturepoint / D. Scot
Scottish Tourist Board / Peyto Slatter / Spectrum / Transglobe / Tom Weir

10 BLAIR CASTLE

9 KILLIECRANKIE

7 CRAIGOWER HILL

6 MOULIN

8 PITLOCHRY

LOCH TUMMEL

5 KIRRIEMUIR

4 GLAMIS CASTLE

RIVER ISLA

12 MENZIES CASTLE

11 ABERFELDY

RIVER TAY

3 MEIGLE

13 TAYMOUTH CASTLE

14 LOCH TAY

BEN CHONZIE
3048

2 SCONE

1 PERTH

FIRTH OF TAY

QUEEN ELIZABETH
FOREST PARK

Ben Manchip

Illustrations: Elsie Wrigley / Richard Hook   Plant Notes: Geoffrey Gilbert   Animals & Birds: Jeremy Johns

1 **PERTH** has been besieged seven times, yet little survives in the city to illustrate the past. St. John's Kirk dates from the 15th Century. It was from this pulpit in 1559 that the Scottish reformer John Knox preached an inflammatory sermon against the "idolatry" of Rome which set the citizens scouring the city for images to destroy. What survived can be seen in the city's museum in George Street or in the kirk itself where the baptismal font is one of the finest examples of English silverwork of the 16th Century.

The Inches of Perth are now parks. They are named from the Gaelic "innis" which means a level grassland on the banks of a river — in this case the Tay. On the North Inch the Battle of the Clans was fought in 1396 between the Clan Chattan and the Clan Kay — 30 champions each side fought to the death. A plaque commemorates the battle.

During the Napoleonic Wars Perth housed thousands of French prisoners. A regiment of hussars was sent from England to help guard them and played cricket on the South Inch much to the amusement of the Scots, who have never taken the game seriously, preferring golf as a national sport.

A house in Curfew Row, now owned by the corporation, has been named as the home of Sir Walter Scott's *Fair Maid of Perth.* Doubtful, because the house is most definitely Victorian, but so enamoured of the story is Perth that the stained glass windows in the City Chambers depict scenes from the book.

Perth's cattle market attracts buyers from all over the world for its bull sales twice a year. Breeders, mainly from Argentina and America, make annual pilgrimage to buy bulls. The sales managed to achieve a peak just after the last war when record prices of 14,500 guineas for a Shorthorn and 60,000 guineas for an Aberdeen Angus were reached.

The Fair Maid's House, Perth

Looking across the Inches to Perth

Pictish stone, about 8th Century

2 **SCONE** (pronounced Skoon) few miles north of Perth, is steepe in Scottish history going back to t reign of Kenneth MacAlpin, first King unite the Picts and the Scots around 84 In the 9th Century, too, a block of san stone was brought to Scone from Iona, relic said to be Jacob's Pillar. This was t Stone of Destiny on which generations Scottish Kings were crowned until Edwa I took it to Westminster at the end of t 13th Century and put it under his ow Coronation Chair. It was sensationa removed from the Abbey in the middle the 20th Century by a group of Scotti Nationalists and returned to Arbroa Abbey, where the Declaration of Indepen ence had been signed by Scottish nobl in 1320. King George VI was known believe that the fate of his dynasty reste with the Stone and was uneasy until it w returned to Westminster Abbey, which was in 1951. The present Scone Palace the home and seat of the Earls of Mansfie Inside the palace is one of the fine collections of French furniture in Scotlar There is also a collection of ivories an china. The gardens are famous for t Pinetum, growing one of the fine collections of rare conifers.

3 MEIGLE has one of the finest collections of early Pictish stones in Scotland housed now in a converted school behind the kirkyard. Controversy still surrounds the stones and dating is insure since there are some unique features which do not occur elsewhere. The subject matter reels from pagan through legendary to Christian. On the main stone which dominates the little whitewashed room of the museum is a carving of three climbing figures, one of which is reaching down to pull up another. The museum is now controlled by the Department of the Environment.

Hunting scene in stone

Triple knot design is symbol of the Trinity

Scone Palace steeped in Scottish history

SACRIFICIAL SHEEP

One of the most remarkable sights in the Park at Scone is a flock of Jacob's sheep. These are reminiscent of Abraham's "ram caught in the thicket". This is the species of ram sacrificed in rituals described in the Old Testament. In the Palace there is a picture of a ram painted in India in the early 18th Century, a further indication of its Eastern origin.

4 **GLAMIS CASTLE** was first occupied by the Bowes-Lyon family in 1372 when Sir John Lyon married Joanna, daughter of King Robert II, who gave them the place as a wedding gift. Their grandson was created 1st Lord Glamis in 1445.

The Queen Mother, herself a Bowes-Lyon — daughter of the 14th Earl of Strathmore in the direct line — spent her childhood at Glamis. Princess Margaret was born there in 1930. The castle, a warren of secret passages and eerie legends, dates from the 11th Century, but was rebuilt in the late 17th Century in the style of a French chateau. In the early 16th Century the widowed Lady. Glamis was accused of witchcraft, imprisoned in Edinburgh Castle and burned at the stake "with great commiseration of the people being in the prime of her years and of singular beauty", says a contemporary report.

The "grey lady of Glamis" has been reported "seen" many times in recent years praying in various rooms and in the garden. A bearded Highlander is said to appear from time to time, striding through walls and passageways looking neither right nor left. Another is said to be the ghost of a "monster" born to a Countess of Glamis which survived for 50 years shut up in a secret room. His screams are said to ring through the darkened castle.

Relics abound of kings and queens who have stayed in the castle. The tartan coat of James VIII, the "Old Pretender", his sword and silver watch, a menu prepared in French for Mary Queen of Scots, documents and jewels, paintings and tapestries.

In the centre of the lawn at Glamis is an ornate sundial with carved facets for each month of the year. It was placed there around 1680 and is calculated to be three degrees west of the Greenwich meridian. It stands 21ft. high and the faceted globe is supported by twisted pillars and rampant lions. Above the globe is a coronet.

In Glamis village is the Angus Folk Museum in the Kirkwynd cottages given by the Strathmore Estates.

Glamis Castle, ghosts and secret passages

Carved fireplace in King Malcolm's room

The drawing room, once the "Great Hall"

The Angus Folk Museum — a but and ben

292

6 MOULIN:

On the edge of the village, just as the traveller moves off the moorland road over the shoulder of Ben y Vrackie, is Kinnaird Cottage surrounded by an overgrown split slate wall. It was here that Robert Louis Stevenson wrote *The Merry Men* and *Thrawn Janet*. A plaque set into the wall records his residence and carries an extract from a letter he wrote to a friend singing the praises of the place. Moulin is an ancient site and, like all villages attached to thriving towns, boasts that it existed as a population centre long before Pitlochry was even a mud hut. The church has a lintel stone with the date 1613 inscribed on it. Perhaps the most interesting relic is an ash tree to which sheep-stealers were chained while awaiting the judgment of the Council of Lairds, a bench of local landowners who administered their own kind of justice. The tree was also used as the gibbet. In the hotel across the road an ancient book recording the names and sentences of the criminals is preserved.

5 KIRRIEMUIR,

the "Thrums" made famous by Sir James M. Barrie, flaunts its weaving origins in its narrow streets. The Barrie museum at his birthplace, 9 Brechin Road, is kept up by the Scottish National Trust. The playwright is almost alive in this little house. The ingle-nook (fireside) chair, which he took to his London flat in the Adelphi is back here. His desk is in the weaving room but it remains a weaving room — the loom is still there with the thrums, the end pieces of the woven material, hanging over the end. Original manuscripts by the author of *The Little Minister*, *Peter Pan* and *The Admirable Crichton* are displayed in an upstairs room with his celebrated address on courage, based on a letter left for him by Scott of the Antarctic.

"Thrums": J. M. Barrie's birthplace

Handloom weaving at Moulin

7 CRAIGOWER HILL,

which rises to 1,300 ft. offers breathtaking views. There are signposts along the way and the National Trust for Scotland has established a viewpoint at the summit from which can be seen Pitlochry, the Tummel valley and, on a clear day, the Lomond Hills of Fife. But perhaps the most striking view is to the west with Schiehallion raising its huge crest 3,547 ft. above the glen.

Looking down on the Tummel valley from Craigower Hill

A winter's day view of Loch Tummel

The Falls of Tummel in the wooded valley near Pitlochry

8 **PITLOCHRY** lies in the wooded valley of the Tummel — take the first left going north for the traditional Road to the Isles of song. It also boasts a man-made loch and it is to the credit of the North of Scotland Hydro-Electric Board that Faskally Loch is now a local beauty spot. Tunnellers bored more than 9,000ft. through hard rock and dug out half-a-million tons of earth to make way for the water to feed the power station. Today the Tummel valley scheme does not jar the eye: the environment is almost unspoiled. In fact new vistas and pleasures have been created, one being the Fresh Water Fishery Research station just north of the town. At the dam is one of the wonders Scotland — the fish pass. Here, deep und the river, is an observation chamber with huge glass wall through which can k seen salmon and trout nosing the glass flashing past on their way to the spawnir grounds. If this were Niagara Falls hug posters would leave the visitor in r doubt about the importance of the spec acle. But, being Scotland, the motori parks his car and finds his own windir way to the wonder.

Pitlochry has its own theatre in the hi with a reputation for quality which attrac thousands to one of the loveliest and mo dramatic settings in Scotland.

Sunset on the Road to the Isles

9 **KILLIECRANKIE:** North of Pitlochry on the way to Blair Castle is the Pass of Killiecrankie, a detour from the route but one worth following for a few miles. On top of the gorge is a National Trust for Scotland information centre. The Battle of Killiecrankie was fought near here in 1689 between the Jacobites and the army of William III under General Mackay. The desperate action was over in a few minutes and the Jacobites of James VII, under the command of Graham of Claverhouse, ("Bonnie Dundee") put the English troops to flight, but Claverhouse himself was killed. One romantic legend from this battle is that of the Soldier's Leap. One of General Mackay's troopers, Donald MacBean, fleeing the Highlanders approached the chasm with his pursuers a few yards from his heels. MacBean took off across a gorge which sceptics used to say was an impossible leap. But in 1912, to confound the critics, an English visitor successfully made the same leap, unscathed.

The Pass of Killiecrankie

The River Garry, near Killiecrankie

ome of the last private army

11 **ABERFELDY** is reached across an iron bridge and along roads which were surveyed by General Wade after the 1715 Jacobite rising. The stone bridge he built here in 1733 is recognised as probably his best. His simple purpose was to create roads so that the Highlands could be pacified. At the southern end of Wade's bridge is a tall cairn topped by a Highland soldier — the Black Watch memorial erected in 1887 to mark the spot where the regiment was formed. After the 1715 Jacobite rebellion the clansmen were forbidden claymore and kilt. Wade formed six independent companies of Highlanders to keep the peace, gave them swords, dirks and pistols and allowed them to wear tartan. They were also given a solemn promise they would never be forced to serve outside the Highlands. Volunteers flocked to the King's colours and were, at first, a watch or police force. Their dark tartans gave them the name of the Black Watch. Now known as the Royal Highland Regiment, the former 42nd Foot has battle honours from the American War of Independence through the Napoleonic campaigns to India, World Wars I and II.

10 **BLAIR CASTLE** is the seat of the Duke of Atholl, who alone in ritain retains the right to a private army. he present Duke, one of Scotland's lected peers, maintains the tradition in a adre known as the Atholl Highlanders. their distinctive uniforms they have ecome a tourist attraction. The castle has een restored to much of its medieval ppearance with the additions of crow-tepped gables, towers and turrets, giving a fairytale look. The oldest part is robably Comyns Tower (13th Century). fter Killiecrankie, the body of Claverhouse as brought to the castle and his cuirass is till preserved there. In 1745 Bonnie rince Charlie stayed at the castle and ueen Victoria's visits are recorded in her ournal during her journey through the ighlands to Braemar.

Moness Burn and the birks o'Aberfeldy

12 **MENZIES CASTLE:** Across the river from Aberfeldy lies this ormer home of the chiefs of Clan Menzies, turretted grey stone, crow-stepped gable house. In Scotland the name is pronounced "Mingis". Part of the castle was built in 1820 but most of it dates back to 1571. The Menzies burial ground at Weem is a little chapel which stands near the modern church. On the walls of the chapel are painted hatchments, lozenge shaped tablets carrying armorial bearings of the chiefs.

urretted greystone Castle Menzies, former home of chiefs of the clan

MOUNTAIN GLORIES

Ben Lawers and the neighbouring peaks have a richer flora than other Scottish mountains. Long known as a place of pilgrimage for botanists, Ben Lawers is now a nature reserve. A good road leads to an information kiosk and car park at 1,800ft providing easy access to the mountain flora.

The flora is dependent on outcrops of the mica-schist. This rock is easily recognised by the glittering crystals of mica. Disintegrating under the action of frost and weather, it contributes to an ideal soil. There are few plants that will not thrive in a pot full of this material.

Soil is not the only requirement of alpine plants, for as rock garden enthusiasts know, they are helpless in competition with quick growing weeds of valley land. In nature a violent climate takes the place of the gardener by eliminating all but small, slow-growing plants. The heroic effort that some alpines make to produce large colourful flowers relates to the need to attract rather scarce insects.

The best place to look for alpines is along rock ledges on the mica-schist outcrops, which may form natural rock gardens packed with interest. You may be lucky enough to find about a dozen within quite a small area, including moss campion.

The best show is possibly provided by the alpine forget-me-not in drifts of sky blue flowers in July. In areas where springs bring up fresh supplies of minerals from the virgin rock and along the sides of brooks, you are likely to find the globe flower. A complete list of local flora can be obtained at the information office.

Taymouth Castle impressed Queen Victoria

13 TAYMOUTH CASTLE was th seat of the Earls of Breadalban the Campbells of Glenorchy. The dashin Sir John Campbell, later the first earl, wer to London to complete his educatio wooed and won an heiress and, so th story goes, sent home for two Highlan ponies. With his bride and himself on or pony and her dowry of 10,000 sovereig on the other, guarded by two clansme he brought her back to his 16th Centu castle. One of their descendants built th present one 150 years ago with its staine glass windows depicting the line of th Campbells of Breadalbane. It lies a mi north-east of Kenmore at the east end Loch Tay. In 1842 Queen Victoria an Prince Albert visited the castle and we impressed by the Earl's regiment, pipe and cheering crowds. She dined in th Great Hall and later wrote in her Journa "It seemed as if a great chieftain in olde feudal times was receiving his sovereig It was princely and romantic." The ente tainment of Highland dancing by torc light, fireworks, bonfires caused her to add "I never saw anything so fairylike".

14 **LOCH TAY** which runs from Kenmore to Killin, is one of Scotland's longest lochs, 14 miles from end to end, and one of the great salmon fishing stretches. A minor road running along the south side of the loch gives a wonderful view of Ben Lawers, 3,984 ft. On the north shore, about four miles from the lovely village of Kenmore, is a hotel which is the best point to start the climb to the summit.

Naturalists will find colonies of rare alpine plants on the slopes but since the mountain is largely owned by the National Trust for Scotland there is an injunction against picking them. The best place to see them is in a corrie called Allt Tuim nam Breac where they carpet the slopes with colour from April to July.

Most prominent are purple and yellow saxifrage, alpine forget-me-nots and the deep blue gentians.

View of Loch Tay from Kenmore

An islet in Loch Tay, one of the great salmon fishing stretches

297

The rushing waters of the River Dochart

15 **KILLIN,** at the foot of Loch Tay, is one of the loveliest villages in Scotland. Here the waters of the Dochart slide darkly through its deep bed to cascade under the bridge south of the village. There is parking a few hundred yards away from the narrow bridge and it is worth exploring the views. Killin is once again the home and seat of the chief of Clan McNab after an absence of almost 150 years when the chief fled to Canada to avoid a debtor's prison.

Kinnell House, where the present chief lives, was owned by the Campbells of Glenorchy from the time of that penniless McNab until 1950 when the uncle of the present chief bought it back. At the house is a famous black vine planted by the Marquess of Breadalbane in 1832 — it is said never to have failed to produce grapes. A visitor may walk from the side of the bridge into the grounds and come to the ancient burial place of the McNab chieftains on the small island of Inchbhuidh.

Francis McNab of McNab, 16th chief, toasted in his heyday as the most rumbustious man in Scotland, was painted by Raeburn and the portrait now hangs in the Scottish National Gallery in Edinburgh. It was said that one of the inducements he offered a potential bride was the chance to lie in "the prettiest burying place in Scotland". He died a bachelor. The McNabs trace their lineage back 13 centuries.

The Dochart by Killin

But it is not the McNabs who are most revered in Killin. It is a priest, St. Fillan, who brought Christianity to the glen. His healing stones — eight of them, each to cure ailments in different parts of the body — lie in a bed of rushes covered by an iron grille by the bridge. The rushes are gathered in a strange ritual each Christmas Eve. The keeper of the stones has to gather the rushes but must not cut them: they must be washed up.

ROB ROY, THE REBEL

The real life of Rob Roy MacGregor ha been befogged by the romantic aura wove about him by Sir Walter Scott. Rob was a old fashioned Highland cattle thief, born o March 3, 1671, in Glen Gyle at the head c Loch Katrine, second son of Lt Col Donal MacGregor of Glengyle, who had his com mission from James VII and II. This wa just ten years after the repeal of penal act ordering the extirpation of all of the nam MacGregor. In 1693 the acts were restorec partly because of Rob Roy's on-goings. B now a grazier on the Braes of Balquidde Perthshire, Rob was really following th ancient Highland trades of cattle lifting an blackmail. This last activity had a differen meaning in those times, indicating tha Rob, for a price, would defend farmers fror cattle thieves — he himself being the mos likely thief. He played off his neighbour. Campbell of Breadalbane and Montrose against each other till the first Duke c Montrose ruined him in a court action burned his home at Inversnaid on th shores of Loch Lomond and turned ou Rob's wife Mary and her family in wil mid-winter. One of Rob Roy's many cave can still be seen above Inversnaid. Fror then Rob turned his brigandry agains Montrose, taking little more than a nomina part in the Jacobite risings of 1715 an 1719. In 1722 he and Montrose wer reconciled, but he was later arrested, take to London and pardoned in 1727 on th eve of transportation to the West Indie. Thereafter he appears to have lived fairi quietly, become a Catholic (itself a rebe lious act at the time) and to have die peacefully in his own bed at Balquidder o December 28, 1734

16 **LOCH LOMOND:** From Killin the road winds to Crianlarich, the junction of three glens, Falloch, Dochary and Strath Fillan. Take a diversion here to Loch Lomond, one of the world's glories, the largest and loveliest loch in Scotland. Here, indeed, is a wealth of forest and mountain, dominated by the mighty shadow of Ben Lomond reflected across the waters to the winding lochside road.

Among the splendours of the loch are 30 wooded islands, the largest of which, Inchmurrin, is still inhabited. The name means "the grassy island" and it was once used as a deer park by the Duke of Montrose. The next largest is Inchcailloch, "the island of old women", which was once the burial place of the Clan Mac-Gregor. The ruins of a nunnery are still visible. It was dedicated to St. Kentigern, Celtic saint, also known as Mungo and patron saint of Glasgow.

The song *By yon bonnie banks* is believed to have been composed by one of Prince Charlie's followers on the eve of his execution. But these bonnie banks have in their time provided a backcloth for the romances and tragedies affecting many of Scotland's greatest clan names — the Buchanans, Colquhouns, Grahams, Mac-Farlanes and MacGregors.

yon bonnie banks of Loch Lomond

7 **LUSS:** Roughly in the middle of the drive south along the shores of [Lo]ch Lomond is the village of Luss which [co]uld be the set for the legendary *[Br]igadoon,* where the inhabitants sleep for [1]00 years. It is one street of white-washed [co]ttages, a tourist centre with a shingle [be]ach and a pier where the pleasure [st]eamer calls in the summer. The church, [bu]ilt in 1887 by Sir James Colquhoun [(p]ronounced Co'hoon) of Luss, houses [re]lics from the family's private chapel and [in] the cemetery is a sarcophagus which [be]ars the effigy of St. Kessog. A few miles [be]yond Luss, just off the new part of the [ro]ad is Duck Bay Marina, a fine modern [co]mplex of hotel, restaurant, shop and [mo]oring for the hundreds of small boats [an]d yachts which sail the loch.

the village of Luss

Ben Lomond across the loch from Luss

18 ARROCHAR

18 ARROCHAR: After returning along Loch Lomondside to Tarbet the road leads to this village, at the head of Loch Long, along the valley where the Viking Haco, or Haakon, dragged his longboats to sack the islands of Loch Lomond. It is worth driving a mile down the road towards Garelochhead to the Ardmay House Hotel, whose kilted owner claims he is the only hotelier who blends and exports his own brand of Scotch whisky.

The hall is loaded with antique weapons and the hotel also boasts one of the most unusual bar games in Scotland — an ice table where a guest can play the ancient game of curling with miniature stones.

The hall of Ardmay House Hotel

Loch Lomond towards Arrochar

THE WILD ONE

The wild cat is three feet long and distinguished from the domestic by i flatter head, longer legs, shorter tail an viciousness. It is only seen in daylight forced from cover.

The new road through Glen Croe in the shadow of the Cobbler

19 GLEN CROE: From Arrochar the road rises along the side of the loch and climbs into the mountain scree. Here, Ben Arthur, better known as The Cobbler since it bears some resemblance to a shoemaker at his last, glowers on the right hand side. The road is now a modern, gentle climb through the pass, less arduous than the military road, ordered by General "Johnny" Cope, in 1745. Cope's steep zig-zag is still used each summer as a hill climb for cars. But in its day it has seen some heavy loads, one of the heaviest being a peal of bells for Inveraray in the nineteen twenties. The three heaviest bells, the biggest one weighing two tons, proved too much for the tractors and had to be left at the roadside for two nights. That two-tonner was the heaviest load to cross the summit of the pass. On the way to the summit a stone bench is inscribed "Re and Be Thankful". After making the clim on foot William Wordsworth wrote:

Doubling and doubling with laborious walk
Who that has gained at length the wished-for height
This brief, this simple wayside call can slight
And rest not thankful?

Looking down Loch Fyne from Inveraray

Argyll Memorial, Inveraray

20 **INVERARAY** nestles on the edge of Argyll, once the ancient Scots kingdom of Dalriada, invaded and conquered by barbarians from Ireland. Today it is a gentle town of whitewash and grey stone. It was first created a burgh in 1473 when it was little more than a huddle of rude huts. In 1648 Charles I, then imprisoned in the Isle of Wight, made it a Royal Burgh to enlist support from the chief of Clan Campbell. It is still little more than a village, but a fascinating one.

The visitor driving into the town past the castle is met by a 500 year old Celtic cross which was brought from Iona. Behind it is an impressive arch which looks like a gateway, but in fact leads to an avenue, more than a mile long, into Essachosan (the Lover's Glen) and All Saints' Episcopal Church.

This church with its tower and a peal of 10 bells was built in 1923 by the 10th Duke of Argyll. The bells ring out each Sunday in memory of the Campbells who fell in the First World War.

The parish church (Presbyterian) has a wall running through the centre which made it possible to hold a service in Gaelic at the same time as an English service on the other side. Nowadays there is no such barrier. Gaelic may be a first language to many in the Outer Hebrides but in Inveraray English is the tongue. The Gaelic side of the kirk is now used as a hall. Another unusual feature of Inveraray is the whitewashed tenements called "lands". One known as "Crombie's Land" was the birthplace of Scottish novelist Neil Munro, who wrote the *Para Handy* stories about the skipper of a small "puffer" which served the needs of the islanders. A memorial to Munro can be seen near Glen Aray.

301

Inveraray Castle, home of the Duke of Argyll

22 LOCH AWE: At the top of th[e] road through Glen Aray fro[m] Inveraray comes the first glimpse of Lo[ch] Awe, which at one time acted as a natur[al] barrier to the Campbells. It is 22 miles lo[ng] and at the most a mile wide. It is the site [of] one of the most ambitious hydro-electr[ic] schemes in the world. It does not intru[de] but adds a new dimension to the scene[ry]. One of the oddities of the villages a[nd] hamlets about the loch is a cluster [of] houses built after the '45 rebellion by t[he] York Buildings Company, a London bas[ed] enterprise which made one of the fi[rst] attempts to develop the Highlands. It [is] called New York, has no colour proble[m] and it is a long time since anyone w[as] mugged there.

Sunset, Loch Awe

21 INVERARAY CASTLE: The castle commissioned by the 3rd Duke of Argyll dates back to the early 16th Century. When the remains of the old castle were demolished the new one was built about 100 yards back from the shore of Loch Fyne. It was completed in 1770 and shows its style in every line, turret and spire. The great hall, armoury and state rooms are open to the public. The castle illustrates the warlike traditions of the clans, great circles of mounted pikes line the hall; ancient muskets match the pattern; claymores and pistols add a counterpoint to the decoration. The castle is set in magnificent gardens and contains Old Masters, tapestries, fine furniture and plate.

Sunrise, Loch Fyne

Autumn tints by Loch Awe

Highland cattle in Loch Awe, 22 miles long and a mile wide

Kilchurn Castle at the head of the loch with Ben Cruachan in the background

Loch Etive and Ben Cruachan

The Brander Pass along the western arm of Loch Awe towards Taynuilt is now an easy and pleasant drive. The village at the head of Loch Etive was at one time an iron mining town and some ruins of the furnaces can still be seen. Near the church there is a standing stone which bears a memorial inscription for Lord Nelson carved before his funeral — certainly the first acknowledgement in stone of the admiral's prowess. Outside Taynuilt, Robert the Bruce routed the men of Lorne in 1308. The whole of Lorne can be seen from the summit of Ben Cruachan which is probably best climbed from Bridge of Awe. Ben Cruachan, the monarch of Lorne, has two main crests, Cruachan Beann (3,689 ft.) and Stob Dearg (3,611 ft.) in the west and six smaller peaks.

A peaceful scene on the loch

24 CONNEL: A few miles through the Brander the River Awe passes the great iron bridge of Connel, the second biggest cantilever bridge in the world after its sister spanning the Firth of Forth. This bridge carried the rail service, now axed. However, what the railway lost the motorist gained and the bridge is now fully open for road traffic. Below the bridge are the Falls of Lora, caused by a ridge of rock across the channel. At low tide the waters of Loch Etive roar over this ridge.

From Connel the road skirts the loch and suddenly swerves inland to Dunstaffnage Bay. Here on a promontory stands Dunstaffnage Castle, ancient stronghold of the Campbells, dating back to the 13th Century. Before that it was a stronghold of the Dalriada Picts and the traditional resting place of the Stone of Destiny before it was moved to Scone. What is left of the castle is more than 800 years old. Some of the walls are 9ft. thick and it is built on a natural shelf of rock. Some of the early Scottish kings were buried here and Alexander III used it in the 13th Century as a base to drive the Vikings from their footholds on the Hebridean islands. When Bruce forced the Pass of Brander he travelled to Dunstaffnage and ousted the MacDougalls who were then holding the stronghold. It was held for the Crown during the Jacobite rebellion and it was here that Flora MacDonald was imprisoned for helping Bonnie Prince Charlie to escape.

Connel Bridge, gain for the motorist

SCARLET EYEBROWS

The male Capercaillie at about three feet is eight inches bigger than the hen, has a large green-black fan tail, the same colour as most of his plumage, but his breast is green and his eyebrows scarlet. The female is a less ostentatious mottled-brown but she also has the red eyebrow. The call of the cock is likened to the "squalls" of fighting cats.

25 **OBAN:** From Pulpit Hill the visitor looks down on the hotels fringed about the bay and across the Firth of Lorne to Mull and Morvern, the islands of Kerrera and Lismore and is in no doubt here that he is in the Highlands. Oban is a busy port with two piers. The North is for the pleasure steamers and the boats to the islands. The south is the fish market, with a constant wheel of gulls overhead.

In 1773 when Dr. Johnson and his biographer Boswell visited it, Oban consisted of a few thatched fishermen's cottages and a "tolerable inn". When Sir Walter Scott was there in 1814 the population was 600. Today it is 7,000.

Beyond the placid harbour lies the northern jut of the island of Kerrera, a natural screen shielding the town from gale and tempest. The town is dominated by McCaig's Folly, modelled on Rome's Colosseum by a local banker and would-be benefactor, John Stewart McCaig. His plan was to make the building a museum to his family with a huge look-out tower sprouting from the middle. He died before it was finished and his tower has a neigh-

bouring folly, on the next hill-top — the unfinished remains of what was intended to be a hydropathic centre where people would come to take the waters. But the project ran out of money and now only the gaunt skeleton remains. Oban is the heart of the Gaelic Mod, a two week festival of song, music and poetry, lubricated with whisky and loved by every Gaelic speaker in the world. It is to the Highland Scot what the Eisteddfod is to the Welsh.

On the outskirts of the town lies Dunollie Castle. It sits on a little headland and was the principal seat of the MacDougalls, Lords of Lorne, and the more recent mansion of the present chief stands beneath the castle. His family once owned a third of Scotland.

Near the Castle is the Dog Stone — in Gaelic, clach-a-choin. It was here that legend says Fingal, the Gaelic hero, tethered his great dog Bran. Scientists have a more mundane explanation for the shape and scoring of the rock. They say that the stone stood at one time in the sea and it was the tide that wore the collar into the neck, not the tether of Bran.

The fishing fleet at Oban, and McCaig's folly

The view across the Firth of Lorne from Pulpit Hill

John Knox: the Bible alone.

Mary Queen of Scots roused Knox's anger.

The original National Covenant of 1638 (right) with the signature of the Earl of Montrose (above). He changed to the King's side in 1644 and raised a Highland Army for his cause

How a nation found its faith

The Covenant, signed in various forms between 1556 and 1689, condemned Papal and Episcopal Church Government and bound by oath members of the reformed Church of Scotland to conserve at all hazards the autonomy of their Church with a form of government sanctioned by "God's plain Word".

John Knox (1515-1572) was the inspiration of the Covenanters. He was in the line of the great religious reformers — Wyclif, Huss, Luther and Calvin. His guiding principle was that the Bible alone is God's plain Word and he pledged his followers to maintain the theological dogmas of the reformed Church "against Pope, King and Parliament". His preaching demanded the repression of all doctrine repugnant to the Gospel, the suppression of idolatry, under which the Mass, invocation of saints and images were included.

When Mary Stuart, the widowed Queen of France, returned as a girl of 18 to assume the sovereignty of Scotland on August 19, 1561, it was inevitable that she should come into conflict with Knox. The murder of her husband, Lord Darnley, and her marriage only three months later to the suspected regicide, the Earl of Bothwell, cost her the throne of Scotland which she abdicated on July 24, 1567. She was followed by James VI (later James I of the United Kingdom) who on January 28, 1581, signed "The King's Confession" affirming that true religion is revealed in the Gospel; abjuring all contrary religion i.e. Popish doctrine, law and ceremonies; and binding the King to obedience to and defence of the doctrine and discipline of "the true, reformed Kirk of Scotland". This Confession formed the first part of the great National Covenant of 1638; the second part specified the Acts of Parliament suppressing Popery and establishing the Protestant religion in Scotland; the third part bound the signatories to defend "the aforesaid true religion".

The signing of this National Covenant in Greyfriars Churchyard, Edinburgh, in 1638 proved to be the most momentous event in the religious struggle between the Stuarts and the people of Scotland. First to sign was the Earl of Montrose, who later changed sides.

In 1639 the bishops appointed by Charles I fled the country and one of the most important General Assemblies of the Presbyterian Church of Scotland met at Glasgow Cathedral in November. This Assembly abolished episcopacy, condemned liturgy, excommunicated the bishops and all anti-Covenant clergy. In the main, the Scottish people accepted the harsh discipline of the Covenant, but it did not penetrate to the Highland Clans, apart from the Campbells; and it was from these hereditary enemies of the Campbells that Montrose drew his support in his campaign for the King in 1644-45. Eventually he was defeated at Philiphaugh, near Selkirk, where the Covenanters' Army stained its record with a massacre of prisoners.

Charles II accepted the Covenant under oath at his Scone Coronation in 1651, but in 1662 he declared it illegal. From then until the Revolution of 1688 the Covenanters were hounded and persecuted but, after the Accession of William of Orange, there was nothing to fight against.

The signing of the Covenant (above) in Greyfriars Kirkyard, Edinburgh. The National Covenant was at once a political document and a declaration of faith. The document was laid out on a flat stone in the Kirkyard and on the first day, Wednesday, February 28, 1638, the nobility and gentlemen signed. According to Archibald Johnston of Warriston, who helped draw up the Covenant, it was "that glorious mariage day of the Kingdom with God". The next day the ministers and leading citizens signed and on March 2 and 3 the general public. By March 5 almost every parish in Scotland had given adherence and in the South-West enthusiasm was so great that it is said men signed with their blood.

The Battle of Bothwell Brig (right) was fought on June 22, 1679, between an army of about 5,000 Covenanters and a Royal Army led by the Duke of Monmouth, bastard son of Charles II. The Covenanters, harangued by their ministers armed with sword in the right hand and Bible in the left, defended the bridge over the Clyde, a few miles from Glasgow, with incredible bravery. They were overwhelmed and 1,200 were marched to Edinburgh and held prisoner in Greyfriars Kirkyard where the Covenant had been signed. The hangings, torture and barbarity of their treatment shocked even Monmouth but his orders did not stop the persecution. It went on through the "killing times" till the coming of William III in 1688.

Charles II accepted the Covenant in 1651. On his Restoration he declared it illegal, restored Episcopacy and persecution of the Covenanters began.

Edinburgh's lofty "lands". The cut-out shows Scotland's "staircase democracy" sweeps in cellars, mechanics in garrets and, nobles, lawyers, shop-keepers and clerks in ascending order.

Banners borne by the Covenanters proclaim their faith in God's plain word. In the "killing times" they wandered the hills of the South of Scotland, boycotted, hunted, half-starved, with prices on their heads, but always fervent.

COVENANT·FOR RELIGEON·ACCORDING TO·THE·WORD·OF·GOD CROWN·AND·KINGDOMS

IEHOVAH·NISSI

FOR GOD AND THE·COVENANTED·WORK·OF·REFORMATION

The Covenant was an answer to the bid by Charles I (right) to restore Episcopacy in Presbyterian Scotland. He correctly believed, however, that the majority of Scottish people wanted him as King and while Cromwell's prisoner at Carisbrooke Castle, Isle of Wight, he made a secret engagement with the Scottish Commissioners. The Scots marched into England, were routed at Preston in 1648. Charles was executed on January 30, 1649

John Graham: "Bluidy Clavers" to Covenanters; "Bonnie Dundee" to Royalists

Northern Scotland – the road to the Isles

CLIFF HANLEY

To most tourists living in Britain, Aberdeen sounds less like the start of a journey than the end. The Granite City is a good 500 miles from London, and as they say in Glasgow, it's a gey long way from everywhere else as well. But these long miles are easily disposed of on today's roads, and every year there are thousands more who are catching the habit. In an age when people are recoiling from the anonymous congestion of big cities, the entire area of Northern Scotland becomes irresistibly alluring.

"This knuckle-end of England," is what a cynical Sassenach called it. Well, nowadays everybody wants to get nearer the knuckle. The light, the colours, the genial tempo of life, even the sheer emptiness, are good medicine. And as cities go, Aberdeen is no heartless sprawl. The place is a tidy size for human beings, with a population of about 180,000, and it has doggedly refused to follow the dreary race towards high-rise living that is blighting so many other cities. It still looks and feels like a place for people to live in.

THE ROYAL ROAD

They call it the Silver City by the Sea, and it's true. Much of it was built in the durable granite which lies deep and rich in the area: a stone that doesn't weather, doesn't decay, and in that clean northern air doesn't go grimy. When sun shine strikes it, it sparkles bravely. And the beaches in the area too are silver rather than gold — splendid generous beaches of a dazzling purity.

Aberdeen grew up as a commercial and a fishing centre with the sea on its doorstep and rich farmland at its back. In modern times it has added engineering and textiles and paper and other industries and the holiday industry is not the least of these. There are attractions in a holiday city which is also a working city, with a thriving harbour to stare at and a feeling of busy-ness and energy.

The discerning traveller will not be content with a brief glance through the windscreen at this strange, homely, flavoursome city, since many travellers are happy to settle comfortably into it for two or three weeks without complaining. But since we are concerned with travelling on, the road lies to the west and the different delights of the open Scottish countryside.

This particular countryside may be surprising, to anyone who is looking forward to the stern masculine landscape of the Scottish north. The land is rich and rolling and feminine through Deeside. Royal Deeside — the adjective belongs with the noun, and it fits. Queen Victoria made this place her own because it looked like paradise to her, and the scene has the kind of spaciousness and graciousness that we associate with that expansive age.

We are not, here, in the Highlands; but in the Northern lowlands, where the land yields bounty and life has always been well organised. Some of the great houses have become hotels and some of the hotels have impersonated the great old houses; and the architectural style is worth looking at. It is a pleasant blend of cosy and magnificent. The cottages huddling into the soil, and the big houses soaring out of it, have a peculiar fitness to the landscape.

Queen Victoria might well have chosen to live in the West Highlands if her first visit there had not been wild and wet and miserable; but that is another story. In Balmoral she chose a right royal retreat and perhaps invented a tradition that is questionable, but agreeable. Cynical Scots call it Balmorality, as a reaction to the prissiness and hypocrisy of Victorian times, and they imply a complacent superficial fakery, a Philistinism, a passion for high-

The Coolins from Elgol in southern Skye

priced romanticism, a rejection of reality. There is some justice i this criticism but Victoria's traditions have their own reality, an they are not to be lightly dismissed.

The great Highland Games nonsense is one of the weapon used by cynics against Balmorality. Today the Highland Game are slickly organised affairs with a travelling circuit of famila champions tossing cabers and blowing bagpipes and dancin against one another. But to be fair to Victoria, she simply loved th Scottish Thing, brawny chaps competing as on a village green an then a wee dance back at the castle where the children could enjo themselves.

Now, the great non-tradition of the Highland Games has estab lished itself as a tradition, and no man in his senses would lightl pass by the Braemar Gathering, the brawny champions, th terrifying business of the caber-tossing and the wild madness the great Highland bagpipe. The tradition may not be as old as seems but the spectacle is magnificent.

But if we are driving on, the road has wilder things ahead of u beginning with the Cockbridge-Tomintoul Road. Nobody Britain can be unfamiliar with these ringing names. If a winter hard, it comes first and hardest to this twisting route betwee Balmoral and Grantown-on-Spey. Forget the lush pastures

Deeside. This is country as bleak and barren as you will find. The road winds and twists and climbs and in winter, if there is snow anywhere, there is snow here. This is the first road in Britain to be announced as closed. Even in summer it is not to be despised.

The marvellous thing about Tomintoul is that when everything else is said about it, it is a pretty place; hard and practical and perched on the roof of the weather forecast, but good to look at and good to stop at. And well supplied with cheer.

FISH, GOLF AND SNOW

Grantown-on-Spey, buried in the north, is almost a bustling metropolis after this moon-landscape journey. It has a thronged main street and several fine hotels and it sits on the fastest-flowing river in Britain; a river irresistible to good fish. Fishing is a pretty expensive business in modern Britain, and it sometimes seems that the fishermen outnumber the fish; but a few pounds will buy an angler the right to work out his mania in Grantown and feel like an emperor. If they don't bite (and it's odd how often we hear that they didn't bite) there is some sporty golf available. There is also the simple feel of the countryside and the vast expanse of sky which is almost the most precious luxury a traveller can enjoy in our times. Grantown is a good place, and if it's difficult to specify why, that is simply because pleasure is not a thing to be catalogued.

Our route leaves here through Carrbridge to Aviemore, the tiny northern village which has hoisted itself into international fame by exploiting the simple attractions of Scottish snow, and set itself up in competition with the traditional winter-ski resorts of France and Switzerland. Easter tends to be more dependable for those who thirst after a rich fall and long runs.

But Aviemore has converted itself into a year-round allure. The old village remains wonderfully unspoiled, but beside it the Aviemore Centre has blossomed, with modern hotels and swimming pools and curling rinks and karting and everything that the jaded 20th Century appetite demands for relaxation or excitement. For travellers with the money and the inclination, Aviemore is entertaining for twelve months in every twelve.

North, then, to Inverness and worth a chapter on its own. In the first place they say that Invernesians speak the purest form of English in the world. Other English-speakers may well dispute this, if anyone can define what pure English is; but there is certainly a kind of purity about the ancient capital of the north. Inverness, oddly enough, is not a Highland town; but kings of Scotland have used it as their high-latitude capital and it has enjoyed a quiet prosperity untouched by many of the skirmishes and blood-baths that tortured Scotland in the past.

It is a settled place, "thrang and thriving" in one of the most beautiful settings God made; an ancient town, a modern town with elegant shops and one-way streets and traffic problems, remote from metropolitan Britain and completely in touch with the 20th Century, the home of the Highlands and Islands Development Board and the jumping-off point for the Loch Ness Monster. A curious town, a place with a flavour hard to define but whose flavour is very positive; seething with history but strangely untouched by history.

If you drive a few miles you will arrive at the village of Beauly. Savour the name—Beau Lieu, the handsome place. Set your face to the west and drive on to Garve, a tiny hamlet where (despite the rusty look of the rails) the trains still run. And from Garve to Strome,

away out west, a local will tell you there is sixteen miles of damn all. If he does, he will be right. Achnasheen on the road is hardly noticeable except for motorists who are also connoisseurs of old railway stations. All else is bleak, barren, and featureless moorland, and, if you've seen an acre of Scottish moor, you have seen the lot.

The next landmark would once have been Stromemore, on the north shore of Loch Carron, and the ferry across the loch to Strome Ferry. Today your road runs along the south shore of the loch without interference by water, on to Balmacara and Kyle of Lochalsh and the Kyle Ferry to the most romantic and perhaps the most beautiful island in the world. The title may be disputed by Hawaiians but no Skye man will listen to their arguments. Skye is the magic, misty isle. Skye is where the bonny boat speeds to. Skye is the paradise in the west.

Well, it's pretty good, there is no doubt. If Skye is your first acquaintance with the Hebrides, you will have no cause to complain. It is not a tiny wee place. It takes well over 100 miles of sporty driving to travel round the island but every mile is worth travelling. From Kyleakin, where the car ferry lands, through Broadford and Sligachan to Portree, you are in the far country of the fairies and the lilting music and the memories of Bonny Prince Charlie and the sad, bitter echoes of the Highland Clearances, and Skye is a world of its own.

In our time, Skye lives by its visitors. It likes to see them, and they come in boatloads. The old firm religion of Calvin and John Knox still stands strong on the island and is not to be easily dismissed or despised, but it has yielded to modern times — the ferry runs on Sundays and, side by side with the hard gospel of the Free Church, goes the genial, witty nature of the Skye folk who love their island and their homes and consequently love other people, too.

The romance is the thing and, mistake it not, it is real. Portree, the main town and port, is a bustling and efficient little place but it is an island place, and Prince Charlie slept here too — in a place where a modern hotel now stands. They say he was not as grateful as he might have been to the gorgeous Flora MacDonald, but there is dispute about that too. You will travel north from Portree and, if the weather is clear, goggle at the bleak majesty of the Storr, and the Old Man of Storr. If you are skilled, or mad, you may even climb one or both.

LANDSCAPE FOR GIANTS

You will sweep round the north of the island, by Staffin to Uig, and be humbled by a landscape that was made for giants and heroes; and across to Dunvegan, where the ancient legend of clan loyalty is enshrined in Dunvegan Castle, the spiritual home of the MacLeods. You will be suitably respectful — there are plenty of MacLeods still living on Skye, and many of them are very large men indeed. The roads will give you no trouble. Skye today is designed for driving. One thing however, you will remember. Courtesy is still valued on this magical island. On the few miles of single-track road you will treat the on-coming motorist as a friend and be at pains to make his journey easy. In the Hebrides anything is forgivable except bad manners and driving is not a competition but a simple necessity; and there is no hurry anyway. Don't stay too long here. You may lose your sense of urgency and never want to go home at all. The saddest sight in life to a Skye man, and in the end to people who have merely visited, is the view from the ferry that leaves Skye behind.

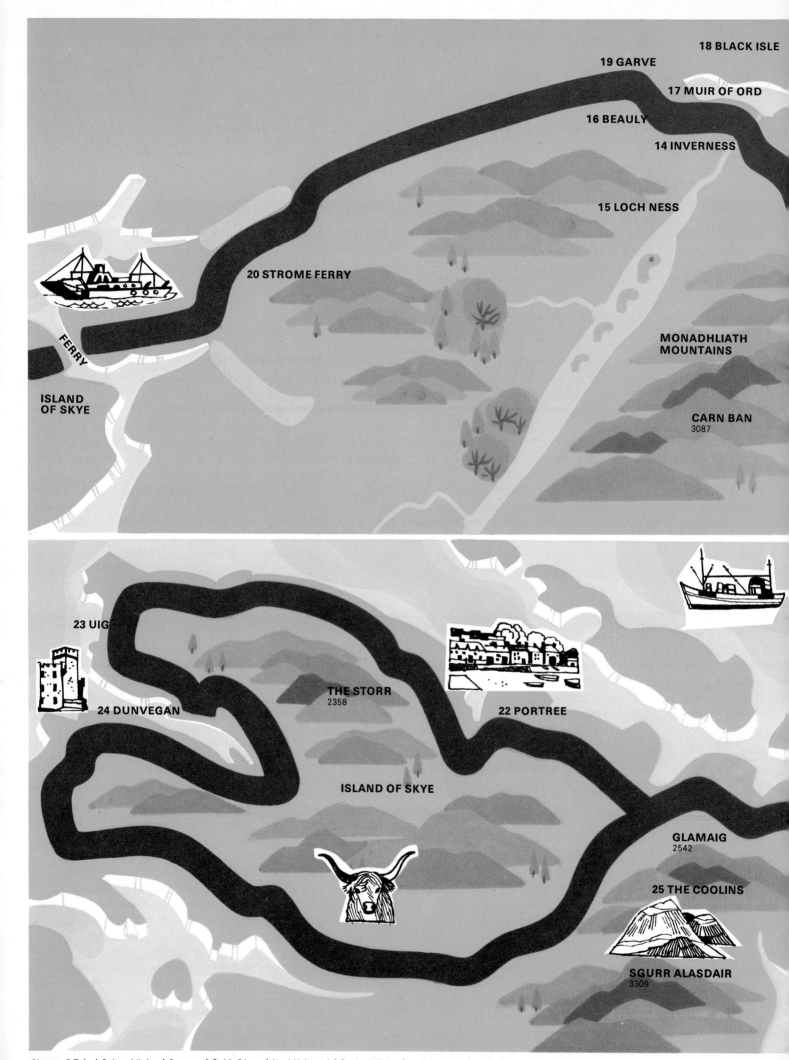

18 BLACK ISLE

19 GARVE

17 MUIR OF ORD

16 BEAULY

14 INVERNESS

15 LOCH NESS

20 STROME FERRY

FERRY

ISLAND
OF SKYE

MONADHLIATH
MOUNTAINS

CARN BAN
3087

23 UIG

24 DUNVEGAN

THE STORR
2358

22 PORTREE

ISLAND OF SKYE

GLAMAIG
2542

25 THE COOLINS

SGURR ALASDAIR
3309

Photos: B.T.A. / Colour Lib Int / Conway / C. M. Dixon / Noel Habgood / Sonia Halliday / A. F. Kersting / H. A. Kistenmacher / F. Melvin / Pictor / Picturepoint / Pix / Michael St Maur Sheil / Scottish Tourist Board / Kenneth Scowan / Spectrum / S. S. Summers / R. J. Westlake / Tom Wright

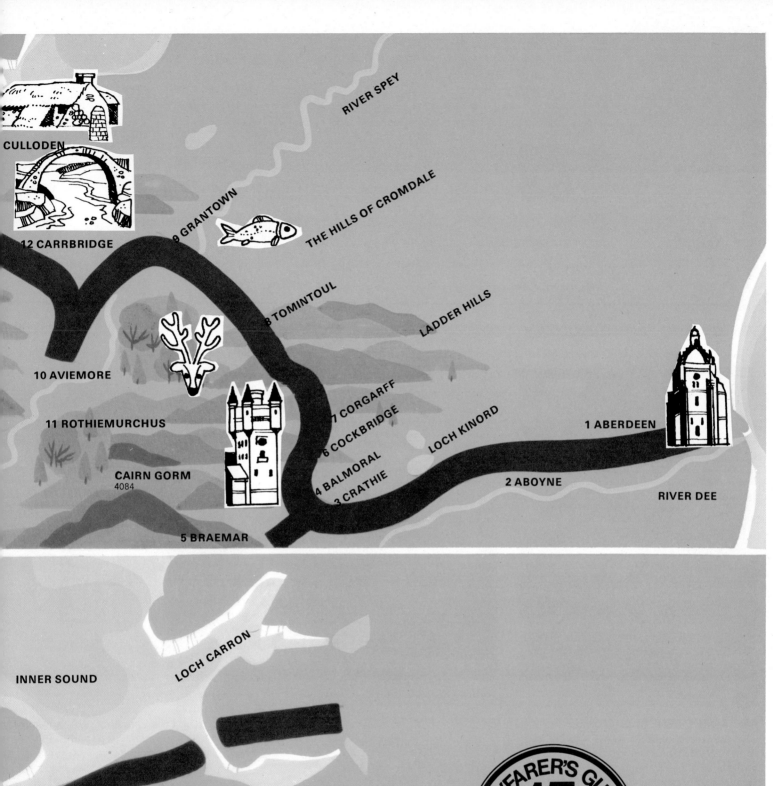

CULLODEN

12 CARRBRIDGE

9 GRANTOWN

RIVER SPEY

THE HILLS OF CROMDALE

8 TOMINTOUL

LADDER HILLS

10 AVIEMORE

7 CORGARFF

11 ROTHIEMURCHUS

6 COCKBRIDGE

LOCH KINORD

1 ABERDEEN

CAIRN GORM
4084

4 BALMORAL

3 CRATHIE

2 ABOYNE

RIVER DEE

5 BRAEMAR

INNER SOUND

LOCH CARRON

21 BROADFORD

SGURR NA COINNICH
2424

SOUND OF SLEAT

Ben Manchip

Illustrations: Elsie Wrigley / Richard Hook   Plant Notes: Geoffrey Gilbert   Animals & Birds: Jeremy Johns

Corner of the harbour at Aberdeen

Aberdeen University

Town Sergeants under the Clock Tower of the Town House

1 **ABERDEEN**: The sheer mass of the stone that built the city is worth studying for its own sake. Union Street, the main street, has a lush variety of granite building which ought to be purely practical and functional but has a reckless amount of variety and ornamentation. Leading off it is Belmont Street, a rather cosier row of low buildings all wilfully individual in flavour.

For a somewhat older spectacle, the enthusiast must certainly see St. Machar's Cathedral, both outside and in. The Cathedral dates from the 14th Century, and the interior is lined with pillars supporting Gothic arches. Marischal College, of stone masonry on granite, is what one feels a university ought to look like. It is, with King's College, one of the two venerable universities now combined to form the University of Aberdeen, it stands in the part of the city known as Aulton — Old Aberdeen — and is very much a part of its surroundings. The district's development was influenced by the existence of the

William Wallace statue

college and the cathedral, expanding into kind of *ville universitaire;* and the student according to their degree of seniority ar still known as magistrands, tertians, semis bajans and bajanellas. (Another form o 'bajan' is found in the bejants of St Andrews University. The word derives from the French *bec jaune* — yellow beak, o baby bird). The supervisor of the non academic staff, head keeper, is the Sacris who still wears an opulent gold-braide uniform on formal occasions.

Until recent times, students invariabl walked to the college in red gowns, an the local children on sighting them shoute "Buttery Willie Collie." Nobody has an idea whatever about where the phras came from or what it's supposed to mear

The statue of William Wallace — modern and daunting work by W. G Stevenson — is not of granite, but it stand proud on a granite plinth. And for wher stone used to be, there is Rubislaw Quarr long abandoned after it had been dug ou

312

King's College, one of two venerable universities

The pride of Aberdeen's Art Gallery at Schoolhill is its collection of artists' self-portraits. There is a good collection of modern art and of sculpture arranged by period. Marischal College has an anthropological museum mainly distinguished by Egyptian and local antiquities; and there is a natural history museum in the Zoology Building in Tillydrone Avenue which can be visited by arrangement with the University. Two old houses have been preserved by the city — Provost Skenes House at Flourmill Brae, where the Duke of Cumberland stayed on his way to Culloden; and by far the oldest house in the city, Provost Ross's House in Shiprow, which was built in 1593.

The Town House, a mid-Victorian building, has an interesting collection of portraits, and its Council Chamber has an impressive heraldic ceiling.

Leaving art and antiquity aside, it is possible to visit on weekday afternoons the Girdleness Lighthouse at Torry. Aberdeen has the advantages of being a bustling commercial centre, a colourful working seaport, and a coastal holiday town with its own beach of absolutely genuine, fine, shining sand. The beach in summer is clearly its *raison d'etre* for masses of visitors, and it has the same gregarious appeal of Brighton beach or the Riviera, where people like to see other people in large numbers.

But beach-lovers who are either shy or misanthropic can find their own pleasures with a very small effort. The same sand is spread with a reckless hand along the coastline and can be found thinly populated a mile or so away. Travel seven or eight miles north from the city and you will discover absolutely stupendous stretches of sand, with great high dunes on the inland side big enough to hide a troop of Bedouin, and running level to the water's edge which at low tide seems miles away. For sheer lavishness there is nothing to surpass this area anywhere in Britain.

2 ABOYNE: On the main road between Aboyne and Ballater, on Royal Deeside, is a massive boulder bearing the inscription "You are now in the Highlands." It was put there fairly lightheartedly by the Deeside Field Club in 1965, and does indeed mark a spot on the long boundary that divides Scottish Lowland from Scottish Highland. The line is not simple, however. It doesn't, as some people imagine, run across Scotland separating north from south. In some places it is more nearly "vertical", marking off the east from the west. Aberdeen and Fraserburgh are not Highland towns, and even Caithness, away up on the roof of Scotland, hardly qualifies either. For that matter, the Orkney and Shetland Islands are *distinctly* not Highland.

The division is between two cultures; the Gaelic-speaking peoples and the Lowlanders who speak "Scots" which is a form of English. Away down south, the Mull of Kintyre, and even the islands of Bute and Arran, in the Firth of Clyde, are Highland by history. The Highland line, in fact, is not so much a physical frontier as an attitude of mind.

Crossing the Highland Line

Aboyne Castle, a Gordon stronghold

3 **CRATHIE:** The original Crathie church was a stark, bare and uncompromising pile built early last century in a stern Presbyterian mood, but it was faithfully attended by Queen Victoria, who liked the hard, simple Church of Scotland services. The present and pretty little kirk was built in 1895 to the design of A. Marshal Mackenzie (the architect of the modern frontage of Marischal College in Aberdeen). Inside, the visitor may see memorials to many of the royal personages who have worshipped there. The gates commemorate the present Queen's father, George VI. The Queen and her family attend services during their Balmoral holidays in August and September, courteously ignored by the local people but enthusiastically watched by visiting subjects to whom these are unique occasions for seeing the monarch informally.

In the nearby graveyard of a ruined church is the monument to John Brown which was erected by Queen Victoria.

Crathie Church

Typical of Highland cattle

6 **COCKBRIDGE:** The Cockbridge Tomintoul road is familiar by name people who have never been within 1 miles of it, because it shares with Shap an a few other places the distinction of gettin the first and the worst of winter snow ice. The road winds through a mounta pass connecting Strathdon with Strathavo Cockbridge itself lies 1,344 ft. above se level, and from there the drive is steeply u to 2,114 ft. In winter the prudent motori takes local advice before setting ou because a sudden change in the weath can close the road in less than an hour, an it is not amusing to be caught on it. Even mild dry conditions it is best approached full daylight; the twists and turns in dark ness are not for the nervous, who cann see but can vividly picture sheer drops disaster on every blind bend. By daylig the road is merely a job asking for attentio and commonsense. The landscape is not s much magnificent as just desolate, like th dark side of a lost planet. Perhaps th greatest attraction in negotiating this pas is to be able to mention it casually later t stay-at-homes who have never dared it.

Balmoral Castle and dark Lochnagar

4 **BALMORAL:** William Topaz McGonagall, the greatest bad poet in the English language, was probably the most loyal subject Queen Victoria ever had. Having received a routine acknowledgment from the Queen's secretary of a poem he had sent to the monarch, McGonagall assumed that he was now under royal patronage, and set out to walk from his home in Dundee to visit Her Majesty at Balmoral. Perfectly awful things happened to him *en route,* as they nearly always did: hunger and pain and attempted robbery, to begin with, and then an officious gatekeeper at the Castle who took his "letter of patronage" inside and returned immediately to say that "they can't be bothered with you." The full sad story can and should, be read in *Poetic Gems.* McGonagall survived

this fresh disappointment without rancour, and has the last word:

> *And Balmoral Castle is magnificent*
> *to be seen*
> *Highland home of the Empress of*
> *India, Great Britain's Queen*
> *With its beautiful pine forests, near*
> *by the River Dee*
> *Where the rabbits and hares do sport*
> *in mirthful glee*
> *And the deer and the roe together*
> *do play*
> *All the live long summer day,*
> *In sweet harmony together,*
> *While munching the blooming*
> *heather,*
> *With their hearts full of glee*
> *In the green woods of Balmoral,*
> *near by the River Dee.*

THE SOLITARY
The Scottish (or blue) hare is a solitar creature usually found on heather moor and craggy hillsides. It changes coat i autumn to help its camouflage in the snov but is never totally white, always havin black tips to its ears.

314

The castle at Braemar where the Jacobite Standard was raised for the '15 rebellion

5 BRAEMAR: Highland Games as we know them today are a fairly modern tradition. The Games enjoyed by Queen Victoria in 1850 were an impromptu "mini" affair. Now we feel entitled to grander spectacles, and we get them. The archetypal spectacle of "The Games" is a giant Highlander heaving a tree across a field, and it happens. The basic object of tossing the caber, however, is not to throw it a mile, but simply to throw it up and out so that when its far end strikes the earth, the great pole falls directly away from the thrower. Attempted by a novice, this odd exercise can do nasty things to the neck muscles, but it is probably inherently less hazardous to onlookers than throwing the hammer. Royal Deeside is hipped on the Games, which can be seen at Ballater in the middle of August, at Aboyne at the beginning of September, followed a few days later by the celebrated Braemar Gathering.

For those interested in much older games: Macbeth died in single combat on Deeside; and the standard of rebellion was first raised at Braemar to launch the 1715 Jacobite Rebellion.

The old bridge of Dee at Braemar

Corgarff Castle, scene of 16th Century atrocity

7 CORGARFF: Less notorious than the Glencoe Massacre, but even more spine-chilling, is the tale of Corgarff Castle in Strathdon, near Cockbridge. First built in the early 16th Century, it was occupied in 1571 by Forbes, laird of Towie, who supported in those political times the claim of James VI as regent of Scotland. A rival chiefling Adam Gordon of Auchindoun took the side of James' mother Mary Queen of Scots; and to prove his point he attacked the castle and set it on fire. Forbes' wife Margaret Campbell was roasted to death, along with 27 others, relatives and servants.

The present-day castle has been completely restored, but only after several other vicissitudes. After its first rebuilding it was fired again in 1689 by the Jacobites, patched up and used still later by the Jacobites as an arsenal for the '45 Rebellion. In the early spring of 1746 an army under Lord Ancrum attacked it, but found it abandoned and yet again set on fire and still smouldering. As recently as 1830, repaired and enlarged, it served as headquarters for an army detachment trying to stop whisky smuggling.

Bridge spanning the River Avon near Tomintoul

A view of Grantown-on-Spey

9 GRANTOWN: A visiting angler can work several miles of the River Spey for a pound a week. If bargain fishing were the obsession of his life he might decide to settle down in Grantown-on-Spey and qualify as a ratepayer for fishing at one pound a *year.*

The Spey is Britain's fastest-flowing river, celebrated for salmon. It also offers seatrout, finnock and brown trout to those who are cunning or lucky enough to get them. The countryside around has other hill burns and lochans well populated with game.

The Strathspey Angling Improvement Association welcomes and encourages visiting anglers. It administers more than 12 miles of fishing on the Spey, and has the rights of another 12 miles on both banks of the River Dulnain, a main tributary. On this narrower water all pools are accessible from the banks and it isn't necessary to wade. An informative brochure on this and other facilities is available from the Grantown-on-Spey Improvements and Tourist Association.

8 TOMINTOUL: A most improbable village. The very idea of planting a community in the remote valley of the Avon seems absurd. But in truth the valley itself is deliciously beautiful, and in old turbulent times must have been a sort of Shangri-La, a faraway haven for the natives who worked the soil and equally for fugitives and outlaws. The glen of the Avon (pronounced Ahn) has been described as scenically the most perfect in Scotland.

The village of Tomintoul is well up from the river and looking down on the valley, and is quite a recent settlement built around 1780 when a new military road made such a village feasible. It is little more than one main street and a village green, but to the traveller who has toiled over the pass from Cockbridge it is one of the world's most welcome sights, and very prettily made of local stone. It has four hotels for the relief of the weary voyager.

Still waters near Aviemore and the bulk of the Cairngorms in the background

Curling rink at the Centre

The nature reserve, Aviemore

10 **AVIEMORE:** The ski season in Scotland opens in December and ends in May. In mild winters the snowfall may be delayed till well into the spring, but in some years the main ski pistes are complete in November. Snow conditions are reported daily to the Glasgow Weather Centre — telephone 041-248 3451 — and are published in Scottish newspapers and broadcast on weekdays by BBC-Scotland TV, Scottish Television and Grampian Television.

The Cairngorm ski-ing business is now highly organised, with interconnected tows and chairlifts totalling over 6,000 ft. Rescue services are provided free by the Cairngorm Ski Patrol. There are nine approved ski schools operating on Cairngorm.

The Aviemore Centre is on modern luxury lines. The whole complex, dreamed up and realised during the sixties, is set in dramatic countryside which gives access to the entertainments organised by the Centre. These include skating, curling, a heated indoor pool and kart racing, children's playground; and facilities outdoors for ski-ing, pony trekking, gliding, canoeing and so on. There are lavish facilities for conferences, and the centre is now very much an all-year-round operation.

11 ROTHIEMURCHUS, variously translated as "the great plain of the pines" and "the fort of the Murdochs" (place-name derivations provide one of Scotland's great guessing games) is a pleasant stretch of the countryside near Aviemore, on the far side of the River Spey. Its principal point of interest is quite modern. A few years after the last war a few reindeer were imported from Lapland to see if they would thrive in the relatively genial climate of northern Scotland. The herd had its initial troubles, but these appear to be over. They are bred on practical lines for meat and skins and for the antlers which are turned into traditional carved ornaments which can be bought locally. For the visitor, however, the simple sight of these handsome visitors is probably a sufficient justification for the short detour to Rothiemurchus.

Loch Morlich, Rothiemurchus

River Dulnan, near Carrbridge

12 CARRBRIDGE: In the little village of Carrbridge a pioneer educational entertainment was launched in 1970 to exploit modern techniques as a means of bringing the ancient past to life. It is called Landmark and lies at the south end of the village among tall pines; a low-slung timber building of rigorously modern style. Inside is a fairly lush carpeted entrance hall with book displays, and there's a glass-roofed restaurant.

The point of the show is firstly a sort of tunnel exhibition with pictures and drawings lighting up automatically and electronic sound effects, and it tells the story of man's development from the Ice Age to the present day. There are also specimens of primitive tools and weapons, and a rotary quern in working order, with which the visitor can actually grind some oatmeal.

13 CULLODEN: Six miles from Inverness lies the tragic, bloody battlefield of Culloden, where the Duke of Cumberland ("Sweet William" to patriotic Englishmen of the time, "Cumberland the Butcher" to Highlanders of the same time) defeated the remains of Prince Charles Edward Stuart's army on April 16, 1746, and finally killed the last hope of the Jacobite cause. In retrospect, the victory can be seen as both inevitable and tragic; inevitable because advanced military armoury (the bayonet) proved invincible against the romantic, obsolete Highland broadsword — tragic because the backlash of the '45 Rebellion made it seem reasonable and prudent to crush any future danger of Highland revolt and started the process that produced the Highland Clearances and turned much of northwest Scotland into a desert where people were supplanted by sheep and then by deer.

The clan graves are marked by headstones, and a small cottage has been preserved from that bloody time in its original condition. A man has to be insensitive to history not to be saddened and thrilled by the atmosphere of this grim place. For the genuinely sentimental there is also an absolutely genuine wishing well (according to people who like wishing wells) which produces fulfilment if one visits it on the first Sunday of May and goes through the proper ritual.

Old Leanach Cottage, Culloden

14 INVERNESS: Probably th[e] earliest artefact of old Inverness [is] the Boar Stone, a rock with Pictish carving on Stratherrick Road. The Picts were th[e] original inhabitants of Scotland, alleged[ly] naked and covered with blue woad, wh[o] were seen but unconquered by the Roma[n] invaders. Very little remains of the[ir] occupation but such carvings as the Bo[ar] Stone, dating from the 7th or 8th Centur[ie]s.

A long time later, but still reasonab[ly] venerable, comes the Clock Tower ne[ar] Shore Street — a relic of the citadel built [by] Cromwell's army in the middle of the 17[th] Century. About 1,000 men of the Commo[n]wealth army were garrisoned here, an[d] when they were withdrawn in 1662 th[e] citadel was torn down by the people [of] Inverness.

Inverness Castle as it stands today [is] nearly contemporary — it was built in [its] present form between 1834 and 1846, an[d] houses the Sheriff Court and other offic[ial] offices. But it is the heir of a much old[er] castle built in 1141, which General Wad[e] reconstructed in 1725 when he move[d] north to pacify the Highlands, and whic[h] Prince Charlie's men destroyed in 174[6] before they in turn were destroyed [at] Culloden.

Inverness has all the services an[d] amenities to be expected of a thrivi[ng] town, and visitors will want to see th[e] tartan, tweeds, knitwear, jewellery an[d] other Highland souvenirs.

Jacobite necklace in the museum

318

The modern castle at Inverness is heir to a much older castle built in 1141

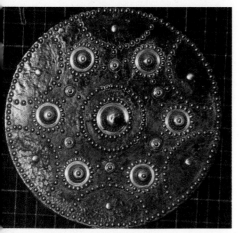

Highland warrior's targe

The cathedral font, Inverness

The River Ness flowing through the heart of Inverness

General view of Loch Ness, home of the monster, with Urquhart Castle in the foreground

16 BEAULY: Beauly — *beau lieu*, the beautiful place. The French associations are sharpened by the fact that the Frasers of Lovat, and this is Lovat country, were — like Robert the Bruce — Norman by origin and proud of it. History is represented by the totally ruined priory at one end of the village, abandoned and left to decay after the Reformation. The priory was built in 1230.

The home of the Lovats, Beaufort Castle, lies about four miles outside the village. It is a fairly recent building in the Scottish baronial style — date 1800. The original Lovat seat, Dounie Castle, was yet another victim of the aftermath of the '45 Rebellion. The Lovat of that time, Simon, was beheaded on Tower Hill. On his way there a woman shouted "You'll get that nasty head of yours chopped off, you ugly old Scotch dog." He smiled and answered, "I believe I shall, you ugly old English bitch."

Beaufort Castle, home of the Lovats, Clan Fraser

LILY OF THE LOCHS

To the botanist the north-western areas deer forest are specially valuable becau they have not yet been catalogued wi the thoroughness of most territories. Perha, the most exciting place to observe th Arctic-alpine flora is Storr (2,360ft.) Skye, where every rock seems to lead something interesting such as moss car pion, globe flower, purple saxifrage, alpi saw-wort and the recently discover koenigia islandica. More sedenta botanists may prefer the drive rour Stoer Head passing Quinag (2,653ft.) Th area, so beset with lily lochan that the seems to be more water than land, is be seen late on June evenings when t lingering northern sun colours its unearth rocks and pools. Each loch has its wa lilies and probably the great royal fe stands six feet high above the wat Interesting plants can be found within few yards of the road.

15 **LOCH NESS** means one thing only to the outside world — the Monster. Even without that bonus, it is a place worth seeing. Scotland is divided obliquely by a great geological fault which has been utilised to form the Caledonian Canal. Loch Ness is the northernmost link in that imposing chain.

The Canal functions, by the way — the string of lochs are threaded by locks and it is possible, and good, to cruise the entire length during the summer on the sturdy boat run by the British Waterways Board, or to sail private yachts all the way from the Moray Firth to Loch Linnhe and the Isle of Mull.

Loch Ness itself is a mile or so broad, more than 30 miles long, and according to legend impenetrably deep. The late John Cobb made his last bids for the world water speed record here, was tragically killed, and has a modest monument erected to his memory on the shore.

The scenery is memorably beautiful on and off the water. There may well be a shy monster minding its own business in the deeps. Why not? *Something* is sighted several times every year — perhaps because he is there, perhaps because we need a nice monster to reassure us.

Murchison (1792-1871)

17 **MUIR OF ORD:** It is easy to imagine the soaring 20th Century highways of Britain being flung across the landscape by the titanic civil engineering companies living in glass towers in London. Just outside the village of Muir of Ord, a few miles beyond Inverness on the road to the Isles, is the headquarters of the Baxters, an almost anonymous family business which demonstrates the canniness and the energy of the Scot on his home ground. John Baxter and Sons are typical of the small-scale Titans who blossom far away from the centres of power.

Their most spectacular undertaking in recent years was the new road linking Tighnabruaich on the Kyles of Bute with the holiday traffic from Glasgow; a road providing fast motoring and the most breathtaking views in Britain. Aberdeen University now has a field study centre at Tarradale House, where Sir Roderick Murchison, the noted geologist, was born in 1792.

18 **THE BLACK ISLE** is neither black nor island. It is a lush peninsula just outside Inverness and worth a detour from the route if there is time to spare. Cradled by the Cromarty Firth and the Moray Firth, its "blackness" derives from the fact that it almost never has snow lying even in the hardest winters. It has, accordingly, long been used for wintering beasts from districts nearby.

The Isle in recent times has developed pleasantly as a holiday area and has several well organised centres for sailing and riding and so on.

Its old Gaelic name was Ardmeanach, and it was under this name that the lordship of the Black Isle was gifted to Henry Darnley by his wife Mary Queen of Scots. The geologist Hugh Miller was born here in 1802 and his cottage is now a museum in which are copies of the newspaper he edited, the *Witness*.

Hugh Miller's cottage in the Black Isle and (right) the paper he edited

A seat by the fireside in Hugh Miller's cottage

19 **GARVE:** At first glance it is difficult to see why anybody built Garve at all, except that there's a railway station. In older days, in fact, it lay on a drovers' road that ran from the West Highlands to markets far south, and where drovers ran there would rise an inn. There is a local tale of a drover who was taking a horse to Ullapool in a snowy winter when he came upon a woman in distress and far gone in pregnancy, trying to walk to reach her sea-captain husband there. As the wind drove fresh snow across the hills, the drover killed his horse, disembowelled it and sheltered the woman inside its body till he could help her to struggle to Ullapool. There must be a sequel, of course. Years later when the same drover was being hauled through the streets of Edinburgh as a Jacobite rebel doomed to die, the same woman saw him and the same woman's husband, now a man of influence and authority, had him freed and sent home. The tale may even be true . . .

Black Water, Garve

Broadford Bay, near the village is the famous Spar Cave

21 **BROADFORD:** The Spar Cave, near the village of Broadford, is less revered today than it once was — principally because successions of visitors have stolen bits of the stalactites which made it splendid and original. It is still a popular spot, and the silly vandalism of visitors is nothing new — it was rife in the 19th Century. When Sir Walter Scott visited Skye in 1814 the then owner of the area had built a 9ft. wall round the entrance to protect the natural treasure. Unable to find the man who would give them the key,

Scott and his friends scaled the wall with the help of a rope, and Scott later wrote: "The floor forms a steep and difficult ascent and might be fancifully compared to a sheet of water which, while it rushed whitening and foaming down the declivity, had been suddenly arrested and consolidated by the spell of an enchanter . . . . there is scarce a form or a group that an active fancy may not trace among the grotesque ornaments which have been gradually moulded in this cavern by the dripping of the calcareous water . . ."

THE SCARS REMAIN

It is impossible to have a sympathetic understanding of the Highlands or the Highlander without knowing something about the great trauma of Highland history, the Clearances. They have left a scar on the consciousness of Highlander and Lowlander alike; they devastated villages and townships and deepened the sense of desolation that you will sometimes feel among the most beautiful landscapes.

The Clearances began properly in the 18th Century, following the Jacobite Rebellions of 1715 and 1745. In the punitive backlash by the Government in London, Highlanders were executed, murdered, shipped abroad to slavery. Some clan chiefs were deprived of land and titles, it was forbidden to own arms or wear tartan, and the old way of life was already being eroded. Worse horrors were to come.

During the Napoleonic Wars there was an urgent need for cheap food for Britain's armies. The answer was found in mutton, and the Highland glens looked ideal for sheep rearing. Now came the great betrayal — not by Englishmen, but by the Highlanders' own surviving chieftains, who realised that the clan lands could produce money from sheep providing they were cleared of people. The process continued after the wars, when Highlanders came home from loyal army service to find their homes being burned and their families driven out, to the hills, to the bleak shelter of the coast, beyond the oceans.

SHEEP FOR PEOPLE

It wasn't merely a question of eviction. In many districts the cottagers were forcibly dragged on to ships that would carry them to America or Canada or Australia whether they liked it or not. The lairds' factors hired thugs to scour the hills for fugitives to be shipped out of Scotland.

So the lands were depopulated; the sheep came; and after them the deer, as estates were bought up by outsiders for sporting holidays. Some lairds grew rich. They sent their children to be educated in England and cut themselves off more completely from their roots.

In a few places, the Highlanders fought the evictions, with sticks and stones, and were defeated. Over most of the area, they submitted numbly to fate, from a sense of despair or loyalty or ingrained discipline.

20 **STROME FERRY** has a new claim to interest: it is no longer Strome Ferry in any functional sense. Until recent years it was a famous bottleneck for motorists because the road from the east ran along the north shore of Loch Carron to Stromemore and the short sail across the loch could be a long, long wait, with no service on the Sabbath. The old road, by the way, was one of the works of the great engineer Thomas Telford.

Now, the new road takes the south shore and moves the traveller briskly towards Kyle and Skye. Having saved so much time, the motorist may care to waste a few moments to look across the mouth of Loch Carron towards the crumbling relics of Strome Castle, from which the MacDonells controlled the district until the fortress suffered the routine fate of being destroyed; in this case by Kenneth Mackenzie of Kintail in 1609.

The tranquil blue waters of Loch Carron from Plockton

Plockton, looking across to the Applecross mountains

323

The River Snizort near Portree

22 PORTREE: It is only eight years since the British Government mounted a punitive expedition against its own citizens at Portree. Poverty and evictions had finally roused the islanders to active protest, and a large force of police was sent from the mainland to arrest the ringleaders. In a head-on collision called the Battle of the Braes, a dozen policemen were wounded. Prisoners were taken, and the islanders were freshly incensed when these prisoners were refused a jury trial. Viewed from a long distance, the situation looked so explosive that the Government actually sent a gunboat to quell the dissidents. Mercifully, it merely showed the flag.

Nothing was solved, the islanders remained stubborn and fierce, and a landlord appealed to the Government for two companies of soldiers. The appeal was refused. The county council then demanded police reinforcements from the mainland, but the grievances of the islanders had by this time roused public opinion all over the country, and what did happen was the establishment of a Royal Commission in 1883 which stimulated legislation to protect crofters' rights all over the Highlands.

The harbour at Portree — once the Government sent a gunboat . . . .

Fishing boats at anchor off Uig — history and legend swirl around here

23 **UIG:** The hamlet is interesting today mainly for its savage sea views; but history and legend swirl around it. Near here, at Bornaskitaig, it is reported of the ancient clan days how the Mac-Donalds acquired their motto *per mare per terras* (by sea and by lands). Donald, son of Reginald MacSomerled, was in dispute with a rival clan for possession of a fairly trivial piece of territory, and agreed on a race by boat, the first man to touch the land to become its master. The MacDonalds rowed stoutly, but a change of weather threatened to cheat them at the last minute. With a splendid Highland gesture, Donald sliced off his left hand with his sword and hurled it ashore to gain the prize.

An equally potent legend concerns the Cave of Gold, into which Macarthur the Piper was lured by a banshee's gift of a silver chanter. He never emerged, naturally, never found any gold and was never heard to play again. In case this story should not be entirely accurate, there is an identical tale told of MacCoitir's cave at Portree — which is also reputed to run right through the Isle of Skye to Loch Bracadale, by the way.

Uig on a quiet day

THE BARLEY BREE

Whisky is Scotland's prime export and the world's favourite tipple. It is produced by one form of modern technology which still contains a mystery, in that no one has ever managed to reproduce the authentic taste of Scotch whisky outside Scotland though people have tried — in Denmark and France and Japan among other places. The mystery ingredient may be the Scottish climate. It certainly has something to do with Scottish water — whiskies made from water drawn from two adjacent streams turn out as quite different whiskies.

By far the bulk of all whisky made today is blended, from malt whiskies or malt-and-grain, or in a few instances from blended pure grain spirits. Blending (also a mystery) maintains a consistency of flavour from year to year.

Single malt whiskies, such as Talisker from the Isle of Skye, are unblended, made by the old processes, and do vary. Among patrons of ordinary blended whiskies, connoisseurship (or whisky snobbery) is a harmless pastime but usually spurious. As they say in the trade, there are no bad whiskies — only good whiskies and better whiskies.

24 **DUNVEGAN:** The old Scottish clans are scattered and their way of life is lost forever, but the ancient loyalties persist, and nowhere more enthusiastically than at Dunvegan Castle, one of the oldest Scottish strongholds to be continuously occupied. The energy and enthusiasm of Dame Flora MacLeod of MacLeod has made Dunvegan a prime attraction for MacLeods from all over the world — but folk of other names and other nations are welcome to visit.

The castle has been modernised inside, but is still an old splendour of original stone.

The relics that can be seen include the mighty two-handed sword of the great chief Rory Mor, the ancient fairy flag, and a lock of Prince Charlie's hair; and there are family portraits by Ramsay and Raeburn.

Samuel Johnson visited Dunvegan on his Scottish tour and actually met the legendary Flora MacDonald; and at that time Lady MacLeod wanted to build a new house and get out of the chilly old place. Johnson dissuaded her. "It is the very jewel of the estate," he said. "It looks as if it had been let down from heaven by the four corners, to be the residence of a chief."

Loch Dunvegan in the MacLeod country

Dunvegan Castle sea gate

25 **THE COOLINS:** The mountains of Skye, the Coolins or Cuillins, were the island's original tourist attraction. Mean, moody and magnificent is a reasonable description. Climbers still flock to the island for no other reason than the challenge of the high peaks.

There are the Black Coolins, and the Red Coolins — red from their red granite screes. They offer exercise on every level from easy hill walks to very severe climbs for the expert. Fifteen of the Black Coolins are "Munros" — Scottish mountains over 3,000 ft. The black rock of their composition is gabbro, attractive to mountaineers because of its rough surface and plentiful handholds and footholds.

One of the most imposing is the Storr, a couple of miles north of Portree, despite its modest height of 2,360ft. Its black basaltic cliffs make man look puny; and below it towers the 150ft. pillar of the Old Man of Storr, which was first climbed in 1955. Treasure-seekers may like to know that a hoard of silver and coins was found in 1891 near the foot of the Old Man — including 10th Century Anglo-Saxon pennies and a handful of coins minted in Samarkand.

The Old Man of Storr on the north east coast

The castle houses the mighty two-handed sword of Rory Mor

MacLeod family portraits by Allan Ramsay

The Coolins rise dramatically above the green fields of Skye

THE HIGH FLYER

The ptarmigan is found high in the Scottish mountains, seldom below 2,000ft. The conditions in which it lives give it a way of life unique amongst British birds. In summer it is a dull mottled-brown colour, so well hidden amongst the rock that it is easily missed. In Autumn it changes colour, the brown becomes flecked with white and its grey underparts become white. By winter the change is complete and the whole bird looks white; even its tail may be hidden by paler brown plumage.

proost Turnhout   (Belgium)

PRINTED IN BELGIUM